The Challenge of Human Rights

The Challenge of Human Rights

Past, Present and Future

Edited by

David Keane

Lecturer in Law, Middlesex University, UK

Yvonne McDermott

Lecturer in Law, Bangor University, UK

Edward Elgar

Cheltenham, UK • Northampton, MA, USA

Published by
Edward Elgar Publishing Limited
The Lypiatts
15 Lansdown Road
Cheltenham
Glos GL50 2JA
UK

Edward Elgar Publishing, Inc.
William Pratt House
9 Dewey Court
Northampton
Massachusetts 01060
USA

A catalogue record for this book
is available from the British Library

Library of Congress Control Number: 2012935307

MIX
Paper from
responsible sources
FSC® C018575

ISBN 978 0 85793 900 5

Typeset by Servis Filmsetting Ltd, Stockport, Cheshire
Printed and bound by MPG Books Group, UK

Contents

Contributors

Kjell Anderson, PhD Graduate, Irish Centre for Human Rights; Special Advisor, International Association of Genocide Scholars

Megan M. Carpenter, Associate Professor of Law and Director, Center for Law and Intellectual Property, Texas Wesleyan School of Law

Joshua Castellino, Professor and Head of Law Department, Middlesex University

Josh Curtis, Doctoral Fellow and PhD candidate, Irish Centre for Human Rights, National University of Ireland Galway

Aoife Daly, Lecturer, School of Law, University of Essex

Shane Darcy, Lecturer, Irish Centre for Human Rights, National University of Ireland Galway

Peter Fitzmaurice, Doctoral Fellow and PhD Candidate, Irish Centre for Human Rights, National University of Ireland Galway

David Keane, Lecturer in Law, Middlesex University

Yvonne McDermott, Lecturer in Law, Bangor University, Wales

Nicholas McGeehan, PhD Candidate, Department of Law, European University Institute

Daragh McGreal, PhD Candidate, DFG-Graduate School in Law and Economics, University of Hamburg

Ray Murphy, Professor and Interim Director, Irish Centre for Human Rights, National University of Ireland Galway

Shannonbrooke Murphy, PhD Candidate, Middlesex University

Majella Ní Chríocháin, MA (International Relations) graduate, Dublin City University; LLM (International Human Rights Law) graduate, Irish Centre for Human Rights, National University of Ireland Galway

Éadaoin O'Brien, Fellow, Human Rights Consortium, School of Advanced Study, University of London

John Reynolds, Government of Ireland Scholar; PhD Candidate, Irish Centre for Human Rights, National University of Ireland Galway

Leila Nadya Sadat, Henry H. Oberschelp Professor and Director of the Whitney R. Harris World Law Institute at Washington University School of Law

William A. Schabas, OC MRIA, Professor of International Law, Middlesex University, London and Part-Time Professor of Human Rights Law, National University of Ireland Galway

Abbreviations

ACHPR	African Court on Human and Peoples' Rights
AHRLR	African Human Rights Law Reports
AJIL	*American Journal of International Law*
CERD	Committee on the Elimination of Racial Discrimination
CESCR	Committee on Economic, Social and Cultural Rights
ECHR	European Convention for the Protection of Human Rights and Fundamental Freedoms
ECtHR	European Court of Human Rights
EJIL	*European Journal of International Law*
HRQ	*Human Rights Quarterly*
ICC	International Criminal Court
ICCPR	International Covenant on Civil and Political Rights
ICESCR	International Covenant on Economic, Social and Cultural Rights
ICISS	International Commission on Intervention and State Sovereignty
ICLQ	*International and Comparative Law Quarterly*
ICMP	International Commission on Missing Persons
ICRC	International Committee of the Red Cross
ICTR	International Criminal Tribunal for Rwanda
ICTY	International Criminal Tribunal for the former Yugoslavia
IJLPF	*International Journal of Law Policy and the Family*
IJRL	*International Journal of Refugee Law*
ILM	*International Legal Materials*
ILO	International Labour Organization
IMT	International Military Tribunal
JICJ	*Journal of International Criminal Justice*
OJLS	*Oxford Journal of Legal Studies*
UDHR	Universal Declaration of Human Rights
UNESCO	United Nations Educational, Scientific and Cultural Organization
Va. J. Int'l L.	*Virginia Journal of International Law*
Web JCLI	*Web Journal of Current Legal Issues*

Foreword

Joshua Castellino

It gives me great pleasure to write the Foreword for this important volume, which addresses a range of human rights issues which are likely to be of enduring interest. It is clear that the world in which we find ourselves in the twenty-first century is significantly different from that which confronted the drafters of the Universal Declaration of Human Rights post-World War Two. Their challenge was to design a system that would be truly universal in coverage, and create the foundations for the prevention of the kinds of atrocities that have regularly occurred in the past. The track record of the Universal Declaration has been mixed; it has generated an important legacy in the creation of an entire system of international human rights law, but with inconsistent results, not only failing to prevent large-scale human rights violations but proving inconsistent in tackling the slower drip of discriminatory treatment of individuals and communities.

In the context of these failures it is significant to note that they are often underpinned by lost opportunities in engaging the entire range of the vision of the drafters of rights. At various points in the history of human rights, sets of norms seeking the emancipation of individuals and communities have been realized. However only a selection of the potential range of human rights has been implemented, usually based on the self-interest of those that have chosen to engage. In addition many of the models derived have emanated from western ideas of law and beliefs in non-interventionist, *laissez faire* governance systems. As a result much of the richness derived through lived experiences has been lost and the discourse of human rights has moved towards a process-oriented regime, unable to address issues outside its specific dimensions.

Professor William A. Schabas is to be commended for the concept of forgotten rights that underlies the Conference that has led to this collection of papers. In academia we sometimes fall prey to the belief that we need to make greater contributions to knowledge that already exists. As a result we often focus on ever greater minutiae, while neglecting the larger questions and unexplored territory. One reason for this could be the research techniques in law; while these derive from the social sciences they are nonetheless restricted, away from theory and towards providing commentary on positivist interpretations of law. As a result there is little room in the discipline for what is euphemistically referred to as 'blue-sky' thinking.

This volume therefore represents a genuine attempt to think beyond the realms of what exists, to reflect on ideas postulated in the past that could be of great salience in the future. It presents the reader with a key question: to what extent are the contemporary concepts of human rights and the systems that support them equipped to address the challenges of a changed world? By thinking through some of the ideas of the past, with a set of promising young scholars alongside more established names, readers will gain a sense of how human rights politics have shaped the current regime while also becoming attuned to the extent to which new directions and mechanisms can be forged in the future.

Many of the individuals whose contributions are encompassed in this volume have strong links to the Irish Centre for Human Rights, at the National University of Ireland, Galway, an institution that has had a significant impact in its first decade of existence under the stewardship of Professor William A. Schabas. This volume celebrates the success of the institution by showcasing some of the talent it has generated, and is likely to be of avid interest to all who care about the future of human rights.

Introduction

David Keane and Yvonne McDermott

When the Universal Declaration of Human Rights in 1948 proclaimed the universality of human rights, this was as much a projection of its future path as a statement of its then status. Human rights has since become as fundamental to political or legal action as mathematics is to physics; a common language to be applied to various problems or situations that arise. There has been a resulting exponential growth of human rights, to the point where it is inextricable from questions of democracy, state legitimacy and state co-operation. This complexity of human rights has seen a fracturing of its origins, motives and influences, and it struggles to be contained within the broad rubric of the UN international legal order or its regional counterparts. The edges of all of the individual rights-specific legal instruments are bursting with new interpretations or applications, as meaning is expanded to draw in wider issues or unforeseen consequences.

The discipline has seeped into 'such exotic and highly specialized'[1] areas of knowledge as international refugee law, minority rights, indigenous rights, children's rights, the international law of armed conflict and individual criminal responsibility, which all have their roots in the protection of the individual. The danger is that an ever-increasing corpus of rights will devalue the existing standards, hard-fought and hard-won, while adding meaningless layers and confusing advocates who seek simple expressions of state responsibilities. In this regard, the expanding range of actors, both state and non-state, has been the almost defining concern of the past two decades of rights scholarship and activism. Corporations among others have seen the need to respond to the barrage of calls for their engagement with the international human rights system.

It is into this cauldron that the present volume seeks to add a number of contributions. They are, like human rights discourse itself, at once

---

[1] International Law Commission, 'Fragmentation of International Law: Difficulties Arising from the Diversification and Expansion of International Law', Report of the Study Group of the International Law Commission finalized by Martti Koskenniemi, UN Doc A/CN.4/L.682, 13 April 2006, para 4.

broad and specific, interdisciplinary and subdisciplinary, ambitious and restrained, technical and political. In other words, they reflect the idiosyncratic nature of human rights, as it has grown in all directions at the insistence of advocates or practitioners, while others try to drag it back to its original goals, whatever they may be. The book is the outcome of one meeting in one human rights centre in one country, and is something of a snapshot of the ability of human rights to stretch across genres.

The aim is to bring disparate ideas under the theme of forgotten rights, with the purpose of mapping future directions. The changing political, economic and legal landscape requires re-interpretation of the fundamental norms that govern international human rights, including the changed emphasis of rights holders and rights bearers and the remedies that can be provided. The ideas that informed the standard-setting period in international human rights law throughout the twentieth century are no longer consistent with contemporary developments, as rights become key to global models of the rule of law. The collection seeks to identify how the past should be re-calibrated to fit with the present; and how the future might look as we re-evaluate the tools of international law.

A common thread within all the pieces is the need to improve the world, as human rights, even in its theory, must always have a discernible measure of effect. The discipline of human rights concerns itself with the dispossessed or the marginal, and represents an attempt to challenge the traditional power structures or privileges within the legal structure. As such, human rights itself is susceptible to majority viewpoints, and within individual rights or within groups of rights, certain elements are emphasized at the expense of others.

Therefore this original collection of 16 essays is exploratory, and seeks to map a future path for human rights. It brings together works which highlight overlooked or forgotten rights and concepts, and contributions which suggest a new course for established rights, as the present century moves into its second decade.

The collection opens with a paper by **Josh Curtis** and **Shane Darcy** on Article 28 of the Universal Declaration of Human Rights (UDHR), the right to a social and international order for the realization of human rights. They ask whether Article 28 has been utilized since 1948 as a means to challenge structural barriers preventing the fulfilment of human rights, given that it has not been translated into legally binding norms like other key provisions of the document. Wider links are made between the aims of Article 28 and the requirements of other, related expressions of international law, such as the Declaration on the Right to Development and Article 2(1) of the International Covenant on Economic, Social and Cultural Rights. In mapping the drafting of this ‘intriguing provision’, the authors highlight the central importance of the concept of international cooperation as an organizational principle of international law. In essence, they see the call in Article 28 for an overarching framework for the realization of all other human rights.

William A. Schabas charts the origins of the right to peace as a corollary of 'freedom from fear', one of the four freedoms proposed by Franklin D. Roosevelt in 1941. He outlines the subsequent marginalization of the right despite its place in the UDHR of 1948, outlining how the growth in two fields that are closely related to human rights law, namely international humanitarian law and international criminal law, may have helped push the issue of peace to the periphery. The successful adoption of amendments to the Rome Statute of the International Criminal Court at the Kampala Review Conference in June 2010, moving the crime of aggression back to centre stage, has added momentum to the importance of peace within the human rights vision. The author criticizes the 'back seat' role taken by NGOs in the adoption of the amendment clarifying the definition of aggression and the conditions where the court can exercise jurisdiction over it. Even though the matter is fundamental to human rights protection, the international NGOs largely eschewed the issue to protect their apolitical character.

Kjell Anderson takes a broader approach to the right to peace, arguing that it is much more than the absence of aggressive war. He sees the emphasis on international conflict stemming from a state-centric model of international relations that has predominated for centuries. Consequently he focuses instead on non-international armed conflict, setting out how the state can violate the right to peace of its citizens through the capricious use of force and how non-state actors may also violate the right to peace through the illegitimate use of force. He also makes the important point that there are reasonable exceptions to the right to peace, including the protection of the rights of others, an idea that is expanded on in the pursuit of a meaningful interpretation of the concept. The aim must be a *jus ad bellum* for intrastate violence that does not asymmetrically remove rights from non-state actors but rather limits the recourse to armed force by states and non-state actors alike.

David Keane completes the triad of contributions on the right to peace by focussing on the role of UNESCO, whose constitution sets out the idea in its preamble that 'since wars begin in the minds of men, it is in the minds of men that the defences of peace must be constructed'. He analyses the initiatives that culminated in the 1997 UNESCO Declaration on the Right to Peace, an attempt to codify the concept that was ultimately rejected by states which perceived that the organization was overstepping its mandate. Parallel to this, the UNESCO-led Seville Statement on Violence 1986, which set out opposition to genetic theories of violence which imply that war is an inevitable product of biological or genetic behaviour, has seen renewed interest in line with developments in behavioural psychology. Retrospectively, UNESCO seems to have accepted the arguments that it overstepped its mandate, but the culture of peace at present represents a withdrawal that belies its historic contribution to the discussion on what has been termed 'mental disarmament'.

Shannonbrooke Murphy opens with a *tour d'horizon* of the roots of the right to resist, seeing its manifestation in writings from the Athenian Decrees of Demophantus and Eucrates, via de Vattel and Grotius, to the writings of twentieth century Marxist scholars. Her piece is premised on the fact that this right has clearly fallen into disfavour, despite the urgency of the need for explicit recognition in the past. The piece is shadowed by the events of the Arab Spring uprisings, which appear to support the argument that the right to resist has its place in the lexicon of international human rights, whether as an hortatory statement or indeed as a legal right to be enforced. The chapter is a closely reasoned, technical examination of a right that has an identifiable pedigree in international law, that has been cited whether it exists or not, and that has increasingly been seen by a variety of actors as critical to the enforcement of all other rights.

Éadaoin O'Brien extends the scope of the collection from the living to the dead, with her examination of the forensic exhumation of mass graves and the legal consequences as experienced by the international criminal tribunals. Inquiries into violations of international criminal law rely on the forensic sciences for evidence on the nature and pattern of crimes committed, and as a result the application of medical and forensic sciences in the investigation of violations of international humanitarian law have come to receive increasing attention by both practitioners and academics in the past number of years. In investigating the nexus between international forensic investigations conducted under the auspices of international criminal tribunals and the rules of international humanitarian law regarding the dead, she sees a potential symbiotic relationship that can satisfy the requirements of the legal system and broader societal needs.

Ray Murphy looks at the consequences of the Israeli occupation of the Golan Heights. The chapter examines the action of the Israeli authorities and argues that certain practices by the Israeli Defence Forces constitute war crimes, which in some cases may amount to grave breaches of the Fourth Geneva Convention governing the protection of civilians. The theme of the piece is the relation between geography, human rights and humanitarian law protections, with a strong sense of the need to understand the complexity of territory in order to arrive at conclusions and remedies. In this regard, the detail involved in establishing the problematic is seen in the contours of the restrictions and violations imposed on the people of the sub-region.

Leila Nadya Sadat provides a glimpse of the machinery behind the elaboration of a potentially major instrument of international law. She highlights how the adoption of the Rome Statute of the International Criminal Court did not obviate the need to fill the lacunae in the legal framework regarding the commission of atrocity crimes, most of which are crimes against humanity and not genocide or war crimes. In 2008, the Whitney R. Harris World Law Institute launched the Crimes against Humanity Initiative, with the aim of drafting a convention on crimes against humanity that will fill the gaps left by the provisions of the Rome Statute. This chapter provides insights into the complex drafting phases that finally establish the principle of state responsibility as well as individual criminal responsibility for crimes against humanity.

Yvonne McDermott assesses the workings of the International Criminal Tribunal for the former Yugoslavia in its approach to the principle of double jeopardy, a rule that has inspired juridical debate at the domestic level but that has not received the same attention at the international level. With a close analysis of relevant case law, she argues that the ICTY has overstepped the boundaries of when a retrial can be ordered on appeal, which may lead to a dilution of the double jeopardy concept in the future. The conclusion is that the Tribunal has stretched the limits of retrial on appeal to such an extent as to find cause for reopening the case when the prosecution is merely unhappy with the outcome, a result that implies the need for greater introspection in terms of prosecutorial strategies at the international level.

John Reynolds looks to the drafting of the *apartheid* convention and asks whether there is scope for its application outside of the South African context. In this regard he undertakes a review of the role *apartheid* has played in the development of human rights, seeing in its prohibition the enunciation of principles which have become central to the application of international law standards. The aim is to caution against restricting *apartheid* to the past, given that it was a form of governmental sanction and practice that can be read into contemporary situations. The example of Palestine and Israel is apparent; other examples include Fiji, between Indo-Fijians and indigenous Fijians, and India's caste system. The chapter defers on whether all these situations amount to *apartheid* or not, instead concentrating on the idea that *apartheid* is not confined to one context, and as a legal lens in which to view control of peoples, is essential to our understanding of human rights, past and present.

Nicholas McGeehan echoes this approach, in questioning a past human rights violation considered 'solved': that is, slavery. He carefully deconstructs the case that slavery can be confined to an historical practice termed 'chattel slavery', and looks to the drafting of the conventions against slavery for answers as to how this international practice can be seen in contemporary situations. The chapter distinguishes between a number of key interrelated concepts, including slavery, forced labour and trafficking, and with an eye on labour practices that represent a high level of control of the individual, such as that witnessed with migrant workers in the Gulf region, he concludes that we cannot say that slavery does not exist anymore. He subsequently looks to the remedies provided in the past conventions and the present expressions of human rights standards, and expresses concern that the law is inadequate in its ability to tackle large-scale exploitative practices that are trapping millions through a combination of debt and other control mechanisms.

Peter Fitzmaurice traces the history of refugee law, from the early *laissez-faire* attitude to immigration to the birth of the 'refugee problem' in Europe in the early twentieth century. He examines the first international refugee legal instruments, with particular reference to the 1933 Convention Relating to the International Status of Refugees. The 1933 Convention had some major limitations, which paralysed its effectiveness in protecting those fleeing from persecution in World War II. Despite its shortcomings, the author argues, there are some interesting aspects to the 1933 Convention which suggest that we should not consign it to the annals of history. These include the fact that the inter-war refugee legal instruments were predecessors to today's international regime for the protection of civil and economic rights; the means in which the Convention established a mechanism through which individual states could supervise human rights violations in other countries, representing a shift from the collective supervision mechanisms that preceded it.

Daragh McGreal provides an innovative application of law and economics to the treaty-drafting process. This is long overdue given the predominance of law and economics theories in some domestic jurisdictions. The arguments in relation to efficiency, including the desire for an optimal number of state ratifications, are factored into drafter decision-making. The assumptions this involves are outlined, as well as the merits of the approach. He notes that combining the disciplines of law and economics with human rights law might initially seem a peculiar concept, with economic tools to analyse laws appearing anathema to the human rights ideal of advancing the security and liberty of individuals. Yet the chapter specifies how there is much merit in using basic economic tools to assess how drafting decisions and ratification decisions are intrinsically linked, ensuring that the approach will be of major interest to those involved in the treaty process.

Aoife Daly asks whether voting rights can be extended to under-18s. While the aim of the chapter is clear, in the course of her analysis as to why voting rights are not extended to under-18s, she uncovers the nature of our assumptions in terms of 'accepted' legal rules. The author unravels the manner in which a commonly held rule can gain the guise of a legal orthodoxy, and argues that it is no longer sufficient to assume that under-18s are incapable of contributing to decision-making processes. Recent events such as the summer riots in London, as well as the role of youth in the Arab Spring, support her views that the disenfranchisement of youth may not be as rational as it is set out to be. In particular, the context of children's rights and the struggle to have them effectively implemented by adults forms a backdrop to the chapter.

Majella Ní Chríocháin rightly asserts that of the five types of rights identified in the UDHR and given legal force in the covenants – civil, political, economic, social and cultural – cultural rights have long been neglected in the discourse. They have suffered from being bundled as economic, social and cultural rights, with the consequent privileging of economic and social rights as they vie for attention against the better protected civil and political rights. Furthermore the spectre of 'cultural relativism' has ensured their demotion. However the chapter perceives a new era for cultural rights, inspired by three key developments: the Committee on Economic, Social and Cultural Rights' General Comment 21 on the right of everyone to take part in cultural life; the appointment of an Independent Expert in the Field of Cultural Rights by the UN Human Rights Council; and the Declaration on the Rights of Indigenous Peoples, which has seen renewed focus on cultural rights as an essential demand of indigenous peoples. The importance of these is highlighted in the idea that cultural rights are fundamental to the survival of minorities and indigenous peoples.

Megan Carpenter takes an issue of commercial law, intellectual property, and gives it a human rights spin. The characterization of intellectual property as a means of protecting corporate or commercial interests has meant that its potential for contributing to human rights protection has been underplayed. The chapter looks to the sources of intellectual property rights in the international human rights treaties, presenting possibilities for a more inclusive approach. In particular, Article 15(1)(c) of the International Covenant on Economic, Social and Cultural Rights, and its authoritative interpretation by the Committee on Economic, Social and Cultural Rights, provides a legal grounding. That the scope of protection of the moral and material interests of authors provided for in Article 15 does not necessarily coincide with what is referred to as intellectual property rights under national legislation or international agreements, provides a departure point for the discussion on the expansion of the range of intellectual property applications.

This collection of essays originated from a conference as part of the Irish Centre for Human Rights 10th Anniversary celebrations, which were held in Galway, Ireland, in November 2010. We are grateful to the organizers of that event, and would like to take this opportunity to thank those in attendance who offered feedback to our authors on their papers. Professor Andrew Clapham of the Graduate Institute, Geneva, and Michael D. Higgins, Adjunct Professor at the Irish Centre for Human Rights and President of Ireland, warrant particular mention. We wholeheartedly thank all of our contributors, and are particularly grateful to **Professor Joshua Castellino** who provided a thought-provoking and insightful Foreword.

1. The right to a social and international order for the realization of human rights: Article 28 of the Universal Declaration and international cooperation

Josh Curtis and Shane Darcy

The United Nations declared in the 1948 Universal Declaration of Human Rights that 'everyone is entitled to a social and international order in which the rights and freedoms set forth in this Declaration can be fully realised'. It is an intriguing provision, in that Article 28 seems to straddle the line between the substantive rights of the Declaration and the last few articles, which do not speak of rights themselves, but rather of duties and limitations. It was important that this foundational document recognized the entitlement of every individual to a social and international order in which the rights and freedoms of the Declaration could be fully realized, for it shows an understanding of how context, both nationally and internationally, impacts on the enjoyment of human rights. The emerging globalization of the post-war world is now a fully fledged reality, and it is clear that the realization of human rights is challenged not just by national set-ups but also by developments at the regional or global level, notably regarding trade, investment and finance, not to mention environmental changes attributable to climate change.

Since the adoption of the Universal Declaration of 1948, we have seen the construction of significant human rights machinery at the international, regional and national levels. Colonialism, the great antithesis of human rights, has formally ended, by and large. But a reading of Article 28 of the Universal Declaration requires a consideration of whether the present social and international orders are adequately designed for the realization of rights and freedoms. For example, does the current international order continue to prioritize states' and even corporate rights, over their existing and potential duties, and thus over the rights and freedoms of individuals and peoples? In particular, has the obligation of international cooperation between states, which is fundamental to the universality of the Declaration and to the human rights system as a whole, been fully recognized, understood and implemented?

In exploring this theme, the essay begins by considering the intention of the drafters who included Article 28 in the Universal Declaration. The Declaration was of course not a legally binding treaty when it was adopted in 1948; its preamble describes it as 'a common standard of achievement for all peoples and all nations'. However, its enormous significance as a human rights instrument is almost unrivalled. In light of its stature, the essay goes on to see if Article 28 has been utilized since 1948 as a means to challenge structural barriers preventing the fulfilment of human rights, or whether it remains a forgotten right, a laudable but unrealized aim in an otherwise celebrated document. In the process, wider linkages between the aims of Article 28 and the requirements of other, related expressions of international law, such as the Declaration on the Right to Development and Article 2(1) of the International Covenant on Economic, Social and Cultural Rights, will be addressed. The central importance here of the concept of international cooperation becomes apparent. The last part of the essay will take a closer look at the meaning of this concept, both as an organizational principle of international law and as a crucial aspect of human rights law. The latter context requires greater specificity and definition of the legal content of this concept than currently exists. Such defined legal content should lead to concrete obligations for states (and possibly other bodies) that could lead to the implementation of the promise of Article 28.

1. THE DRAFTING HISTORY OF ARTICLE 28

The Universal Declaration itself was seen as part of a larger human rights project at the United Nations. Eleanor Roosevelt, who had presided over the Commission on Human Rights, stated prior to the Declaration's adoption that, although it was a great step forward in the protection and promotion of human rights, it was 'only the first step in the elaboration of the human rights programme of the Charter; it was essential that it should be followed by a covenant on human rights, drafted in the form of a treaty and containing provisions for implementation.'[1] The Declaration itself was adopted by the General Assembly with 48 votes in favour and

---

[1] *Yearbook of the United Nations*, 1948–49, V. Social, Humanitarian and Cultural Questions, 527.

8 abstentions; a voting statistic that was most closely followed by the previous vote on Article 28 itself (then Article 29) during voting on the preamble and individual articles.[2]

With regard to the origins of Article 28, the distinguished Lebanese member of the Commission, Charles Malik, had proposed the provision in order to resolve the debate surrounding the so-called 'old rights' – the civil and political – and the 'new rights' – economic, social and cultural rights. Progress on the drafting of the Universal Declaration had been delayed for several days while these rights were discussed in debates described as being 'amongst the most emotional in the Commission's history.'[3] According to Mary Ann Glendon, the debate was largely between the United States and the Soviet Union; and '[f]or the two superpowers it was a face-off between central planning and programs that left substantial room for the free operation of the market.'[4] Malik's proposal was seen as an attempt to:

> contextualize the relationship between the new rights and the old: a provision for the right to a social and political order in which all the Declaration's rights and freedoms could be realized. This proposal met with general approval and eventually became the Declaration's Article 28, but it did not resolve the impasse.[5]

The original proposal by Charles Malik had been for 'the right to a good social and international order'. This was disfavoured by several participants: Mr. Pavlov of the USSR felt that 'a "good" social order could not be achieved except through a socialistic society in which there was real equality'.[6] The proposal of substituting 'such' for 'good' was rejected when put to a vote,[7] and the Article was adopted with the inclusion of the phrase 'good social and international order'.[8] 'Good' remained in Article 26 of the Draft International Declaration of the Commission of Human Rights of June 1948,[9] but was dropped in the Third Committee's draft.

---

2 *Ibid.*, 534–5.

3 Mary Ann Glendon, *A World Made New; Eleanor Roosevelt and the Universal Declaration of Human Rights* (New York: Random House, 2001) 116.

4 *Ibid.*

5 *Ibid.*

6 United Nations, Economic and Social Council, Commission on Human Rights, Third Session, Summary Record of the 78th Meeting, UN Doc E/CN.4/SR.78, 24 June 1948, 9.

7 *Ibid.*, 10.

8 *Ibid.*, 10–11.

9 United Nations, Economic and Social Council, Report of the Third Session of the Commission on Human Rights, UN Doc E/800, 28 June 1948, 13.

The rationale for the inclusion of Article 28 seems to have been to emphasize that no particular existing national order could be favoured, and that the full realization of rights and freedoms was also dependent on a certain international order. Malik himself later explained his understanding of the provision that 'the Declaration should clearly set forth the right of mankind to have a United Nations a world organization, as well as a social order, in which the rights and freedoms could be realized'.[10] The organization was already in existence while the Declaration was being drafted, and perhaps the idea was that it would have a more prominent role in the protection of human rights. René Cassin, the French member of the Commission, had proposed a similar provision, but addressed specifically at socio-economic rights, the fulfilment of which 'should be made possible by the State separately or by international collaboration'.[11] This became Article 22 of the Universal Declaration:

> Everyone, as a member of society, has the right to social security and is entitled to realization, through national effort and international co-operation and in accordance with the organization and resources of each State, of the economic, social and cultural rights indispensable for his dignity and the free development of his personality.

This article illustrates the thinking that an effective international order must be based on international cooperation, and it complements Charles Malik's more general article which was included as Article 28 of the Universal Declaration:

> Everyone is entitled to a social and international order in which the rights and freedoms set forth in this Declaration can be fully realised.

It may be asked whether the language of Article 28 connotes a human right to a social and international order or an entitlement to such. During the drafting process, the original phrase used had been that 'everyone has a right', although this was replaced by 'everyone is entitled', upon the suggestion of Mr. Chang of China. His view was that this was a necessary stylistic alteration because 'the terminology of rights occurred twice in the article'.[12] There seems not to have been any opposition or indeed

---

[10] United Nations, Economic and Social Council, Commission on Human Rights, Third Session, Summary Record of the 78th Meeting, UN Doc E/CN.4/SR.78, 24 June 1948, 9.

[11] Glendon, *A World Made New* (n3) 116.

[12] Johannes Morsink, *The Universal Declaration of Human Rights; Origins, Drafting and Intent* (Philadelphia: University of Pennsylvania Press, 1999) 232.

substance to this change. If understood as a right in and of itself, Article 28 prompts consideration as to where the corresponding duty may lie, bearing in mind the declaratory and aspirational nature of the Universal Declaration itself.

2. EXPLORING ARTICLE 28

From the Universal Declaration's drafting history, the text of the instrument itself and subsequent references to Article 28 in other United Nations instruments, it is possible to develop an understanding of the content of the right to a social and international order for the realization of human rights. 'Social order' is seen as referring to national regimes[13] and Article 28 as a whole 'emphasises the political, legal and economic relations within . . . and between states'.[14] Both the social and international order should be founded on the rule of law, mention of which is made in the Universal Declaration's preamble. The preamble of the 1993 Vienna Declaration elaborated on the requirements of an international order, which it described as an aspiration of all peoples:

> an international order based on the principles enshrined in the Charter of the United Nations, including promoting and encouraging respect for human rights and fundamental freedoms for all and respect for the principle of equal rights and self-determination of peoples, peace, democracy, justice, equality, rule of law, pluralism, development, better standards of living and solidarity.[15]

It can also be concluded that an order for the realization of rights necessarily entails corresponding duties.[16] Some of the general duties of states are clear under the present international order – refraining from the use of force or intervening in the domestic affairs of other states. Article 28 can be said to encapsulate these more general duties; it is seen as echoing 'the main Preamble's insistence on the rule of law and friendly relations

---

[13] Thomas Pogge, *World Poverty and Human Rights: Cosmopolitan Responsibilities and Reforms* (Cambridge: Polity Press, 2008) 130.

[14] Emily Logan, 'Article 28', in Donncha O'Connell (ed.) *60 Years, 30 Perspectives: Ireland and the Universal Declaration* (Dublin: Amnesty International/New Island, 2009) 184.

[15] World Conference on Human Rights, UN Doc A/CONF.157/23, 12 July 1993.

[16] Mary Ann Glendon, '*Propter Honoris Respectum*: Knowing the Universal Declaration of Human Rights' (1998) 73 *Notre Dame L. Rev.* 1153, 1169: 'Two features of the order are spelt out in Article 29 and 30 – duties and limitations'.

among nations.'[17] Notably, General Assembly Resolution 60/163 (2005) on the 'Promotion of peace as a vital requirement for the full enjoyment of human rights by all' specifically invokes Article 28:

> *Recalling* that everyone is entitled to a social and international order in which the rights and freedoms set forth in the Universal Declaration of Human Rights can be fully realized.

In the context of the realization of human rights, the duties of states internationally, as opposed to within their own domestic spheres, are perhaps not as clearly enunciated. This is particularly so when one considers state action, either individually or collectively, which harms human rights extraterritorially. This essay accordingly focuses on the nature of the international order, as opposed to domestic orders, and its impact on the realization of human rights. International cooperation with regard to human rights should clearly be embedded in such an international order.

A number of United Nations instruments have emphasized that it is not only states that have a role to play with regard to the fulfilment of Article 28, in keeping with the Universal Declaration's reference to 'every individual and organ of society' in its preamble. The Declaration on the Right and Responsibility of Individuals, Groups and Organs of Society to Promote and Protect Universally Recognized Human Rights and Fundamental Freedoms states that:

> individuals, groups, institutions and non-governmental organizations also have an important role and responsibility in contributing, as appropriate, to the promotion of the right of everyone to a social and international order in which the rights and freedoms set forth in the Universal Declaration of Human Rights and other human rights instruments can be fully realized.[18]

Interestingly, these instruments refer to everyone's right to a social and international order and also extend the scope of that right to other rights and freedoms beyond those set out in the Universal Declaration.[19]

---

17 Glendon, *A World Made New* (n3) 190.

18 Declaration on the Right and Responsibility of Individuals, Groups and Organs of Society to Promote and Protect Universally Recognized Human Rights and Fundamental Freedoms, UN GA Res 53/144, UN Doc A/RES/53/144, 8 March 1999.

19 See also Draft Declaration on Human Social Responsibilities (2003) Art. 11, Human rights and responsibilities, *Final report of the Special Rapporteur, Miguel Alfonso Martínez, on the Study requested by the Commission*, UN Doc E/CN.4/2003/105, 17 March 2003, referring to the duty of individuals to contribute to the creation of an international and social order.

A key aspect of the international order envisaged by Article 28, which Malik himself recognized, was the presence of supranational organizations that could exercise oversight of states in relation to human rights. There had been some debate during the drafting of the Universal Declaration on the question of international enforceability of the rights in the document, as well as the supremacy of an international body over the jurisdiction of individual nations.[20] Although issues of enforcement were put aside in the end, the delegates did generally agree that national authority is supreme and will remain so, yet it is to 'no longer be exclusive'.[21] Since 1948, highly developed human rights machinery has been put in place at the international, regional and, depending on the individual state, the national level. Various bodies exercise oversight of a state's human rights record via state reporting, individual complaints, litigation and now Universal Periodic Reviews before the United Nations Human Rights Council. Accountability for the most serious human rights abuses, those designated as international crimes, has developed significantly in the past two decades, with a permanent International Criminal Court now in place and operational. It has been observed that these human rights treaties and monitoring systems have helped to shape the existing international order.[22] It is argued that:

> more has been achieved by the existence of international standards and monitoring mechanisms than could have been achieved by domestic pressure alone. International human rights standards provide objective benchmarks around which criticism of the state can be framed.[23]

It must be conceded, however, that the human rights machinery currently in place is generally neither universal nor consistent. The numerous human rights courts and bodies have varying jurisdictions, limited by geographic reach and the types of rights they can adjudicate on, and differing enforcement powers. Asia, most notoriously, lacks a regional human rights mechanism, and the recent subregional body set up under ASEAN is considered to be weak and flawed from the outset.[24] Substantively, it is only in the past couple of years that an individual complaints mechanism has been put in place under the International Covenant on Economic,

---

20 Glendon, *A World Made New* (n3) 95.

21 *Ibid.*, 114.

22 Logan (n14) 185.

23 *Ibid.*, 186.

24 See generally Tan Hsien-Li, *The ASEAN Intergovernmental Commission on Human Rights* (Cambridge: CUP, 2011).

Social and Cultural Rights, and it was only in 2010 that the General Assembly explicitly acknowledged the right to water as a fundamental human right. In general, it can be stated that human rights bodies lack the effective enforcement of other international bodies, such as the World Trade Organization and the International Centre for the Settlement of Investment Disputes. Of particular note is that the human rights bodies almost exclusively focus on the conduct of states themselves, usually to the exclusion of other actors whose actions and policies impact on human rights, specifically multinational corporations and international financial and trade institutions. Such bodies play a significant role in the shaping of the present international order.

Discussions at the international level regarding business, trade and human rights have seen reference made to the need for an acceptable international order respectful of human rights. In his Report to the General Assembly in 2000 on 'Globalization and its impact on the full enjoyment of all human rights', the Secretary-General considered that 'an international and social order is one that promotes the inherent dignity of the human person, respects the right of people to self-determination and seeks social progress through participatory development and by promoting equality and non-discrimination in a peaceful, interdependent and accountable world'.[25] He specifically identified the Global Compact, the corporate social responsibility model put forward by the United Nations, as a way of bringing trade, business and human rights together to realize the promise of Article 28.[26] In response to this report, the High Commissioner for Human Rights commented that:

> Achieving fair and equitable trade liberalization by adopting human rights approaches to WTO rules will be an important step in establishing a just international and social order and a failure to do so could perpetuate or even exacerbate existing inequalities.[27]

The High Commissioner felt specifically that 'the reduction and eventual elimination of export subsidies will be an important step in achieving a just international and social order as envisaged under article 28 of the Universal Declaration.'[28]

---

[25] United Nations Secretary-General, Report to General Assembly, UN Doc A/55/342, 'Preliminary Report', 2000, para 7.

[26] *Ibid.*, para 8.

[27] *Globalisation and its impact on the full enjoyment of human rights*, Report of the High Commissioner for Human Rights submitted in accordance with Commission on Human Rights Resolution 2001/32, UN Doc E/CN.4/2002/54, 15 January 2002, para 9.

[28] *Ibid.*

Business interests have underpinned the development of the international trade system, with transnational corporations and related bodies instrumental in determining the direction of developments. Moreover, it can be said that they have played a role in stifling more effective regulation of corporate activities affecting human rights. A UN Report from 1978 stated that:

> The effective regulation of multinational corporations which could make them more acceptable instruments of international prosperity and cooperation has yet to be devised.[29]

Little seems to have changed since then. From the perspective of business and human rights, efforts aimed at holding corporate entities to account for human rights abuses have been piecemeal to date: some prosecutions of individual company officers (as happened after the Second World War), various civil claims against companies in national courts (such as under the Alien Torts Claims Statute in the United States), and occasional criticism by human rights bodies of states for failing to control corporate activities (for example, the African Commission on Human Rights in relation to Shell's operations in Nigeria). The United Nations has focused more on this issue in recent years and the Secretary-General appointed a Special Representative, John Ruggie to examine the question of business and human rights. Ruggie left behind the broad brush approach of the 2003 *Draft Norms on the Responsibilities of Transnational Corporations & Other Business Entities with regard to Human Rights,* and prepared a framework which emphasizes the state duty to protect human rights, the business responsibility to respect human rights and the need for effective remedies.[30]

In an address to the General Assembly, Ruggie stated that 'the era of declaratory [corporate social responsibility] is over'.[31] Nevertheless, what

---

[29] United Nations Committee for Development Planning, Official Records of the Economic and Social Council, 1978, Supplement No. 6, para 27 cited in Report of the Secretary-General, *The International Dimensions of the Right to Development as a Human Right in Relations with Other Human Rights based on International Co-operation, including the Right to Peace, taking into account the requirements of the New International Economic Order and the Fundamental Human Needs,* UN Doc E/CN.4/1334, 2 January 1979, 145.

[30] Report of the Special Representative of the Secretary-General on the issue of human rights and transnational corporations and other business enterprises, John Ruggie, *Guiding Principles on Business and Human Rights: Implementing the United Nations 'Protect, Respect and Remedy' Framework*, UN Doc A/HRC/17/31, 21 March 2011.

[31] Statement by Professor John Ruggie, Mandate of the Special Representative of the Secretary-General on the Issue of Human Rights and Transnational

remains lacking is a United Nations framework for business and human rights with a binding legal basis, clearly necessary for curbing corporate abuses. Recent economic turmoil seems to provide proof that the existing international and national orders have failed to place meaningful regulation on corporate actors. Such entities enjoy rights within national legal systems and under international law, but without sufficient responsibilities, and given the record of corporate complicity in human rights abuses, the international order as demanded by Article 28 is notably wanting in this respect.

Article 28 of the Universal Declaration has been described as an 'enabling' right, 'one that is necessary so that the other rights can be attained'.[32] Richard Falk has commented on the 'normative promise' of the provision, which, in his view, embraces 'a commitment to establish a just world order premised on humane governance'.[33] Stephen Marks takes this even further, referring to the 'revolutionary proposition in Article 28, according to which everyone has a "right" to a social and international order in which all human rights can be assured'.[34] If this is taken seriously he writes,

> then everyone has a right to a *radical change in power relations both domestically and internationally*, for no political economy or legal system on earth today adequately ensures all human rights for everyone, and the structures of international relations often inhibit their full enjoyment. After the great ideological battles of the twentieth century, we are confronted in this century with the same unjust structures that contribute to world poverty, exacerbated by the negative impacts of globalization.[35]

In describing this right as one which requires certain changes for the realization of all rights, the echoes with the right to development are striking and it is in relation to this right that Article 28 has provided noticeable

---

Corporations and Other Business Entities, 65th Session of the United Nations General Assembly, 26 October 2010, 3, available online at: http://www.business-humanrights.org/media/documents/ruggie-statement-to-un-gen-assembly-26-oct-2010.pdf

[32] Victor W. Sidel, 'The Right to a Just and Peaceful Social and International Order' (1998) 3(2) *Health and Human Rights* 111.

[33] Richard Falk, *On Humane Governance: Toward a New Global Politics* (Pennsylvania University Press, 1995) cited in Sidel, 'The Right to a Just and Peaceful Social and International Order' (n32) 111.

[34] Stephen Marks, 'Foreword', in Margot E. Salomon, *Global Responsibility for Human Rights – World Poverty and the Development of International Law* (Oxford: OUP, 2007) x.

[35] *Ibid.*, [emphasis added].

traction. Asbjørn Eide described Article 28 as the embryo for the 1986 Declaration on the Right to Development.[36] Indeed in 1979, this provision was referred to in a Report of the Secretary-General on the Right to Development as one of the legal norms relevant to this right, specifically in connection with the issue of international cooperation.[37] The preamble of the Declaration on the Right to Development states:

> *Considering* that under the provisions of the Universal Declaration of Human Rights everyone is entitled to a social and international order in which the rights and freedoms set forth in that Declaration can be fully realized.[38]

Margot Salomon notes that an earlier draft and the work of the drafting committee reveal that 'the right to development is "*based upon* Article 28 of the Universal Declaration of Human Rights".'[39] Alongside Articles 55 and 56 of the UN Charter, Article 28 is seen as providing 'the intellectual origins and legal claims' of the Declaration on the Right to Development.[40] The right to development itself can be viewed as 'a commitment to Article 28'.[41]

The Declaration on the Right to Development lays the primary responsibility upon states for the creation of national and international conditions favourable to the realization of the right to development. Moreover, it recognizes that the realization of this right requires changes to the existing international order. In particular, Article 3, paragraph 3 of the Declaration sets out the importance of international cooperation:

> States have the duty to co-operate with each other in ensuring development and eliminating obstacles to development. States should realize their rights and fulfil their duties in such a manner as to promote a new international economic order based on sovereign equality, interdependence, mutual interest and co-operation among all States, as well as to encourage the observance and realization of human rights.

---

36 Asbjørn Eide, 'Human Rights Requirements to Social and Economic Development' (1996) 21(1) *Food Policy* 23, 25.

37 Report of the Secretary-General, *The International Dimensions of the Right to Development as a Human Right in Relations with Other Human Rights based on International Co-operation, including the Right to Peace, taking into account the requirements of the New International Economic Order and the Fundamental Human Needs*, UN Doc E/CN.4/1334, 2 January 1979, 145.

38 UN GA Res 41/128, Declaration on the Right to Development, 4 December 1986.

39 Salomon, *Global Responsibility for Human Rights* (n34) 50, n215.

40 *Ibid.*, 4.

41 Daniel Aguirre, *The Human Right to Development in a Globalized World* (Aldershot: Ashgate, 2008) 68.

The United Nations Special Rapporteur on Human Rights and Responsibilities, Miguel Alfonso Martínez, has stated that:

> Directly linked with the achievement of that more just and humane international and social order to which the world aspires, the Declaration on the Right to Development proclaims, in so many words, the duty of States to cooperate among themselves so as to realize this extremely important and inalienable human right, which is both individual and collective in essence.[42]

The idea that the realization of human rights is not solely within developing states' own control was also recognized by the Committee on Economic, Social and Cultural Rights in the context of poverty reduction. The Committee has stated that it is 'deeply aware' of the 'structural obstacles to the eradication of poverty in developing countries', some of which 'lie beyond their control in the contemporary international order'.[43] In its view:

> . . . it is imperative that measures be urgently taken to remove these global structural obstacles, such as unsustainable foreign debt, the widening gap between rich and poor, and the absence of an equitable multilateral trade, investment and financial system, otherwise the national anti-poverty strategies of some States have limited chance of sustainable success. In this regard, the Committee notes article 28 of the Universal Declaration of Human Rights, as well as the Declaration on the Right to Development, in particular article 3.3.[44]

Exploration of the right set down in Article 28 of the Universal Declaration and its application by various United Nations bodies and scholars very quickly demonstrates the significant structural barriers within the present international order that hinder the realization of human rights globally.

---

42 *Human rights and responsibilities*, Final report of the Special Rapporteur, Miguel Alfonso Martínez, on the Study requested by the Commission, UN Doc E/CN.4/2003/105, 17 March 2003, para 57.

43 Statement adopted by the Committee on Economic, Social and Cultural Rights on 4 May 2001, *Poverty and the International Covenant on Economic, Social and Cultural Rights:* 10/05/2001/10, E/C.12/2001/10, para 21.

44 *Ibid.* See also *Millennium Development Goals,* 'Goal 8 – Develop a Global Partnership for Development: Target 8.A: Develop further an open, rule-based, predictable, non-discriminatory trading and financial system; Target 8.D: Deal comprehensively with the debt problems of developing countries; Target 8.E: In cooperation with pharmaceutical companies, provide access to affordable essential drugs in developing countries.' On the relationship between the MDGs and human rights see Philip Alston, 'Ships Passing in the Night: The Current State of Human Rights and Development as Seen Through the Lens of the Millennium Development Goals' (2005) 27 *HRQ* 3.

The next section tentatively examines means for the possible realization of this article.

3. REALIZING ARTICLE 28

To realize the right set out in Article 28 of the Universal Declaration, two key approaches have been identified: improving international cooperation amongst states for the realization of human rights and reforming the existing international order itself, particularly those institutions and laws regarding trade and finance. Both of these are complementary and, as will be shown, if international cooperation is to be taken seriously to the extent of affecting power relations, then reform of the existing order clearly becomes imperative.

3.1 International Cooperation in Human Rights Law

International cooperation has of course been seen as an essential element of the international human rights system since its inception. However, the concept already had a pedigree in public international law, with a general shift having taken place from an international politico-legal system founded on the principles of states' independence and coexistence, to one currently based on the principles of interdependence and cooperation.[45] Edward McWhinney traces the origins of what was termed the 'new International Law of Cooperation' to the end of the nineteenth and beginning of the twentieth centuries.[46] The effects of the industrial revolution, colonialism, an international division of labour, increasing complexity and sophistication of technology, and the resultant standards of living, have all meant that the well-being and security of one state is increasingly dependent and reliant on the actions of other states, individually and collectively.[47] The fundamental purpose of the League of Nations was 'to promote international cooperation and to achieve international peace and

---

45 See Wolfgang Friedmann, *The Changing Structure of International Law* (New York: Columbia University Press, 1964).

46 Edward McWhinney, 'The Concept of Cooperation', in Mohammed Bedjaoui (ed.) *International Law: Achievements and Prospects* (Leiden: Martinus Nijhoff Publishers, 1991) 425–36.

47 See David Held and Anthony McGrew (eds) *The Global Transformations Reader: An Introduction to the Globalization Debate* (Cambridge: Polity Press, 2003).

security.'[48] A commentator at the time wrote that 'a shifting of emphasis from rights of States to responsibilities of States is the fundamental change which the Covenant will make in international law.'[49] The new assumption underlying international law and motivating the move towards responsibilities can be seen in the principle of international cooperation.

The Charter of the United Nations similarly sets this principle at the heart of the organization, which has the stated purpose of seeking:

> to achieve international co-operation in solving international problems of an economic, social, cultural, or humanitarian character, and in promoting and encouraging respect for human rights and for fundamental freedoms for all without distinction as to race, sex, language, or religion.[50]

Chapter IX of the Charter obliges states to take 'joint and separate action in co-operation with the Organization for the achievement of . . . universal respect for, and observance of, human rights and fundamental freedoms for all'.[51] The constitutional document of the organization recognizes that international cooperation is essential to address human rights, amongst the other goals of the United Nations.

International human rights law also gives detailed legal expression to the requirement of international cooperation. Article 28 of the Universal Declaration preceded a number of human rights treaties which expressly include international cooperation as a necessary component. Margot Salomon has observed that:

> The steadily-emerging international law of cooperation is rooted in Article 28 – an early formal expression by the international community that human rights involve claims on our global order; that our global order is to be assessed, developed and reformed principally by reference to its relative impact on human rights fulfilment.[52]

The concept of international cooperation was elaborated upon in documents such as the 1968 Tehran Declaration[53] and the 1993 Vienna

---

48 League of Nations, *Covenant of the League of Nations*, 28 April 1919, Preamble.

49 Quincy Wright, 'Effects of the League of Nations Covenant' (1919) 13(4) *American Political Science Review* 556, 556–8.

50 Charter of the United Nations, 24 October 1945, 1 UNTS XVI, Art. 1(3).

51 *Ibid.*, Arts 55 and 56.

52 Salomon, *Global Responsibility for Human Rights* (n34) 75.

53 Proclamation of Teheran, Final Act of the International Conference on Human Rights, Teheran, 22 April to 13 May 1968, UN Doc A/CONF. 32/41 at 3 (1968).

Declaration and Programme of Action,[54] and has also been included in binding treaties,[55] particularly in relation to economic, social and cultural rights. That said, the concept of cooperation as a legal requirement under international law, as opposed to a political aspiration, remains relatively novel and not well understood or implemented in practice. While its place in politics is well established, its place in international law has remained embryonic.[56]

It is instructive to consider Article 2(1) of the International Covenant on Economic, Social and Cultural Rights, the general implementation article applying to all the Covenant rights which obliges:

> Each State Party to the present Covenant . . ., to take steps, individually and *through international assistance and co-operation*, especially economic and technical, to the maximum of its available resources, with a view to achieving progressively the full realization of the rights recognized in the present Covenant by all appropriate means, including particularly the adoption of legislative measures.[57]

---

54 Vienna Declaration, World Conference on Human Rights, Vienna, 25 June 1993, UN Doc A/CONF.157/24 (Part I) at 20 (1993).

55 See, for example, International Covenant on Economic, Social and Cultural Rights (adopted 16 December 1966, entered into force 3 January 1976) 993 UNTS 3 (ICESCR); Declaration on the Right to Development, UN Doc A/RES/41/128, 4 December 1986; Convention on the Rights of the Child, adopted and opened for signature, ratification and accession by UN GA Res 44/25 of 20 November 1989, entered into force 2 September 1990; Convention on the Elimination of Discrimination Against Women, adopted and opened for signature, ratification and accession by UN GA Res 34/180 of 18 December 1979, entered into force 3 September 1981; Organization of American States, Additional Protocol to the American Convention on Human Rights in the Area of Economic, Social and Cultural Rights ('Protocol of San Salvador') adopted 17 November 1998, entered into force 16 November 1999.

56 Sigrun Skogly, *Beyond National Borders: States' Human Rights Obligations in International Cooperation* (Antwerp: Intersentia, 2006) 4 and 13. Though the legal content of international cooperation has long been overlooked in this context it is now receiving far more attention. See for example: Fons Coomans and Menno Kamminga (eds), *Extraterritorial Application of Human Rights Treaties* (Antwerp: Intersentia, 2004); Wouter Vandenhole, 'Third State Obligations under the ICESCR: A Case Study of EU Sugar Policy' (2007) 76(1) *Nordic J Int'l L* 73; International Council on Human Rights Policy, *Duties sans Frontières: Human Rights and Global Social Justice* (ICHRP, Geneva, 2003); Mark Gibney et al., 'Transnational State Responsibility for Violations of Human Rights' (1999) 12 *Harvard Human Rights J* 267; Sigrun Skogly and Mark Gibney, 'Transnational Human Rights Obligations' (2002) 24 *HRQ* 781; Smita Narula, 'The Right to Food: Holding Global Actors Accountable Under International Law' (2005–6) 44 *Columbia J Transnat'l L* 691.

57 UN GA Res 2200A (XXI) 21 UN GAOR Supp. (No. 16) at 49, UN Doc A/6316 (1966) 993 UNTS 3, entered into force Jan. 3, 1976 [emphasis added].

The incorporation of international cooperation into Article 2(1) could be said to give expression in treaty law to Article 28's vision of a collaborative international order for the realization of human rights, albeit limited to economic, social and cultural rights. The inclusion of the phrase 'and through international assistance and cooperation' in the Covenant was a recognition that developing countries would be unable to fulfil their primary obligations on their own. During the drafting of the Covenant the representatives from Egypt and India stated respectively, that 'the available resources of the smallest countries, even if utilised to the maximum, would be insufficient, [and] as a result, those countries would have to fall back on international cooperation', and that 'international cooperation [was] a point which was of cardinal importance to the under-developed countries, which needed help if they were to be capable of implementing economic rights'.[58]

On the basis of their analysis of the drafting history of Article 2(1), Philip Alston and Gerard Quinn suggest an understanding of the meaning of international cooperation based on a requirement that wealthy states should:

> . . . conduct their economic policies in a manner which takes into account the interests of other countries by appropriate procedures of consultation; in the legitimate exercise of their economic sovereignty, they should seek to avoid any measure which causes substantial injury to other States, in particular to those interests of developing States and their peoples.[59]

An acceptable legal understanding of the requirement of Article 2(1) cannot be limited to simply providing assistance to poorer countries to offset the negative effects of an unjust international order. It is necessary to address the nature of the order itself, and the concept of international cooperation is fundamental to this deeper analysis. In this respect, it mandates an analysis of the power disequilibrium existing at the level of state interaction in the formulation of the international order. As was stated on several occasions in the drafting process,[60] the policies and actions of the

---

[58] Skogly, *Beyond National Borders* (n56) 85.

[59] Philip Alston and Gerard Quinn, 'The Nature of States' Parties Obligations Under the International Covenant on Economic, Social and Cultural Rights' (1987) 9 *HRQ* 191–2, quoting from the 'Draft declaration on the progressive development of principles of public international law relating to a new international economic order', submitted by the Committee on the Legal Aspects of the New International Order to the 62nd Conference of the International Law Association, Seoul, August 1986.

[60] For example, the Chilean representative argued that, 'the economic devel-

wealthy developed states have a substantial impact on the economic and financial well-being of developing states, and thus on their ability to realize the socio-economic rights of their people. As such, international cooperation can be characterized as a means of addressing the power differential between wealthy influential states and those states unable to realize the rights of their people. The concept of cooperation would then be fundamentally linked to this power differential, and obligations to cooperate would be based on any given state's relative power to effect the realization of rights in any other given state. This necessitates the removal of structural obstacles to the realization of rights that are themselves a manifestation of the existing power imbalance.

The Committee on Economic, Social and Cultural Rights has made some attempt in its work to address the phrase 'international assistance and cooperation'. In General Comment 3, the Committee confirmed that available resources 'refer to both the resources existing within a State and those available from the international community'.[61] It emphasized the 'essential role of such cooperation in facilitating the full realization of the relevant rights'[62] and went further to state that international cooperation 'is an obligation of all States' grounded in the United Nations Charter and 'well-established principles of international law'.[63] The Committee's General Comment 12 contains a section on international obligations, addressed at States Parties acting individually and through international organizations, such as the United Nations and associated institutions.[64] In General Comment 15 on the right to water, the Committee states:

> To comply with their international obligations in relation to the right to water, States parties have to respect the enjoyment of the right in other countries. International cooperation requires States parties to refrain from actions that interfere, directly or indirectly, with the enjoyment of the right to water in other countries.[65]

---

opment of the less developed countries was bound up with the factors over which the highly industrialised countries had more control than the developing countries themselves.' UN Doc A/C.3/SR.1203, para 12, as quoted in Alston and Quinn (n59) 189.

61 General Comment 3, 'The Nature of States Parties Obligations', CESCR 5th Session, 14 December 1990, para 13.

62 *Ibid.*

63 *Ibid.*, para 14.

64 General Comment 12, 'The Right to Adequate Food', CESCR 20th Session, UN Doc E/C.12/1999/5, 12 May 1999.

65 General Comment 15, 'The Right to Water', CESCR 25th Session, UN Doc E/C.12/2002/11, 20 January 2003, para 31.

Due diligence is urged in the negotiation and structuring of international agreements:

> With regard to the conclusion and implementation of other international and regional agreements, States parties should take steps to ensure that these instruments do not adversely impact upon the right to water. Agreements concerning trade liberalization should not curtail or inhibit a country's capacity to ensure the full realization of the right to water.[66]

The same can be seen to apply to the operations of those organizations formulating the structure of the international economic order:

> States parties should ensure that their actions as members of international organizations take due account of the right to water. Accordingly, States parties that are members of international financial institutions, notably the International Monetary Fund, the World Bank, and regional development banks, should take steps to ensure that the right to water is taken into account in their lending policies, credit agreements and other international measures.[67]

Taking into account the drafting history of the International Covenant on Economic, Social and Cultural Rights and the deliberations of the Committee, it is possible to set out the legal parameters of international cooperation. It is based on the need for addressing the global power and resources imbalance amongst states, which is fundamental for the universal realization of socio-economic rights, as is the removal of structural obstacles within the international order hindering such realization. Most significantly, and controversially, the resources of wealthy developed countries must be considered as part of those which should be available for the realization of socio-economic rights in developing countries. As a minimum, states must respect the human rights of persons in other countries, while also seeking to prevent their violation by third parties.[68] Furthermore, socio-economic rights should be respected and protected in the formulation of international agreements and in the operations of international financial and economic institutions of which states are members, both in their individual actions and in the policies and activities of the given institution as a

---

66 *Ibid.*, para 35.

67 *Ibid.*, para 36.

68 This can be distinguished from situations where states exercise effective control over individuals or the territory of another state and can thus directly violate human rights, triggering their international human rights obligations. See generally Fons Coomans and Menno Kamminga (eds), *Extraterritorial Application of Human Rights Treaties* (n56).

whole. The provision of humanitarian assistance and development aid are also incumbent on those states with the resources to do so.

3.2 Further Theoretical Development and Practical Application

The emerging legal definition of international cooperation is somewhat short on clearly binding obligations, although certain requirements have been enunciated, albeit in the language of best practice. These would include the requirement that states *should take steps* to ensure that international agreements do not cause rights violations.[69] It seems clear that the way forward is to at least strengthen those already outlined requirements into binding obligations. For example, if it were a binding obligation that states *must ensure* that socio-economic rights are not violated by the negotiation, creation and implementation of agreements forming the structure of the international economic order, then a number of procedural mechanisms would have to be put in place to ensure compliance. Possible mechanisms could assess particular negotiating positions and the proposed agreements as a whole for possible negative effects on human rights. Equally important would be procedures to create and disseminate information, increase transparency and facilitate genuine consultation and participation. The fundamental process of negotiating and creating the structure of the international order would have to be changed dramatically. These procedural mechanisms would inevitably coalesce to act as checks and balances, ensuring that the exercise of power in the formulation of the international economic order, at the least, does not inhibit another state's capacity to realize the Covenant rights of its people.

If international cooperation necessarily involves an analysis of power relations and their impact on human rights, then reform of the international order will clearly become imperative. Given the ever increasing weight of evidence that structural obstacles are the root cause of the failure of 60 years of 'development', and given the clear fact that the wealthy states have far greater influence over this structure, the increasing differential in the wealth and power of the world's nations is hard to justify. The disparity is remarkably clear in a simple balance-sheet comparison of financial flows between developed and developing countries. For example, in 2008 total Official Development Assistance amounted to US$100 billion,[70] yet overall there was a net financial transfer of US$900

---

[69] See n65 and accompanying text.

[70] See Eckhard Deutscher, *Development Co-operation Report 2010*, OECD, 2010, Figure 8.2, 98. On the practice and effectiveness of aid, see Fatoumata

billion from developing to developed countries.[71] The current regime of international trade, finance and investment arrangements in effect moulds a reality where 44 per cent of the world's population, living on less than US$2 a day, benefit from only 1.3 per cent of the global product; while those living in high income countries have an 81 per cent share of that product.[72] The former 2,735 million people would need an increase of only 1 per cent share to lift them over this poverty threshold as defined by the World Bank.[73] As Thomas Pogge notes, some have attempted to justify this differential by allusion to 'explanatory nationalism'.[74] This argument attempts to locate the differing levels and rates of development of the world's nations in factors internal to those nations. In this way it explains the under-development of poor nations by reference primarily to domestic corruption, governmental incompetence and the oppression of ruling elites. Yet once it is recognized that these factors certainly play a part it also becomes obvious that they do not tell the whole story. To complete the story, Pogge points back to this growing weight of evidence regarding structural obstacles. For example:

> In the WTO negotiations, the affluent countries insisted on continued and asymmetrical protections of their markets through tariffs, quotas, anti-dumping duties, export credits, and huge subsidies to domestic producers. Such protectionism provides a compelling illustration of the hypocrisy of the rich states that insist and command that their own exports be received with open markets. And it greatly impairs export opportunities for the very poorest countries and regions. If the rich countries scrapped their protectionist barriers against imports from poor countries, the populations of the latter would benefit greatly: hundreds of millions would escape unemployment, wage levels would rise substantially, and incoming export revenues would be higher by hundreds of billions of dollars each year.[75]

Jawara and Aileen Kwa, *Behind the Scenes at the WTO: The Real World of International Trade Relations – The Lessons of Cancún* (London: Zed Books, 2004) 149; UNDP, *Human Development Report 2005: International Cooperation at a Crossroads – Aid, Trade, and Security in an Unequal World,* UNDP-New York, 2005, 73–110; Gilles Carbonnier, 'Official Development Assistance Once More Under Fire From Critics' (2010) *International Development Policy* Series 1; Dambisa Moyo, *Dead Aid: Why Aid is not Working and How there is a Better Way for Africa* (London: Penguin, 2009).

[71] See United Nations, *World Economic Situation and Prospects: 2010*, UN-New York, 2010, ix.

[72] Thomas Pogge, 'World Poverty and Human Rights' (2005) 19(1) *Ethics and International Affairs* 1.

[73] *Ibid.*

[74] *Ibid.*, 6.

[75] *Ibid.*

The unbalanced outcome of these negotiations reflects the imbalance in power between the negotiating states and the bias in decision-making procedures. The United Nations Development Programme has stated that the WTO system perpetuates mass poverty and deepening inequality and concluded that its rules are based on a foundation of hypocrisy and double standards between wealthy and poor nations.[76] The WTO is said to operate by consensus; however the process by which this 'consensus' is reached is one of exclusion, arm-twisting and side-line bilateral deals aimed at destroying the coherence of developing country interests and preventing them from acting as a bloc.[77] Collectively, 'the Quad' (US, EU, Canada and Japan) determine the agenda for negotiations and draft the texts of future WTO Declarations behind closed doors at interim meetings with a small number of other countries present by invitation only. Known as 'mini-Ministerials',[78] these meetings are not a part of the *modus operandi* set out in the original constitutional document of the organization.[79] The imbalance is also crucially reflected in the number of staff making up each country's permanent trade mission in Geneva; the US has 14 staff devoted solely to WTO meetings (around 1000 per year, many held in parallel), most developing countries have between two and five staff which must cover the WTO and the activities of 20 other international agencies based in Geneva, and 20 of the poorest nations have no permanent mission at all.[80] The imbalance of power becomes even more acute when regional trade negotiations are considered, as is the case in past efforts to

---

[76] UNDP, *Human Development Report 2005* (n70).

[77] See Jawara and Kwa (n70); Aileen Kwa, *Rethinking the Trading System,* Dialogue on Globalisation – Occasional Papers, No. 32 (Geneva: Friedrich-Ebert-Stiftung, 2007); Eric Burt, 'Developing Countries and the Framework for Negotiations on Foreign Direct Investment in the World Trade Organisation' (1997) *American University Journal of International Law and Policy* 12; Ernst-Ulrich Petersman (ed.), *Developing Countries in the Doha Round: WTO Decision-making Procedures and Negotiations on Trade in Agriculture and Services* (Robert Schuman Centre for Advanced Studies – European University Institute, 2005).

[78] Jawara and Kwa (n70) 50–79. On the substantive as well as the procedural aspects of imbalance see Bernard Hoekman, 'Operationalising the Concept of Policy Space in the WTO: Beyond Special and Differential Treatment', in Ernst-Ulrich Petersman (ed) *Developing Countries in the Doha Round* (n77) 163.

[79] Marrakesh Agreement establishing the World Trade Organization (with final act, annexes and protocol) Concluded at Marrakesh on 15 April 1994, UNTS Vol. 1867, No. 31874.

[80] Jawara and Kwa (n70) 20–1.

establish a Free Trade Area of the Americas[81] and current negotiations on a Trans-Pacific Partnership, both involving the US and a group of other, by far economically weaker nations. In the latter case the Special Rapporteur on the right to health has been asked to intervene in the negotiations by a group of civil society organizations and individuals, stressing a lack of transparency and the exploitation of uneven bargaining power.[82]

Completing what are sometimes referred to as the three pillars of the international economic order, the IMF and the World Bank are in many ways far more obviously biased in favour of the wealthy nations of the North. Within these institutions there is not even a pretence of egalitarianism in the process of decision-making, as is at least partially defended by the formal notion of consensus in the WTO. As constitutionally determined, the decision-making power of states in both these institutions is based on their relative wealth. Voting power is effectively assigned according to the size of the state's share in the global economy, which is related directly to its wealth. Within the World Bank, for instance, the US holds the greatest share of the vote, at 17 per cent, followed by Japan, Germany, the United Kingdom and France. Together these five members control 40 per cent of the vote. At the other end the poorest 48 African countries control 5.5 per cent.[83] Such disparities are exacerbated by disconnection and unaccountability, as the wealthiest nations are not dependent on these institutions and so the policies and conditions which they set do not apply to them. This demonstrates clearly that any legal theory of international obligations towards the realization of human rights must focus on interstate power relations and the structural obstacles to eliminating poverty and guaranteeing human rights.

---

[81] Maude Barlow, *The Free Trade Area of the Americas and the Threat to Social Programs, Environmental Sustainability and Social Justice in Canada and the Americas* (The Council of Canadians, 2001).

[82] International Centre for Trade and Sustainable Development, 'IP Provisions in Trans-Pacific Partnership Negotiations Raise Public Health Concerns', *Bridges Weekly Trade News Digest,* 15(10) (23 March 2011). See also Knowledge Ecology International, Letter to Anand Grover and Basis for Request that the Special Rapporteur for the United Nations on the right of everyone to the enjoyment of the highest attainable standard of health Issue an Urgent Appeal with Regard to the Trans-Pacific Partnership Agreement Negotiation, 22 March 2011, available at http://haieurope.org/wp-content/uploads/2011/03/22-Mar-2011-KEI-Complaint-to-UN-Rapporteur-Trans-Pacific-Partnership-Agreement-HAI-Endorsed.pdf, accessed 17 August 2011.

[83] See Margot Salomon, *International Economic Governance and Human Rights Accountability*, London School of Economics, Law, Society and Economy Working Papers – 9/2007, 20.

Margot Salomon has developed such a theory on the legal content of international cooperation in light of economic global governance and the power and influence which wealthy states exercise. She echoes Pogge in stating that 'it is also the very *design* of the economic order, which contributes to the perpetuation of world poverty',[84] and that poverty is 'a product of a system that repeated findings demonstrate benefits some by virtue of its *structure* while disadvantaging others.'[85] For Salomon the process of developing the legal content of international cooperation must be pursued by

> facilitating methods of determining state responsibility for global structural impediments to the exercise of basic socio-economic rights of people in far off places . . . since this is essential to establishing a process of remedying existing violations manifested in world poverty, and preventing further ones.[86]

Salomon notes in particular the 'concentration of power among certain states that design, and give effect to, this economic system.'[87] She seeks to address this power differential within her theory of how responsibility should be assigned to individual state actors under an obligation to cooperate internationally, and proposes an allocation based on

> the state's weight and capacity in the world economy; its relative power and influence over the direction of finance, trade, and development; and the degree to which it benefits from the existing distribution of global wealth and resources.[88]

Applying this theory in practice would obviously need to overcome the hostility of those wealthy states that would seek to protect their self-interest.

This problem is substantial as there are a wide variety of circumstances in which the legal requirements of international cooperation could be

---

[84] Resulting in the death of around 18 million people worldwide every year (Thomas Pogge,'World Poverty and Human Rights' (n72) 1).

[85] Salomon, *Global Responsibility for Human Rights* (n34) 9 [original emphasis].

[86] *Ibid.*

[87] *Ibid.*, 45.

[88] *Ibid.*, 200. Elsewhere Salomon has noted that 'the independence and autonomy formally afforded states as sovereign equals under international law does not endow them with functional equality in the shaping or enforcement of the rules of the game. Disparities in size, population, and particularly, wealth create power differentials between and among states that mock notions of substantive sovereign equality.' Margot Salomon, 'Poverty, Privilege and International Law: The Millennium Development Goals and the Guise of Humanitarianism' (2008) 51 *German Yearbook of International Law* 39, 41.

practically applied, meaning that a broad spectrum of state's actions could be affected. Sigrun Skogly identifies at least four main areas of states' foreign policy in which the legal obligation to cooperate could apply: trade, development cooperation, participation in intergovernmental institutions and security cooperation.[89] Specific circumstances where the distinct aspects of an obligation to cooperate would create legal requirements on states are many, and only a few can be mentioned here. Reform of the WTO Agreement on Trade-Related Aspects of Intellectual Property Rights may be mandated given the problem of HIV anti-retroviral drugs in sub-Saharan Africa.[90] Disproportionate agricultural subsidies in the EU and the US may not be legally sustainable given their effects on the living standards of small-scale producers in the South.[91] Loans for development projects via state banks or the World Bank itself may be restricted given the proven detrimental effects of certain projects on human rights, notably those of indigenous peoples.[92] International investment law may need to be redesigned given its clear prioritization of the property rights of foreign companies over the socio-economic rights of local communities and individuals.[93]

As alluded to above, one potentially far-reaching application that is worth mentioning in particular could be the development of a set of guidelines based on the legal parameters of international cooperation that would frame and legitimize the process of negotiations on international economic agreements. The current international economic order is the result of power dominance. A set of guidelines informed by a concept of cooperation based on an accurate assessment of the power disequilibrium at the level of the international order, and aimed at creating a balance through certain procedures, could ground the negotiations and the agreements in human rights concerns. General principles of transparency, equality of arms and participation could be applied, and negotiating positions could be assessed by a prior human rights impact analysis. The guidelines could operate through mandatory procedural mechanisms and

---

89 Skogly, *Beyond National Borders* (n56) 189–201.

90 Emily Mok, 'International Assistance and Cooperation for Access to Essential Medicines' (2010) 12 *Health and Human Rights* 73.

91 Vandenhole, 'Third State Obligations under the ICESCR' (n56) 73–100.

92 FIAN, *Globalising Economic and Social Human Rights by Strengthening Extraterritorial State Obligations: Seven Case Studies on the Effects of German Policies on Human Rights in the South*, March 2005.

93 Luke Peterson, *Human Rights and Bilateral Investment Treaties: Mapping the role of human rights law within investor-state arbitration* (Montreal: Rights and Democracy, 2009).

deliberative feedback. Certain positions that could foreseeably result in rights violations would be deemed illegitimate and discarded, and only an agreement that was a product of a negotiating process that adhered to the guidelines and the procedures would be taken as legitimate and legally enforceable under international law. Though this would not immediately change the current order, it would ensure that at least that order would degenerate no further from a human rights standpoint.

3.3 Concrete Obligations to Cooperate as Implementation of Article 28

In these and other ways, implementing concrete requirements for states that could be derived from the international obligation to cooperate in human rights law can be seen as a form of implementation of the entitlement of Article 28. That entitlement to a rights-enabling social and international order is worded simply and is vast in its scope. The work that has been and remains to be done on delineating the legal content of international cooperation, in a sense breaks down that entitlement into a number of more manageable requirements to be implemented, which, taken together, can be viewed as delivering on the promise of Article 28.

It is argued, by Thomas Pogge in particular, that much could be achieved in terms of poverty reduction and development, if states simply corrected the existing inequalities in the international economic order. According to Pogge we are living in a world where

> current global institutional arrangements as codified in international law constitute a collective human rights violation of enormous proportions to which most of the world's affluent are making uncompensated contributions.[94]

He sees Article 28 as forming a 'moral plank' to underscore the need for change:

> Article 28 should be read as holding that the moral quality, or justice, of any institutional order depends primarily on the extent to which it affords all its participants secure access to the objects of their human rights; any institutional order is to be assessed and reformed principally by reference to its relative impact on the realization of the human rights of those on whom it is imposed.[95]

The author proposes various solutions, such as the elimination of affluent country protectionism (quotas, tariffs, subsidies, export credits etc.) and

---

[94] Thomas Pogge, 'Recognized and Violated by International Law: The Human Rights of the Global Poor' (2005) 18(4) *LJIL* 717, 721.

[95] *Ibid.* (footnote omitted).

more symmetrical rules of free and open competition, as a means of correcting the inequalities in the existing international order.[96] This would certainly go towards the implementation of Article 28.

While Article 28 may provide the moral plank, the obligation to cooperate internationally could provide the practical and legal planks. Pogge's analysis could be built upon to show how international institutions could be restricted or redirected so that they do not contribute to human rights violations, and then remain that way. Article 28 prompts many questions for which answers may not easily be gleaned. Even if we can identify now some aspects of the international order that should be changed, and we change them without a principled basis and a clear procedure for doing so, how do we ensure the same inequities are not reverted to in the future? What would stop power dominance from reasserting itself? This is where it becomes obvious that it is not sufficient to simply change the law, we must also change the way the law is made. For this we need principled guidelines and a procedural mechanism for framing the legitimacy of negotiations. The concept of international cooperation, with the leverage of its position in positive law, can help to provide them.

4. CONCLUSION

Article 28 is not a forgotten right, nor a forgotten concept and its demand has been reiterated in other United Nations declarations and has provided an impetus for scholarly critique of the existing global order. That being said, it is important that its plain message is not forgotten, that everyone has a right to a social and international order in which their rights can be realized, continues to be highlighted. Article 28 should act as a reminder to human rights advocates and scholars that the realization of specific human rights requires consideration of the national and international contexts. As Margaret Salomon has observed, 'Article 28 reflects a view that is now widely endorsed – that methods for the meaningful protection and promotion of human rights cannot be disassociated from the wider global environment'.[97]

There is no doubt that considerable advances have been made in the human rights machinery since 1948. But if we use Article 28 as a lens, we can see that considerable structural problems remain. Some of the current debate carries echoes of the proposed New International Economic Order

---

96 *Ibid.*, 725.

97 Salomon, *Global Responsibility for Human Rights* (n34) 73.

of the 1970s, referred to in the Declaration on the Right to Development, given the continued problems for human rights associated with protectionist barriers, such as export credits, debt and structural adjustment policies.[98] The Secretary-General of the UN acknowledged in 2000 that '[t]he challenge of article 28 of the Universal Declaration of Human Rights . . . remains.'[99] Article 28 has taken on a life outside of this document, which although aspirational in 1948, has become the authoritative statement of principles for human rights. The concept of an international and social order for the realization of human rights is explicit in various other human rights documents and implicit throughout the system as a whole.

Any discussion involving Article 28 focuses much-needed attention on the existing inequalities in the international order, where competition often seems the order of the day rather than cooperation. It prompts difficult questions of how to restructure or redirect international institutions such that they do not contribute to human rights violations, and how to assess the international order according to human rights norms. It is argued here that the concept of international cooperation and the further development of its legal content can provide some answers. It clarifies certain steps and delineates certain procedures that could help pave the way to the implementation of a just international order. International cooperation is an essential element for realizing Article 28. It demands not only a change in existing international law that perpetuates inequality, but also in the process by which that law, and thus the international order itself, is created.

---

[98] Sidel (n32) 119.

[99] United Nations Secretary-General Report to General Assembly, 'Preliminary Report', 2000 (n25) para 48.

2. Freedom from fear and the human right to peace

William A. Schabas

The human right to peace may be one of the best examples of a forgotten right. It was central to the vision of Franklin D. Roosevelt, who launched the modern process of recognition and codification of human rights with his 'Four Freedoms' speech. It was actually his 'State of the Union Address' to the United States Congress in 1941. The first three rights, freedom of speech and expression, freedom of worship, and freedom from want, were well-anchored in domestic legal provisions, many of them constitutional. Freedom from fear, on the other hand, could not be ensured by national law alone. It required international recognition and protection. Of course, the list of four freedoms was really a form of political shorthand. Roosevelt knew that many other rights were needed to complete the catalogue.

When the codifiers at the Commission of Human Rights put flesh on the skeleton that Roosevelt had produced, they required 30 distinct provisions, adding to the list rights to privacy, the protection of the family, association, scientific progress, torture, fair trial and many more. The 'right to peace', labelled 'freedom from fear' according to Roosevelt's nomenclature, is included in the Universal Declaration of Human Rights (the preamble, for example, explicitly cites the four freedoms). But it does not have the same prominence given in the speech to the first three freedoms. Roosevelt's attention to 'freedom from fear' cannot be challenged, however. What is difficult to understand is how 'freedom from fear' became somewhat marginalized in the years to follow.

The expression 'freedom from fear' is today invoked in a range of contexts, including counter-terrorism and mental health. It is helpful to return to Roosevelt's 1941 speech, because he briefly explained what was meant by the terse slogan. In Roosevelt's words: 'The fourth is freedom from fear – which, translated into world terms, means a world-wide reduction of armaments to such a point and in such a thorough fashion that no nation will be in a position to commit an act of physical aggression against any neighbour – anywhere in the world.' Roosevelt was talking about the human right to peace.

Peace has often been viewed as a 'peoples' right' rather than as a 'human right'. The African Charter on Human and Peoples' Rights recognizes the peoples' right to peace ('All peoples shall have the right to national and international peace and security'),[1] but there is nothing comparable in the universal human rights instruments, or the other main regional instruments of general application. In 2008, 2009 and 2011, the Human Rights Council adopted Resolutions on the promotion of 'the peoples' right to peace'. The Council was divided, with countries of the global south by and large voting in favour, while those of the north were opposed. On both sides, there seems to be no great clarity about what this right entails.

There is, to be sure, no suggestion that human rights law is in some sense opposed to peace. Yet the growth in two fields that are closely related to human rights law, namely international humanitarian law and international criminal law, may have helped push the issue of peace to the periphery. The relationship between international humanitarian law and human rights law has been addressed by the International Court of Justice on three occasions in recent years. It is said by some that human rights law, like the law of armed conflict, only speaks to the *jus in bello* and not to the *jus ad bellum*. This suggests that peace, though not *per se* undesirable, has no place in the priorities of human rights law and practice. The implication is that peace belongs to another agenda, such as that of political bodies like the United Nations Security Council or the General Assembly. Issues not unrelated to this debate have also manifested themselves at the International Criminal Court in the efforts to properly incorporate the crime of aggression, which in an earlier iteration was called 'crimes against peace', into the subject-matter jurisdiction provisions of the Rome Statute. Advocates of international criminal law argue that justice, not peace, is their real concern. The successful adoption of amendments to the Rome Statute at the Kampala Review Conference in June 2010 has added momentum to the importance of peace within the human rights vision.

1. THE 'PEOPLES' RIGHT TO PEACE'

In 1984, the United Nations General Assembly adopted a Resolution on 'The Peoples' Right to Peace'.[2] The context was the final years of the Cold

---

1 Art. 23(1) African Charter on Human and Peoples' Rights (adopted 27 June 1981, entered into force 21 October 1986) (1982) 21 ILM 58 (African Charter).

2 Declaration on the Right of Peoples to Peace, UN Doc A/RES/39/11, Annex. Somewhat earlier, the General Assembly had 'reaffirme[ed] the right

War, although nobody at the time understood it as such. The Resolution was proposed by Mongolia. The text proclaimed that 'the peoples of our planet have a sacred right to peace' and that 'the preservation of the right of peoples to peace and the promotion of its implementation constitute a fundamental obligation of each State'.[3]

There were periodic efforts to reinvigorate the Declaration. In 2002, a Resolution of the Commission on Human Rights affirmed 'the solemn proclamation that the peoples of our planet have a sacred right to peace'. The Commission stated 'that the preservation of the right of peoples to peace and the promotion of its implementation constitute a fundamental obligation of each State'.[4] That instrument led, the following year, to a Resolution in the General Assembly entitled 'Promotion of the right of peoples to peace'.[5] In 2005, the Commission adopted a Resolution entitled 'Promotion of peace as a vital requirement for the full enjoyment of all human rights by all'.[6] It was again echoed subsequently by a Resolution in the General Assembly along the same lines.[7] All of these Resolutions referred to the 1984 Declaration.

In 2008, the Human Rights Council adopted a Resolution entitled: 'Promotion of the right of peoples to peace'.[8] Like previous resolutions, it failed to obtain consensus and a recorded vote was required. The European Union explained that it voted against the Resolution, but noted the Resolution's call for a seminar which could provide 'a more comprehensive and open debate' on the subject.[9] No seminar took place, however, the ostensible reason being a lack of budget provisions for the event.[10] The following year, another Resolution was adopted along similar

---

of individuals, States and all mankind to life in peace' (Declaration on the Preparation of Societies for Life in Peace, UN Doc A/RES/33/73).

3 *Ibid.*, paras 1–2.

4 'Promotion of the right of peoples to peace', UN Doc E/CN.4/RES/2002/71. Adopted by 33 votes to 15, with 5 abstentions (UN Doc E/2002/23, 305).

5 'Promotion of the right of peoples to peace', UN Doc A/RES/57/216. Adopted by 116 votes to 53, with 14 abstentions (UN Doc A/57/PV.77, p. 26).

6 UN Doc E/CN.4/RES/2005/56. Adopted by 32 votes to 15, with 6 abstentions (UN Doc E/2005/23, p. 230).

7 'Promotion of peace as a vital requirement for the full enjoyment of all human rights by all', UN Doc A/RES/60/163. Adopted by 116 votes to 53, with 8 abstentions (UN Doc A/60/PV.64, p. 16).

8 'Promotion of the right of peoples to peace', UN Doc A/HRC/RES/8/9.

9 Explanation of vote by Slovenia (on behalf of EU) concerning UN Doc A/HRC/8/L.13, 18 June 2008 (http://www.un.org/webcast/unhrc/archive.asp?go=080618).

10 'Implementation of Human Rights Council resolution 8/9 on the promotion of the right of peoples to peace, Note by the Secretariat', UN Doc A/HRC/11/38.

lines.[11] Explaining the negative vote of the European Union members of the Council, the delegate from Germany said:

> The European Union supports some of the principles set out in this draft resolution and recognizes the linkage between peace and enjoyment of human rights. However, the draft resolution omits to state that the absence of peace cannot justify failure to respect human rights. Besides, it deals almost exclusively with the relationship between states and not with the relationship between the state and its citizens, and the state's respect for human rights, which is the core mandate of this council. We believe that most of the issues raised in this resolution are better dealt with in other fora which have the competence to do so and which are already dealing with these issues.[12]

This time the seminar took place, in December 2009. The keynote address was delivered by Antônio Cançado Trindade, the distinguished Brazilian human rights scholar and judge, recently elected to the International Court of Justice.[13]

Similar Resolutions were adopted in 2010[14] and 2011,[15] with virtually

---

11 'Promotion of the right of peoples to peace', UN Doc A/HRC/RES/11/4. In favour: Angola, Argentina, Azerbaijan, Bahrain, Bolivia (Plurinational State of), Brazil, Burkina Faso, Cameroon, Chile, China, Cuba, Djibouti, Egypt, Gabon, Ghana, Indonesia, Jordan, Madagascar, Malaysia, Mauritius, Mexico, Nicaragua, Nigeria, Pakistan, Philippines, Qatar, Russian Federation, Saudi Arabia, Senegal, South Africa, Uruguay, Zambia. Against: Bosnia and Herzegovina, Canada, France, Germany, Italy, Japan, Netherlands, Republic of Korea, Slovakia, Slovenia, Switzerland, Ukraine, United Kingdom of Great Britain and Northern Ireland. Abstaining: India.

12 Explanation of vote by Germany (on behalf of EU) concerning UN Doc A/HRC/11/L.11, 17 June 2009 (http://www.un.org/webcast/unhrc/archive.asp?go=090617).

13 UN Doc A/HRC/14/38.

14 'Promotion of the right of peoples to peace', UN Doc A/HRC/RES/14/3, 17 June 2010. In favour: Angola, Argentina, Bahrain, Bolivia (Plurinational State of), Brazil, Burkina Faso, Cameroon, Chile, China, Cuba, Djibouti, Egypt, Gabon, Ghana, Indonesia, Jordan, Madagascar, Mauritius, Mexico, Nicaragua, Nigeria, Pakistan, Philippines, Qatar, Russian Federation, Saudi Arabia, Senegal, South Africa, Uruguay, Zambia. Against: Belgium, Bosnia and Herzegovina, France, Hungary, Italy, Japan, Netherlands, Norway, Republic of Korea, Slovakia, Slovenia, Ukraine, United Kingdom of Great Britain and Northern Ireland, United States of America. Abstaining: India.

15 'Promotion of the right of peoples to peace', UN Doc A/HRC/RES/17/6. In favour: Angola, Argentina, Bahrain, Bangladesh, Brazil, Burkina Faso, Cameroon, Chile, China, Cuba, Djibouti, Ecuador, Gabon, Ghana, Guatemala, Jordan, Kyrgyzstan, Malaysia, Maldives, Mauritania, Mauritius, Mexico, Nigeria, Pakistan, Philippines, Qatar, Russian Federation, Saudi Arabia, Senegal, Thailand, Uganda, Uruguay, Zambia. Against: Belgium, France, Hungary, Japan,

identical results on recorded votes. The 2010 Resolution requested the Advisory Committee, which is subordinate to the Council, 'in consultation with Member States, civil society, academia and all relevant stakeholders, to prepare a draft declaration on the right of peoples to peace, and to report on the progress thereon to the Council'. The Advisory Committee produced a 38-page report that included more than 40 proposals on standards that might be included in the draft declaration.[16] The 2011 Resolution noted the ongoing work by the Advisory Committee and asked for a further progress report at the 20th session of the Council.

The Human Rights Council Resolutions take note of the 1984 Declaration of the General Assembly as well as the United Nations Millennium Declaration[17] and the Purposes and Principles enshrined in the Charter of the United Nations. They also speak of the obligation to refrain from the threat or use of force in international relations, and the importance of friendly relations and cooperation among states, with a reference to the Declaration on Friendly Relations.[18] The concept of the peoples' right to self-determination, drawn from common article 1 of the human rights covenants, is also reaffirmed. The preamble of the Resolutions '[r]ecogniz[es] that peace and security, development and human rights are mutually interlinked and reinforcing'. Echoing Article 28 of the Universal Declaration of Human Rights, it also '[r]ecall[s] that everyone is entitled to a social and international order in which the rights and freedoms set forth in the Universal Declaration of Human Rights can be fully realized'.[19] The 2011 Resolution includes a paragraph recalling the Declaration on the Right to Development.[20]

In the operative paragraphs, the Resolutions of the Human Rights

---

Norway, Poland, Republic of Korea, Republic of Moldova, Slovakia, Spain, Switzerland, Ukraine, United Kingdom of Great Britain and Northern Ireland, United States of America.

[16] 'Progress Report of the Human Rights Council Advisory Committee on the Right of Peoples to Peace', UN Doc A/HRC/17/39, 28 March 2011.

[17] 'United Nations Millennium Declaration', UN Doc A/RES/55/2, 18 September 2000. There are many references to peace in the declaration, but there is no mention of a 'right to peace' *per se*.

[18] 'Declaration on Principles of International Law Concerning Friendly Relations and Cooperation among States, in accordance with the Charter of the United Nations', UNGA Res 2625 (XXV).

[19] For an in-depth analysis of this provision, see Shane Darcy and Josh Curtis, 'The Right to a Social and International Order for the Realization of Human Rights: Article 28 of the Universal Declaration and International Cooperation', Ch 1 in this volume.

[20] UN Doc A/RES/41/128.

Council affirm 'that the peoples of our planet have a sacred right to peace'. They stress 'the importance of peace for the promotion and protection of all human rights for all'. The issue of the peoples' right to peace is linked to 'the deep fault line that divides human society between the rich and the poor and the ever-increasing gap between the developed world and the developing world'. The Resolutions insist that 'the policies of States be directed towards the elimination of the threat of war, particularly nuclear war, the renunciation of the use or threat of use of force in international relations and the settlement of international disputes by peaceful means on the basis of the Charter of the United Nations'.

There have been other, related initiatives over the years related to the 'right to peace', although they have not explicitly taken their bearings from the 1984 General Assembly Declaration. In 1996 and 1997, the now-defunct Sub-Commission on the Promotion and Protection of Human Rights adopted resolutions that affirmed: '[i]nternational peace and security as an essential condition for the enjoyment of human rights, above all the right to life.'[21] During the 1980s and 1990s, UNESCO held a number of meetings on the subject of solidarity rights and, specifically, the right to peace.[22] In 1995, the General Conference of UNESCO adopted the 'Declaration of Principles of Tolerance', which states that humans 'have the right to live in peace and to be as they are'.[23] In 1998, Director-General Federico Mayor convened a meeting of representatives and experts to aid in drafting a declaration for the right to peace. While some state representatives voiced doubts about the content of the right during the 1998 conference, they all supported the right to peace as a moral principle.[24] However, the resulting draft was edited to omit any explicit reference to the right to peace, and remained rather ambiguous. For example, the General Conference spelled out its goal 'to build the defences of peace in the minds of human beings in everyday life', rather than explicitly recognizing the right to peace.[25]

---

21 UN Doc E/CN.4/Sub.2/RES/1996/16; UN Doc E/CN.4/Sub.2/RES/1997/36.

22 Philip Alston, 'Peoples' Rights: Their Rise and Fall', in Philip Alston (ed.) *People's Rights* (Oxford: OUP, 2001) 260, 280.

23 Janusz Symonides, 'New Human Rights Dimensions, Obstacles and Challenges: Introductory Remarks', in Janusz Symonides (ed.) *Human Rights: New Dimensions and Challenges* (Paris: UNESCO, 1998) 1, 8.

24 Director-General of UNESCO, *Report on the Result of the International Consultation of Governmental Experts on the Human Right to Peace*, para 13, *delivered to Executive Board*, UN Doc 154 EX/40 (17 April 1998).

25 *Ibid.*, Annex 5, section I, para 1.

2. THE 'HUMAN RIGHT TO PEACE'

International law seems to distinguish between 'peoples' rights' and 'human rights'. The idea of 'peoples' rights' is often associated with 'group rights'.[26] Philip Alston, who is not an enthusiast for the concept, describes peoples' rights as 'the elevation of the well-recognized, but nonetheless vague and open-ended, duty of states to cooperation to achieve the objectives of the United Nations Charter, in combination with an emerging principle of solidarity, so as to transform the correlative duties that attach to human rights into concrete obligations upon governments to transfer resources to those in need'.[27]

There is, of course, a close relationship between peoples' rights and human rights. Thus, for example, the African Charter is concerned with both human and peoples' rights. Its preamble says that 'the reality and respect of peoples' rights should necessarily guarantee human rights'. The two United Nations Covenants on human rights enshrine the 'right of peoples to self-determination' in common article 1. It has been held by the Human Rights Committee that this provision does not give rise to an individual right of petition, because only 'individuals can claim that their individual rights have been violated'. However, common article 1 may be relevant in the interpretation of other rights in the International Covenant on Civil and Political Rights, especially democratic rights (Article 25), non-discrimination (Article 26) and minority rights (Article 27).[28]

There is also some support for this in academic writing, including the relevant chapter in the commentary by Gudmunder Alfredsson and Asbjørn Eide: 'It does not take much reflection to recognize that violence and war negatively affect the enjoyment of human rights. A social and political order in which all the rights in the Universal Declaration could be enjoyed would be possible only if there were peace on both the international and the national levels.'[29]

Article 20(1) of the International Covenant on Civil and Political Rights requires that '[a]ny propaganda for war shall be prohibited by law'.[30] In its

---

[26] Ian Brownlie, 'The Rights of Peoples in Modern International Law', in James Crawford (ed.) *The Rights of Peoples* (Oxford: Clarendon Press, 1988) 1.

[27] Philip Alston, 'Introduction', in Alston (ed.) (n22) 1.

[28] E.g., *Gillot* v. *France*, UN Doc CCPR/C/75/D/932/2000, para 13.4.

[29] Asbjørn Eide, 'Article 28', in Gudmundur Alfredsson and Asbjørn Eide (eds) *Universal Declaration of Human Rights* (Dordrecht: Kluwer Academic Publishers, 1999) 620.

[30] See further, Michael Kearney, *The Prohibition of Propaganda for War in International Law* (Oxford: OUP, 2007).

first General Comment on the right to life, the Human Rights Committee invoked Article 20(1) in support of a more general proposition about the right to life and armed conflict:

> The Committee observes that war and other acts of mass violence continue to be a scourge of humanity and take the lives of thousands of innocent human beings every year. Under the Charter of the United Nations the threat or use of force by any State against another State, except in exercise of the inherent right of self-defence, is already prohibited. The Committee considers that States have the supreme duty to prevent wars, acts of genocide and other acts of mass violence causing arbitrary loss of life. Every effort they make to avert the danger of war, especially thermonuclear war, and to strengthen international peace and security would constitute the most important condition and guarantee for the safeguarding of the right to life. In this respect, the Committee notes, in particular, a connection between article 6 and article 20, which states that the law shall prohibit any propaganda for war (para. 1) or incitement to violence (para. 2) as therein described.[31]

This paragraph on the right to life is rarely invoked today, and would probably not reappear were the Committee to revise its general comment. The context of adoption of the general comment seems to be associated with the 1984 General Assembly Declaration, and it also resonates in the academic literature of the time.[32]

The evolving discussions of the right to peace within the Human Rights Council reflect both the appropriateness of its place on the agenda and hesitations about the importance that it should be given. Possibly those who are sceptical about the usefulness of a right to peace would adjust their views if they saw its potential to influence and frame the interpretation of other fundamental rights.

3. THE DEBATE ABOUT AGGRESSION

Since its revival in the early 1990s, international criminal law or international criminal justice has been closely associated with human rights law.

---

[31] 'General Comment 6', UN Doc CCPR/C/21/Add.1, para 2. See also: 'General Comment 14', UN Doc E/C.12/2000/4 (2000) para 2.

[32] For support for a 'right to peace', see: Ved P. Nanda, 'Nuclear Weapons and the Right to Peace Under International Law' (1983) 9 *Brooklyn J. Int'l L.* 283; Amynmohamed B. Sajoo, 'Human Rights Perspectives on the Arms Race' (1982) 28 *McGill L. J.* 628; A.A. Tickhonov, 'The Inter-Relationship Between the Right to Life and the Right to Peace: Nuclear Weapons and Other Weapons of Mass-Destruction and the Right to Life', in B.G. Ramcharan (ed.) *The Right to Life in International Law* (Dordrecht: Martinus Nijhoff, 1985) 97. *Cf.* Philip Alston, 'Conjuring Up New Human Rights: A Proposal for Quality Control' (1984) 78 *AJIL* 607.

The initial impetus for the creation of the *ad hoc* tribunals and related activities derived much energy from normative developments within bodies like the United Nations Sub-Commission on the Promotion and Protection of Human Rights, and creative interpretations of international human rights treaties where the obligation to prosecute gross and systematic violations, especially those involving the right to life and the prohibition of torture, were developed.[33] The campaign for the International Criminal Court was strongly supported by human rights NGOs, both large and small. The subject-matter jurisdiction of the Court reflects language derived from human rights norms, especially with regard to genocide and crimes against humanity.

Nevertheless, the Rome Conference of 1998 at which the Statute of the Court was adopted could not reach agreement on provisions that would enable prosecution of the crime of aggression. A half-baked compromise provision in effect postponed the matter. Article 5(1) of the Rome Statute listed aggression as a crime within the jurisdiction of the Court, along with genocide, crimes against humanity and war crimes, but adds, in Article 5(2): 'The Court shall exercise jurisdiction over the crime of aggression once a provision is adopted in accordance with articles 121 and 123 defining the crime and setting out the conditions under which the Court shall exercise jurisdiction with respect to this crime. Such a provision shall be consistent with the relevant provisions of the Charter of the United Nations.'

The somewhat cryptic language of Article 5(2) indicates that the real obstacle was not with the definition of aggression so much as with the conditions for exercise of jurisdiction. Article 39 of the Charter of the United Nations says '[t]he Security Council shall determine the existence of any threat to the peace, breach of the peace, or act of aggression'. The five permanent members believed that this meant the Security Council had a monopoly on such determinations. The head of the United Kingdom delegation, Franklyn Berman, said this quite clearly in the final plenary of the Rome Conference. The permanent members were only prepared to agree with incorporating aggression into the Rome Statute if the Council's approval of prosecutions was a prerequisite. This had not been a problem at Nuremberg.

The vast majority of states at the Rome Conference were unwilling to let the Court's Statute be used to reaffirm, reinforce or strengthen the interpretation of the Charter of the United Nations favoured by the permanent

---

33 *Velasquez Rodriguez v. Honduras*, Series C, No. 4. More recently: *Rantsev v. Cyprus and Russia* (App. No. 25965/04) Judgment, 7 January 2010.

five. For many, the goal was the opposite: use the Rome Statute to do indirectly what they had been unable to do directly, and trim the prerogatives of the Security Council. The debate about incorporating the crime of aggression in the Rome Statute concealed a much larger controversy about the post-Second World War world order and the architecture of the United Nations.

Over the decade or so that followed the 1998 Diplomatic Conference, a determined group of states and individuals pursued the incorporation of the crime of aggression in the Rome Statute. Organized through much of this period in the 'Special Working Group on the Crime of Aggression', they experimented with various formulae and approaches. Eventually, the Special Working Group reached broad agreement on a definition of aggression but no clarity whatsoever on the conditions for the exercise of jurisdiction. In the course of its work, the negotiators discovered that the dysfunctional amendment provisions of the Statute presented an additional problem. To the surprise of most and the joy of many, their work culminated in the crafting of a set of amendments to the Rome Statute that was adopted at the Kampala Review Conference, in early June 2010. By general agreement, the Conference accepted provisions that define the crime of aggression and that establish the conditions for exercise of jurisdiction. In a radical development, they contemplate prosecution for aggression by the Court without any prior authorization from the Security Council.

The president of the Review Conference had put the package before delegates just before midnight on the final day of the meeting. All that was required to defeat the proposal was for one delegation to call for a vote, given the near certainty that there were not enough voting delegations left in the room to make the two-thirds requirement set out in the Statute. But neither of the two permanent members of the Security Council that were also States Parties to the Rome Statute, France and the United Kingdom, raised their flags to ask for a vote. They had repeatedly insisted that any amendment allowing the Court to proceed without a Security Council blessing would be unthinkable. Now, *in extremis*, they meekly allowed the provision to be adopted without protest. Had the inflexible pronouncements been nothing but a bluff from London and Paris? Or were the tectonic plates of world politics shifting, pulverizing prerogatives of the permanent members of the Security Council that had existed since 1945?

The 2010 amendments to the Rome Statute provide a definition of the crime of aggression inspired by General Assembly Resolution 3314(XXIX). The list of 'acts of aggression' in that Resolution is nevertheless conditioned on contextual factors, principally the requirement in the amendments to the Rome Statute that such an act, 'by its character, gravity and scale, constitutes a manifest violation of the Charter of the United Nations'. An 'understanding' agreed to at the Kampala Conference specifies that 'aggression is the most serious and dangerous form of the illegal use of force; and that a determination whether an act of aggression has been committed requires consideration of all the circumstances of each particular case, including the gravity of the acts concerned and their consequences, in accordance with the Charter of the United Nations'. The Conference rejected an American proposal for an additional understanding intended to prevent any use of force motivated by humanitarian purposes from being labelled aggression. In effect, the Conference was saying that self-appointed proponents of humanitarian intervention (or the 'responsibility to protect') risk prosecution if they proceed without Security Council authorization.

Pursuant to the amendments, the Security Council retains the initiative in determining whether the Court should prosecute the crime of aggression. The Court must wait for six months before proceeding if it does not receive a green light from the Security Council. The Security Council also retains the right to block a prosecution, but only temporarily, by adopting Resolutions on an annual basis. The jurisdictional scope of the aggression amendments is narrower than is the general rule for crimes under the Rome Statute. Only a State Party (or rather, the leaders of that state) can be subject to prosecution for aggression committed against another State Party. By contrast, leaders and other nationals of a non-party state may be prosecuted under the Statute for genocide, crimes against humanity and war crimes where the acts are perpetrated on the territory of a State Party. A broader scope of jurisdiction would have been desirable, allowing the Court to address aggression committed against a State Party by a non-party state. But consensus was probably impossible on this more radical vision. Sometimes, the best can be the enemy of the good. And, perhaps, the unique jurisdictional regime for aggression may provide an incentive to non-party states to join the Court. It is the only way they can give the Court the authority to prosecute aggression of which they may be the victim if it is perpetrated by a State Party.

The most enigmatic dimension of the 2010 amendments concerns the formula for amendment and entry into force. Article 121 of the Rome Statute offers two options, depending upon the nature of the amendment. Each of these had its own problems and shortcomings. In the end, the Kampala Conference appears to have adopted a third approach to amendment, which may or may not be judged compatible with Article 121. There is no problem, of course, with a Review Conference deciding to create a new amending formula, but it seems that it is locked in by the existing one. It can only amend the amending formula by respecting the provision that already exists. With a bit of imagination and creativity, the new amendment may fit rather approximately within Article 121. Only time will tell whether the creative amendment adopted at Kampala can resist judicial scrutiny.

The 2010 amendments require ratification by 30 States Parties, and cannot enter into force in any case prior to 2017. Then, an additional two-thirds vote of States Parties is required. These conditions should not present much difficulty. Once fulfilled, they give the Court jurisdiction with respect to the crime of aggression over all States Parties that have ratified the amendment, at a minimum, and probably over all States Parties generally, depending upon how one interprets the amendment. A State Party unhappy with the amendments may make a declaration withdrawing from the jurisdiction over aggression. Though a simple matter procedurally, this is likely to be politically unpalatable for most states and few such declarations are to be expected. The price to be paid *vis à vis* public opinion for an admission that a state fears prosecution for the crime of aggression is likely to be judged to be too high.

It may be decades before there are any prosecutions for the crime of aggression. Few events that have taken place since 1945 actually respond to the definition, and there is no reason to think that this situation will change in the future. That observation is merely a tribute to the effectiveness of the Charter of the United Nations and the collective security regime that it establishes. The jurisdictional scheme of the aggression provisions of the Rome Statute may complicate matters still further, because several of the 'usual suspects' will remain outside the system. Eventually, the Rome Statute will achieve universal ratification. But even if the amendments adopted in 2010 are not applied by the Court, they still perform a vital declaratory function that may, in some situations, act as a deterrent. Perhaps prosecutors and judges will return to the insights of their predecessors at Nuremberg who saw wars of aggression as the 'supreme international crime'. If so, this may influence decisions about the priorities of international justice and its relationship with the constant quest for lasting peace.

3.1 Indifference from the Big NGOs

The major international human rights NGOs, generally highly devoted to the creation and work of the International Criminal Court, were surprisingly indifferent to the issue of the crime of aggression. Although present at the Kampala Conference, they concentrated their attention on the 'stocktaking' sessions, a series of panel discussions held during the first days of the meeting on thematic issues such as complementarity and cooperation. This was an environment where NGOs felt right at home and where they could thrive. There were persuasive speeches and eloquent declarations about fighting impunity. States were hectored about living up to their responsibilities. Policy papers were distributed. But when the foreplay was over and the Conference shifted its attention to the main act, which was the crime of aggression, most of the NGOs retreated. Many of them simply returned to their homes in Europe or America. Those that stayed behind were out of sorts, probably frustrated by their self-imposed irrelevance to the profound developments that were under way.

How did they explain their positions? Amnesty International said it had not 'taken a stance on the definition of the crime of aggression because its mandate – to campaign for every person to enjoy all of the human rights (civil and political and economic, social and cultural rights) enshrined in the Universal Declaration of Human Rights and other international human rights standards – does not extend to the lawfulness of the use of force'.[34] This assessment of the Universal Declaration of Human Rights is simply mistaken, as has been explained earlier in this essay.

Human Rights Watch took a more pragmatic, policy-oriented view: 'Human Rights Watch's institutional mandate includes a position of strict neutrality on issues of *jus ad bellum*, because we find it the best way to focus on the conduct of war, or *jus in bello*, and thereby to promote our primary goal of encouraging all parties to a conflict to respect international humanitarian law. Consistent with this approach, we take no position on the substance of a definition of the crime of aggression.' In a footnote to its explanation, Human Rights Watch added: 'The only exceptions that Human Rights Watch has made to this policy is to call for military intervention where massive loss of human life, on the order of genocide, can be halted through no other means, as was the case in Bosnia and Rwanda in the 1990s.'[35]

The footnote in the Human Rights Watch statement may provide a useful clue to understanding the reticence of the big NGOs in this area. A militaristic tendency has crept into human rights discourse in recent years, encouraged by talk of 'humanitarian intervention' and the 'responsibility to protect'. Of course, human rights law has never been pacifistic, in the sense of a principled and intransigent opposition to the use of force under

---

[34] Amnesty International, 'International Criminal Court, Concerns at the seventh session of the Assembly of States Parties', October 2008, Index: IOR 40/022/2008, 22.

[35] Human Rights Watch, 'Memorandum for the Sixth Session of the Assembly of States Parties of the International Criminal Court'.

all circumstances. The preamble of the Universal Declaration of Human Rights says that human rights must be protected by the rule of law so that 'man is not to be compelled to have recourse, as a last resort, to rebellion against tyranny and oppression'. But there has been a growing willingness to contemplate military interventions as the ultimate solution to serious human rights violations. In these discussions, it seems that an appeal to the Pentagon (or, often, an *ex post facto* rationalization), albeit framed in reluctant language, is rarely very distant.

Another influence may be the debates about the relationship between peace and justice in the context of prosecutorial strategy at the International Criminal Court. In situations where there is an arguable case that peace negotiations may be jeopardized by prosecution, such as northern Uganda and even Darfur, there has been political pressure on the Court to back off out of respect for the interests of promoting peace. Encouraged by human rights NGOs, the Prosecutor of the Court has taken the view that the quest for peace should not condition his decisions about selection of cases. In a policy paper issued in September 2007, the Prosecutor cited paragraph 3 of the preamble to the Rome Statute ('Recognizing that such grave crimes threaten the peace, security and well-being of the world'), noting that '[t]he ICC was created on the premise that justice is an essential component of a stable peace'. He wrote that 'there is a difference between the concepts of the interests of justice and the interests of peace and that the latter falls within the mandate of institutions other than the Office of the Prosecutor'. Furthermore, 'the broader matter of international peace and security is not the responsibility of the Prosecutor; it falls within the mandate of other institutions'.[36]

Yet there is also much to be said for the view that the rationale of the International Criminal Court is to promote peace, just as it was for the *ad hoc* tribunals. The latter were, after all, created by the United Nations Security Council in pursuit of its mandate to promote international peace and security, with Chapter VII of the Charter invoked in support. According to the first annual report of the International Criminal Tribunal for the former Yugoslavia:

> it would be wrong to assume that the Tribunal is based on the old maxim *fiat justitia et pereat mundus* (let justice be done, even if the world were to perish). The Tribunal is, rather, based on the maxim propounded by Hegel in 1821: *fiat justitia ne pereat mundus* (let justice be done lest the world should perish). Indeed, the judicial process aims at averting the exacerbation and aggravation

---

[36] Office of the Prosecutor, Policy Paper on the Interests of Justice, September 2007.

> of conflict and tension, thereby contributing, albeit gradually, to a lasting peace.[37]

These words suggest that the pursuit of peace lies at the heart of international justice. The idea dovetails neatly with the approach of the International Military Tribunal, for which a war of aggression was the supreme international crime, an overarching paradigm within which the other atrocity crimes, crimes against humanity and war crimes, find their place.

In suggesting that it should confine its activity to the *jus in bello*, Human Rights Watch transposes to the field of human rights law a concept that is well accepted in the law of armed conflict. For a century and a half, the International Committee for the Red Cross has insisted that its work of civilizing the conduct of hostilities imposes a duty of neutrality. In order to intervene effectively on the battlefield, it cannot be seen to favour one side over the other. It is the very essence of the law of armed conflict that both sides be held to the same normative standards. But why should this logic apply to human rights law, which is concerned primarily with the protection of individuals from violations attributable to a state? This is not a matter of choosing sides so much as one of determining that the use of force by a state, which inexorably results in human suffering of huge proportions, violates the human rights of the victims to the extent that such use of force is unlawful. The problem with the contrary view – the one proposed by Human Rights Watch – is that it accepts rather too easily the loss of human life and the destruction of property resulting from the use of force by an aggressor, to the extent that this may be deemed 'collateral damage'. The law of armed conflict tolerates 'incidental' loss of life and destruction of property as an inevitable accompaniment of war. When the war is itself unlawful, the law of human rights should not tolerate loss of life and destruction of property based upon the trite proposal that it is unconcerned about *jus ad bellum*.

4. CONCLUSION

The amendments to the Rome Statute move the crime of aggression back to centre stage in the constantly expanding field of international criminal law. They helpfully focus our attention not only on the state as the

---

[37] First Annual Report of the International Criminal Tribunal for the former Yugoslavia, UN Doc A/49/342-S/1994/1007, annex, para 18.

primary source of human rights violations but also on the importance of peace. They will only enter into force in 2017, and only then if certain conditions are met. The jurisdictional scope of the provisions is narrower than for other international crimes. But even if the message is only symbolic, it is an important one.

The notion of a right to peace provides a unifying principle that assists in bringing human rights law, international criminal law and international humanitarian law closer together. Unstated or understated in human rights law, it is nevertheless implicit. The right to peace very usefully puts other rights into perspective. Similarly, it rounds off the corners of international humanitarian law, so that a body of norms that sometimes looks like rules to govern killing and destruction takes on a more anti-war dimension. The overarching theme of a right to peace was important at the dawn of international prosecutions, at Nuremberg and Tokyo, but later it seemed to lose its way. The adoption of amendments to the Rome Statute at the Kampala Review Conference in June 2010 brings the crime of aggression back to centre stage and with it the mission of international criminal justice as well as international human rights as a civilizer not only of individuals but also of nations.

3. The universality of war: *Jus ad bellum* and the right to peace in non-international armed conflicts

Kjell Anderson*

Much of the focus of the right to peace seems to be on the prohibition on aggressive war. Yet peace, understood as the absence of hostility, encompasses much more than the absence of aggressive war. In order for peace to be fully realized the threat of war must also be removed through measures such as arms control, confidence building, and mediation. International efforts to prohibit war have focussed on aggressive wars between states (the crime of aggression or 'crimes against peace' as it was dubbed at the Nuremberg Tribunal). Indeed, at Nuremberg all the crimes charged required a nexus with the waging of a war of aggression. This emphasis on international conflict stems from the state-centric model of international relations that has predominated for centuries. States had no interest in limiting power within their own domain – they only wanted to make the international environment (and perhaps their own power) more secure. However, most wars are now fought within states. Surely these wars, with their often dire humanitarian consequences, are a violation of the peoples' right to peace.

Both domestic law and international law recognize that there are situations where the use of violence may be legitimate. The right to self-defence is present in both domestic criminal law and international law. Moreover, in both the domestic and international spheres, it is recognized that legitimate authorities may use force. Thus, beyond self-defence, authorities have a monopoly on the legitimate use of force.[1] Yet, there are some fundamental differences between this monopoly on force in the domestic

* With thanks to Nathan Derejko for his very helpful comments on my draft.

[1] This conception of the state was first elucidated by Max Weber in his 1919 essay 'Politics as a Vocation' published in Hans Gerth & C. Wright Mills (eds) *From Max Weber: Essays in Sociology* (New York: OUP, 1946) 77 (essay first published in 1919).

and international systems. Domestically, power is centralized in the hands of state authorities – the state is a unitary actor that uses force as it deems fit, with some limitations imposed by international human rights law and international humanitarian law. This force is authorized by leaders, whether democratically elected or not, and exercised by agents such as police officers. In some sense, action under the United Nations Security Council through a Chapter VII resolution, due to threats to international peace and security, is the policing function of the state transposed to the international context. Yet the use of force on the international level is decentralized – the United Nations may only act if states decide that action is necessary. Moreover, such recourse to force may only occur through the agents of states – the United Nations has no agents of its own to apply legitimate force.

There is no question that the illegitimate use of force, in the sense of an aggressive war, is a violation of the right to peace. But because of the legitimacy of state authority, it is impossible for the state to violate the right to peace of its own citizens. Intrastate violence does not entail the crossing of international borders in order to deprive foreign nationals of their rights to self-determination and peace. However some forms of violence that a state commits against its own citizens may be unlawful under international human rights law and international humanitarian law, such as genocide and crimes against humanity. Is the state's use of illegitimate force against its own citizens also a violation of the right to peace? This conceptual question will be analysed throughout the rest of this chapter.

It will be set out that: 1) the right to peace is applicable to intrastate violence; 2) the state can violate the right to peace of its citizens through the capricious use of force; 3) non-state actors may also violate the right to peace through the illegitimate use of force; 4) there are reasonable exceptions to the right to peace, including the protection of the rights of others; and 5) we must move towards the prohibition of all forms of unnecessary and disproportionate violence.

1. THE HUMAN RIGHT TO PEACE

War has brought humankind incalculable suffering. Few people would dispute this assessment; yet the end of all war belongs more to the hallowed ground of platitude than it does to earthy human endeavour. It is a triumph of civilization that the existence of human rights is now taken as a given. It is widely recognized that every individual on this planet, from Tierra del Fuego to Tokyo, is born with certain inalienable rights. There is some disagreement on which rights are the most important but there is no question that human rights, as a concept, have achieved nearly universal acceptance. Human rights have become human ethics and even gross violators of rights will reframe or conceal their actions rather than attack the validity of rights as a concept.

The right to life is a bedrock right without which the exercise of all other human rights is impossible. War, of course, requires the denial of this right to life. At its worst, taking lives may be an objective of war itself. Nevertheless the right to peace is often held to be ephemeral and lacking in true substance. It is the stuff of aspirations, a different species than concrete measurable rights like *habeas corpus* and the prohibition on torture. It is only in recent decades that the state's unequivocal right to take life has been challenged. Yet, in spite of the advancements of human rights norms, there has been little discussion of the state's recourse to collective violence against its own citizens; instead the focus has been on the type of violence used, and even those discussions have been curtailed by conservative interpretations of state sovereignty.

If the right to peace is merely conceptual then it is not really a human right at all. The so-called third generation rights such as the right to peace, the right to a clean environment, and the right to development appear to be rights without remedies. This is not really the case though. Human rights are normally about the obligations which states have towards their citizens. The state which commits war (or just aggressive war) is violating the rights of its citizens to live in peace. States which make use of widespread or systematic violence against their own citizens, without good cause, are also violating the rights of their citizens to peace. The right to peace *can*, therefore, be precisely defined and implemented.

Another important question is whether the struggle for peace is best situated in the normative structures of human rights law. The limited utility of the law as an instrument to address social problems flows from the tension between the reductionism of the law and the complexity of the real world. The law is a system of rules for regulating behaviour; the law seeks to reduce harm to individuals and groups by restricting harmful behaviour. But in spite of the aspirations of the law, individual and collective behaviour are difficult to dictate, especially when other social or psychological factors are influencing behaviour in ways contrary to the aims of the law. Yet even if the law fails in its mission to absolutely deter wrongful behaviour, it may succeed in changing the norms that enable harmful acts. This is certainly the case with the right to peace – the first step in undermining the death grip which war has on the human race is to clearly define the waging of war as wrongful and to take concrete steps to reduce such behaviour. The definition and implementation of the right to peace has the potential to set new norms that will gradually erode the culture of militarism. However, in order for the right to peace to be meaningful it must also cover intrastate violence.

Although the right to peace is not well-defined in international law the prohibition on the use of force, especially in the waging of aggressive war, is well-established.[2] Such a prohibition exists because of recognition of the harmfulness of war. There are already many treaties regulating the conduct of states towards each other and towards their own citizens. The right to peace is recognized in the UN Charter which aspires in its preamble that people should 'live together in peace'. Moreover, Article 28 of the Universal Declaration on Human Rights stipulates that 'everyone is entitled to a social and international order in which the rights and freedoms set forth in this Declaration can be fully realized.' This is not an explicit endorsement of the right to peace but there is little doubt that the presence of war disrupts the full realization of human rights.

The other side of the coin, the importance of human rights for the maintenance of peace, is recognized in the preamble of the Universal Declaration on Human Rights which states that 'the inherent dignity and of the equal and inalienable rights of all members of the human family is the foundation of freedom, justice and peace in the world.'[3] Furthermore Article 26 of the Declaration (the right to education) also emphasizes the importance of education for the maintenance of peace. Article 23 of the African Charter on Human and Peoples' Rights recognizes that all peoples 'shall have the right to national and international peace and security'.

The right to peace was also affirmed by the UN General Assembly in declaration 39/11 of 12 November 1984. The annexed Declaration on the Rights of Peoples to Peace:

> 1. Solemnly proclaims that the peoples of our planet have a sacred right to peace;
> 2. Solemnly declares that the preservation of the right of peoples to peace and

---

[2] For example, see: the Kellogg–Briand Pact (Treaty between the United States and other Powers providing for the renunciation of war as an instrument of national policy, signed 27 August 1928, proclaimed 14 July 1929) and the Charter of the United Nations, 24 October 1945, 1 UNTS XVI. This prohibition on the use of force was supplemented by the so-called Stimson doctrine, which set out the non-recognition of territorial changes effectuated by force. This doctrine was incorporated into international legal instruments such as the Rio de Janeiro Anti-War Treaty of Nonaggression and Conciliation, 10 October 1933, 49 Stat 3363 (1935–36) TS 906, and ILA, Budapest Articles of Interpretation Final Text, Report of the 38th Conference 66–67 (1934).

[3] Moreover, CCPR General Comment 6, 'The Right to Life', 16th Session, 30 April 1982, recognizes the harmful effects of war (including the arbitrary deprivation of life) and the link between war and human rights violations.

> the promotion of its implementation constitute a fundamental obligation of each State;
> 3. Emphasizes that ensuring the exercise of the right of peoples to peace demands that the policies of States be directed towards the elimination of the threat of war, particularly nuclear war, the renunciation of the use of force in international relations and the settlement of international disputes by peaceful means on the basis of the Charter of the United Nations;
> 4. Appeals to all States and international organizations to do their utmost to assist in implementing the right of peoples to peace through the adoption of appropriate measures at both the national and the international level.

Thus the right to peace must include more than just the renunciation of war itself; it must also involve the full removal of the threat of war through the progressive realization of measures such as disarmament.

War is harmful to human rights, not only because it results in significant 'arbitrary deprivation of life', but also because a state of war undermines many other fundamental rights.[4] War diverts resources from the public good and pervasively undermines human security. Moreover, war and the threat of war often lead to the deprivation of many rights as the threat of the 'enemy' justifies the concentration of power and oppressive measures such as states of emergency. This is illustrated well by the derogability of almost all human rights provisions during times of war. The realization of most rights is impossible in the state of fundamental insecurity that characterizes war.

2. THE STATE AS A VIOLATOR OF THE RIGHT TO PEACE

The state is not only protector but also prison warden to its citizens. In fact, the state is the most egregious institutional perpetrator of human rights abuses. Political scientist R.J. Rummel estimates that governments intentionally killed 169 million people in the twentieth century

---

4 Of course, not all deprivation of life during war is arbitrary. The deaths of combatants is permissible under most circumstances in international humanitarian law (with certain exceptions such as those *hors de combat*) and the death of civilians may also be permissible if these deaths adhere to the principles of proportionality, humanity, and discrimination. In a sense then, *jus ad bellum* takes careful consideration of civilian deaths; thus this deprivation of life is not 'arbitrary.' However, from a broader philosophical perspective, all civilian deaths in war are arbitrary as they are not actively participating in hostilities; thus, they are not subject to the notion of the moral equality of combatants. For more information on these questions consult: Jeff McMahan, *Killing in War* (New York: OUP, 2009).

alone.[5] Much of this mass killing was done by authoritarian regimes against their own citizens.[6] Consequently, liberal thinkers have long acknowledged that the state, with its monopoly on power and coercive force, is the greatest threat to the rights of its citizens.[7]

This reality, the fundamental recognition that the state is not always a benign presence acting in the best interests of its citizens, has led to a re-imagining of state sovereignty. The international human rights regime originally emerged out of the self-interest of great powers which sought to reciprocally ensure the rights of their ethnic confederates in other states. However, in the post-World War Two era, the corpus of human rights has shifted its focus to the fundamental rights of individuals.

At the domestic level, the state's monopoly on violence is carried out through the disarming of private citizens and the arming of state organs. State authority itself rests upon violence and the threat of violence (force). In effect the state, particularly the illiberal state, exercises the right to life and death including the use of capital punishment and the waging of war. As Michel Foucault argues, 'if genocide is indeed the dream of modern powers, this is not because of a recent return of the ancient right to kill; it is because power is situated and exercised at the level of life, the species, the race, and the large-scale phenomenon of population.'[8] This system is granted legitimacy and authority through the law. In contrast, the international system is anarchical precisely because there is no international monopoly on violence, no super-state. Through the threat of potential violence the state creates a 'pacified space'; this operates internationally through multilateral treaties.[9] International human rights law is also rooted in multilateral treaty-making; it militates against the unlimited coercive power of the state and locates sovereignty in individuals.[10] Such

---

[5] R.J. Rummel, *Death by Government* (Piscataway, NJ: Transaction Publishers, 1997) 15. A later estimate by Rummel claims a figure of 262 million deaths: see 'Freedom, Democracy, Peace; Power, Democide, and War', available online at: http://www.hawaii.edu/powerkills/. Rummel uses the term 'democide' to denote such mass killing by governments.

[6] Examples abound, but some of the more prominent cases include the mass killings of Hitler, Mao and Stalin.

[7] See, for example, the writings of Michel Foucault.

[8] Michel Foucault, 'Right of Death and Power over Life' in Nancy Scheper-Hughes and Philippe Bourgois (eds) *Violence in War and Peace* (Malden, MA: Blackwell Publishing, 2004) 80.

[9] Reinhart Kössler, 'Violence, Legitimacy and Dynamics of Genocide – Notions of Mass Violence Examined' (2008) 50 *Development Dialogue* 40.

[10] Kofi A. Annan, 'Two Concepts of Sovereignty' *The Economist*, 18 September 1999.

treaties are consensual, yet over time treaties may become customary and therefore non-consensual.

The ideal of the state is that citizens concede a measure of legitimate authority to the state in return for security and cooperation towards the greater good. The state must also manage conflict through the appropriate distribution of resources. Yet there are many states where this compact has been broken; these states operate much like individual criminals in society and through their deviant acts they subvert shared values and collective interests.

When the state uses force illegitimately, i.e. to commit genocide or to attack political opponents, this is arguably also a violation of the right to peace. Historian Martin Shaw argues that genocide is actually a form of warfare in which social groups are the enemy.[11] In such wars entire social groups may be criminalized. This is reflected in a proposed draft of a Human Rights Council declaration on the right to peace which states that 'all peoples and individuals have the right not to be regarded as enemies by any state.'[12] This right is a broad reformulation of the prohibition on collective punishment. Similarly, crimes against humanity are an attack on a civilian population. Therefore, the illegal use of mass force by the state against its citizens is a violation of their right to peace.

The application of human rights (unlike humanitarian law) to armed conflict should be universal. In other words, all the protections of human rights should apply equally to individuals regardless of whether an individual's right to peace has been violated by an international or a non-international armed conflict; by a foreign power or a tyrannical domestic regime. In contrast, international humanitarian law extends different protections to individuals on the basis of whether the violation occurred during an international armed conflict or a non-international armed conflict and whether the individual targeted was a protected person (i.e. a civilian, medic, etc.) or a combatant.

2.1 Inter-State and Intra-State Violence Compared

Collective violence is a human social phenomenon rooted in elements of social interaction such as aggression and tribalism. As a social phenomenon, it is not surprising that violence has occurred at different levels of human social organization including the interpersonal level (violence

---

11 Martin Shaw, *War and Genocide* (Cambridge: Polity Press, 2003).

12 Progress Report of the Human Rights Council Advisory Committee on the Right of Peoples to Peace, UN Doc A/HRC/17/391, April 2011.

between individuals) and the collective level (violence between groups within the state or between states within the international system). Violence at these different levels is treated differently, both in terms of policy and the legal regime. At the small-scale, interpersonal level violence is regulated by domestic criminal law while collective violence may be regulated by international criminal law and the law of state responsibility. The principle of state sovereignty has historically precluded lawful external intervention in cases of violence occurring within the state.

This state-centric system of international relations, which recognized the nearly absolute right of states to sovereignty, emerged with the Treaty of Westphalia in 1648. Sovereignty is the principle that a state has the exclusive right to exercise power within its borders. In the context of international relations this means non-intervention in the internal affairs of other states. Sovereignty has always been at the heart of international law. Article 2(7) of the UN Charter states: 'nothing contained in the present Charter shall authorise the United Nations to intervene in matters that are essentially within the domestic jurisdiction of any state or shall require the Members to submit such matters to settlement under the present Charter.'

However, in the 50 years since the development of the Charter, levels of internal conflict have been steadily increasing, while levels of international conflict have remained relatively constant.[13] Moreover, the damage inflicted and number of states affected by internal conflicts has also steadily increased.[14] With the increasing number of internal conflicts there have been increasing numbers of civilian deaths. In fact, of the four million war-related deaths of the 1990s, approximately 90 per cent were civilian.[15] The United Nations and the international community have responded to these challenges in part through the use of peace support operations (authorized under Chapter VI and Chapter VII of the UN Charter). The Security Council has condemned gross violations of human rights and humanitarian law in internal conflicts such as Bosnia, Kosovo, Libya, Côte d'Ivoire, and Sierra Leone. Moreover, the Security Council now routinely uses humanitarian concerns as justifications for

---

13 Ted Robert Gurr, Monty G. Marshall, and Deepa Kholsa, *Peace and Conflict 2001: A Global Survey of Armed Conflicts, Self-Determination Movements, and Democracy* (College Park, MD: University of Maryland Center for International Development and Conflict Management, 2000) 7.

14 *Ibid.* 8–9.

15 United Nations, 'United Nations Press Kit: Small Arms Backgrounder,' (Geneva, United Nations Department of Public Information, 1998) 1.

intervention.[16] This was ostensibly the case with the recent intervention in Libya, authorized by Resolution 1973. Therefore, a new paradigm is emerging in international security discourse that legitimizes intervention in situations of gross violations of rights. Such interventions are authorized by the UN Security Council and are therefore an exception to the prohibition on the use of force, analogous to self-defence.

One component of this emerging paradigm is a new conception of sovereignty that emphasizes *human security* rather than just *national security*. The development of human rights is an explicit limitation on the right of the state to exercise unlimited sovereignty. People are deemed to have rights on the basis of their humanity, rather than on the basis of their citizenship in a particular state. The development of international humanitarian law, which places rules and limitations on the conduct of armed conflict, is another aspect of the evolving international norms. Yet the legal regime that applies to non-international armed conflicts is, in certain respects, more limited in scope than that which applies to international armed conflicts.[17]

When comparing international and non-international conflicts one can find similar structural factors underlying the propensity to conflict. These include things such as relative deprivation, environmental pressures, authoritarian government (the democratic peace theory) and the proliferation of weapons (the availability hypothesis). But theories of the causation of international conflict also focus on the nature of the international system and the relations between states. For example, the security dilemma posits that when one state increases its security (such as through the procurement of advanced weapons) this decreases the security of other states.[18] Thus, an arms race may ensue.

---

[16] The word 'humanitarian' appeared 18 times in Resolution 794 authorizing the use of force in Somalia. The definition of 'threats to international peace and security' has broadened so much that in January 2000 the Council considered the issue of AIDS in Africa as coming within its mandate.

[17] The difference between the legal regimes applying to non-international and international armed conflicts in international humanitarian law is quite a complicated issue. In non-international armed conflicts there is no combatant status for individuals fighting the state – thus there is no combatant immunity and individuals may be prosecuted just for the fact that they took up arms (for example, for crimes such as treason). However, once an individual in a non-international armed conflict takes 'direct part in hostilities' they are considered to be *de facto* combatants. It is debatable whether such individuals (as with combatants in international armed conflicts) may be killed at any time (with the exception of individuals who surrender or are *hors de combat*).

[18] John H. Herz, *Political Realism and Political Idealism* (Berkeley: University of California Press, 1951).

Explanations for internal armed conflicts tend to focus more on ethnic antagonisms and alienation from oppressive governments. Nationalism may foment both internal and international conflict in the form of secessionist movements or irredentism – both attempts to make the nation synonymous with the state. In spite of differences in causation, the effects of international and non-international armed conflicts are nearly identical: the denial of the right to peace and the widespread deprivation of human rights.

2.2 The Right to Peace and the Crime of Aggression

It is a consequence of this state-centric nature of international relations that the crime of aggression, a central element of the right to peace, has only been considered in terms of international conflicts. As stated earlier, it is not possible for the state to aggress against its own citizens as the violation of borders is implied in the definition of aggression. For example, Article 2(4) of the United Nations Charter prohibits the 'threat or use of force against the territorial integrity or political independence of any state.' The definition of the crime of aggression in Article 8*bis* of the Rome Statute, adopted by the Review Conference of the International Criminal Court in 2010, follows from the UN Charter [italics added for emphasis]:

> 1. For the purpose of this Statute, 'crime of aggression' means the planning, preparation, initiation or execution, by a person in a position effectively to exercise control over or to direct the political or military action of a State, of an act of aggression which, by its character, gravity and scale, constitutes a manifest violation of the Charter of the United Nations.
> 2. For the purpose of paragraph 1, 'act of aggression' means the use of armed force by a State against the sovereignty, territorial integrity or political independence of *another State*, or in any other manner inconsistent with the Charter of the United Nations.

Thus, the crime of aggression only encompasses conflicts between states. The recourse to the use of force in international law (*jus ad bellum*) is only permitted in self-defence or under the authority of the United Nations Security Council. The Security Council has the authority, under Chapter VII of the UN Charter, to authorize the use of force where there are threats to 'international peace and security'. In some sense, all uses of military force can be said to be violations of the peace. Yet it is well-recognized in both domestic and international law that it is reasonable for individuals and states to be able to defend themselves from wrongful violence (i.e. violence not authorized by legitimate authorities). This right to self-defence is also customarily recognized in many sources including the Bible and

Talmud.[19] Moreover, the UN Charter stipulates in Article 51 there is an 'inherent right of individual or collective self-defence.'

There are customary restrictions to the use of self-defence. For example, Thomas Aquinas put forward the *double effect* doctrine that the main effect (intention) of self-defence should be to ward off attack; harming the attacker is only a secondary (double) effect.[20] This lines up neatly with the principle that self-defence must be proportional. Ohlin and Fletcher set out six criteria for the permissible use of self-defence: the attack must be overt, unlawful and imminent; and the use of defensive force must be necessary, proportional and intentional (directed at the attack).[21] In other words there must be a clear need for the victim to act in self-defence and this self-defence must be directed at this need rather than other objectives. These elements of self-defence are relevant whether the victim of the attack is an individual or a state. Yet individual self-defence generally requires that the target of an attack retreat, except when in their home. States have a territorial dimension so attacks on states are always attacks on the 'home' of the state, thus, there is no obligation to retreat.

In a sense one can conceive of these elements of self-defence as representing both *jus ad bellum* (the ends of the use of force – that self-defence must be in response to an overt, imminent and unlawful attack) and *jus in bello* (the means utilized – that they must be proportional, necessary and intentional). Necessity and proportionality are core principles of international humanitarian law, along with distinction (that force must be directed at combatants, i.e. that it must be intentional) and humanity.[22] The UN Charter provision on self-defence (Article 51) does not specifically name these elements as being necessary for lawful self-defence, but it is reasonable to extend their application to the use of force by states acting in self-defence, as similar considerations apply. The use of the wording 'if an armed attack occurs' in the Charter indicates that the exercise of self-defence must be in response to an attack which is overt and imminent. Imminence means that self-defence is unlawful if a state responds too

---

19 George Fletcher and Jens David Ohlin, *Defending Humanity: When Force is Justified and Why* (New York: OUP, 2008) 26. It is interesting that the Talmud also stipulates that self-defence may only be used in the case of violent acts.

20 *Ibid*. 26.

21 *Ibid*. 86.

22 These principles are embodied in instruments such as the Geneva Conventions (12 August 1949) 75 UNTS 35, entered into force 21 October 1950 and the Hague Convention (IV) Respecting the Laws and Customs of War on Land and its annex: Regulations Concerning the Laws and Customs of War on Land (18 October 1907); 1 Bevans 631, entered into force 26 January 1910, as well as customary law.

early (pre-emptive self-defence) or too late (retaliatory violence).[23] The UN Charter makes no mention of whether self-defence may be used in response to lawful attacks. Yet presumably if the use of force is authorized under Chapter VII of the United Nations Charter, the state subject to this use of force has no right to self-defence.[24]

2.3 Towards a *Jus ad Bellum* for the Use of Force within States

It is well established that many of the *jus in bello* principles applicable during non-international armed conflicts such as distinction, necessity and proportionality, also apply to the use of force in non-international armed conflicts. More importantly, the limitations on the use of force in non-international armed conflicts have been entrenched as customary international law.[25] However, the notion that there is a *jus ad bellum* for non-international armed conflicts has been little discussed. One of the most fundamental rights (and prerogatives) of the state is its ability to exercise control within its own borders. This means that it can deal with rebels and other threats to its security however it wishes, provided it does so within the bounds of humanitarian law, international criminal law and human rights law.

If the right to peace entails the removal of the threat of war, then it is imperative that the threat of internal wars be removed at the same time as the threat of international war. After all, as argued above, the humanitarian consequences are similar and the violation of the right to peace is equal. Thus, there must be some *jus ad bellum* restrictions on the use of force by states within their own borders. If the prohibition of the use of force is not absolute in the international context (i.e. states may use force in self-defence, against regimes of foreign occupation, and under the authorization of the UN Security Council), the recourse to force must also be permissible in the domestic context under certain limited circumstances. What might these circumstances be?

It seems logical to extend the exceptions found at the international level, and the individual level, to the state level. Thus, the state should be allowed to use force internally in situations of self-defence and for the maintenance of peace and security. Self-defence can only occur where

---

23 Fletcher and Ohlin (n19) 90.

24 *Ibid.* 47.

25 See: *Prosecutor v. Tadić*, Interlocutory Appeal on Jurisdiction, Case No. IT-94-1, 2 October 1995, para 97; See also: Jean-Marie Henckaerts and Louise Doswald-Beck (eds) *Customary International Humanitarian Law, Volume 1: Rules* (London: ICRC and CUP, 2009).

there is an overt, imminent and unlawful attack. Thus the state's invocation of self-defence for its exercise of force against its own citizens must be in response to an open attack which threatens its territorial integrity or political independence. Such a threat may be calculated on the basis of the level of organization of the threatening group, its tactics (i.e. is it using violence), and its objectives (such as the installation of a fascist dictatorship). Thus the use of military force would not be permissible against protests or political groups which are peacefully campaigning for a change in the political order. Moreover, the state should be permitted to use force only as a last resort and it has a strong obligation to attempt to peacefully resolve all internal conflicts. In cases like the political conflicts in Syria and Egypt in 2011, where peaceful movements for political reform were met with state-directed violence, the right to peace has clearly been violated.[26]

Needless to say these restrictions on force are already embodied in other human rights norms. For example Article 6 of the ICCPR prohibits the 'arbitrary deprivation of life'. It is lawful to restrict certain human rights such as the right to free expression (ICCPR Article 19), freedom of assembly (ICCPR Article 21), and the freedom to associate with others (ICCPR Article 22) in the name of 'public order', 'national security' and 'public safety.' The UN Code for the Conduct of Law Enforcement Officials stipulates that force may be used by law enforcement officers only according to requirements such as: 1) sufficient legal basis; 2) necessity; 3) proportionality; and 4) precaution. Once again we see a parallel here with international humanitarian law and the criminal law justification of self-defence (i.e. the inclusion of necessity and proportionality). Moreover, the precautionary principles regulate under what circumstances force may be used, i.e. only in self-defence or for the defence of others. In effect the human rights norms relating to the use of force constitute a sort of skeletal *jus ad bellum* for violence within the state, restricting violence to the maintenance of public order. The utility in using the language of *jus ad bellum* is that it emphasizes that intrastate violence must be a last resort. Moreover, rather than the current management of violence approach embodied in international humanitarian law norms such as proportionality and military necessity, we can envision moving towards the prohibition of violence.

The core contribution of the right to peace framework is that we move from a *management of violence* approach to a *prohibition of violence*

---

[26] The situation in Libya is somewhat different as those opposing the regime have effectively declared war on the state and all who support it (although such a rebellion may be considered to be a legitimate exercise of the right to resist).

approach. The prerogative of the state must be further restricted. Such a shift is crucial to ending the threat of war.

3. NON-STATE ACTORS, THE RIGHT TO RESIST AND THE RIGHT TO PEACE

Non-state actors are involved in most armed conflicts worldwide – therefore the right to peace must also restrict the recourse to the use of force by non-state actors. Non-state actors must only use force in situations of self-defence and extreme oppression – where the very life of the group is threatened. The right to resist oppression may constitute an exception to the prohibition on the use of force which binds non-state actors and states alike.

The legal basis of the right to resist is tenuous, grounded in the open language of Article 51 of the UN Charter. The preamble of the Universal Declaration of Human Rights also sets out that 'it is essential, if man is not to be compelled, to have recourse, as a last resort, to rebellion against tyranny and oppression.' Generally this right to resist only extends to regimes of foreign occupation, colonial oppression and legitimate claims of self-determination.[27] It does seem logical however to extend the right to resist to cover resistance against your own state in situations of tyranny such as a genocidal regime. There is some basis to a right to resist unlawful arrest in American jurisprudence.[28] This seems to be indicative of some basis of a right to resist the arbitrary exercise of state power. Furthermore, British jurisprudence upholds the 'lawful excuse' defence where offences may be excused in order to prevent more serious crimes.

If there is a right to resist, it is difficult to conceptualize how such a right would relate to the right to peace. If a non-state actor takes up arms against the state, is it acting in violation of the right to peace of all citizens within that state, even as it is lawful under the right to resist? It seems that the right to resist can only exist as an exception to the *jus ad bellum* prohibition

---

[27] For example, UN GA Res 3070 of 14 December 1960 'reaffirms the legitimacy of the people's struggle for liberation from colonial and foreign domination and alien subjugation by all available means, including armed struggle.' See also the progress report of the Human Rights Council Advisory Committee on the Right to Peace (n12) 10, which reaffirms the right to resist foreign domination and occupation, as well as crimes against humanity and genocide.

[28] Craig Hemmens and Daniel Levin, 'Resistance is Futile: The Right to Resist Unlawful Arrest in an Era of Aggressive Policing' (2000) 46(4) *Crime and Delinquency* 472.

on the use of force. Currently the use of force by non-state actors is of very questionable legality. Article 2(4) of the UN Charter prohibits the 'threat or use of force against the territorial integrity or political independence of any states.' The actions of many non-state actors certainly violate this principle. Moreover, the effect of such recourse to violence by non-state actors has socially similar effects to the violation of the right to peace by the state; thus, it is as much a violation of the rights of individuals to peace as war waged by states.

Nicholas Fontion sets out the tenets of just war theory as: 1) just cause; 2) last resort; 3) proportionality; 4) likelihood of success; 5) right intentions (that the waging of war be linked only to just causes like self-defence and no other objectives), and 6) legitimate authority. Just war theory was conceived with states in mind and the principles of likelihood of success and legitimate authority are not easily transposed to non-state actors.[29] Given the usual asymmetry between states and non-state actors the likelihood of success of non-state actors would always appear to be low. Moreover, the taking of arms against the state by non-state actors is inherently illegitimate unless we consider that certain states behave as deviants and thus lose their legitimacy. Attacks on the state may be conceived of as attacks on the citizenry of the state but this is not necessarily the case. The use of force by non-state actors should be permissible in situations of self-defence or to overthrow extremely oppressive regimes.

4. THE DEFENCE OF OTHERS (THE RESPONSIBILITY TO PROTECT) AS A LAWFUL EXCEPTION TO THE PROHIBITION ON THE USE OF FORCE

The right to peace is closely intertwined with the prohibition on the use of force. As argued above, this prohibition on the use of force contains a number of legitimate and lawful exceptions such as self-defence and action by the UN Security Council. The Security Council seems to be taking a far more activist role in response to abuses of state power than it has in the past. It is important that we consider whether the seemingly lawful use of force by the UN Security Council under the auspices of the responsibility to protect doctrine is also legitimate in terms of the content and objectives of the right to peace.

Another important aspect of the right to peace is to consider whether

---

29 Nicholas Fontion, *War and Ethics* (London: Continuum Books, 2007) 88–9.

the right of self-defence might also include the right, or duty, to defend others. The unlawful use of force is by its very nature deviant within the international legal order. If the right to peace is to be brought to fruition this prohibition on the use of force must extend beyond the international use of force to encompass the unlawful use of force in domestic contexts. This may include crimes such as genocide and crimes against humanity but also any collective force which is unnecessary and disproportionate.

Public international law sets out numerous illegal acts for states including the breach of treaty obligations and the commission of wrongful acts such as genocide, crimes against humanity, war crimes, piracy and terrorism. Aggression, a *jus cogens* norm and *erga omnes* obligation, is prohibited by customary international law.[30] These are more than mere legal norms but are actually representative of the shared values of the international community.

Critical theorists sometimes argue that the international system, and the norms it embodies, are entirely the product of power relations and specifically the domination of the peripheral 'less developed countries' by the core 'more developed countries.' There is some validity to this disputation – states are political objects within a political system and any determination of the legality of the use of force is going to have an inevitable political aspect. This is precisely why multilateral institutions need to be made more effective. Moreover, the notion of security must continue to be interpreted broadly to encompass threats to the fundamental human rights and security of human beings. States that commit gross human rights violations are clearly deviant within the international legal and moral order.

States which violate the right to peace in the international or domestic context may be addressed under the notion of the 'defence of others' which is present in some iterations of self-defence.[31] Fletcher and Ohlin make the novel argument that the use of the term '*légitime défense*' in the official French language version of the UN Charter rather than the English term 'self-defence' indicates that the broader French concept of

---

[30] *East Timor (Portugal v. Australia)* Judgment, ICJ Reports 1995, 90, para 29. *Legality on the Threat or Use of Nuclear Weapons*, Advisory Opinion, ICJ Reports 1996, 226, para 83. *Application of the Convention on the Prevention and Punishment of the Crime of Genocide*, Preliminary Objections, Judgment, ICJ Reports, 1996, 595, paras 31–2.

[31] The defence of property is also sometimes considered to be a part of the right to self-defence. However, in international criminal law self-defence is a permissible defence for the protection of property only in the case of war crimes, not crimes against humanity or genocide.

legitimate defence may be legally applicable.[32] Legitimate defence includes, in addition to self-defence, the defence of others. Moreover, the notion of 'collective self-defence' found in the UN Charter may include the defence of others, rather than just regional security arrangements.[33] Fletcher and Ohlin also contend that the right to self-determination applies to nations and that nations also have the right to self-defence, ergo the defence of others extends to a right (or even duty) to defend nations.[34]

Traditionally, there has been no widespread *duty* to rescue others in either domestic or international legal contexts. In most common law jurisdictions there is a duty to rescue only in the case of family members 'and a set of persons with whom one has a special relationship of trust and responsibility.'[35] This provision has evolved in common law and a general duty to rescue others also seems to be emerging in international law with the emergence of the responsibility to protect doctrine.

However, in many continental legal jurisdictions there is also a duty to protect others. For example, Article 223 – 6 of the French Penal Code stipulates that:

> Anyone who, being able without risk to himself or to third parties to prevent by immediate action a felony or a misdemeanour against the bodily integrity of a person, wilfully abstains from doing so, is punished by five years' imprisonment and a fine of €75,000.
>
> The same penalties apply to anyone who wilfully fails to render to a person in danger any assistance which, without risk to himself or to third parties, he could render him either by his own action, or by initiating rescue operations.

Similar provisions are found in Article 15 of the Swiss Penal Code and Article 195 of the Spanish Penal Code.

In the international context the idea of imposing a duty to intervene in defence of others was proposed in the UN charter drafting process by New Zealand and rejected.[36] Moreover, in the *Military and Paramilitary Activities in and against Nicaragua* case, the International Court of Justice qualified the notion of the self-defence of others by arguing that a state under attack must declare its desire for the intervention of a third state in order for such intervention to be lawful.[37] However, there has been much

---

32 Fletcher and Ohlin (n19) 64.
33 *Ibid.* 67.
34 *Ibid.* 152.
35 *Ibid.* 53.
36 *Ibid.* 77.
37 *Case Concerning Military and Paramilitary Activities in and against Nicaragua*, Judgment, ICJ Reports, 27 June 1986, para 165.

recent debate about military intervention in defence of others (the so-called 'responsibility to protect' doctrine).

As things now stand, there is no legal provision explicitly permitting humanitarian intervention; however, some commentators argue that customary international law may have evolved to allow for humanitarian intervention in certain circumstances.[38] The approach of the International Commission on Intervention and State Sovereignty (ICISS) is that states have a 'responsibility to protect' their citizens from 'avoidable catastrophe . . . but when they are unwilling or unable to do so, that responsibility must be borne by the broader community of states.'[39] In other words, intervention to protect against human rights violations must be *complementary* – it can only occur in situations where the state has failed to act, or where the state itself is acting as a perpetrator such as when the state is waging an internal war without adequate efforts for peaceful resolution.

The responsibility to protect is more than just an authorization for intervention; it is also a guideline to restrain unjustifiable humanitarian intervention. The ICISS sets six criteria for legitimate intervention. The first is *just cause* – a large scale loss of life through deliberate state action, state neglect, or inability to act, or gross human rights violations ('actual or apprehended').[40] Secondly, *right intention* – the primary purpose of the intervention should be humanitarian. Thirdly, *proportionality* – the means of intervention should be the 'minimum necessary' to achieve the objective. The fourth prerequisite is that military intervention should be the *last resort*. Fifthly, there must be a '*reasonable chance of success* in halting or averting the suffering.'[41] The final criterion is *right authority* – the United Nations Security Council is the most appropriate body for the authorization of intervention. The United Nations is the only authority in the international system that has a sufficiently broad membership and the appropriate institutional mandate to authorize the use of force. Moreover, there are checks and balances inherent in multilateralism.

The risks of the responsibility to protect doctrine are manifest. Firstly,

---

38 See, for example, Art. 4 of the United Nations Security Council Resolution 1674 (adopted on 28 April 2006) which: '*Reaffirms* the provisions of paragraphs 138 and 139 of the 2005 World Summit Outcome Document regarding the responsibility to protect populations from genocide, war crimes, ethnic cleansing and crimes against humanity'.

39 International Commission on Intervention and State Sovereignty (ICISS), *The Responsibility to Protect* (Ottawa: International Development Research Centre, 2001) viii.

40 *Ibid.* 5.

41 *Ibid.* 3.

one might consider the risk that state sovereignty is continuously and substantially eroded, as such an erosion of sovereignty may also erode human rights if states violate each other's sovereignty in order to commit human rights abuses.[42] There is also a risk that an increasingly intrusive international system could be controlled by the deviant states themselves and abused to negative ends. Nonetheless, the waging of an unjustified war is an uncontested social ill within the international community. Action against such crimes is consistent with the aims of the United Nations – to counteract threats to international peace and security and foster international cooperation.

One can question whether humanitarian intervention is itself a violation of the right to peace. After all, it is the recourse to armed force. Yet such intervention, under the correct circumstances, must be legitimate as it is intended as a policing action to remove the threat of war, rather than to perpetuate war – thus it does not violate the right to peace. Interestingly an International Committee of the Red Cross (ICRC) survey conducted in 1999 found that fully two-thirds of civilians in 12 war zones were in favour of military intervention.[43] In other words, those who suffer the violation of the right to peace most acutely, those subject to war, support military intervention to interdict violations as an exception to the prohibition on the use of force.

5. BEYOND AGGRESSION: DISMANTLING STRUCTURES OF VIOLENCE AND MILITARISM

The right to peace encompasses more than just the unlawful or illegitimate use of force. Thus the UN General Assembly Resolution on the right to peace speaks of the 'threat of war' and not just war itself. The implementation of the right to peace must also involve dismantling the structures of violence and militarism that undermine the exercise of the right to peace. This means that civilian control over the military must be affirmed, as must the exclusion of children from military service. Moreover, the right to conscientious objection must be internationally recognized.

States which produce, stockpile and trade arms in large quantities are surely acting in violation of the right to peace. After all, weapons are

[42] Germany between the world wars is one such society where the concept of deviancy was continuously and ruinously expanded.

[43] Thomas G. Weiss, *Humanitarian Intervention* (Cambridge: Polity Press, 2007) 153.

created for the express purpose of doing violence. Even if we consider that weapons are used for lawful purposes such as the maintenance of public order, the number and power of weapons in the world is far excessive to meet these modest goals. Nowhere is this truer than with nuclear weapons, which have the potential to kill every human being on the planet.

Furthermore, implementing the right to peace must involve not only the cessation of existing conflicts, but also the prevention of future conflicts. The cessation of current conflicts will require extensive mediation and negotiation efforts. Many conflicts seem to come to an end only once parties have reached a hurting stalemate – where the potential for gains is low and costs of continuation high for both parties to a conflict. The resolution of existing conflicts is essential if states are to implement the right to peace.

Conflict prevention is likewise a complex exercise that must target the root causes of violence. In other words governance must be made more equitable, democratic and just. Moreover, ethnic and other identity conflicts must be managed with a spirit of toleration. Of course, the resolution of these issues will result in the improvement of numerous human rights. This underscores the importance of the right to peace for the realization of other human rights. Propaganda for war is already prohibited in Article 20 of the International Covenant on Civil and Political Rights. The UN Human Rights Council Advisory Committee on the Right to Peace proposes expanding this prohibition to cover all 'glorification of violence and its effects'.[44] In short, all factors which contribute to the number and intensity of armed conflicts must be addressed for the implementation of the right to peace.

6. CONCLUSION: A WORLD WITHOUT WAR?

One might still argue that through legitimizing state efforts to protect the rights of others we are only seeking to unwisely universalize the demonstrably non-altruistic state. Inevitably, discussions about the failings of state altruism lead us to the failure of individual altruism. After all, states are led by individuals and comprise individuals. Is the state a vehicle of human desire? If this is the case, then the sinister manifestations of state power are ultimately attributable to the imperfection of *homo sapiens*. We must face the reality that we might be our own worst enemy, the instrument of our own destruction.

---

[44] Advisory Committee on the Right of Peoples to Peace (n12) 14.

The altruistic rhetoric of human rights must not be grounded in naivety about the flawed character of human motivation but rather a desire to respond to the threat of mass violence in a progressive and effective manner. What are needed are realistic structures built around a core of idealism. The failings of globalized altruism necessitate enduring and robust structures of international mobilization within a framework of human rights.[45] The international system must be transformed into a true system of social control grounded on state responsibilities. This system of social control would operate through political interaction, as states are the main subjects of the system rather than individuals. Even if states cannot be reformed, they can at least be restrained. Such a system to counteract state deviancy, in situations of the unlawful use of force, requires both constraints on the power of states to abuse their own citizens and constraints on their boundless power to ignore the abuse of citizens in other states.

Kant argued that states are moral equals, so the idea of one state punishing another is impossible.[46] Yet, what is being proposed here is not an international system acting as a 'philosopher king' in the Platonic sense of a benign dictator, but rather a system of rights and responsibilities grounded in democratic participation within each state and between states within the global community. Such action will be grounded in the equality between states, but also the recognition of the rights of individuals. Intervention of any type must be purposefully restricted to the safeguarding of shared values and collective interests.

There must be a shift from the management-based approach to armed conflict to a prohibition-based approach. There is inherent tension between the lofty goals of human rights law and the 'lesser evil' approach of international humanitarian law. For example, the doctrine of military necessity in international humanitarian law is itself inimical to the realization of the right to peace, and the use of force should never be deemed to be necessary except in the case of self-defence or the defence of others. The lack of immunity for combatants in non-international armed conflicts is indicative of the linkages between *jus in bello* and *jus ad bellum*, particularly

---

[45] Also material to this debate is the possibility of pacifism in a militarized world. In his book *Mass Hate: The Global Rise of Genocide and Terror* (Cambridge, MA: Westview, 2002) 242, Neil Kressel approvingly quotes columnist Michael Kelly when he writes: 'pacifism can be inescapably and profoundly immoral, "on the side of the murders, and . . . on the side of letting them murder again."' Such hyperbole shows a profound lack of understanding of pacifism. It is frequently, and wrongly, misrepresented as passivity.

[46] Fletcher and Ohlin (n19) 57.

in the case of non-international armed conflicts.[47] These linkages must be strengthened to reflect the fact that the disproportionate use of force invalidates a just cause for going to war.[48] Proportionality considerations are even greater in the case of the responsibility to protect doctrine, where the disproportionate use of force by intervening powers would completely invalidate the humanitarian objectives of the mission.[49]

What is needed is a *jus ad bellum* for intrastate violence that does not asymmetrically remove rights from non-state actors but rather limits the recourse to armed force by states and non-state actors alike. Human rights are largely an exercise in norm-setting so we must recognize that the right to peace may be a generational endeavour. Nonetheless, our ultimate goal must be the dismantling of all structures of violence and the end of all war.

---

[47] Francois Bugnion, '*Jus ad Bellum, Jus in Bello* and non-international armed conflicts' (2003) 6 *Yearbook of International Humanitarian Law* 167.

[48] Larry May, *Aggression and Crimes against Peace* (New York: CUP, 2008) 113.

[49] Frédéric Mégret, '*Jus in Bello* as *Jus ad Bellum*: "Humanitarian Intervention" as a rare case where bringing *jus in bello* and *jus ad bellum* closer together makes sense' *The Relationship Between* Jus ad Bellum *and* Jus in Bello, *Past, Present, Future – Proceedings of the ASIL, 2006*.

4. UNESCO and the right to peace

David Keane

The right to peace as a human right has been incidentally mentioned in various documents. As early as 1969, the Istanbul Declaration, adopted during the 21st International Conference of the Red Cross, proclaimed the right to lasting peace as a human right. In January 1997, the Director-General of UNESCO prepared the Oslo Draft Declaration on the Human Right to Peace, which proclaimed that 'every human being has the right to peace, which is inherent in the dignity of the human person'. The 1997 Oslo Draft Declaration proved to be the apex of UNESCO's 'right to peace' initiative, which quickly met with determined state opposition.

The organization turned instead to the concept of a 'culture of peace', which had been developing in tandem with the right to peace movement. The 'culture of peace' subsumed elements of the right to peace initiative, without the legal character that the Oslo Draft Declaration had been attempting. However the original 'culture of peace' idea had an interesting origin, including a UNESCO document called the Seville Statement on Violence 1986. The Seville Statement represented an exploration of the link between aggressive behaviour and genetics, and sought to challenge a number of alleged biological findings that have been used to justify violence and war.

This aspect of the 'culture of peace' has been marginalized, as the concept has instead been used to promote the more mainstream ideas inherent in the notion of the right to peace. The paper will explore the right to peace from the UNESCO perspective, outlining the reason for its failure; the origin and meaning of the 'culture of peace'; and will finally trace the work of UNESCO in linking human rights and genetics. It will be argued that the future of the concept of a right, or indeed a culture, of peace, may lie in a resurrection of the ideas proposed in Seville in 1986.

1. CODIFYING THE RIGHT TO PEACE

The work already accomplished in the United Nations system to develop the concept of the human right to peace has been described as 'one of the world's best kept secrets'.[1] The right to peace as a human right has formed part of various international documents, although none of them was entirely devoted to the elaboration of this right.[2] Thus a 1969 Red Cross conference passed the Istanbul Declaration which proclaimed the right to lasting peace as a human right,[3] and in 1976, the Commission on Human Rights passed a resolution stating that everyone has the right to live in conditions of peace.[4] In 1978, the General Assembly adopted Resolution 33/73 on the Preparation of Societies for Life in Peace which provides: 'Every nation and every human being, regardless of race, conscience, language or sex, has the inherent right to life in peace.'[5] Subsequently, the UN General Assembly adopted the Declaration on the Right of Peoples to Peace in 1984, which proclaims that the peoples of our planet have a sacred right to peace.[6]

In 1946, the first General Conference of UNESCO approved the constitution of the organization, which begins with the declaration: 'since wars begin in the minds of men, it is in the minds of men that the defences of peace must be constructed', with the first half of the sentence attributed to Clement Attlee and the second half to the American poet Archibald McLeish.[7] Thus UNESCO was established to promote peace through the application of education, science and culture.[8] Valderrama's history of UNESCO emphasizes this essential aim:

> the original idea that guided and still guides the work of UNESCO [is] that of peace, a peace which is something more than the mere absence of declared

---

[1] Douglas Roche, 'The Human Right to Peace', Address to Koerner Lecture Series, 31 October 2003, available online at: http://roche.apirg.org/public_html/writings/documents/socialjustice/KorenerLectures2003Oct31.pdf

[2] UNESCO, Report by the Director-General on the Human Right to Peace, UNESCO Doc 29C/59, 29 October 1997, available online at: http://unesdoc.unesco.org/images/0011/001100/110027E.pdf

[3] *Ibid.*, para 7. 21st International Conference of the Red Cross and Red Crescent, Resolution 19: Istanbul Declaration, Istanbul, 1969, reprinted in (1969) 104 *International Review of the Red Cross* 620–1.

[4] UNESCO Doc 29C/59 (n2). UN Human Rights Commission Resolution 5 (XXXII) 27 February 1976.

[5] UNESCO Doc 29C/59 (n2). UN GA Res 33/73.

[6] UNESCO Doc 29C/59 (n2) para 6. Declaration on the Right of Peoples to Peace, approved by UN GA Res 39/11, 12 November 1984, Art. 1.

[7] Clare Wells, *The UN, UNESCO and the Politics of Knowledge* (London: Macmillan, 1987) 26. Of course wars can also begin in the minds of women, from Zenobia of Palmyra to Margaret Thatcher.

[8] Fernando Valderrama, *A History of UNESCO* (Paris: UNESCO Publishing, 1995) 25.

> hostilities, a peace involving solidarity, concord and a concerted effort by free men to achieve security and happiness, the aim being to make war impossible by instituting truly human relations among all peoples of the world and to vanquish its causes through the social, material and moral progress of mankind.[9]

Clare Wells concurs: 'UNESCO's prime task was thus to be the promotion of peace at the level of intellect and conscience, or what could be termed mental and moral disarmament.'[10] Its central mandate under its Constitution was therefore 'knowledge for peace', indicating a concern with the goals of knowledge in all fields, at all levels, and by whatever means of communication.[11]

In July 1989, the International Congress on Peace in the Minds of Men was held in Yamoussoukro (Ivory Coast), in cooperation with the Houphouet-Boigny International Foundation for Peace, with the aim of formulating the concept of a 'culture of peace'. It approved the Yamoussoukro Declaration, which defined peace positively, not as the mere absence of war. The objectives of the Congress were to draw attention to the positive aspects of the activities designed to build peace and to the contribution of UNESCO to that task within its areas of competence and in discharge of the mission assigned to it by its constitution.[12]

Federico Mayor, then Director-General of UNESCO, led the way in an early attempt to codify the right to peace.[13] The idea of proclaiming the human right to peace was formulated in Mayor's declaration of January 1997. It received a positive response and was discussed at an international meeting of experts at Las Palmas, Spain in February 1997.[14] The meeting expressed the view that the human right to peace should be recognized, guaranteed and protected at the international level through the preparation and adoption of a Declaration on the Human Right to Peace for UNESCO's General Conference in November.[15]

On the initiative of Asbjørn Eide, Director of the Norwegian Institute of Human Rights, a meeting on the human right to peace was held in Oslo from 6 to 8 June 1997.[16] The main objective of the meeting was to prepare

---

9 *Ibid.*, 30.

10 Wells (n7) 45.

11 *Ibid.*, 46.

12 Valderrama (n8) 325–6.

13 Douglas Roche, 'The Human Right to Peace', Address to Liu Institute for Global Issues, 2 April 2003, available online at: http://roche.apirg.org/public_html/writings/documents/nuclear/LiuCentrePresentation.pdf

14 UNESCO (n2) Outline and Background.

15 *Ibid.*, para 12.

16 *Ibid.*, para 13.

a Draft Declaration on the Human Right to Peace. They elaborated a text which was presented to the Norwegian press and radio by the UNESCO Director-General, who took part in the final session of the meeting.[17] The Oslo Draft Declaration on the Human Right to Peace has a preamble and three interrelated provisions: Article 1, Peace as a Human Right; Article 2, Peace as a Duty; and Article 3, Peace through the Culture of Peace. It proclaims that 'every human being has the right to peace, which is inherent in the dignity of the human person'.[18]

After Oslo, further meetings were held at which the need to recognize the human right to peace was affirmed. Those meetings resulted in the Bamako Declaration (Mali) which proclaims that the human right to peace is a fundamental right. Likewise the Maputo Declaration (Mozambique) adopted by the International Conference on the Culture of Peace and Governance in September 1997, stated that 'the human right to peace is an inalienable right'.[19]

Opposition to the concept emerged at UNESCO's General Conference on 6 November 1997, where a 'remarkable debate' on the Draft Declaration took place.[20] Many European states attacked or expressed reservations on the concept of a right to peace, accusing Mayor of overstepping his mandate.[21] The debate split North and South, with developing states accusing the North of wanting to protect their arms industries.[22] Paraguay noted that 'perhaps peace is a greater concern in the South where scarce resources are being diverted to war.'[23]

The participants also questioned whether the human right to peace really falls within the competence of UNESCO.[24] Some were of the view that the matter lay more properly within the competence of the General Assembly of the United Nations, and that UNESCO should focus its efforts on its own fields of competence, fostering collaboration, understanding and respect among nations in the fields of education, science, culture and communication, rather than on a declaration relating to human rights.[25] Some of these concerns were examined in Mayor's 1997 Report, where he notes that the special role of UNESCO in the

17 *Ibid.*, para 14.
18 *Ibid.*, Annex II.
19 *Ibid.*, para 17.
20 Roche (n1).
21 *Ibid.*
22 *Ibid.*
23 *Ibid.*
24 UNESCO (n2) para 8.
25 *Ibid.*, para 22.

implementation of the human right to life in peace was, in fact, recognized by the Declaration on the Preparation of Societies for Life in Peace (1978), which, in Part III, paragraph 2, called for 'concerted action on the part of governments, the United Nations and the Specialized Agencies, in particular UNESCO'.[26]

Eventually the idea was abandoned by Mayor in the absence of a consensus, leaving residual scepticism as to the potential for the elaboration of a human right to peace, whether under the leadership of UNESCO or not.[27] Consequently the concept of a 'culture of peace' has come to define UNESCO efforts in this sphere. According to Doug Roche:

> attention in UNESCO shifted back from a 'right' to peace to the 'culture' of peace. This was easier to digest for those who did not want their 'right' to make war impeded. Everyone, after all, could be for peace in general. UNESCO showed its wisdom by treading slowly and developing the concept of the culture of peace into a series of programs that would, at least in the minds of those who truly understood the dimensions of the culture of peace, prepare the groundwork for a later acceptance of the human right to peace.[28]

Following a proposal from UNESCO, the General Assembly in 1998 established a separate agenda item entitled 'Towards a Culture of Peace', defined as consisting of values, attitudes and behaviours that reject violence and endeavour to prevent conflicts by addressing their root causes, with a view to solving problems through dialogue and negotiations between individuals, groups and nations.[29] In 1999, the General Assembly adopted the Declaration and Programme of Action on a Culture of Peace (Resolution A/53/243) defining eight action areas to be linked through the concept of a culture of peace and non-violence into a single coherent approach.[30] UNESCO was the focal point for the International Year for the Culture of Peace, in 2000, while 2001–2010 was declared the

---

26 *Ibid.*, para 9.

27 Roche (n1).

28 *Ibid.*

29 UNESCO, 'Mainstreaming the Culture of Peace' (Paris: UNESCO Publishing, 2002) available online at: http://www3.unesco.org/iycp/uk/uk_sum_cp.htm.

30 UN Doc A/RES/53/243, 6 October 1999, Declaration and Programme of Action on a Culture of Peace. The eight areas are: a culture of peace through education; sustainable economic and social development; respect for all human rights; equality between men and women; democratic participation; advance understanding, tolerance and solidarity; free flow of information and knowledge; international peace and security.

International Decade for a Culture of Peace and Non-violence for the Children of the World, with UNESCO as lead agency.[31]

2. FROM A 'RIGHT TO PEACE' TO A 'CULTURE OF PEACE': THE LOSS OF 'RIGHTS STATUS'

In a 1984 article in the *American Journal of International Law*, Philip Alston proposes a 'quality control' for examining claims as to whether a human right exists or not.[32] Beginning with a quote from Richard Bilder that 'in practice, a claim is an international human right if the United Nations General Assembly says it is',[33] Alston emphasizes that this truth is in danger of being undermined by related UN agencies that have superseded the General Assembly's role in elaborating, or 'conjuring up', new human rights. Furthermore the General Assembly has on several occasions proclaimed new rights without setting out the required criteria for achieving such status. The ease with which such rights have emerged threatens to undermine the integrity of the entire process of human rights recognition and enforcement.[34] Some examples cited are the right to tourism, supported by the intergovernmental World Tourism Organization,[35] the right to sleep and the right to be free to experiment with alternative ways of life, the latter two among a list said to be 'on the world waiting list for processing into rights' in an ambitious UNESCO document.[36]

The right to peace forms part of a stronger push towards a 'third generation' of 'solidarity rights'. The notion of 'solidarity rights' was proposed by Karel Vasak in a 1979 lecture to the International Institute of Human Rights. He stated that such rights 'can be realized only through the concerted efforts of all the actors on the social scene: the individual, the State, public and private bodies and the international community.'[37] Vasak

---

31 *Ibid.*

32 Philip Alston, 'Conjuring Up New Human Rights: A Proposal for Quality Control' (1984) 78 *AJIL* 607.

33 Richard Bilder, 'Rethinking International Human Rights: Some Basic Questions' (1969) *Wisconsin L. Rev.* 171, 173.

34 Alston (n32) 607.

35 UN Doc E/1978/98, quoted in Alston (n32) 611: 'tourism has become increasingly a basic need, a social necessity, a human right'.

36 Johan Galtung and Anders Helga Wirak, 'On the Relationship between Human Rights and Human Needs', UNESCO Doc SS-78/CONF.630/4, 48, quoted in Alston (n32) 610.

37 Quoted in Stephen Marks, 'Emerging Human Rights: A New Generation for the 1980s?' (1980–81) 33 *Rutgers L. Rev.* 435, 441.

distinguished the three generations of rights as corresponding to each of the elements of the motto of the French revolution, *liberté, égalité, fraternité*, with the third generation being the generation predicated on human brotherhood, or *fraternité*.[38]

Solidarity is a prerequisite to action to address certain planetary concerns,[39] and 'solidarity rights' include, principally, the right to development and the right to a healthy environment.[40] The right to development was made explicit in the 1986 Declaration on the Right to Development,[41] although no comparable standard-setting General Assembly proclamation exists for the right to a healthy environment.[42] Their exalted status among candidates for 'rights status' is evident from the fact that all three have been recognized in the African Charter of Human and Peoples' Rights of 1981.[43] On the right to peace, Alston writes:

> The status of the right to peace is similar to that of the right to development. It has been proclaimed in varying formulations by both the Commission and the Assembly, but neither its status as a human right nor its precise formulation, let alone its content, has ever been formally debated. This did not, however, deter the General Assembly from adopting in 1978 . . . a declaration proclaiming the principle that 'every nation and every human being . . . has the inherent right to life in peace'.[44]

He notes that the 1978 Resolution was passed on the recommendation of the First Committee of the General Assembly, without reference to the Third Committee, the body normally charged with human rights matters. Similarly the Commission on Human Rights was bypassed in the proclamation of the right.[45] Stephen Marks highlights the Cold War machinations behind the push towards a right to peace in the late 1970s:

> the sponsors for the resolution of the Commission on Human Rights were the USSR and other socialist countries and . . . the Declaration on the Preparation

---

38 Cited in Marks, *ibid.*

39 *Ibid.*

40 Alston (n32) 610–11. Marks (n37) 441, lists 'peace, development, ecological balance and communication' as forming part of the list of 'solidarity rights'.

41 See further http://www.unhchr.ch/development/right.html

42 The 'Stockholm Declaration' of 1972 recognizes the nascent right to a healthy environment. While endorsed by the General Assembly in general terms, it has never specifically proclaimed the right to a clean environment. Alston (n32) 612.

43 Text approved by OAU Ministerial Conference in January 1981, reprinted in 21 *ILM* 59 (1982).

44 Alston (n32) 612.

45 *Ibid.*

> of Societies to Live in Peace was a Polish initiative. Moreover, the study made for UNESCO on the right to peace for its contribution in 1978 to the work of the Commission was prepared by Alexander Tichonov of the Institute of State and Law of the Soviet Academy of Sciences. May we conclude that the so-called right to peace is merely a preoccupation of some countries?[46]

Marks, writing in the early 1980s, decided that such a conclusion was not justified, and pointed to a certain degree of international recognition sufficient to characterize the right to peace as 'one of the emerging human rights of the 1980s.'[47] On the content of the right, he offered an 'illustration of the sort of definitions that should go into the definition of this right': the right of every individual to contribute to efforts for peace, including refusal to participate in the military effort; the collective right of every state to benefit from the full respect by other states of the principles of non-use of force, of non-aggression, of peaceful settlement of disputes, of the Geneva Conventions and Additional Protocols and similar standards, as well as from the implementation of policies aimed at general and complete disarmament under effective international control.[48]

The evolution of the right to peace reached a high point in 1997 with the Oslo Draft Declaration on the Right to Peace. The vehement opposition to the concept expressed at the UNESCO conference underlines serious misgivings among certain states as to the viability of a human right to peace. UNESCO had gone too far, seeking 'rights-status' for a poorly-defined and understood concept. The parallel concept of a 'culture of peace', which was being investigated as part of the broader right to peace movement, was instead embraced as the focal point of UNESCO efforts in this sphere. The emergence of a 'culture of peace' agenda has been readily endorsed by the General Assembly in the 1999 Declaration and Programme of Action. As a result, the 'culture of peace' has come to embrace the wider ideas associated with the right to peace, although originally it appears to have been much more focused. Its contemporary position as a substitute for the right to peace movement obscures the task it was originally assigned.

3. A 'CULTURE OF PEACE' EXPLORED

The 1997 UNESCO Report on the Human Right to Peace states that 'there is also another intimate dimension of peace, the need for internal peace,

46 Marks (n37) 446.
47 *Ibid.*
48 *Ibid.*

for the prohibition of violence of all kinds.'[49] The accompanying footnote refers to a speech by the UN Secretary-General in which he stated that 'in the broadest sense we seek to establish a culture of peace. UNESCO . . . is founded on the premise that "since wars being in the minds of men, it is in the minds of men that the defences of peace must be constructed".'[50] Article 3 of the Oslo Draft Declaration on the Right to Peace divided the culture of peace into two provisions:

> (a) The culture of peace, whose aim is to build the defences of peace in the minds of human beings every day through education, science and communication, must constitute the means of achieving the global implementation of the human right to peace;
> (b) The culture of peace requires recognition and respect for – and the daily practice of – a set of ethical values and democratic ideals which are based on the intellectual and moral solidarity of humanity.[51]

The meaning of a 'culture of peace' is different, pre- and post-Oslo. Originally a subset of the right to peace, the concept has been thrust into the centre of UNESCO's efforts to secure peace given the failure to codify a rights-based approach. Prior to the Oslo Draft Declaration, a 'culture of peace' was more closely aligned to the notion of 'internal peace', or the 'minds of men' referred to in UNESCO's Constitution. The 2002 UNESCO brochure, 'Mainstreaming the Culture of Peace', highlights the origin of the notion of the culture of peace:

> The idea to use the term 'culture of peace' was inspired by an educational initiative called *Cultura de paz* developed in Peru (1986), and by the Seville Statement on Violence (1986) adopted by scientists from around the world, which stated that war is not a fatality determined by genes, violent brains, human nature or instincts, but is rather a social invention. Therefore, 'the same species that invented war is capable of inventing peace'.[52]

The Seville Statement on Violence challenges a number of alleged biological findings that have been used to justify violence and war.[53] Recalling Valderrama's assertion that UNESCO's aim was 'to make war

---

49 UNESCO (n2) para 10.

50 *Ibid.*, para 10, n1.

51 *Ibid.*, Annex II.

52 UNESCO (n29).

53 UNESCO, Seville Statement on Violence, 16 May 1986, adopted at the twenty-fifth session of the General Conference on 16 November 1989, available online at: http://www.unesco.org/cpp/uk/declarations/seville.pdf. A list of the natural and social scientists involved in drafting the Statement may be found at:

impossible',[54] this approach is undermined by the belief that war is natural or somehow part of our genetic constitution. It is divided into five propositions which link violence, war and evolutionary biology, and all begin with the phrase '[I]t is scientifically incorrect (. . .)':

1. It is scientifically incorrect to say that we inherited a tendency to make war from our animal ancestors. Predatory feeding upon other species cannot be equated with intraspecies violence, and warfare is a peculiarly human phenomenon that does not occur in other animals. The fact that warfare has evolved radically means that it is a product of culture rather than biology. War is 'biologically possible but it is not inevitable.'[55]
2. It is scientifically incorrect to say that war and violence is genetically programmed into our human nature. While genes are co-involved in establishing our behavioural capacities, they do not produce individuals predisposed to violence; neither do they determine the opposite.[56]
3. It is scientifically incorrect to say that in the course of human evolution there has been a selection for aggressive behaviour over other forms of behaviour. In all studied species, status is achieved through cooperation and fulfilling social functions rather than use of superior physical power. Violence is neither an evolutionary legacy nor in our genes.[57]
4. It is scientifically incorrect to say that humans have a 'violent brain'. While we have the neural apparatus to act violently, it cannot be triggered automatically by certain stimuli. We have the capacity to filter stimuli and there is nothing in our neurophysiology to compel us to react violently.[58]
5. It is scientifically incorrect to say that war is caused by a single motivation or 'instinct'. Modern war involves institutional use of personal characteristics such as obedience, suggestibility, idealism and social skills. The technology of modern war has exaggerated traits associated with violence both in the training of combatants and in the preparation of support for war in the general population. Such traits are often mistaken to be the causes rather than the consequences of the process.[59]

According to the final paragraph:

> We conclude that biology does not condemn humanity to war, and that humanity can be freed from the bondage of biological pessimism . . . Although these tasks are mainly institutional and collective, they also rest upon the

---

http://portal.unesco.org/education/en/ev.php-URL_ID=3247&URL_DO=DO_TOPIC&URL_SECTION=201.html

54 Valderrama (n8) 30.
55 UNESCO (n53).
56 *Ibid.* An exception for 'rare pathologies' is accepted.
57 *Ibid.*
58 *Ibid.*
59 *Ibid.*

> consciousness of individual participants for whom pessimism and optimism are crucial factors. Just as 'wars begin in the minds of men', peace also begins in our minds. The same species who invented war is capable of inventing peace. The responsibility lies with each of us.[60]

In a 1989 article in the *Journal of Peace Research*, David Adams charts the historical significance and progress of the Seville Statement on Violence.[61] The initial idea for the project came from the UNESCO Statements on Race, dating from 1950, which gave a scientific foundation to the political work of the UN against racial discrimination by challenging the notion of biologically-determined racial categories. The unofficial drafting body in Seville was the International Society for Research on Aggression (ISRA),[62] under the auspices of the Spanish National UNESCO Commission. All participants were asked to answer the following question: 'Does modern biology and social science know of any biological factors, including those concerned with the biology of violent behaviour of individuals, that constitute an insurmountable or serious obstacle to the goal of world peace . . . including an ultimate goal of general and complete disarmament through the UN?'[63]

The objective need for the Statement was quantified in a study presented at the meetings, in which it was found that if a person believes that war is an intrinsic part of human nature they are much less likely to engage in activities for peace.[64] On the content and style of the Statement, Adams notes that 'we have received remarkably little criticism'.[65] The historical contribution of the document is reflected in the fact that it confronts active resistance in the mass media to biological determinism: 'The myth that war is part of human nature does not appear to be so much an inherent component of "common sense" so much as it is the end result of a campaign of psychological propaganda that has been promulgated in the

---

60 *Ibid.*

61 David Adams, 'The Seville Statement on Violence: A Progress Report' (1989) 26(2) *Journal of Peace Research* 113, available online at: http://www.culture-of-peace.info/ssov/title-page.html

62 The International Society for Research on Aggression, founded in 1972, is premised on the notion that 'any serious study of aggression had to be international in scope and interdisciplinary in character.' See further 'Brief History', available online at: http://www.israsociety.com/history.html

63 Adams (n61) 115.

64 *Ibid.*, 116. See also Alfie Kohn, *Psychology Today* (1988) available online at: http://www.alfiekohn.org/miscellaneous/aggression.htm in which a Finnish study reached similar conclusions.

65 Adams (n61) 119.

mass media in order to justify political policies of militarism.'[66] The author draws cogent parallels with the myths that surrounded race:

> It would be interesting to compare the present situation to earlier use of racist myths to justify slavery and colonialism. There was a great deal of racist propaganda in mid-19th century US at the time of the abolition of slavery and in mid-20th century at the time of the dismantling of colonialism. Such racist propaganda may be seen as a last-resort effort by those who had a vested interest in slavery and colonialism to defend these institutions by appealing to the vulnerable belief systems of individual psychology at a time when they could no longer justify the institutions by economic or political arguments. Does today's propaganda about the biological basis of warfare derive from a similar effort by those with a vested interest in militarism and who can no longer justify it on economic and political grounds?[67]

The Statement is part of a 'psychological war'. Adams concludes that the difficulty will become greater as time goes on, for 'the more the political and economic justifications for war are discredited, the more we may expect these sectors to fall back on the psychological justifications for war.'[68]

The Seville Statement on Violence has subsequently been criticized in light of more recent developments in the psychological realm. An article in *Nature* in February 2008 by Dan Jones begins by quoting the Seville Statement, and claims that the decades since have not been kind to these beliefs.[69] The author traces the emergence post-Seville of evolutionary psychology, which seeks an evolutionary account of violent behaviour. While researchers have not figured out the characteristics of 'homicidal adaptations', it is proposed that the murder of members of one group by those of another could be an adaptive behaviour that has been encouraged by evolution.[70] The article concludes that humans may have what the Seville Statement called a 'violent brain', in that evolution may favour those who go to war. However we have also been furnished with a moral sense by evolution, and it is understanding the relationship between morality and violence that future research should explore.[71]

---

66 *Ibid.*, 120.
67 *Ibid.*, 121.
68 *Ibid.*
69 Dan Jones, 'Human Behaviour: Killer Instincts' (2008) 451 *Nature* 512.
70 *Ibid.*, 513–14.
71 *Ibid.*, 515.

4. THE SCIENCE OF PEACE

The International Committee for Intellectual Cooperation (ICIC) created under the auspices of the League of Nations, was an elitist organization run by the French and designed to be an assembly of world luminaries that would rise above conflicts, politics and ideology.[72] UNESCO by contrast was conceived of as an intergovernmental organization which would promote political consensus, rather than a non-governmental organization concerned only with technical knowledge.[73] This was 'the outcome of Anglo-American "populism" during the initial negotiations.'[74]

The inclusion of the 'S' in UNESCO was an innovation introduced at the end of the Constitutional Conference held in London in 1945, taken up as a result of lobbying by a group of influential British scientists.[75] On the final days of the negotiations, and against the backdrop of the launching of US atomic bombs over Hiroshima and Nagasaki in August 1945, the British Minister of Education, Ellen Wilkinson, stressed the importance of scientists in the post-war era: 'In these days, when we are all wondering, perhaps apprehensively, what scientists will do to us next, it is important that they should be linked closely with the humanities and should feel that they have a responsibility to mankind'.[76]

Clare Wells charts the loss of part of UNESCO's constitutional mandate in the first decade of its existence. She notes that 'while retaining unquestioned jurisdiction with respect to "education for peace", narrowly understood, UNESCO had by the early 1950s for all practical purposes surrendered to the UN that portion of its constitutional mandate bearing upon "information for peace" defined more broadly to include news and the press.'[77] This was due to an informal division of labour in the early years between the 'political' and the 'technical' in which the UN had competence in the former while UNESCO had competence in the latter sphere. UNESCO maintained unchallenged jurisdiction over 'education for peace' within the UN system, but this was a narrow concept regarded

---

72 Aant Elzinga, 'UNESCO and the Politics of Scientific Internationalism', in Aant Elzinga and Catharina Landstrom (eds) *Internationalism and Science* (London: Taylor Graham, 1996) 89.

73 *Ibid.*, 90.

74 Alexis de Greiff, 'The Politics of Noncooperation: The Boycott of the International Centre for Theoretical Physics' (2006) 21 *Osiris* 86, 108.

75 Elzinga (n72) 89.

76 Quoted in *ibid.* 93.

77 Wells (n7) 183.

as less political than 'war propaganda'.[78] For example in the field of news, UNESCO would concentrate on improving technical conditions for production and exchange, while the UN would have responsibility for news content given its essentially political character.[79] She surmises that if the word 'war' appeared in the title of a motion, it was referred to a 'political' organ.[80] Similarly Western questioning of UNESCO standard-setting activities and the rejection of normative approaches, such as the right to peace model, in favour of more 'technical' solutions is a reflection of a false technical/political dichotomy.[81]

The right to peace has been designated a 'forgotten' right, but there is a forgotten aspect of this forgotten right. Thus the right to peace had two components; the right itself, elaborated in the draft Declaration, and the parallel exploration of violence and the need to engage with biological explanations for violent behavior, designated the 'culture of peace' project. With the failure of the Oslo right to peace process, that movement has been subsumed under the 'culture of peace' banner, while the study of militarist propaganda or the psychological justifications for war have been dropped from UNESCO's agenda. Meanwhile evolutionary biology is rapidly accelerating in terms of its explanatory reach, and we are now witnessing attempts to explain the growth and development of law and human rights itself in terms of biology, genetics and evolution.[82]

The production of genetic truths evidently raises fundamental questions as to what level issues of justice, fairness and equality are raised.[83] Arneson and Hjorleiffson critically examine the concept of 'geneticization', which warns of the dangers of researchers becoming preoccupied with the transformative effect of genetics, and call for greater analysis of the socio-cultural preconditions under which genetics is operating.[84] Importantly, geneticization draws the attention of philosophers and social scientists to challenges that are 'beyond the scope of mainstream

---

78 *Ibid.*, 50–1.

79 *Ibid.*, 49.

80 *Ibid.*, 51.

81 *Ibid.*, 185.

82 See further Edwin S. Fruehwald, 'A Biological Basis of Rights', Hofstra University Legal Studies Research Paper 9/17 (2010) available online at: http://papers.ssrn.com/sol3/papers.cfm?abstract_id=1440247

83 Antoinette Rouvroy, *Human Genes and Neoliberal Governance: A Foucauldian Critique* (New York: Routledge, 2008) 142.

84 Vilhjalmur Arnason and Stefan Hjorleifsson, 'Geneticization and Bioethics: Advancing Debate and Research' (2007) 10 *Medicine, Healthcare and Philosophy* 417.

bioethics',[85] perceived as providing a legitimating cover for biotechnology while claiming to regulate its application and, as a result, too narrow in its parameters. This debate, once central to the 'culture of peace' idea, is now bypassing UNESCO.

The website on the culture of peace indicates a clear shift from the early commitment to 'internal peace'. In line with the broader mandate assigned to the concept of the culture of peace, the project covers eight specified 'action areas', beginning with fostering a culture of peace through education.[86] The aim is to create a 'global movement' and many laudable initiatives are listed on the website, notably in the field of peace and human rights education, women's initiatives, community media, intercultural dialogue and mediation.[87] These clearly fall within the educational sphere of UNESCO's mandate, but the scientific element is absent.

The failure of the right to peace movement in 1998 is behind the shortcomings in the contemporary culture of peace project. UNESCO has subsumed broad ideas into what was originally a specialized undertaking. The present work on peace education should continue, and many of the projects documented throughout the world in this field have great value.[88] However UNESCO should also re-orient itself towards the scientific aspect of its project, as conceived in Seville. Insufficient links between evolutionary biology and genetics, and the universal movement for peace, have been made since the pioneering Seville Statement. As a result UNESCO should re-visit the Seville Statement in light of new research and advances in genetics. Considering it dates from 1986, there is a major gap in our understanding which is being filled by attacks on some of the conclusions of the Seville drafters.

A re-assessment of the five Seville propositions in light of new research would be a far more engaging and important activity. This was the concept behind the 'culture of peace', the so-called 'internal peace' to be found in the 'minds of men'. UNESCO should return to explore the realm of scientific research, in line with its ethos. In that manner it would be fulfilling its established role and making a far more lasting contribution to peace

---

85 *Ibid.*, 429.

86 UNESCO (n29).

87 *Ibid.*

88 For example the 2002 Report charts a number of educational initiatives; international public–private partnerships for young people were also implemented in Côte d'Ivoire, Guatemala and the occupied Palestinian territories that aim at empowering disadvantaged youth in conflict and post-conflict situations through improved access to, and use of, information and communication technologies and web-based social networking tools. (*Ibid.*, para 56).

in the world. In a preview to his recent monograph outlining the decline of global violence,[89] psychologist Steven Pinker writes: 'Instead of asking "Why is there war?" we might ask, "why is there peace?"'[90] The roots of violence are complex and at present, evolutionary psychology is increasingly orienting itself as the foundational explanatory discipline for tracing the origins of violent behaviour. This is problematic and the primacy of evolutionary psychology ought to be challenged, but there is little evidence that UNESCO is engaging with this aspect of its work in terms of promoting the culture of peace, or indeed in its wider aim of a binding right to peace.

Similarly the concept of militarist propaganda, likened by Adams to nineteenth-century racist propaganda in its recourse to biology, should form part of the culture of peace project. The prohibition of propaganda for war in Article 20 of the International Covenant on Civil and Political Rights has received recent attention,[91] and the role of propaganda has been examined by both the International Criminal Tribunal for Yugoslavia and the International Criminal Tribunal for Rwanda.[92] Inevitably, evolutionary psychology is also making its contributions on propaganda, linking the suggestiveness of the human brain to evolution. For example, a recent study sought to investigate the notion of 'indoctrination' as an evolutionary adaptation or predisposition: 'to what extent can the ethnonationalist conflicts that have so marred the twentieth century be attributed to an evolved trait of indoctrination? How is this predisposition exploited by politicians?'[93]

Since the abandonment of the right to peace project, its various strands have unraveled leaving a vague culture of peace dialogue that appears light in comparison with the initial aims. There are elements of the right to peace that are beyond the remit of UNESCO; for example there are compelling arguments for a legal right to refuse to participate in the

---

89 Steven Pinker, *The Better Angels of Our Nature* (London: Allen Lane, 2011).

90 Steven Pinker, 'Why is there Peace?' (2009) *Greater Good: The Science of a Meaningful Life*, available online at: http://greatergood.berkeley.edu/article/item/why_is_there_peace/

91 See further Michael G. Kearney, *The Prohibition of Propaganda for War in International Law* (Oxford: OUP, 2007).

92 See for example Judith Armatta, 'Milosevic's Propaganda War', *Global Policy Forum*, 27 February 2003, available online at: http://www.globalpolicy.org/component/content/article/163/29237.html and *Prosecutor v. Nahimana, Barayagwiza and Ngeze*, Case No. ICTR-99-52-T.

93 Irenäus Eibl-Eibesfeldt and Frank Salter, *Ethnic Conflict and Indoctrination: Altruism and Identity in Evolutionary Perspective* (New York & Oxford: Berghahn, 1998) 5.

military effort which have nothing to do with education, science or culture. Similarly the principles of non-use of force, of non-aggression, of peaceful settlement of disputes, and policies aimed at general and complete disarmament, named by Marks as components of the realization of a right to peace, clearly do not engage the competency of UNESCO.

Yet UNESCO has played a central role, initiating the codification of the right to peace even if this process failed. Retrospectively, UNESCO seems to have accepted the arguments that it overstepped its mandate, but the culture of peace at present represents a withdrawal that belies its historic contribution to the discussion. It is apparent that UNESCO lost vital state support for the initiative post-Oslo. This does not imply however that it ignores important achievements. As the principal international forum on science, it needs to re-engage with the science of peace.

5. The right to resist reconsidered

Shannonbrooke Murphy

The right to resist has ancient, cross-cultural and pan-ideological origins. Its antecedent legal and normative concepts include the doctrine of tyrannicide codified in Solon's Law and the Athenian Decrees of Demophantus and Eucrates, transmitted into Roman law and advocated by jurists and philosophers including Cicero, Seneca and Plutarch,[1] and manifested in the Confucian twin concepts of *tianming* (mandate of heaven) and *geming* (removal of the mandate).[2] Of course it is also one aspect of the broader concept of *jihad* (struggle against oppression) in Islamic law.[3] It has roots in the earliest conceptions of international law and in a wide spectrum of philosophical traditions. The right of 'the people' to resist 'the sovereign' under conditions of misrule is acknowledged in the just war theories of Grotius[4] and de Vattel,[5] as well as in the liberal democratic

---

[1] James F. McGlew, *Tyranny and Political Culture in Ancient Greece* (New York: Cornell University Press 1993) 88, 185–7. See also Oscar Jászi and John D. Lewis, *Against the Tyrant: The Tradition and Theory of Tyrannicide* (Glencoe, IL: The Free Press, 1957).

[2] *Mencius* (D.C. Lau trans, rev. edn, Beijing: Chinese University Press, 2003) for example book 1 part B:8, book II part B:14, book VII part A:31. See also Chung-Shu Lo, 'Human Rights in the Chinese Tradition', in UNESCO, 'Human Rights: Comments and Interpretations' (July 1948) UNESCO Doc PHS/3(rev.) 25, 185–6.

[3] *The Qur'an* (M.A.S. Abdel Haleem trans, Oxford: OUP, 2004) 4:75 with explanation at xxii.

[4] 'Jus belli dari posse in principem populi liberi' ('that the right to make war may be conceded against him who has the chief authority among a free people'). Hugo Grotius, *The Law of War and Peace: Selections From* De Jure Belli ac Pacis (W.S.M. Knight trans, London: Peace Book Co., 1939) book I chapter IV i3, vii4, viii4; book II chapter XXV viii2.

[5] Subjects have a legal right to resist their sovereign 'if by his insupportable tyranny he brings on a national revolt against him'. Emmerich de Vattel, *The Law of Nations: Or, Principles of the Law of Nature Applied to the Conduct and Affairs of Nations and Sovereigns* (Charles G. Fenwick trans, Washington, DC: Carnegie Endowment, 1916) book I chapter IV 54.

social contract theory of Locke in particular.[6] A 'right to struggle' against capitalism and colonialism specifically may be found in Marxist thought.

At various points in the history of the development of the human rights movement from the eighteenth through to the twentieth century, explicit legal recognition of the right to resist has been considered urgent. By the beginning of the twenty-first century, however, this idea had not only fallen into disfavour, it had all but disappeared from international human rights law discourse. Today the right to resist is not included in the curricula of most programmes teaching human rights law, nor can it be found in the indexes of seminal survey works on that subject. It is not codified in the treaties of the United Nations (UN) system and its general status within international human rights law is at best precarious. Indeed there is not even an agreed legal definition. Given its distinguished pedigree, its weak position in contemporary international human rights law and discourse begs the question: has this right, previously characterized as the 'supreme' human right by one of the most distinguished international jurists,[7] been forgotten or discarded because it is now obsolete? This chapter argues that, although the right to resist is as relevant as ever and, moreover, has a basis in positive law, it has been progressively marginalized over time by the emergence of a predominant paradigm in human rights that disavows both its validity and its very existence. The chapter concludes that this 'doctrine of disavowal' of the right to resist disregards the law, is ethically wrong and deserves reconsideration.

1. FROM AMBIVALENCE TO AMBIGUITY TO A DOCTRINE OF DISAVOWAL

The doctrine of disavowal of the right to resist is most clearly manifested in the widely acclaimed Declaration on Human Rights Defenders ('the Declaration') adopted by the UN General Assembly in 1998. Insofar as this Declaration purports to principally reaffirm rights already protected in law, any reader of it could be forgiven for assuming that a 'right to resist' does not exist *per se*. Article 1 at first appears to define human

---

6 See Locke's 'Doctrine of the lawfulness of resisting all unlawful exercises of power'. John Locke, *Two Treatises of Government* (Peter Haslett ed., Cambridge: CUP, 1988) especially the Second Treatise chapter XVIII 'Of Tyranny' and chapter XIX 'Of the Dissolution of Government'; chapter XIX [226] 415; chapter XIX [243] 427-428; chapter XVIII [206] 402; chapter XVIII [207] 403.

7 Hersch Lauterpacht, *International Law and Human Rights* (London: Stevens and Sons Ltd, 1950) 116.

rights defenders broadly and to protect their activities in general, on the basis of intent, by stating that '[e]veryone has the right, individually and in association with others, to promote and to strive for the protection and realization of human rights and fundamental freedoms'.[8] However Articles 12 and 13 make it very clear that, regardless of context and even with respect to 'mass, flagrant or systematic violations such as those resulting from apartheid, all forms of racial discrimination, colonialism, foreign domination or occupation, aggression . . . [or] the refusal to recognize the right of peoples to self-determination',[9] if a person or group does not use exclusively peaceful means to defend human rights then that person or group is not actually a 'human rights defender'. Article 12(1) specifies that '[e]veryone has the right, individually and in association with others, to participate in peaceful activities against violations of human rights and fundamental freedoms',[10] so no actions taken in defence of human rights that are not peaceful are worthy of protection according to the Declaration. Furthermore Article 13 of the Declaration does not recognize any right to solicit, receive or use support to defend human rights by any other than peaceful means, regardless of context or circumstance.[11]

There is no real room for interpretation on this point. A review of statements by some of the Declaration's leading proponents shows there is no mistaking that it goes beyond mere non-inclusion or non-recognition of the right to resist in favour of an active disavowal. For example, while the UN Special Rapporteur on Human Rights Defenders states on the one hand that '[t]here is no specific definition of who is and can be a human rights defender' and that '[h]uman rights defenders must be defined and accepted according to the rights they are defending', this is strongly qualified by the assertion that there is a 'minimum standard' for recognition under which only peaceful actions will be found to comply with the Declaration and therefore qualify as protected acts.[12] In its guide to the Declaration, the International Service for Human Rights, whose core mission is to support

---

[8] Declaration on the Right and Responsibility of Individuals, Groups and Organs of Society to Promote and Protect Universally Recognized Human Rights and Fundamental Freedoms, UNGA Res 53/144 (9 December 1998) UN Doc A/RES/53/144 (Declaration on Human Rights Defenders) Art. 1.

[9] *Ibid.* preamble, para 4.

[10] *Ibid.*, Art. 12.

[11] *Ibid.*, Art. 13.

[12] UN Special Rapporteur on the Situation of Human Rights Defenders, 'Who Are Human Rights Defenders?' available online at: http://www2.ohchr.org/EN/Issues/SRHRDefenders/Pages/Defender.aspx.

human rights defenders, defines them exclusively as those who accept and respect the principle of non-violence. This requires that 'any actions taken by human rights defenders must be peaceful. Violence cannot be used to protect or promote human rights under any circumstances.'[13] This despite the repressive conditions within which human rights defenders frequently act or the extreme consequences they may face, which the organization acknowledges:

> The abuses to which human rights defenders are subjected include killings, death threats, torture, arbitrary arrest, criminal prosecution, harassment, defamation and various forms of attacks often coupled with impunity for the perpetrators of these acts.[14]

Is it reasonable to have a right to defend and realize human rights that either stops with the acceptance of failure if one cannot achieve this through peaceful means, or else requires one to proceed unto torture, prison or death? Moreover, is this desirable? If previous defenders of the human rights to freedom from slavery, colonialism, or apartheid had followed these rules it is highly unlikely that these rights would have been won to the extent that they have. Indeed, if all the defenders of the rights to freedom from aggression, genocide, crimes against humanity and other human rights violations by Nazi Germany and the Axis Powers had complied with this standard, would there be a United Nations, or a Universal Declaration on Human Rights or, for that matter, human rights at all?

In the real world, not all human rights defenders are content with either failure or martyrdom under such circumstances. As one founder of a rebel guerrilla army intent on defending and realizing the human right to equality famously expressed at his trial:

> All lawful modes of expressing opposition . . . had been closed by legislation, and we were placed in a position in which we had either to accept a permanent state of inferiority, or to defy the Government. We chose to defy the law. We first broke the law in a way which avoided any recourse to violence; when this form was legislated against, and then the Government resorted to a show of force to crush opposition to its policies, only then did we decide to answer violence with violence . . . This conclusion was not easily arrived at. It was only when all else had failed, when all channels of peaceful protest had been barred to us, that the decision was made to embark on violent forms of political

---

[13] International Service for Human Rights, 'Defending Human Rights Defenders: A Short Guide' available online at: http://www.protectionline.org/IMG/pdf/WHRD_booklet_EN.pdf, 4.

[14] *Ibid.*, 3.

> struggle . . . We did so not because we desired such a course, but solely because the Government had left us with no other choice.[15]

Notwithstanding the eloquent explanation of the last resort context of these decisions after approximately 50 years of constitutionalism and non-violence, it is clear that by the Article 12 and 13 definitions, Nelson Mandela himself would not be considered a 'human rights defender' taking actions worthy of protection or support in relation to his work founding and leading, raising funds and planning campaigns for Umkhonto we Sizwe.[16]

The Declaration on Human Rights Defenders is an important document and contains a great many provisions and ideas that should not be undermined. However, by actively negating the right to resist, Articles 12 and 13 are fundamentally flawed in that they not only ignore the existing law (as will be established in the following section) but are also ethically questionable as they abandon many human rights defenders operating in the most repressive and extreme situations. The Declaration's approach is typical of a contemporary human rights movement so categorically averse to violence in all its forms that it imposes excessive limits on the scope of action of human rights defenders, using a moralistic reductivism that evaluates strategies and tactics in defence of human rights out of context and in a way that is not only too simplistic but paternalistic. Indeed, the real net effect of this doctrine of disavowal is to perpetuate currently unequal patterns of access to universal human rights in a manner prejudicial to the most vulnerable.

The disavowal position taken in the Declaration amounts to a distortion of the ambivalent or ambiguous treatment of the right to resist in other UN instruments, none of which contain an express provision either permitting or prohibiting resistance. Rather, there is sufficient ambiguity in the law that some credible scholars maintain that this right is actually either implied or latent in the International Bill of Human Rights,[17]

---

[15] Nelson Mandela, 'I Am Prepared to Die: Nelson Mandela's Statement from the Dock at the opening of the defence case in the Rivonia Trial' (Pretoria Supreme Court, 20 April 1964, Nelson Mandela Foundation Speech Archive unique ID NMS010) available online at: http://db.nelsonmandela.org/speeches/pub_view.asp?pg=item&ItemID=NMS010&txtstr=Statement%20from%20the%20dock.

[16] See Mandela's own account of his activities in Nelson Mandela, *Long Walk to Freedom* (New York: Little Brown and Co, 1994) particularly 320–7, 336–40, 342–59, 362–5.

[17] Universal Declaration of Human Rights, UNGA Res 217 A(III) UN Doc A/810 91, UN General Assembly, 10 December 1948; International Covenant on Civil and Political Rights (adopted 16 December 1966, entered into force 23 March

although such claims have yet to be judicially tested and may or may not hold up to scrutiny.

As becomes obvious from a close reading, the right to resist is not actually codified as a right in the Universal Declaration on Human Rights ('the Universal Declaration'). Instead its preamble merely acknowledges resistance as an outcome when rights are denied.[18] Paragraph 3 of the preamble states that 'whereas it is essential, if man is not to be compelled to have recourse, as a last resort, to rebellion against tyranny and oppression, that human rights should be protected by the rule of law.'[19] The form of its wording and its placement in a preambular position rather than as an article and thus without direct effect, suggest that it is actually formulated as a non-right. Nevertheless there is a theory that the right to resist is an implied right in customary international law as reflected in the Universal Declaration,[20] closely linked to a right to democracy or 'internal self-determination'.[21] This result is derived from reading across paragraph 3 of the Universal Declaration preamble and Article 21(3) on the 'will of the people' as the basis of legitimate State authority.[22] Others assert that while it may not be a primary right in the Universal Declaration, the preamble

---

1976) 999 UNTS 171 (ICCPR); International Covenant on Economic, Social and Cultural Rights (adopted 16 December 1966, entered into force 3 January 1976) 993 UNTS 3 (ICESCR).

[18] Johannes Morsink, 'The Philosophy of the Universal Declaration' (1984) 6(3) *HRQ* 325, n94.

[19] Universal Declaration of Human Rights (n17) preamble, para 3.

[20] See for example Walter Kälin and Jorg Künzli, 'Article 1F(b): Freedom Fighters, Terrorists and the Notion of Serious Non-Political Crime' (2000) 12(Supp) *Int'l J. Refugee L* 46, 51. Though many presume the Universal Declaration of Human Rights' status as customary law, Eide and Alfredsson conclude that there is actually no agreement on this. Asbjørn Eide and Gudmundur Alfredsson, in Asbjørn Eide, Gudmundur Alfredsson, Göran Melander and ors (eds) *The Universal Declaration of Human Rights: A Commentary* (Oslo: Scandinavian University Press, 1992) 7. For a thorough treatment of the issue of its legal status see Hurst Hannum, 'The Status of the Universal Declaration of Human Rights in National and International Law' (1995/1996) 25 *Ga J. Intl. and Comp.* 287.

[21] This use of terminology follows the approach in Antonio Cassese, *Self-Determination of Peoples: A Legal Reappraisal* (Cambridge: CUP, 1995) bisecting the right to self-determination into its 'internal' and 'external' dimensions.

[22] Proponents of this theory include Jordan J. Paust, 'The Human Right to Participate in Armed Revolution and Related Forms of Social Violence: Testing the Limits of Permissibility' (1983) 32 *Emory LJ* 545, 565–6; Allan Rosas, 'Article 21', in Gudmundur Alfredsson and Asbjørn Eide (eds) *The Universal Declaration of Human Rights: A Common Standard of Achievement* (Leiden: Nijhoff, 1999) 442, 449; Johannes Morsink, *The Universal Declaration of Human Rights: Origins, Drafting and Intent* (Pittsburgh: University of Pennsylvania Press, 1999) 308.

nevertheless implicitly recognizes resistance as a valid remedy for violations, or a secondary right.[23]

Although appealing, the argument that the Universal Declaration is a source of the right to resist in international human rights law is less convincing after reviewing the *travaux préparatoires* (preparatory works), which reveal both an acknowledgement of the right and a conscious decision to exclude an express provision for pragmatic reasons.[24] Proposals to include a specific article on the right to resist were made during the drafting debates on the right to political participation. It was included in both the 'Humphrey draft' as Article 29 '[e]veryone has the right, either individually or with others, to resist oppression and tyranny,'[25] and the later 'Cassin draft' as Article 25 '[w]henever a government seriously or systematically tramples fundamental human rights and freedoms, individuals and peoples have the right to resist oppression and tyranny, without prejudice to their right of appeal to the United Nations.'[26] When these met with opposition the proposals were eventually withdrawn, so in the end no votes were taken on the issue. Significantly, however, an alternate joint Colombian-Costa Rican proposal to include a 'right of opposition' by exclusively legal means was actually voted down.[27] A number of subsequent formulations including an express right to resist also failed,[28] and the more ambivalent compromise wording and preambular placement were adopted instead. Therefore, while logically possible, any finding that the Universal Declaration contains an implied right to resist would

---

[23] For example Tran Van Minh, 'Political and Juridical Sanctions Against Violations of Human Rights', in *Violations of Human Rights: Possible Rights of Recourse and Forms of Resistance* (Paris: UNESCO 1984) 157–66, 163; J.L. Taulbee, 'Political Crimes, Human Rights and Contemporary International Practice' (1990) 4 *Emory Int'l L. Rev.* 43, 47.

[24] See Morsink's accounts in *The Universal Declaration of Human Rights: Origins, Drafting and Intent* (n22) 308–12 and 'The Philosophy of the Universal Declaration' (n18) 322–5.

[25] 'Draft Outline of an International Bill of Human Rights (Prepared by the Division of Human Rights of the Secretariat)' reprinted in 1947 *UN Ybk Hum. Rts* 484 (Annex A).

[26] 'Suggestions Submitted by the Republic of France for Articles of the International Declaration of Human Rights' reprinted in 1947 *UN Ybk Hum. Rts* 495–8 (Annex D).

[27] UNGA Third Committee (3rd Session) (9 October 1948) UN Doc A/C.3/248.

[28] A revised version submitted jointly by Cuba, Chile and France was also rejected, but is very close to what ultimately became the third preambular paragraph. UNGA Third Committee (3rd Session) (30 Nov 1948) UN Doc A/C.3/382/Rev.1.

represent a significant evolutive interpretation that deliberately departs from the *travaux*.

Likewise, some scholars propose what could be termed a theory of constructive ambiguity regarding a right to resist latent in the core international human rights treaties.[29] This involves a complex formula by which a right to resist derives from Article 1 common to the International Covenant on Civil and Political Rights and International Covenant on Economic, Social and Cultural Rights on the right to political and economic self-determination (now partly enforceable through resort to force under limited conditions in customary international law, as set out below) and/or Article 25 of the International Covenant on Civil and Political Rights on the right to political participation, when read together with the right to an effective remedy at Article 2(3)(a), combined with the lack of an express prohibition on resistance in these instruments.[30]

Again, despite the appeal, this conclusion is difficult to share. If anything, the *travaux préparatoires* suggest the opposite.[31] The UN Human Rights Committee General Comments also give no positive indication[32] and none of its case law to date considers this claim. In order for this theory to accord with reality, significant evolutive interpretation of the relevant provisions within these instruments amounting to advocacy would be required. Admittedly there may be scope here for future expansion. For example, it is certainly true that what constitutes an effective remedy under the International Covenant on Civil and Political Rights is apparently not limited to legal or judicial remedies,[33] and that forceful or peaceful but otherwise illegal action on the part of non-State actors is also not expressly prohibited. In addition, the UN Human Rights Committee has been careful to point out that the prohibitions on propaganda for war

---

29 See Manfred Nowak, *UN Covenant on Civil and Political Rights – CCPR Commentary* (Kehl, Germany: NP Engel Publishers, 1993) 23, 34; Rosas (n22) 432, 441–2, 449, 451.

30 See in particular Rosas (n22) 432, 441–2, 449, 451. See International Covenant on Civil and Political Rights (n17) Arts 1, 2(3)(a) and 25.

31 M.J. Bossuyt, *Guide to the 'Travaux Préparatoires' of the International Covenant on Civil and Political Rights* (Leiden: Nijhoff, 1987) 24, 32; UNGA Third Committee (10th Session) (1955) UN Doc A/3077, cited in Bossuyt, *ibid.*, 35.

32 UNCCPR 'General Comment 12 – Article 1: The Right to Self-Determination of Peoples' (1984) UN Doc A/39/40; UNCCPR 'General Comment 25 – Article 25: The Right to Participate in Public Affairs, Voting Rights and the Right of Equal Access to Public Service' (1996) UN Doc A/51/40 vol 1; UNCCPR 'General Comment 3 – Implementation at National Level: Article 2 (1981) UN Doc 29/07.

33 UNCCPR 'General Comment 3' (n32) para.1.

'do not prohibit advocacy of the sovereign right of self-defence or the right of peoples to self-determination and independence in accordance with the Charter of the United Nations.'[34] For now, the International Bill of Human Rights remains at best a source of *lacunae* in the law on the right to resist. Likewise the Slavery Convention, the Genocide Convention, the Apartheid Convention, the Convention Against Torture and the other major international human rights treaties as they neither protect nor prohibit the right to resist violations relevant to their provisions.[35] Nor, for that matter, does the UN Declaration on the Right of Peoples to Peace.[36] It is more likely that the absence of an express right denotes overall ambivalence rather than either acceptance or rejection within the UN human rights system, at least at this point.

A more distinct doctrine of disavowal of the right to resist emerges from the European and Inter-American regional human rights treaties. Like the International Covenant on Civil and Political Rights there is no express provision on the right to resist in the European Convention for the Protection of Human Rights and Fundamental Freedoms ('the European Convention'), the American Convention on Human Rights ('the American Convention') or the American Declaration on the Rights and Duties of Man ('the American Declaration'), though all other political means short of resistance get explicit (albeit limited) protection in the democratic rights cluster: freedom of expression, freedom of peaceful assembly, freedom

---

[34] UNCCPR 'General Comment 11 – Article 20: Prohibition of Propaganda for War' (1983) UN Doc A/38/40 2.

[35] Convention on the Prevention and Punishment of the Crime of Genocide (adopted 9 December 1948, entered into force 12 January 1951) 78 UNTS 277; Slavery Convention (1926, amended by Protocol 1953) (entered into force 7 July 1955) 212 UNTS 17; Convention on the Elimination of All Forms of Racial Discrimination (entered into force 4 January 1969) 660 UNTS 195; International Convention for Suppression and Punishment of the Crime of Apartheid (adopted 30 December 1973, entered into force 18 July 1976) 1015 UNTS 243; Convention on the Elimination of All Forms of Discrimination Against Women (entered into force 3 September 1981) UNGA Res 34/180, UN Doc A/34/46; Convention Against Torture and Other Cruel, Inhuman or Degrading Treatment or Punishment (adopted 10 December 1984, entered into force 26 June 1987) 23 ILM 1027; Convention on the Rights of the Child (entered into force 2 September 1990) 1577 UNTS 3; International Convention on the Protection and Promotion of the Rights and Dignity of Persons with Disabilities (adopted 13 Dec 2006, entered into force 3 May 2008) UNGA Res 61/106 Annex 1, UN Doc A/RES/61/106 (2006).

[36] UN General Assembly Declaration on the Right of Peoples to Peace, UNGA Res 39/11 Annex (1984) UN Doc A/39/51.

of association and the right to participation in the political process.[37] However the European and Inter-American systems depart from the UN system in three important ways. First, there is no analogous right to self-determination in these three regional instruments. Second, in contrast to the International Covenant on Civil and Political Right's open-ended provision on the right to an effective remedy, the European Convention and American Convention clauses are specifically limited to a remedy provided by the State.[38] Third, in this different context, the codified (albeit limited) right of the State to resist under these instruments – the derogation regimes at Article 15 of the European Convention, and Article 27 of the American Convention – suggests instead an apparent position that the State has an absolute monopoly on exceptional measures including force, which is not necessarily implied in the International Covenant on Civil and Political Rights despite its own derogation provision at Article 4.[39] The express right of the State under the European Convention at Article 2(2)(c) to use lethal force where 'absolutely necessary' to quell an insurrection and the American Convention's explicit specification that the right to assembly must be exercised 'without arms' provide further reinforcement. If there may be room for an implied or latent right to resist in an ambivalent or ambiguous UN system, the European and Inter-American systems have, in contrast adopted what can only be described as an implied or latent disavowal, and it is actually this Euro-American position that the Declaration on Human Rights Defenders consolidates.

The combination of the above factors could lead one to reasonably conclude that the right to resist does not exist. However that conclusion presents a legal-factual problem: it is simply not correct – not least because, as shown below, the other two regional (African and Arab) human rights systems have taken a different position. Likewise any presumption that the

---

[37] The provisions are, respectively: ICCPR (n17) Arts 19, 21, 22, 25; European Convention for the Protection of Human Rights and Fundamental Freedoms (4 November 1950, entered into force 3 September 1953) 213 UNTS 222 (ECHR) Arts 10, 11 and Art. 3 of Protocol 1 to the ECHR; American Convention on Human Rights (Pact of San José) (signed 22 November 1969, entered into force 18 July 1978) OASTS 36, OAS Off Rec OEA/Ser. L/V/11.23 doc. 21 rev. 6 (1979) (ACHR) Arts 13, 15, 16, 23; the American Declaration of the Rights and Duties of Man (1948) OEA/ Ser L/V/11.71 at 17 (1988) Arts 4, 20, 21, 22, and the unique Art. 24 (right to petition).

[38] See ECHR (n37) Art. 13; ACHR (n37) Art. 25.

[39] Under these derogation regimes the State may suspend certain rights but not others, provided the State complies with the other conditions. In the ICCPR and ECHR the 'derogable' rights include the full democratic cluster. In the ACHR, however, Art. 27(2) makes the right to vote non-derogable.

right to resist cannot exist: it does. The separate conclusion that a right to resist should not exist presents a further ethical problem: if true, it means that the law is prevented from effectively assisting those most vulnerable, whose defenders cannot stop human rights violations or achieve human rights compliance by such restrictive means as otherwise permitted.

2. A DISTINGUISHED PEDIGREE AND A BASIS IN POSITIVE LAW

The doctrine of disavowal described above has undoubtedly marginalized the right to resist to the point where it is either overlooked or actively avoided by too many human rights scholars and remains either unknown or misunderstood among too many human rights advocates. However this right has not only a distinguished pedigree but also a basis in contemporary positive law. A review of this positive law shows that the doctrine of disavowal has produced two apparent disconnects: one between international human rights law and both domestic constitutional law and customary international law, and the other within the international human rights law regional systems on a north–south basis.

In contrast to its status in the international treaties, the right to resist has a well-established place in domestic constitutional law. Perhaps the earliest provision is found in Clause 61 of the Magna Carta, which activates a right to resist in the event of failure to redress within 40 days a grievance regarding a violation of one of its provisions.[40] Today the right to resist is codified in numerous countries cross-continentally, following four distinct constitutional waves: revolutionary republican, post-fascist, post-colonial and post-Soviet. It remains to be seen whether a new wave will follow the Arab Spring.

As demonstrated by the following sample, the constitutional provisions vary considerably in scope: some protect only the right to resist a foreign invasion or domestic coup, others authorize a potentially much broader right to resist oppression and human rights violations. The revolutionary republican provisions of the eighteenth century clearly establish the right as inextricably linked to an emerging concept of human rights. For example, according to the second preambular paragraph of the American Declaration of Independence 'whenever any Form of Government becomes destructive [to the ends of securing unalienable rights], it is the Right of

---

[40] Magna Carta (1215) Art. 61, reprinted in James C. Holt, *Magna Carta* (2nd edn, Cambridge: CUP, 1992) Appendix 6, 448–73.

the People to alter or to abolish it, and to institute new government'.[41] Similarly, Article 2 of the French Declaration of the Rights of Man and the Citizen lists 'resistance to oppression' among the 'natural, unalienable, and sacred rights'.[42] In the twentieth century, the post-fascist formulations develop the idea of the right as a law of exception, linked to effective remedy; for example, Article 20 of the Basic Law for the Federal Republic of Germany: '[a]ll Germans shall have the right to resist any person seeking to abolish [the] constitutional order, if no other remedy is available,'[43] and Article 21 of the Constitution of the Portuguese Republic: '[e]veryone shall possess the right to resist any order that infringes their rights, freedoms or guarantees and, when it is not possible to resort to the public authorities, to use force to repel any aggression.'[44] Variations in the post-colonial formulations often reflect more strongly the particular experiences of the countries in question. For example, the right under Article 3 of the Constitution of the Republic of Cuba is limited to defence of the communist system: '[w]hen no other recourse is possible, all citizens have the right to struggle through all means, including armed struggle, against anyone who tries to overthrow the political, social and economic order established in this Constitution.'[45] Article 3(4) and (5) of the Constitution of the Republic of Uganda is specifically directed towards defence against coup d'état, and establishes an explicit legal licence reminiscent of ancient tyrannicidal law. Not only do Ugandan citizens have 'the right and duty at all times . . . to defend this Constitution, and in particular, to resist any person or group of persons seeking to overthrow the established constitutional order' but moreover '[a]ny person or group of persons who, as required . . . resists the suspension, overthrow, abrogation or amendment of this constitution commits no offence.'[46] Finally Article 32 of the Constitution of Slovakia, a post-Soviet provision, is among the broadest and most interesting: '[c]itizens have the right to put up resistance to anyone who would eliminate the democratic order of human rights and basic liberties listed in this Constitution, if the activity of constitutional bodies and the effective use of legal means are rendered impossible.'[47]

Returning to international human rights treaty law, in contrast with the ambivalence and ambiguity of the UN system or the disavowal of the

---

41 American Declaration of Independence (1776) preamble para 2.
42 Declaration of the Rights of Man and of the Citizen (1789) Art. 2.
43 Basic Law for the Federal Republic of Germany (1949) Art. 20.
44 Constitution of the Portuguese Republic (1976) Art. 21.
45 Constitution of the Republic of Cuba (1992) Art. 3.
46 Constitution of the Republic of Uganda (1995) Arts 3(4), 3(5).
47 Constitution of Slovakia (1992) Art. 32.

European and Inter-American systems, there are now express provisions on the right to resist in both the African and Arab regional human rights treaties. If the Universal Declaration provides the first intimation that the right to resist might have a place in international human rights law, the African Charter on Human and Peoples Rights ('the African Charter') is the first international human rights instrument to actually codify it.[48]

Within the context of Article 20 on the right to self-determination, Article 20(2) of the African Charter asserts that '[c]olonized or oppressed peoples shall have the right to free themselves from the bonds of domination by resorting to any means recognized by the international community.'[49] Article 20(3) goes further, providing that '[a]ll peoples shall have the right to the assistance of the States Parties . . . in their liberation struggle against foreign domination, be it political, economic or cultural.'[50] There are three important elements to the right to resist in the African Charter. Firstly, Article 20(2) is a broad formulation that extends the right to all 'oppressed' peoples in Africa. Secondly, it provides that those resisting oppression may have recourse to 'any means' provided these are 'recognized by the international community'. This has the positive effect of ensuring that exercise of the right is consistent with international norms and subject to regulation by international human rights, humanitarian and criminal law. Unfortunately it also makes the entire provision dependent on the legal status of the right to resist elsewhere, and thus impossible to interpret from the African Charter alone. Thirdly, the right to assistance from other African States is also an express right implying State duty, though this is restricted to those resisting 'foreign domination', meaning that most of those resisting oppression by a domestic power probably do not share this specific sub-right. Despite its unique place in international human rights law, the right to resist oppression at Article 20(2) of the African Charter has not yet received sufficient attention from commentators, most of whom have given it only cursory consideration, if any.[51] Such under-examination is only partially explained by the fact

---

48 For a more detailed analysis see Shannonbrooke Murphy, 'Unique in International Human Rights Law: Art. 20(2) and the Right to Resist in the African Charter on Human and Peoples' Rights' (2011) 11(2) *African Hum. Rts L.J.* 465.

49 African Charter on Human and Peoples' Rights (adopted 27 June 1981, entered into force 21 October 1986) (1982) 21 ILM 58 (African Charter) Art. 20(2).

50 *Ibid.*, Art. 20(3).

51 See U. Oji Umozurike, *The African Charter on Human and Peoples' Rights* (Leiden: Nijhoff, 1997) 126; Christof Heyns, 'Civil and Political Rights in the African Charter', in Malcolm D. Evans and Rachel Murray (eds) *The African Charter on Human and Peoples' Rights: The System in Practice 1986–2000* (Cambridge: CUP, 2002); Clive Baldwin and Cynthia Morel, 'Group Rights',

that the African Commission on Human and Peoples' Rights has yet to consider any cases which specifically concern Article 20(2), as the three key Article 20 cases all make findings relevant to its future interpretation.[52]

Like the African Charter, the Revised Arab Charter on Human Rights also includes an express provision directly linked to the right to self-determination.[53] The 'right to resist foreign occupation' at Article 2(4) is significantly narrower than the African Charter provision but on the other hand it is also unqualified. Though this treaty has only recently come into force the development is notable, not merely because its right to resist is a new right that was not present in the predecessor 1994 Arab Charter of Human Rights but because it has become the clearest assertion available in any human rights treaty of one aspect of this right, considered by many to be based on otherwise well-established customary international law (as set out below).

Since the two regional treaty provisions have not been subject to either judicial or thorough scholarly analysis, and are also dependent on other sources of international law to varying degrees for their interpretation, the full scope of these rights to resist has yet to be determined. They nevertheless represent a significant departure from the approach of all the other main human rights treaties on this issue and a challenge to the doctrine of disavowal.

In addition to the constitutional and treaty sources, the right to resist is also found in customary international law, although this too has yet to be fully and systematically explored in legal scholarship and its boundaries therefore remain somewhat contested. Most however can agree that the UN General Assembly's interpretative Declaration on Principles of International Law Concerning Friendly Relations and Cooperation Among States in Accordance with the Charter of the United Nations ('UN

---

in Malcolm Evans and Rachel Murray (eds) *The African Charter on Human and Peoples' Rights: The System in Practice, 1986–2006* (Cambridge: CUP, 2008) 279–82. In this context, see the exceptional substantive contribution of Fatsah Ouguergouz, *The African Charter on Human and Peoples' Rights: A Comprehensive Agenda for Human Dignity and Sustainable Democracy in Africa* (Leiden: Nijhoff, 2003) 215–65, 267.

[52] *Katangese Peoples' Congress v Zaire* (2000) AHRLR 72 (ACHPR 1995); *Jawara v The Gambia* (2000) AHRLR 107 (ACHPR 2000) 28–40; 72–73; Communication 266/03, *Kevin Mgwanga Gunme et al v Cameroon*, Twenty-sixth Annual Activity Report (ACHPR 2009) 169, 171; 174; 178–9; 181; 188; 190–1; 194; 197; 199–200. Again, for more detailed analysis see Murphy (n48).

[53] Arab Charter on Human Rights, League of Arab States (adopted 22 May 2004, entered into force 15 March 2008) *Int'l Hum. Rts Rep.* 893 (2005) (Arab Charter) Art. 2(4).

General Assembly Resolution 2625'),[54] setting out the customary law on the right to self-determination, also contains a form of a related secondary collective right to resist violations of this law involving the use of force.[55] According to paragraph 7 of the first principle, paragraph 3 of the third principle, and paragraph 5 of the fifth principle set out in UN General Assembly Resolution 2625, States have a basic obligation to refrain from forcible action depriving peoples of the right to self-determination, and hence an obligation to refrain from supporting other States involved in such conduct. Peoples have a corresponding implied right to resist in order to enforce their right to self-determination, insofar as they furthermore have the right to request assistance in this regard from other States according to paragraph 5 of the fifth principle.[56] This peoples' right may extend to the use of force in such resistance, albeit in compliance with the law on the use of force.[57] Likewise while States have an obligation to support such assistance requests, they must do so in accordance with the UN Charter as well as other recognized customary rules.[58]

---

[54] Declaration on Principles of International Law Concerning Friendly Relations and Co-operation Among States in Accordance with the Charter of the United Nations, UNGA Res 2625 (XXV) UN GAOR 25th Session Supp 28 UN Doc A/5217 (1970) 121–4 (UNGA Res 2625).

[55] See Georges Abi-Saab, 'Wars of National Liberation and the Laws of War' (1972) 3 *Annales d'Études Internationales* 93, 100; Bert V.A. Röling, 'The Legal Status of Rebels and Rebellion' (1976) 13(2) *Journal of Peace Research* 149; 152–5; 159; Asbjørn Eide, 'The Right to Oppose Violations of Human Rights: Basis, Conditions and Limitations', in *Violations of Human Rights: Possible Rights of Recourse and Forms of Resistance* (Paris: UNESCO, 1984) 44–5, 58; Christian Tomuschat, 'The Right of Resistance and Human Rights', in *Violations of Human Rights: Possible Rights of Recourse and Forms of Resistance* (Paris: UNESCO, 1984) 26. See also the more equivocal Heather A. Wilson, *International Law and the Use of Force by National Liberation Movements* (Oxford: Clarendon, 1990) 98–105, 136; Cassese (n21) 150–4; Christine Gray, *International Law and the Use of Force* (3rd edn, Oxford: OUP, 2008) 61–4.

[56] This interpretation is affirmed by Art. 7 of the UN General Assembly Resolution on the Definition of Aggression, which refers non-exclusively but 'particularly' to 'peoples under colonial and racist regimes or other forms of alien domination [and] the right of these people to struggle to that end and to seek and receive support, in accordance with the principles of the [UN] Charter and in conformity with [UNGA Res 2625].' UNGA Res 3314 (XXIX) (17 December 1974) UN Doc A/9619 and Corr. 1.

[57] See for example Abi-Saab (n55); Tomuschat (n55) 18; 'Meeting of experts on the analysis of the basis and forms of individual and collective action by which violations of human rights can be combated, Freetown, Sierra Leone, 3–7 March 1981: Final Report' in *Violations of Human Rights: Possible Rights of Recourse and Forms of Resistance* (Paris: UNESCO, 1984) 223.

[58] For example, the customary prohibitions on aggression and intervention

From the wording of UN General Assembly Resolution 2625 it is clear that this exceptional right applies to situations demanding 'external self-determination', that is where peoples are subject to foreign invasion and occupation, and colonial or other racist rule by force (termed foreign 'subjugation, domination and exploitation'), as these are understood by law. Consequently, International Court of Justice determinations, UN Security Council resolutions or even certain UN General Assembly resolutions recognizing a right to self-determination, or finding that a State is engaged in aggression, occupation or colonization in contravention of international law or is contravening the prohibition against apartheid,[59] or findings by these bodies or other competent courts that connected international crimes have taken place, can therefore also have the effect of indirectly authorizing the customary right to resist affirmed under UN General Assembly Resolution 2625 in specific cases,[60] provided the forcible deprivation condition is also met. However it is equally clear on the other hand that UN General Assembly Resolution 2625 does not authorize a generalized right of resistance by, much less a secession remedy for, minority peoples or movements, insofar as it furthermore asserts at paragraph 7 of the fifth principle that the right to resist forcible deprivation of the right

reflected in UNGA Resolution 2625, Principle 1, paras 8–9; Principle 3, paras 1–2; and customary legal limits on State assistance to rebels as enumerated by the International Court of Justice in *Case Concerning Military and Paramilitary Activities In and Against Nicaragua (Nicaragua v United States of America)* (Merits) [1986] ICJ Reports 14 195, 228; see also 86, 108–116, 176.

59 As defined at Art. 2 of the International Convention for Suppression and Punishment of the Crime of Apartheid (n35). This includes a series of 'inhuman acts committed for the purpose of establishing and maintaining domination by one racial group of persons over any other racial group of persons and systematically oppressing them' which may include, but is not limited to, 'similar policies and practices of racial segregation and discrimination as practiced in southern Africa.'

60 For example, Cassese cites two examples of the UN General Assembly affording this rare 'licence' to resist: to the Palestinians (UNGA Res 32/14, 7 November 1977) and to the people of Namibia (UNGA Res 39/50A, 12 December 1984 and UNGA Res 39/72A, 13 December 1984). Cassese (n21) 151, n9. The International Court of Justice has not made any direct determination on the right to resist but relevant jurisprudence regarding the right of certain peoples to self-determination includes *Legal Consequences for States of the Continued Presence of South Africa in Namibia (South West Africa) Notwithstanding Security Council Resolution 276 (1970)* (Advisory Opinion) [1971] ICJ Reports 16; *Western Sahara* (Advisory Opinion) [1975] ICJ Reports 54–9, 75–83, 162–3; *Case Concerning East Timor (Portugal v Australia)* (Merits) [1995] ICJ Reports 31, 37; *Legal Consequences of the Construction of a Wall in the Occupied Palestinian Territory* (Advisory Opinion) [2004] ICJ Reports 131.

to self-determination cannot be construed as 'authorising or encouraging any action which would dismember or impair . . . the territorial integrity or political unity of sovereign and independent States.'[61] The exception to this would be, also according to paragraph 7 of the fifth principle, where the State in question is not conducting itself 'in compliance with the principle of equal rights and self-determination of peoples . . . and thus possessed of a government representing the whole people belonging to the territory without distinction as to race, creed or colour',[62] and again, where the forcible deprivation condition is met.

Unfortunately this is where the legal clarity ends. Given the vagueness of the language of UN General Assembly Resolution 2625, it is less obvious exactly what the customary law is in relation to forcible deprivation of the right to 'internal self-determination' by way of undemocratic, unconstitutional, tyrannical, oppressive or otherwise corrupt or unresponsive governments and therefore whether and under what conditions this could be logically and reasonably construed as extending a right to resist misrule by a 'domestic' regime. Some argue that a right to resist forcible deprivation of the right to internal self-determination is consistent with the letter of UN General Assembly Resolution 2625, but concede that such an interpretation probably cannot yet be considered established in customary international law.[63] That a *lacuna* in the customary law persists in this regard would appear proven by the lack of direct language on the right to resist crimes against humanity or other systematic violations of human rights in the UN Security Council 2011 resolutions on Libya which implicitly supported or in any event did not criticize the Libyan resistance.[64] This is corroborated by the subsequent controversy among States over whether the resolutions also authorized direct support to the rebels, and the failure of the UN Security Council to agree similar resolutions in analogous and contemporaneous situations related to other Arab Spring uprisings wherein peoples were forcibly deprived of their rights to 'internal' self-determination.

As a consequence of the foregoing, even though areas of legal uncertainty remain, Articles 12 and 13 of the Declaration on Human Rights Defenders which arise from and typify the now predominant doctrine

---

61 UNGA Res 2625 (n54) 124.

62 *Ibid.*

63 See discussion in Ouguergouz (n51) 230–6.

64 See UN Security Council resolutions and related debates records UNSC Resolution 1970 (26 Feb 2011) UN Doc S/Res/1970 (2011); UNSC Verbatim Record (26 February 2011) UN Doc S/PV.6491; UNSC Resolution 1973 (17 March 2011) UN Doc S/Res/1973 (2011); UNSC Verbatim Record (17 March 2011) UN Doc S/PV.6498.

of disavowal of the right to resist are of doubtful legality because they either oversimplify or ignore other established sources of law. Advocates of the disavowal perspective also cannot ignore that at least the right to resist occupation now has some very high level exponents within the UN system. For example, two major reports recently commissioned by the UN Human Rights Council have explicitly affirmed this right in relation to the Palestinian case: the Report of the UN Special Rapporteur on the Situation of Human Rights in the Palestinian Territories Occupied Since 1967[65] and the Report of the United Nations Fact-Finding Mission on the Gaza Conflict.[66] Former UN Secretary-General Kofi Annan also cited the 'right to resist occupation'.[67] These developments demonstrate that, despite its current predominance, the penetration of the doctrine of disavowal is not absolute.

3. AN ETHICAL NECESSITY: TOWARDS FRESH CONSIDERATION AND A STRONGER POSITION IN THE HUMAN RIGHTS LEXICON[68]

If the idea that a legal right to resist does not or cannot exist is factually incorrect, any contention that the right to resist should not exist is ethically questionable from a human rights perspective. The failure to accord firmer recognition to this right, to broaden its scope appropriately and responsibly, or even to apply what thin provisions do exist, has led to a perverse situation whereby international human rights law effectively abandons the majority of people facing grave or massive human rights violations, including crimes against humanity or genocide, those facing 'oppression' by way of tyranny or other dictatorship, and those facing systematic and

---

65 UNHRC, 'Human Rights Situation in Palestine and Other Occupied Arab Territories: Report of the Special Rapporteur on the situation of human rights in the Palestinian territories occupied since 1967', UN Doc A/HRC/10/20 (the Falk Report) 11 February 2009, 18; 40–1.

66 UNHRC, 'Human Rights Situation in Palestine and Other Occupied Arab Territories: Report of the United Nations Fact Finding Mission on the Gaza Conflict', UN Doc A/HRC/12/48 (the Goldstone Report) 15 September 2009, 520 part 5 XXX A 1672.

67 Report of the UN Secretary-General to the UN General Assembly, 'In Larger Freedom: Towards Development, Security and Human Rights for All', UN Doc A/59/2005, 21 March 2005, 26 B91.

68 The usage here of the term 'human rights lexicon', after Susan Marks and Andrew Clapham, *International Human Rights Lexicon* (Oxford: OUP, 2005) is not intended as critical comment on this particular work.

serious violations of 'lesser' rights, if their human rights defenders cannot resolve these situations using exclusively peaceful means. Particularly when considered against the international community's persistent inability to protect or to prevent, this is surely not acceptable. Permitting the ongoing absence of a clear legal framework for the right to resist and consequent duties on third parties risks either further legal paralysis at international level or politicized distortion of international law amounting to norm abuse. Clarifying and strengthening the legal protection but also regulation of the right to resist as a self-help remedy and means of enforcement when other mechanisms have failed is therefore an ethical necessity. Yet because discussions of the law on the right to resist have been largely neglected or avoided for the past 20 years,[69] some rather basic conceptual work remains to be done.

For example, despite its long tradition, a review of the literature shows that there is still no agreed standard legal definition of this right, and in general the use of terminology lacks precision.[70] Elements borrowed from Honoré probably provide the most useful starting point: the 'right to resist' is the right, given certain conditions, to take action intended to effect social, political or economic change, including in some instances a right to commit acts that would ordinarily be unlawful.[71] It is an individual or collective right, exercised either on one's own behalf or on behalf of a group, or by a smaller group on behalf of a mass movement or 'people', generally against a State or other authority.[72] It can embrace a full spectrum of objectives from overthrow and replacement of a given political, social or economic order, to more modest objectives such as specific

---

69 Exceptions include Bertil Dunér, 'Rebellion: The Ultimate Human Right?' (2005) 9(2) *Int'l J. Hum. Rts* 247; David B. Kopel, Paul Gallant and Joanne D. Eisen, 'Is Resisting Genocide a Human Right?' (2005) 81(4) *Notre Dame L. Rev.* 1275; David B. Kopel, Paul Gallant and Joanne D. Eisen, 'The Human Right of Self-Defence' (2008) 22 *BYU J. Public L.* 43; Frédéric Mégret, 'Causes Worth Fighting For: Is There a Non-State *Jus Ad Bellum*?', in Aristotle Constantinides (ed.) *Essays in Honour of Prof. Kalliopi K. Koufa* (Leiden: Nijhoff, 2009); Frédéric Mégret, 'Civil Disobedience and International Law: Sketch for a Theoretical Argument' (2010) 47 *Canadian Ybk Int'l L.*; Frédéric Mégret, 'Not "Lambs to the Slaughter": A Program for Resistance to "Genocidal Law"' in René Provost and Payam Akhavan (eds) *Confronting Genocide* (Dordrecht: Springer Verlag, 2011) 195.

70 For example, it is common to use the cognate terms 'resist/resistance', 'rebel/rebellion' and 'revolt/revolution' interchangeably, or offer incomplete explanations of the distinctions between them.

71 Tony Honoré, 'The Right to Rebel' (1988) 8(1) *OJLS* 34, 35–6.

72 *Ibid.*, 37.

violation or grievance redress.[73] It also encompasses a full spectrum of illegal tactics from the peaceful to the forceful.[74] It is effectively a law of exception applicable to non-State actors.[75]

For the purposes of international human rights law, the right to resist must also be a secondary, conditional and limited right. 'Secondary' because it should activate only in the context of violations of recognized primary rights,[76] meaning that it falls into the smaller category of 'rights as remedies' and is not an end unto itself.[77] It thereby remains inseparable from the core proposition that governments are instituted to protect human rights, providing an alternative form of protection and enforcement only when they do not.[78] The corresponding duty it imposes on third parties is to either assist (within the limits of the law), or not obstruct.[79] It is 'conditional' because within a human rights framework it can only be justified in pursuit of specific aims that are internally consistent with international human rights law,[80] and 'limited' because the right cannot be invoked or otherwise used to intentionally suppress the rights of others.[81] This is important because as a concept divorced from human rights a 'right to resist' has no inherent moral content and has been invoked by claimants across the full political spectrum, from human rights defenders to history's grossest human rights violators.[82] It would need to be subject to other valid limitations such as a necessity test that can demonstrate that other effective remedies are not available,[83] and a proportionality test as to the specific means employed in context

[73] Eide (n55) 39; Minh (n23) 160–61; Honoré (n71) 52-3.

[74] Eide (n55) 54; Minh (n23) 161–2; Tomuschat (n55) 25; Rachael E. Schwartz, 'Chaos, Oppression, and Rebellion: The Use of Self-Help to Secure Individual Rights Under International Law' (1994) 12 *BU Int'l L.J.* 255, 256–7.

[75] It is thus characterized in Arthur Kaufmann, 'Small Scale Right to Resist' (1985–6) 21(3) *New Eng L. Rev.* 571, 573–5; Giorgio Agamben, *State of Exception* (Kevin Attell trans, Chicago, IL: University of Chicago Press, 2006) 10.

[76] Tomuschat (n55) 24; Honoré (n71) 38.

[77] Eide (n55) 44–53; Minh (n23) 157, 163; Tomuschat (n55) 20; Honoré (n71) 39–40.

[78] Honoré (n71) 53–4; Morsink, *The Universal Declaration of Human Rights: Origins, Drafting and Intent* (n22) 302.

[79] Honoré (n71) 36.

[80] Eide (n55) 54–5; Honoré (n71) 43, 52.

[81] Paust (n22) 569.

[82] Guenter Lewy, 'Resistance to Tyranny: Treason, Right or Duty?' (1960) 13(3) *West Pol. Q.* 581, 588–9.

[83] Tomuschat (n55) 19, 27, 30; Paust (n22) 569; Schwartz (n74) 265–9, 273–6, 278–84.

and against objectives,[84] and it would have to be exercised otherwise in compliance with international human rights, humanitarian and criminal law.[85] In this way, such a secondary, conditional and limited right to resist can remain fully consistent with the principle of respect for the rule of law.

Both the potential benefit and risk associated with this legal right deserve careful and thorough exploration. What would it mean in practice to respect, protect and fulfil such a right? What would in practical terms constitute a violation? What are the implications of such a right for guiding UN and member State responses? What is the potential role of a right to resist in making the right to an effective remedy real? What is its nexus with the right to dignity? How does it relate to enforcing the right to self-determination, as that concept evolves, or indeed as advocates push for contemporary and evolutive interpretations of modern manifestations of colonialism, slavery and apartheid (topics explored in subsequent chapters)? The potential clashes between a right to resist and other fundamental rights and international norms including in particular the prohibition on intervention, and its potentially symbiotic relationship with a right to peace and the right to a social and international order in which human rights may be realized (topics explored in previous chapters), also need more careful analysis. Is it analogous to a right of self-defence and therefore complementary or alternative to the responsibility to protect? Could it constitute a more coherent basis for a clarified concept of protected political activity that can be applied both within and beyond extradition and refugee law? What would it mean for the legal validity or interpretation of sedition or treason laws, or for the availability of defences otherwise within criminal law? Could it have a positive preventative role, enhancing human security by providing an effective deterrent to violator states? Should there also be a right to resist powerful corporate or other private actors that systematically abuse human rights but are currently even less accountable than States within the international system?

Given that two express formulations of the right to resist have now been included in two regional human rights treaties, legal scholarship needs to take seriously and explore what the African and Arab Charter right to resist provisions mean, or could mean, how they should be applied and what the relevant legal tests should be.

The strong correlation with contemporary armed conflicts and other conflicts that do not reach the armed conflict thresholds demands more

---

84 Eide (n55) 54–6, 60–3; Kaufmann (n75) 574.
85 Eide (n55) 34–5, 55, 58.

than abstract debate. As amply documented in quantitative studies,[86] a great many groups around the world, motivated by a wide diversity of objectives, claim the right to resist legitimately or otherwise, and act upon such claims using the full spectrum of tactics from illegal but non-violent protest to full-scale war. Indeed, we now live in an era when every active armed conflict involves non-State actor rebel forces.[87] Either by pure choice or perceived necessity, social movements demanding human rights or protecting themselves against violations do not always limit themselves to peaceful means. Actions under these presumptive claims frequently have implications for the international community. Yet international law still lacks sufficient clarity to address most situations due to ongoing *lacunae* where resistance is neither permitted nor prohibited. International law in general and international human rights law in particular should be in a position to adjudicate, but currently are not due to deficits in the law and legal scholarship. As has been shown, any purported answer to the question of whether any particular individual or group has a right to resist derived from the conclusions reached by proponents of the disavowal perspective, is based on reasoning that is not merely incomplete, but relies on wrong assumptions. A clearer, more rational and more just legal and analytical framework for adjudicating a right to resist could make a positive contribution to how we understand and achieve not only human rights but through that vehicle, human security. It could also reduce the contradictions and dangers posed by actions taken in the name of the responsibility to protect without the benefit of such frameworks.

In this context, the initiative of the UN Human Rights Council to codify the right to peace is of considerable significance, with the potential to revive and advance both the debate and the law on the right to resist.

---

86 See for example, data reported in *Human Security Report Project, Mini-Atlas of Human Security* (New York: World Bank, May 2008); J. Joseph Hewitt, Jonathan Wilkenfeld, Ted Robert Gurr and Birger Heldt, *Peace and Conflict 2012* (Maryland: University of Maryland 2012); J. Joseph Hewitt, Jonathan Wilkenfeld and Ted Robert Gurr, *Peace and Conflict 2010* (London: Paradigm Publishers 2009); J. Joseph Hewitt, Jonathan Wilkenfeld and Ted Robert Gurr, *Peace and Conflict 2008* (London: Paradigm Publishers, 2007); Monty G. Marshall and Ted Robert Gurr, *Peace and Conflict 2005: A Global Survey of Armed Conflicts, Self-Determination Movements, and Democracy* (Center for International Development and Conflict Management, University of Maryland, 2005). See also the regularly updated Minorities at Risk (MAR) Data, 'Minorities at Risk Project' at the Center for International Development and Conflict Management University of Maryland, available online at: http://www.cidcm.umd.edu/mar/.

87 J. Joseph Hewitt, 'Trends in Global Conflict 1946–2007', in Hewitt, Wilkenfeld and Gurr, *Peace and Conflict 2010* (n86) 19.

In its recommendations tabled at the 17th session in June 2011, the UN Human Rights Council's Advisory Committee proposed to include an express right to resist provision in a new 'Declaration on the Human Right of Peoples to Peace', and later advanced this broad formulation that both respects and arguably goes beyond the existing law:

> Article 7. Resistance and Opposition to Oppression
> 1. All peoples and individuals have the right to resist and oppose oppressive colonial, foreign occupation or dictatorial domination (domestic oppression).
> 2. Everyone has the right to oppose aggression, genocide, war crimes and crimes against humanity, violations of other universally recognized human rights, and any propaganda in favour of war, or incitement to violence or violations of the right to peace as defined in the present declaration.[88]

For its part, the UN Human Rights Council deferred substantive consideration of the report's proposals until 2012.[89] Without constructive intervention and advocacy, a number of less than positive scenarios are possible, reminiscent of the Universal Declaration outcomes. States could continue to avoid this complex issue and quietly push the proposal into convenient obscurity. The debate could bring the existing schism to the surface but widen it and end without agreement. Or the disavowal advocates could prevail, either freezing the law in place or worse, narrowing or eliminating existing protections. None of these results would advance human rights beyond the present position.

For all of these reasons, the time has now come for fresh consideration of the right to resist by the current generation of human rights scholars, advocates and activists. This right deserves a stronger position in the human rights lexicon of the twenty-first century. A new development in the universal system now makes this prospect real. Addressing the deficiencies in the law at both international and regional levels will undoubtedly raise a host of complex jurisprudential and practical questions, and the challenge should not be underestimated. It is crucial that this work is done in a considered and well-informed way, with due regard to the realities facing human rights defenders at the front lines.

---

88 UNHRC, 'The right of peoples to peace progress report prepared by the Drafting Group of the Advisory Committee' (9 December 2011) UN Doc A/HRC/AC/8/2 (2011), Annex Draft Declaration on the Right to Peace, 7. This includes significantly improved wording from that originally tabled to the UN Human Rights Council in UNHRC, 'Progress report of the Human Rights Council Advisory Committee on the right of peoples to peace' (1 April 2011) UN Doc A/HRC/17/39 (2011) 9–10; 35–7, sec D 'proposed standards'.

89 UNHRC, 'Resolution on Promotion of the Right of Peoples to Peace' (10 June 2011) UN Doc A/HRC/17/l.23 (2011) 14–17.

6. Forensic science, international criminal law and the duties towards persons killed in war

Éadaoin O'Brien*

In recent decades, the forensic exhumation of mass graves and other deposition sites containing the bodies of victims of war crimes, and the subsequent forensic analysis of the remains retrieved from such graves have been a notable feature of international criminal tribunals. For example, the *ad hoc* tribunals established in the 1990s, the International Criminal Tribunal for the former Yugoslavia ('ICTY'), which was established by Resolution 827 of the Security Council on 25 May 1993,[1] and the International Criminal Tribunal for Rwanda ('ICTR'), established in November 1994 pursuant to United Nations Security Council Resolution 955[2] incorporated forensic techniques into their investigatory and prosecutorial strategy. The use of forensic methodologies, including the forensic exhumation of mass graves, is only one element of the international criminal investigation process but it is a very valuable one. Enquiries into violations of international criminal law rely on the forensic sciences 'for critical evidence that establishes the nature and pattern of crimes committed'[3] as well as for providing methods for human identification.[4] Forensic analysis pertaining to death investigations concentrates on specific crimes falling with the broader categories under the jurisdiction of the tribunals. For example, in the context of war crimes the forensic examination will pertain

* The research on which this chapter is based has been supported by a postgraduate scholarship awarded by the Irish Research Council for the Humanities and Social Sciences.

1 UN Doc S/RES/827 (1993).

2 UN Doc S/RES/955 (1994).

3 Erin H. Kimmerle, 'Current Trends in Forensic Investigations of Human Rights Abuse: Human Identification of Mass Graves', in Matthias I. Okoye and Cyril H. Wecht (eds) *Forensic Investigation and Management of Mass Disasters* (Tuscon, AZ: Lawyers and Judges Publishing Company Inc., 2007) 221.

4 *Ibid*. 221.

to 'acts of wilful killing, directing attacks against a civilian population or protected persons, killing of surrendered combatants, physical mutilations and medical experiments, intentional starvation, and extrajudicial executions'.[5] Such forensic enquiries will, by their very nature, require the examination of bodies of war dead and, if recovered from a burial site, the contents of the graves from which they have been exhumed.

Issues pertaining to the application of medical and forensic sciences in the investigation of violations of international humanitarian law have come to receive increasing attention by both practitioners and academics in the past number of years. In addition, in recognition of the value attached to utilizing forensic techniques in the movement to combat impunity, a number of international bodies are currently focusing attention on how the synergy between the respective disciplines can be improved.[6] A related topic which to date has received less attention pertains to the nexus between international forensic investigations conducted under the auspices of international criminal tribunals and the rules of international humanitarian law regarding the dead. Utilizing examples from the work of the ICTY, this chapter will explore the relationship by examining how forensic investigations can assist in ensuring compliance with the legal obligations towards the dead as codified in international law.

This chapter consists of three parts. The first section outlines rules in international humanitarian law pertaining to obligations towards the dead during and following armed conflict. The second section provides a short overview of the forensic programme operated by the ICTY and outlines the purpose of gathering forensic evidence for international criminal trials. The third and final section explores how the work of forensic programmes

---

[5] Helena Ranta and Kari T. Takamaa, 'Crimes against Humanity and Other War Crimes', in Tim Thompson and Sue Black (eds) *Forensic Human Identification: An Introduction* (Boca Raton/London/New York: CRC Press, 2007) 445, 448.

[6] See for example, *Report of the Office of the United Nations High Commissioner for Human Rights on the right to the truth and on forensic genetics and human rights,* UN Doc A/HRC/15/26, 24 August 2010. The report was submitted pursuant to Human Rights Council Resolutions 9/11 and 10/26, in which the Council requested the High Commissioner's Office to 'prepare a report, to be presented to the Council . . . on the use of forensic experts in case of gross violations of human rights with a view to identifying trends and best practices in this regard' and 'to request information from States, intergovernmental and non-governmental organizations on best practices in the use of forensic genetics for identifying victims of serious violations of human rights and international humanitarian law with a view to considering the possibility of drafting a manual that may serve as a guide for the application of forensic genetics . . .', *Ibid.,* 'Summary'.

can augment the practice in states with regard to the appropriate treatment of war dead.

1. INTERNATIONAL HUMANITARIAN LAW OBLIGATIONS PERTAINING TO THE DEAD

1.1 The Ethical, Social and Legal Significance of the Dead Body

When a person has died, why do we care about how the dead body is treated? The explanation for the continuing concern for the person who was once living lies in the lingering connection between the living and the dead. As D. Gareth Jones and Maja I. Whitaker indicate the dead body has ethical significance and most people have deep moral intuitions which induce us to bestow value on other human beings like ourselves.[7] This is why, they contend, 'most people are horrified by pictures of corpses being dumped in mass graves after a holocaust. It touches something very deep in their sense of what is right and wrong; they recognize this as a form of indignity, and would be even more distressed if one of the bodies was that of someone known to them'.[8] All cultures throughout time have developed forms of mortuary rituals, of which a central feature is disposal of the dead in a respectful manner and funeral rites focused around a reverent final resting place.[9] Behaviour that is regarded as deviating from cultural notions of respect and dignity can prompt strong moral outrage.[10]

---

[7] D. Gareth Jones and Maja I. Whitaker, *Speaking for the Dead: The Human Body in Biology and Medicine* (2nd edn, Aldershot: Ashgate, 2009) 21.

[8] *Ibid.* 22.

[9] There is a wealth of anthropological studies on death and cultural practices surrounding death. See, for example, Peter Metcalf and Richard Huntington, *Celebrations of Death: The Anthropology of Mortuary Ritual* (2nd edn, Cambridge: CUP, 1991); Antonius C.G.M. Robben, *Death, Mourning and Burial: A Cross-Cultural Reader* (Malden-Oxford-Carlton: Blackwell Publishing, 2004); Douglas James Davies, *Death, Ritual and Belief: the Rhetoric of Funerary Rites* (2nd edn, London: Continuum, 2002).

[10] There are numerous examples to draw upon but I will give just one here. It was reported in the British media in February 2011 that a borough council in Worcestershire in the United Kingdom was considering proposals to re-use energy at its crematorium to heat a nearby swimming pool at a leisure centre run by the council, as part of a commitment to reduce carbon dioxide emissions. 'The heat would otherwise be exhausted into the atmosphere'; a wasteful scenario in an age of austerity. Opponents to the plan branded it as 'sick' and the council was called upon to apologize for 'the insulting and insensitive proposals'. Danielle Dwyer, PA 'Council defends crematorium plan to heat pool', *The Independent*, 24 January

For Jones and Whitaker, there are several related components to this moral intuition. First of all, our recognition of each other is dependent on recognizing distinctive physical characteristics that are not immediately obscured at the time of death. What is done to the dead body therefore 'has relevance for our feelings about that person when alive; the cadaver and the person cannot be totally separated'.[11] A second component relates to the memories that are formed between the person when alive and those who knew him or her. The cadaver, the authors contend, represents a collection of built-in memories that can never be entirely divorced from it. For most people, these memories lead to 'a sense of respect for a cadaver and its enshrined associations'.[12] The final component centres on the deceased person's prior relationships. The deceased was someone's friend or relative who is now grieving the death. Respect shown to the cadaver is therefore to show respect for the survivors' grief.[13]

Although armed conflicts can present substantial difficulties in fulfilling traditional mortuary rituals, this does not mean to say that such practices are abandoned entirely during periods of war. On the contrary, funerary rites and commemoration ceremonies have been modified and adapted in order to take into account the exigencies of armed conflict.[14] In recognition of the importance of treating the dead body with respect and facilitating the grief and mourning of families and communities left behind, a number of obligations have been codified in international humanitarian law (IHL). The requirements include the obligation to search for, collect, identify, handle with dignity and dispose of the dead in a culturally appropriate manner. The imperative to implement such legal obligations pertains not just to reasons of a cultural and religious nature, but also to legal and psycho-social concerns. Failure to follow the obligations outlined in IHL can have serious consequences and as reflected upon by Tidball-Binz, '[t]he trauma suffered by bereaved families and affected communities as a result of the neglect and mismanagement of their dead, including lack of news of missing relatives, often lasts much longer than the more conspicuous physical effects of catastrophes'.[15]

2011, available online at: http://www.independent.co.uk/news/uk/home-news/council-defends-crematorium-plan-to-heat-pool-2193188.html.

11 Jones and Whitaker (n7) 22.

12 *Ibid.* 22.

13 *Ibid.* 22.

14 Luc Capdevila and Danièle Voldman, *War Dead: Western Societies and the Casualties of War* (English translation, original publication in French, 2002) (Edinburgh: Edinburgh University Press, 2006) 114–79.

15 Morris Tidball-Binz, 'Managing the Dead in Catastrophes: Guiding

In the former Yugoslavia, following the mass executions and clandestine burial of approximately 7500 men and boys in the area surrounding Srebrenica, Bosnia in July 1995, the ongoing uncertainty as to the fate of the missing has given rise to a newly recognized psycho-social pathology category known as 'Srebrenica Syndrome'.

> The Trial Chamber heard that the survivors of Srebrenica have unique impediments to their recovery and staff members at Vive Zene speak of the 'Srebrenica Syndrome' as a new pathology category. One of the primary factors giving rise to the syndrome is that, with few exceptions, the fate of the survivor's loved ones is not officially known: the majority of men of Srebrenica are still listed as missing. For Bosnian Muslim women it is essential to have a clear marital status, whether widowed, divorced or married: a woman whose husband is missing does not fit within any of these categories. Moreover, on a psychological level, these women are unable to move forward with the process of recovery without the closure that comes from knowing with certainty what has happened to their family members and properly grieving for them.[16]

Relatives who do not have conclusive proof of death or a body to mourn over remain in a state of limbo which can have a debilitating effect on their quality of life. Without confirmation of death, the missing person lies somewhere between life and death and the survivor is often in an indeterminate state caught between the traumatic past and an uncertain future. Apart from the obvious psycho-social effects such a state of affairs must bring there are issues of a more practical nature that arise.[17] For example, there will be direct consequences on the ability of the individual to remarry should they wish and make claims to pension entitlements.[18] Indeed the right of the family to know the truth of what happened to their loved one underpins the *raison d'être* for the provisions pertaining to the dead in modern international humanitarian law.[19] Analogous protections can also

---

Principles and Practical Recommendations for First Responders' (2007) 89(866) *International Review of the Red Cross* 421, 422.

16 *Prosecutor v. Krstić*, Trial Judgement, Case No. IT-98-33-T, 2 August 2001, para 93.

17 Erin D. Williams and John D. Crews 'From Dust to Dust: Ethical and Practical Issues Involved in the Location, Exhumation and Identification of Bodies from Mass Graves' (2003) 44(3) *Croatian Medical Journal* 251, 252.

18 For an account of the difficulties facing survivors who still search for the remains of their loved ones in Bosnia-Herzegovina, see further Wojciech Tochman, *Like Eating a Stone: Surviving the Past in Bosnia* (London: Portello Books, 2008, English translation).

19 Marco Sassòli and Antoine A. Bouvier (in cooperation with Susan Carr, Lindsey Cameron and Thomas de Saint Maurice), *How Does Law Protect in War: Cases, Documents and Teaching Materials on Contemporary Practice in*

be identified in the regime developed in international human rights law on preventing enforced disappearances, which includes the United Nations International Convention for the Protection of All Persons from Enforced Disappearance which entered into force on 23 December 2010.[20]

1.2 International Humanitarian Law and Treatment of the Dead

The proper treatment of the dead body in war has been a concern for centuries with reference found in ancient texts as well as in contemporary international legal instruments.[21] Prior to the codification of provisions in modern laws of war, a number of ancient texts addressed this issue. For example, the *Mahābhārata*, one of the two major Sanskrit epics of ancient India, required burial of enemy fighters with full military honours, for 'with death our enmity has terminated'.[22] During the latter part of the

International Humanitarian Law (2nd edn, Geneva: ICRC, 2006) 170. The source of this right is Art. 32 of the Protocol Additional to the Geneva Conventions of 12 August 1949, and Relating to the Protection of Victims of International Armed Conflicts (Protocol I) of 8 June 1977 (First Additional Protocol).

[20] Available online at: http://treaties.un.org/Pages/ViewDetails.aspx?src=TREATY&mtdsg_no=IV-16&chapter=4&lang=en. For further information on the legal framework pertaining to the crime of enforced disappearance, including the Declaration on the Protection of all Persons from Enforced Disappearances, the International Convention for the Protection of All Persons from Enforced Disappearance, and General Comments on elements of this crime including General Comment on the definition of enforced disappearance, General Comment on Enforced Disappearance as a crime against humanity, General Comment on Enforced disappearance as a continuous crime and General Comment on the Right to the Truth in Relation to Enforced Disappearances and on the work of the Working Group on Enforced or Involuntary Disappearances, which comes under the auspices of the United Nations Office of the High Commissioner for Human Rights, see: http://www.ohchr.org/EN/Issues/Disappearances/Pages/DisappearancesIndex.aspx. On the origins of the crime in the laws of war see, further, Brian Finucane, 'Enforced Disappearance as a Crime under International Law: A Neglected Origin in the Laws of War' (2010) 3 *Yale J. Int'l L.* 171.

[21] In more recent years, the question of the legal standing of the body has come to the fore in international human rights law as legal scholars attempt to establish whether the dead have human rights. This gives rise to a number of philosophical and indeed practical questions which are outside the scope of this current chapter. For an analysis on the rights of the dead in the context of international forensic investigations see further, Adam Rosenblatt, 'International Forensic Investigations and the Human Rights of the Dead' (2010) 32(4) *HRQ* 921.

[22] Leslie C. Green, 'What One May Do In Combat – Then And Now', in Astrid J.M. Delissen and Gerard J. Tanja (eds) *Humanitarian Law of Armed Conflict Challenges Ahead: Essays in Honour of Frits Kalshoven* (Dordrecht: Nijhoff, 1991) 269, 279.

Middle Ages, the victor was expected to provide a Christian burial and listing of the dead.[23] Classical literary works further illustrate the philosophy of the time regarding chivalry in warfare. Homer and Shakespeare both addressed the issue of the honourable treatment of dead bodies of defeated enemies through their writings.[24]

In terms of the movement to codify modern humanitarian law, a number of texts published in the nineteenth century are of note, as these represent 'first thoughts considering the treatment of enemy dead'[25] prior to the enshrining of principles in treaty form. In *Un souvenir de Solferino,* Henry Dunant discussed how the dead were abandoned on the battlefields in Solferino and in an 1867 report to international conferences of agencies engaged in aid to soldiers and sailors, he discussed this point in an article about prisoners who died in captivity. He called for them to be given 'individualised graves', the rationale being that the families would be able to trace the remains in order to facilitate repatriation.[26] At a conference held in Berlin in 1869 a proposal was made by the International Committee of the Red Cross (ICRC) delegates that victorious armies should, whenever possible, identify bodies on the battlefield and opposing parties should exchange information on the deceased. A number of years later, a manual on the laws of warfare drafted by Gustave Moynier and adopted by the Institute of International Law in Oxford on 9 September 1880 again showed concern for dead combatants. Article 19 of the text forbade the plundering and mutilation of the dead left on the battlefield, and Article 20 provided that measures should be adopted to identify the dead before burial and that information was to be passed on to their army or government.[27] These texts were used as reference documents at the drafting stage of the proceedings of the conference at the Hague in 1899 and at Geneva in 1906, when recommendations were made that belligerents should inform each other of the death of prisoners and of the identity of enemy dead in the area under the respective control of the parties to the conflict.[28]

In the past century the provisions affording protection to the dead have been consolidated as the experiences of major conflicts such as the Great War, the Second World War and numerous non-international armed

---

23 *Ibid.* 279.

24 Theodor Meron, *Bloody Constraint: War and Chivalry in Shakespeare* (Oxford: OUP, 1998) 63.

25 Capdevila and Voldman (n14) 78.

26 Henry Dunant, *Un souvenir de Solferino* (Lausanne: l'Âge d'Homme, 1986 [1st edn, 1862]) 134, cited in Capdevila and Voldman (n14) 77.

27 Capdevila and Voldman (n14) 77–8.

28 *Ibid.* 78.

conflicts demonstrated the need to codify clear instructions binding on the parties to armed conflict.[29] Of particular note are the obligations codified in the four Geneva Conventions and the Additional Protocols.[30] A number of provisions pertaining to the deceased are now recognized as constituting customary international humanitarian law. These rules of IHL reflect both treaty law and practice, and as such they are recognized as having the status of customary law and are binding on all states, regardless of the

---

[29] For an outline of the treaty obligations pertaining to the war dead in international humanitarian law texts, see further Dietrich Schindler and Jiri Toman, *The Laws of Armed Conflicts: A Collection of Conventions, Resolutions and Other Documents* (Leiden/Boston: Nijhoff, 2004).

[30] Geneva Convention for the Amelioration of the Condition of the Wounded and Sick in Armed Forces in the Field of August 12, 1949 (First Geneva Convention) Arts 4, 12, 15, 16, 17; Geneva Convention for the Amelioration of the Condition of Wounded, Sick and Shipwrecked Members of Armed Forces at Sea of August 12, 1949 (Second Geneva Convention) Arts 18, 19, 20, 21; Geneva Convention Relative to the Treatment of Prisoners of War of August 12, 1949 (Third Geneva Convention) Arts 13, 120, 121; Geneva Convention Relative to the Protection of Civilian Persons in Time of War of August 12, 1949 (Fourth Geneva Convention) Arts 16, 129, 130, 131, 136, 139; Protocol Additional to the Geneva Conventions of 12 August 1949, and First Additional Protocol (n19) Arts 32, 33, 34, 61; Protocol Additional to the Geneva Conventions of 12 August 1949, and Relating to the Protection of Victims of Non-International Armed Conflicts of 8 June 1977 (Second Additional Protocol) Art. 8. There are two provisions in the Geneva Conventions and Additional Protocols that make reference to exhumation. Art. 17 of the First Geneva Convention provides *inter alia* that:

> Parties to the conflict shall . . . ensure that the dead are honourably interred, if possible according to the rites of the religion to which they belonged, that their graves are respected, grouped if possible according to the nationality of the deceased, properly maintained and marked so that they may always be found. For this purpose, they shall organize at the commencement of hostilities an Official Graves Registration Service, to allow subsequent exhumations and to ensure the identification of bodies, whatever the site of the graves, and the possible transportation to the home country.

Art. 34(4) of the First Additional Protocol authorizes exhumations in situations where overriding public necessity demands such action, including circumstances of an investigatory nature. It provides that:

> A High Contracting Party in whose territory the grave sites referred to in this Article are situated shall be permitted to exhume the remains only:
> (a) . . ., or
> (b) where exhumation is a matter of overriding public necessity, including cases of medical and investigative necessity, in which case the High Contracting Party shall at all times respect the remains, and shall give notice to the home country of its intention to exhume the remains together with details of the intended place of reinterment.

status of ratification of the treaties in which these rules originate. Thus, they can be considered as constituting the *minimum legal obligations* for the treatment of those killed as a result of armed hostilities – both combatants and civilians. The customary rules of international humanitarian law as documented by the ICRC, relevant to the appropriate handling of the dead, will now be discussed.

1.3 Search for and Collection of the Dead

> Whenever circumstances permit, and particularly after an engagement, each party to the conflict must, without delay, take all possible measures to search for, collect and evacuate the dead without adverse distinction [Rule 112].[31]

Respect for this rule is considered as a condition *sine qua non* of respect for the subsequent rules 113–116, requiring return of remains, decent burial and identification of the dead.[32] As deduced by the ICRC, in its customary international humanitarian law study, state practice and a review of case law from a number of jurisdictions indicate that these rules are equally applicable to combatants and civilian decedents. Indeed, in contemporary armed conflict the boundaries between soldier and civilian can be blurred. For example, a civilian may directly participate in hostilities and be classified as an unprivileged belligerent who for the purpose of such activities may not enjoy the protection of IHL afforded to civilians. Such actors may indeed be classified as terrorists, depending on who is framing the terms of reference.[33] In this light it is important to place the emphasis on the humanitarian aspect of these legal prescriptions rather than attempting to establish what duties are owed to the dead in accordance to the category of decedent. As recognized by the Israeli High Court in the *Jenin (Mortal Remains)* case in 2002:

> The location, identification, and burial of bodies are important humanitarian acts. They are a direct consequence of the principle of respect for the dead – respect for all dead.[34]

---

31 Jean-Marie Henckaerts and Louise Doswald-Beck, *Customary International Humanitarian Law; Volume 1: Rules* (Cambridge: CUP, 2005) 406.

32 *Ibid.* 407.

33 On the question of civilians and direct participation in hostilities, see further Nils Melzer, *Interpretative Guidance on the Notion of Direct Participation in Hostilities under International Humanitarian Law* (Geneva: ICRC, 2009).

34 *MK Mohammed Barake v. The Minister of Defense et al.*, HCJ 3114/02, *MK Ahmed Tibi v. The Prime Minister et al.*, HCJ 3115/02, *Adalah et al. v. The*

This obligation is considered to be an obligation of means – each party to the conflict is expected to take all measures possible to locate the dead. There will be a wide diversity relating to the available resources of any given party to a conflict, which are necessary in order to execute these obligations. A component of this requirement includes permitting the search for and collection of the dead by humanitarian organizations or calling on the assistance of the public. In practice such organizations, which include organizations such as the ICRC, or national Red Cross organizations, need the permission of the party in control of the area to be searched. However, such permission must not be arbitrarily denied.[35]

A topic closely related to that of the dead in armed conflict is the subject of the missing. During the course of armed conflict a considerable number of individuals or groups of people can fall into the category of 'missing' – their whereabouts is unknown and additionally it is usually not established whether they are living or deceased. The missing can be members of the armed forces, but increasingly in contemporary armed conflicts, can belong to the civilian population. Regardless of what category the missing or dead fall in to, the humanitarian rationale behind the provisions on the deceased or missing is the same: 'It is not primarily to protect the dead and the missing themselves that International Humanitarian Law (IHL) contains specific rules concerning them. The main consideration is the right of families to know the fate of their relatives'.[36]

1.4 Treatment of the Dead

> Each party to the conflict must take all possible measures to prevent the dead from being despoiled. Mutilation of dead bodies is prohibited [Rule 113].[37]

The disdain for the practice of mutilation of dead bodies was first codified in modern humanitarian law in the Hague Convention of 1907 (X).[38] The prohibition has been consolidated through codification in the Geneva Conventions, found in numerous military manuals and reaffirmed in a number of criminal cases.[39] The need for this provision arose due to the

Commander of the IDF Forces in the West Bank, HCJ 3116/02, Judgment, 14 April 2002, para 9.

[35] Henckaerts and Doswald-Beck (n31) 407.

[36] Sassòli and Bouvier (n19) 170.

[37] Henckaerts and Doswald-Beck (n31) 409.

[38] Convention (X) for the Adaptation to Maritime Warfare of the Principles of the Geneva Convention, The Hague, 18 October 1907, Art. 16.

[39] Henckaerts & Doswald-Beck (n31) 407.

perpetual maltreatment of the bodies of the dead. Laws drafted to govern the treatment of the dead body, from religious law, to national law, to rules of international humanitarian law, often require, as a very basic, that the mortal remains are treated in a dignified and respectful manner. Armed conflicts, past and present, have seen many instances where the dead have been mutilated and maltreated, for a variety of reasons, including the practice of using enemy bodies as a weapon,[40] taking parts of the body as a 'souvenir',[41] and using the body to terrorize members of the civilian population.[42] As Meron discusses:

> In antiquity, in the Middle Ages, but even in our times in Vietnam, Cambodia, Korea, the Middle-East, the former Yugoslavia and elsewhere, sworn enemies desecrate their enemies' bodies in violation of international humanitarian law. Often, return of the bodies for an honourable burial is treated as a bargaining chip, as shameful leverage for what is in effect ransom.[43]

A recent expression of the prohibition of the mutilation of the dead is found under the Rome Statute of the International Criminal Court. The Rome Statute includes the imperative that remains must be handled in a dignified manner and as such recognizes that the mutilation of the deceased is prohibited in both international and internal armed conflicts. Under the Statute of the ICC, the prohibition of mutilating dead bodies is covered by the crime of 'committing outrages upon personal dignity'. According to the Elements of Crimes, this proscription also applies to dead persons.[44] Thus, this represents a positive law codification reflecting the gravity of this offence.

1.5 Return of the Remains and Personal Effects of the Dead

> Parties to the conflict must endeavour to facilitate the return of the remains of the deceased upon request of the party to which they belong or upon the request of their next of kin. They must return their personal effects to them [Rule 114].[45]

---

[40] Capdevila and Voldman (n14) 84–90.

[41] Simon Harrison, 'Skull Trophies of the Pacific War: Transgressive Objects of Remembrance (2006) 12(4) *Journal of the Royal Anthropological Institute (N.S.)* 817.

[42] Capdevila and Voldman (n14) 98–107.

[43] Meron (n24) 75.

[44] Elements of Crimes for the ICC, Definition of committing outrages upon personal dignity as a war crime (ICC Statute, footnote 49 relating to Art. 8(2)(b)(xxi) for international armed conflict and footnote 57 relating to Art. 8(2)(c)(ii) for internal armed conflict).

[45] Henckaerts and Doswald-Beck (n31) 411.

Rule 114 recognizes the importance of the repatriation of the remains of the deceased. The customary nature of this rule in international armed conflict is well established.[46] In regards to non-international armed conflicts, although there are no treaty obligations requiring measures to transfer the remains of decedents to their families, it is identified that there is a 'growing trend' towards the recognition of this obligation. Additionally, the fact that this rule is in keeping with the obligation of respect for family life implies its dual applicability in international and internal armed conflicts.[47]

1.6 Disposal of the Dead

> The dead must be disposed of in a respectful manner and their graves respected and properly maintained [Rule 115].[48]

In national jurisdictions, mortuary procedures are regulated through legal codes. In war time, although there are many more challenges to be faced in ensuring appropriate interment or other forms of mortuary procedures, these mortuary rituals are no less important. Thus it is identified that Rule 115 'reflects a general principle of law requiring respect for the dead and their graves'.[49] Depending on the circumstances of each individual scenario, those responding to the scene at which the fatality has occurred may or may not be a professional, trained in body handling and forensic methods appropriate to the identification of the deceased. To this end the ICRC has published guidelines on operational best practices for the handling of the dead by non-specialist personnel.[50]

1.7 Accounting for the Dead

> With a view to the identification of the dead, each party to the conflict must record all available information prior to disposal and mark the location of the graves [Rule 116].[51]

This rule emphasizes the importance of human identification so that each individual death is recorded and it also ensures the families of the deceased

---

[46] *Ibid.* 411.
[47] *Ibid.* 412.
[48] *Ibid.* 414.
[49] *Ibid.* 416.
[50] *Operational Best Practices Regarding the Management of Human Remains and Information on the Dead by Non-Specialists: for all armed forces; for all humanitarian organizations* (Geneva: ICRC, November 2004).
[51] Henckaerts and Doswald-Beck (n31) 417.

can be directed to the whereabouts of their relatives' remains. As identified in the ICRC study, the rule is reinforced by two other rules, the requirement of respect for family life (Rule 105) and the right families have to know the fate of one's relatives (Rule 117).[52] Again, this is an obligation of means, and parties to the conflict are not obliged to identify all bodies that have been found; in many conflict situations this would be a monumental if not impossible task. Each party must try though to collect information which will aid in the identification of the deceased. However, States are not precluded from obtaining assistance from humanitarian organizations who can, when appropriate, apply sophisticated and more forensically accurate methods of identification, such as DNA analysis, in lieu of, or in addition to, efforts made by High Contracting Parties.

2. FORENSIC INVESTIGATIONS BY INTERNATIONAL CRIMINAL TRIBUNALS WITH PARTICULAR REFERENCE TO THE ICTY

The exhumation programme operated by the ICTY had four main objectives:

- to obtain evidence regarding the identity of victims killed during the conflict;
- to establish the circumstances and causes of death;
- to link primary and secondary mass graves;
- to reveal attempts to cover up the crimes.[53]

The exhumation programme commenced in July 1996[54] and largely ceased in 2001, with only a residual forensic programme remaining.[55] The *modus operandi* for exhuming the mass graves varied; initially work was conducted by external agencies such as non-governmental organizations

---

52 *Ibid.* 417.

53 ICTY – UNICRI, *ICTY Manual on Developed Practices* (Turin: United Nations Interregional Crime & Justice Research Institute, 2009) 17.

54 Third Annual Report of the International Tribunal for the Prosecution of Persons Responsible for Serious Violations of International Humanitarian Law Committed in the Territory of the Former Yugoslavia since 1991, UN Doc A/51/292- S/1996/665, 16 August 1996, 26.

55 Ninth Annual Report of the International Tribunal for the Prosecution of Persons Responsible for Serious Violations of International Humanitarian Law Committed in the Territory of the Former Yugoslavia since 1991, UN Doc. A/57/379-S/2002/985, 4 September 2002, 39.

and specialists donated by states, with Tribunal staff in attendance. Over time the ICTY developed internal forensic capacity. The 2009 manual prepared by the ICTY and the United Nations Interregional Crime and Justice Research Institute which provides an overview of the practices established at the Tribunal highlights that exhumations are expensive and complex exercises and it found that the 'most cost-effective exhumations [were] those conducted by external agencies with tribunal staff in attendance'.[56]

Forensic investigation of complex crimes such as war crimes, crimes against humanity and genocide requires a multidisciplinary approach. Experts drawn from the fields of science, medicine, law and criminal justice will ideally be deployed. A number of disciplines are regarded as central to the investigation with other, more specialized experts becoming engaged in the work as the need arises. Skinner and Sterenberg advocate that minimally, complete teams are composed of core expertise from 'crime scene managers, archaeologists, anthropologists and pathologists'.[57] Additionally, further professionals may be employed including 'evidence officers, logisticians, heavy equipment operators, photographers, surveyors, dentists, [and] mortuary managers'.[58] Once a suspected grave site has been located, the forensic investigation of the mass grave takes place in several stages.[59] The process entails site assessment, survey, excavation and post-mortem examination of the remains.[60] To obtain forensically defensible conclusions from the exhumation, the process may take weeks or even months.[61] Notwithstanding the fact that the examination of mass graves entails a particular *modus operandi*, it should not be seen in isolation from the broader investigation and will indeed be focused by factors such as prosecutorial strategy and directed by intelligence gathered from a number of sources.[62]

From an international criminal law perspective, the number of bodies recovered from a mass grave can range from a minimum number of

---

56 *ICTY Manual on Developed Practices* (n53) 17.

57 Mark Skinner and Jon Sterenberg, 'Turf Wars: Authority and Responsibility for the Investigation of Mass Graves' (2005) 151 *Forensic Science International* 221, 222.

58 *Ibid*. 222.

59 Note that the place of execution and the deposition site may not be the same location. Victims may be killed in one or numerous places and the bodies then transported to the grave site for disposal.

60 Skinner and Sterenberg (n57) 222.

61 Mark Skinner, 'Planning the Archaeological Recovery of Evidence from Recent Mass Graves' (1987) 34 *Forensic Science International* 267.

62 Skinner and Sterenberg (n57) 231.

three, as per the definition put forward by the United Nations Special Rapporteur on extra judicial, summary or arbitrary executions,[63] to numbers in the hundreds or even thousands. In criminal investigations, the primary goal of the excavation is the recording and full recovery of all evidence, including human remains, in the best possible physical condition. Although further disruption to the bodies may inevitably occur during the process of exhumation, the more complete the body remains, the more information the forensic pathologist and forensic anthropologist will have available for making an identification, for evaluating the cause and manner of death and making other related analysis.[64]

Traditionally, identification of decedents in armed conflict was achieved via methods such as visual identification, examination of clothing and personal effects on the remains, including identification bracelets or 'dog tags' worn by members of some military forces. For a number of reasons, including lack of resources or specialization, in many contemporaneous conflicts the deceased continue to be identified through presumptive methods. In contrast, international criminal tribunals will have means at their disposal that enable them to obtain positive identifications using more sophisticated techniques such as through DNA analysis, in addition to utilizing conventional identification methods such as odontology and anthropology. Forensic examinations conducted by or on behalf of international criminal tribunals will seek to identify the remains of the decedents but primarily in the context of the criminal charges being investigated, and failure to achieve individual identification will not necessarily preclude the use of evidence obtained as a result of the examination. In the context of some prosecutions, particularly those relating to

---

[63] The United Nations Special Rapporteur on extra-judicial, summary or arbitrary executions has defined mass graves as locations where three or more victims of extrajudicial, summary or arbitrary executions were buried, not having died in combat or armed confrontations UN Doc E/CN.4/1993/50, 10 February 1993: *Situation of Human Rights in the Territory of the Former Yugoslavia*. Report on the situation of human rights in the territory of the former Yugoslavia submitted by Mr. Tadeusz Mazowiecki, Special Rapporteur of the Commission on Human Rights, pursuant to Commission resolution 1992/S-1/1 of 14 August 1992. Annex I: Summary of the report of the Special Rapporteur on extrajudicial, summary or arbitrary executions on his mission to investigate allegations of mass graves from 15 to 20 December 1992, available at http://www.unhchr.ch/Huridocda/Huridoca.nsf/0/313049964d7549ec802567900054cf88?Open Document

[64] Hugh Tuller and Marija Đurić, 'Keeping the Pieces Together: Comparison of Mass Grave Exhumation Methodology' (2006) 156 *Forensic Science International* 192, 193.

genocide charges, establishing group identity may be more pertinent than determining individual identifications.[65]

Forensic pathology is a specialization in the discipline of pathology that concerns the investigation of deaths where there are medico-legal implications, for example, where it is suspected that the death occurred as a result of homicide. It is the responsibility of the forensic pathologist to perform an autopsy of the human remains.[66] The forensic anthropologist can play a valuable role in the course of the exhumation of the bodies as well as during the period of mortuary examination after the bodies are removed from the mass grave. Forensic anthropology entails the application of methodology in physical anthropology to a medico-legal context. Forensic anthropological analysis generally involves the examination of human skeletal remains, although experts may also be trained in soft tissue anatomy. Their expertise is called upon to differentiate human skeletal remains from non-human material, provide estimation of sex, ancestry, living stature, age at death, estimate the post-mortem interval, provide an interpretation of taphonomic factors, document activity that may have been of a criminal nature, document ante-mortem trauma, distinguish ante-mortem injuries from peri-mortem and post-mortem damage to the body and record any other details that may assist in identification.[67]

Post-mortem analysis of both fleshed and skeletal remains by forensic pathologists and forensic anthropologists helps provide contextual analysis of the manner of death in war crime trials. Examination of wounds and wounding patterns can be revealing particularly when interpreted in conjunction with information on how the bodies were disposed; for example if disposed of in clandestine grave sites the evidence may point towards attempts to conceal unlawful death. Lethal use of force coupled with attempts to conceal and destroy the remains lends robust credence to prosecutorial theories that contend, for example, that the victims were unarmed civilians as opposed to legitimate combatants killed in armed confrontation.[68]

---

65 Debra Komar, 'Is Victim Identity in Genocide a Question of Science or Law? The scientific perspective, with special reference to Darfur' (2008) 48 *Science and Justice* 146–52.

66 'Forensic pathology', The Royal College of Pathologists, available at www.rcpath.org/index.asp?PageID=444. Accessed 18 April 2011.

67 Douglas H. Ubelaker, 'Evolution of the Relationship of Forensic Anthropology with Physical Anthropology and Forensic Pathology: A North American Perspective' (2006) 4 *Studies in Historical Anthropology* 199.

68 Jose Pablo Baraybar and Marek Gasior, 'Forensic Anthropology and the Most Probable Cause of Death in Cases of Violations against International

The crucial investigative decisions taken by international criminal tribunals – first, whether to instigate a forensic programme and second, how many graves should be exhumed – can be influenced by a number of factors, including whether and how the exhumations will contribute to the aims of the investigation, prosecutorial strategy and the availability of funding. Exhumations and what they entail in terms of logistics, personnel, equipment and running costs can be prohibitively expensive. Tribunals do not exhume mass graves for humanitarian reasons but rather the purpose of exhuming the bodies of the war dead is driven by a necessity to locate evidence to forensically prove a crime. To be clear, it is not and should not be the purpose of a tribunal to exhume, identify and repatriate *all* human remains relating to the conflict unless the demands of the criminal proceedings so require. Criminal tribunals have not the resources, the time nor the mandate to carry out this task. Criminal tribunals conduct exhumations with clear objectives in line with a strategy devised by the prosecution. These objectives seek to recover evidence that indicates the identity of the victims, establish circumstances and causes of death, link primary and secondary graves, uncover any attempts made to cover up the crime[69] and establish whether events as described in the indictments fit into the legal categorization being applied to the crime.[70] Forensic investigations are important as fulfilling these objectives and applying the evidence recovered to a prosecutorial case goes towards proving the crime base as well as indicating intent, motives and culpability of the accused.

3. HOW TRIBUNALS CAN ASSIST IN UPHOLDING INTERNATIONAL HUMANITARIAN LAW OBLIGATIONS TOWARDS THE DEAD

Outside the context of international criminal investigations, the motivation for organizing exhumations frequently fulfils a humanitarian mandate to recover and identify victims' remains and return them to their family and community who can then conduct culturally appropriate mortuary rituals, thus providing a form of closure for survivors. The two

---

Humanitarian Law: An Example from Bosnia and Herzegovina' (2006) 51(1) *Journal of Forensic Science* 103–8.

69 *ICTY Manual on Developed Practices* (n53) 17.

70 For example to prove that the category of decedents (civilians, combatants *hors de combat* etc.) and cause and manner of death (e.g. gunshot wounds and homicide) link evidentially to the charges made in the indictment e.g. that civilians were targeted for persecution and their deaths constitute a crime against humanity.

overall objectives of evidence-motivated investigations versus humanitarian searches are not necessarily mutually exclusive and both can be fulfilled in a complementary fashion.

During armed conflict the deceased may be immediately recovered and the remains treated according to the obligations outlined in IHL. However, not all bodies are treated with appropriate respect and some, particularly the remains of victims of war crimes or other violations of international law, may be disposed of in a clandestine manner. In countless conflicts, bodies of civilian and combatant decedents have been callously discarded into mass graves. As Adam Rosenblatt succinctly notes, the dead bodies that remain buried as a consequence of heinous crimes '[form] an underground map of atrocity that stretches across the planet's surface'.[71] The efforts required to search for, locate and recover these remains may overwhelm local capacity, particularly in circumstances where the national medico-legal system is rudimentary or has been disrupted due to the conflict. Through their investigatory activities, tribunals can play a role in fulfilling some of the obligations towards the deceased, in particular in the search for the dead and the subsequent identification of the deceased.

The ICTY has facilitated the recovery of human remains from the Yugoslav conflict in a number of ways. Firstly, the ICTY has cooperated with organizations functioning on the ground in the region and established a reciprocal relationship that has satisfied some of the needs of both the Tribunal and the humanitarian organizations working on identifying the missing. A number of dedicated organizations have been established in the region to operate under a purely humanitarian mandate to recover, identify and repatriate the remains of the war victims to their surviving families and communities. Prominent in fulfilling a role to ensure the cooperation of governments in the location and identification of the missing is the humanitarian organization the International Commission on Missing Persons (ICMP). The ICMP was established in 1996 at the initiative of US President Bill Clinton at the G-7 Summit in Lyon, France, and it utilizes DNA, as well as more traditional identification techniques, in the identification of large numbers of the war missing.[72] The ICTY

---

71 Rosenblatt (n21) 924.

72 International Commission on Missing Persons, website online at: http://www.ic-mp.org/. For an account of the search for the remains of the men missing following the Srebrenica massacre and the use of DNA in this endeavour see further, Sarah E. Wagner, *To Know Where he Lies: DNA Technology and the Search for Srebrenica's Missing* (Berkeley, CA: University of California Press, 2008).

has been able to utilize information compiled by the ICMP through its exhumation and identification work in order to calculate statistical data on the missing and dead from areas in the Balkans, notably those related to the fall of Srebrenica.[73] The ICTY has also utilized lists of missing persons compiled by the non-governmental organization Physicians for Human Rights, who conducted a number of exhumations on behalf of the ICTY.[74]

As discussed above, international organizations such as the ICRC have highlighted the imperative to retrieve the remains of the dead for reasons other than criminal justice requirements i.e. for the social, psychological and legal needs of the deceased's families and communities, and have instigated important programmes directed towards body recovery during periods of armed conflict and other mass casualty crises.[75] The work of the ICRC on reuniting families separated by conflict and disasters assists families in ascertaining what happened to their missing relatives, the fulfilment of this right to know thus alleviating the anguish of uncertainty.[76] For the former Yugoslavia, the ICRC gained access to information gathered by the ICTY that concerned closed cases or incidents not being used for trial purposes. The ICRC was able to analyse the information in order to select useful data for the clarification of the fate of missing persons, particularly 'indications of the locations of remains, lists of persons presumed dead and documentation on alleged grave sites'.[77]

Conversely, the Tribunal was able to utilize data compiled by the ICRC on missing persons and the deceased. Missing person lists have been described as 'an important component of the source material acquired and used by the OTP (Office of the Prosecutor) in all stages of [its] work, i.e. in investigation, trial preparation, trial and even post-trial (i.e. appeal)

---

73 Helge Brunborg, Ewa Tabeau and Arve Hetland, Office of the Prosecutor, International Criminal Tribunal for the Former Yugoslavia, *Missing and Dead from Srebrenica: The 2005 Report and List, Expert Report for the Case of Vujadin Popović et al. (IT-05-88)* 16 November 2005, available online at: http://www.icty.org/x/file/About/OTP/War_Demographics/en/popovic_srebrenica_050916.pdf

74 *Ibid.*

75 Morris Tidball-Binz (n15) 421–42.

76 International Committee of the Red Cross, 'Reuniting families separated by conflict and disasters' 29 October 2010, http://www.icrc.org/eng/what-we-do/reuniting-families/overview-reuniting-families.htm, last accessed 8 June 2011.

77 Monique Crettol and Anne-Marie La Rosa, 'The Missing and Transitional Justice: the Right to Know and the Fight Against Impunity' (2006) 88(862) *International Review of the Red Cross* 355–62, 359.

stage, are compared with other OTP sources related to victims of the IHL violations in question'.[78]

During the course of the investigatory phase, the lists are scrutinized for potential leads in connection with victims and incidents. The lists are also evaluated to ascertain crime patterns. The lists are further cross-referenced with associated sources on victims in order to establish the number of missing also reported dead and the circumstances of the deaths. Regarding the indictments, names of the missing have been frequently included as victims, based on the outcome of the investigation stage. Records of missing persons may be presented to the court during the trial phase as confirmed victims of incidents outlined in the indictment, as corroborated by other evidentiary sources. Missing person lists have also been used during the trial and appeal stage as a reference source for victims' names cited by witnesses, documents or by the Defence. ICRC lists of missing persons from Bosnia and Herzegovina have been valuable in trials at the Yugoslav Tribunal particularly in relation to Srebrenica cases such as *Krstić*,[79] *Blagojevic et al.*,[80] *Vujadin Popovic et al.*[81] and the *Slobodan Milosevic*[82] trial.[83] Individual cases from missing person lists were cross-referenced with cases reported in other sources that related to the same incidents, with the aim of ascertaining whether the missing individuals could be confirmed as victims or as survivors. The intention of this exercise was that the end result would mean an increase in 'the quantity and quality of OTP information about individual cases'.[84] This was required for 'trial purposes in the first place, but at the same time the end result of these searches can be beneficial to the families of the missing who can learn from these results about the fate of the missing'.[85]

Second, although the ICTY only conducted exhumations for evidentiary

---

78 Ewa Tabeau, 'ICRC lists of missing persons as part of the OTP information system on victims of IHL violations committed in the 1990s conflict in the former Yugoslavia', in Maria Teresa Dutli and Noreen Majeed (eds), *Report of the Second Universal Meeting of National Committees on International Humanitarian Law, Geneva, 10–21 March 1997, Legal Measures and Mechanisms to Prevent Disappearances, to Establish the Fate of Missing Persons, and to Assist Their Families* (Geneva: ICRC, September 2007, 162).

79 *Prosecutor v. Radislav Krstić*, Case No. IT-98-33.

80 *Prosecutor v. Vidoje Blagojevic and Dragon Jokic*, Case No. IT-02-60-T.

81 *Prosecutor v. Vujadin Popović, Ljubiša Beara, Drago Nikolić, Ljubomir Borovĉanin. Radivoje Miletić, Milan Gvero, Vinko Pandurević*, Case No.IT-05-88-T.

82 *Prosecutor v. Slobodan Milosovic*, Case No. IT-02-54.T.

83 Tabeau (n78), 168, n78.

84 *Ibid.*, 163.

85 *Ibid.*

purposes,[86] these activities contributed to the humanitarian endeavours to locate and identify remains. Even though the forensic activity was initially conducted as part of a criminal investigation, exhumations uncovered valuable information which the national authorities and humanitarian organizations operating in the region have been able to utilize in the search for the dead and missing. In some cases suspected grave sites transpired not to contain human remains, or were considered irrelevant to the Tribunal's on-going investigations; however, the site excavations nonetheless 'served a valuable purpose because they helped to inform relatives that their loved ones were not in the place they were thought to be'.[87]

Another manner in which the ICTY has contributed to national efforts to locate and identify the missing is through the transfer of specialized material to relevant organizations in the Balkans. When the forensic programme of the Tribunal was drawn to a close in accordance with the initial completion strategy of the Tribunal, valuable resources were transferred to organizations working in the area:

> In support of initial completion strategy activities, the General Services Section planned and organized the orderly closure of the forensics programme of the Office of the Prosecutor and the Tribunal's field offices in Skopje, Macedonia and Pristina, Kosovo. Surplus assets, including special equipment and vehicles, were transferred to agencies with compatible mandates such as UNMIK, the International Commission on Missing Persons and the European Union Police Mission in Bosnia and Herzegovina.[88]

However, satisfactorily fulfilling the needs of the criminal justice system and the needs of the families can pose some challenges and it can be difficult to strike a balance between both sets of interests.[89] Exploring the friction between the requirements of victims' families and the war crime

---

[86] As expressed by the first chief prosecutor of the Yugoslav tribunal, Richard Goldstone: 'We are only interested in grave sites relevant to our indictment or indictments we may issue in future. It is not our business to exhume mass graves other than for forensic reasons relating to prosecution charges', ICTY – Bulletin No 8.

[87] ICTY Manual on Developed Practices (n53) 17.

[88] Eleventh Annual Report of the International Tribunal for the Prosecution of Persons Responsible for Serious Violations of International Humanitarian Law Committed in the Territory of the Former Yugoslavia since 1991, UN Doc A/59/215.S/2004/627, 16 August 2004, para 388.

[89] Eric Stover and Rachel Shigekane, 'The Missing in the Aftermath of War: When do the Needs of Victims' Families and International War Crimes Tribunals Clash?' (2002) 84(848) *International Review of the Red Cross* 845; Eric Stover and Rachel Shigekane, 'Exhumation of Mass Graves: Balancing Legal and Humanitarian Needs' in Eric Stover and Harvey M. Weinstein (eds) *My*

tribunals, Stover and Shigekane have highlighted that '[i]deally, the relationship between the families of the missing and international war crimes tribunals should be symbiotic, benefiting both the relatives *and* the courts but, in reality, it rarely is'.[90] Discussing exhumations relating to the graves of Srebrenica the authors convey that:

> Rather that initiating or encouraging another international entity to make a long-term effort to identify the Srebrenica victims, the OTP opted to turn over the remains to local forensic scientists who lacked both the resources and skills to do efficient investigative work themselves and thus set back the identification process by years.[91]

It must be remembered, however, that the work of the Yugoslav Tribunal was in many ways unprecedented. The Tribunal was a unique institution composed of staff from a multitude of different countries and jurisdictional backgrounds. In 1996, the year the forensic programme commenced, the chief Prosecutor Richard Goldstone's then staff of 180 personnel – lawyers, police and military investigators, computer technicians, administrative assistants and analysts – came from almost 40 countries. As Goldstone revealed '[t]hat has never been done before; it was not done at Nuremberg . . . This is the first time in history that there has been an international prosecutor's office investigating international war crimes.'[92] The forensic investigations conducted for the *ad hoc* tribunals were a learning curve for all involved. As voiced by one of the forensic anthropologists working in the Balkans exhuming graves for the Yugoslav Tribunal:

> This is a new thing for all of us . . . Archaeologists have experience digging up many skeletons, but exhuming decomposing bodies in situations like we have here poses new problems and ways of approaching them.[93]

Likewise, there was no existing template to guide the relationship between the Tribunal and humanitarian organizations which sought to recover the

---

Neighbour, My Enemy: Justice and Community in the Aftermath of Mass Atrocity (Cambridge: CUP, 2004) 85.

90 Stover and Shigekane, 'The Missing in the Aftermath of War' (n83) 847.

91 *Ibid.* 856.

92 Richard Goldstone, 'Assessing the Work of the United Nations War Crimes Tribunal' (Address of the Honorable Justice Richard Goldstone, Former Chief Prosecutor for the *Ad Hoc* International Tribunals for the Former Yugoslavia and Rwanda, and Justice of the Constitutional Court of South Africa, Stanford Law School, October 12, 1996) (1997) 33(1) *Stanford J. Int'l L.* 1, 4–5.

93 Quote from William Haglund, speaking to Stover in Eric Stover and Gilles Peress, *The Graves: Srebrenica and Vukovar* (Zurich/Berlin/New York: Scalo, 1998) 154–5.

war dead. Practice developed through experience gained on the ground. Whilst mistakes may have been made, the knowledge gained over the course of the life of the Tribunal will make a valuable contribution to future forensic investigations conducted by other international institutions. In this way the forensic programme of the ICTY and the synergy formed with humanitarian organizations working in accordance with the obligations toward the dead as outlined in international humanitarian law forms an important legacy of this institution.

4. CONCLUSION

The obligations codified in international humanitarian law regarding the war dead are of considerable importance as the consequences of impropriety to the dead can result in detrimental effects on the living. Rules guiding the appropriate conduct towards the dead in the aftermath of war have evolved over centuries, with the need to treat the dead with respect and to facilitate the mourning and grief of the families and communities of the deceased recognized by states, non-governmental organizations and civil society. In more recent years bodies of the war dead come to have instrumental value as post-mortem examinations of the bodies of victims recovered from clandestine burial sites can provide valuable evidence at war crimes trials. The principles underpinning the rules pertaining to the dead remain, however, of a humanitarian intent.

Looking to the future, it is highly likely that forensic investigations will continue to be a feature of international criminal justice mechanisms, including the International Criminal Court (ICC). The desirability of maintaining a forensic programme that simultaneously can contribute to humanitarian obligations towards the deceased and their families has been observed by the ICRC in the context of the work of the ICC. In a statement submitted at the Review Conference of the Assembly of State Parties, the Committee highlighted the importance of:

> . . . the role of justice mechanisms – including the ICC – in the effective realisation of the 'Right to know' what has happened to one's loved ones. Many victims of armed conflicts tell the ICRC that what they want to know, above all, is the fate and whereabouts of their loved ones who have disappeared. The work carried out by judicial mechanisms, including forensics activities such as exhumations, can be particularly valuable and relevant in this regard.[94]

---

[94] *The impact of the Rome Statute system on victims and affected communities, Statement submitted by the International Committee of the Red Cross*, 1 June 2010,

The examples outlined in this chapter concerning the obligations towards the dead from armed conflicts and the practice of the ICTY demonstrate that when a reasonable level of cooperation is established between an international tribunal and humanitarian agencies established to locate, identify and repatriate the missing from armed conflict, a symbiotic relationship can be established that satisfies the requirements of both the legal system and broader societal needs. The experiences of the ICTY and its working relationship with organizations in the former Yugoslavia is specific to this context but it does demonstrate *how* the work of tribunals can help fulfil the humanitarian obligations of states. The ICTY has contributed to efforts to locate and identify the deceased and missing through information sharing and national capacity building. In this way it represents an important legacy of the work of this institution.

---

available online at: http://www.icc-cpi.int/iccdocs/asp_docs/RC2010/Stocktaking/RC-StocktakingVictims-ICRC-statement-ENG.pdf

7. Forgotten rights: Consequences of the Israeli occupation of the Golan Heights

Ray Murphy*

The area known as the Golan Heights is a mountainous region and plateau in southwest Syria. The overall landmass of the Golan Heights is 1860 square kilometres, which is approximately one per cent of the total landmass of Syria.[1] Reference to 'the Golan Heights' has typically described the portion of the Syrian Golan that has been occupied by Israel since 1967.[2]

Successive Israeli governments have adopted a number of policies to control and contain the Syrian population since Israel began its occupation. Numerous villages have been destroyed, thousands driven from their homes, private and public property expropriated, the remaining Arab villages have been prevented from expanding and the free movement of people curtailed. In 1981, Israel enacted legislation that purported to annex the territory.[3] This move was widely condemned.[4]

This chapter outlines the background to the occupation and the consequences for the local population. It examines the action of the Israeli authorities and argues that certain practices by the Israeli Defence Forces constitute war crimes, which in some cases, may amount to grave breaches of the Fourth Geneva Convention governing the protection of civilians.

---

* Based on Ray Murphy and Declan Gannon, 'Changing the Landscape: Israel's Gross Violations of International Law in the Occupied Syrian Golan' (2008) 11 *Yearbook of International Humanitarian Law,* 139–74, and a report by Al-Marsad (2008).

[1] Permanent Mission of the Syrian Arab Republic to the UN, 'The Syrian Golan' available online at: http://www.un.int/syria/golan.htm.

[2] *Ibid.*

[3] Golan Heights Law, Israeli Ministry of Foreign Affairs, 14 December 1981, available online at: http://www.mfa.gov.il/MFA/Peace+Process/Guide+to+the+Peace+Process/Golan+Heights+Law.htm.

[4] UN Security Council Resolution 497 (1981) UN Doc S/Res/497, 17 December 1981.

Source: United Nations website.

Fig. 7.1 Israel, Occupied Golan, West Bank and Gaza

1. THE OCCUPIED SYRIAN GOLAN: BACKGROUND

The Syrian Golan region is important for a number of reasons. From a military perspective, the Golan offers geo-strategic value with commanding positions, overlooking much of southern Lebanon, Syria and northern Israel. From an agricultural perspective, the Syrian Golan is a fertile volcanic plateau.[5] Following Israel's occupation, Israeli agricultural settlements have been established and are producing wine, beef, fruit and mineral water for the Israeli domestic and export market.[6] The Syrian Golan is also a vital source of water for the region.[7] Israel harvests all the water from the Banyas River, estimated at 121 million cubic metres per year.[8] Exploitation of water resources by Israeli companies, Tahal and Mekerot, is having a dramatic effect on the livelihoods of the Arab population and their agricultural yields.[9] According to reports, the Occupied Golan is now supplying Israel with a third of its water consumption.[10]

Israel viewed the Golan as a Syrian military stronghold that posed a serious threat to Israel's security.[11] A further factor in compounding the tensions was the belief of Israel's former Prime Minister Ben-Gurion that the Golan Heights and parts of south-western Syria were part of biblical Palestine and ought to be restored by historical and religious right to the state of Israel.[12]

After the Six Day War of 1967, tensions remained high in the Middle East.[13] Then on 6 October 1973, to Israel's surprise, both Syria and Egypt

---

[5] Sakr Abu Fakhr, 'Voices from the Golan' (2000) 29(4) *Journal of Palestine Studies* 6.

[6] UN General Assembly, Economic and Social Council Report (2007) UN Doc A/62/75-E/2007/13, 3 May 2007, para 68.

[7] David W. Lesch, *The New Lion of Damascus: Bashar al-Asad and Modern Syria* (New Haven and London: Yale University Press, 2005) 20.

[8] UN General Assembly, *Report of the Special Committee to Investigate Israeli Practices Affecting the Human Rights of the Palestinian People and Other Arabs of the Occupied Territories* (2006) UN Doc A/61/500, 9 October 2006, para 84.

[9] *Ibid.*

[10] UN General Assembly Economic and Social Council Report (n6) para 72.

[11] Mitchell Bard, 'The Golan Heights' (Jewish Virtual Library 2008) available online at: http://www.jewishvirtuallibrary.org/jsource/Peace/golan_hts.html.

[12] Moshe Shemesh, 'Prelude to the Six Day War: the Arab-Israeli Struggle Over Water Resources' (2004) 9(3) *Israel Studies* 1, 2.

[13] For an Israeli perspective, see Chaim Herzog, *The Arab Israeli Wars* (London: Arms and Armour Press, 1982) 285–306.

launched a coordinated attack.[14] Syria's attempt to recapture the Golan ultimately proved unsuccessful and in 1974, Syria and Israel signed an armistice agreement.[15] In the negotiations that followed, Israel conceded some territory captured in 1967, including Qunaytra, which the Israelis destroyed as they withdrew.[16] A demilitarized zone that runs north–south along the eastern edge of the Occupied Golan was also established and a UN peacekeeping force deployed to monitor the disengagement agreement.[17]

Proponents of Israel's continued presence in the area consider that the Syrian Golan is of 'little military importance' so long as it remains in the hands of Israel or its allies.[18] If controlled by a country hostile to Israel, however, some believe that the area has the potential to be a strategic threat to Israel.[19] In an era of advanced missile and rocket systems, such arguments have less weight.

Prior to occupation, the Golan was somewhat ethnically and religiously diverse, with Syrian Arabs constituting the majority of the population.[20] The most serious impact suffered by the local population subsequent to Israel's occupation in 1967 was the 'uprooting and expulsion of the local Syrian population.'[21] According to reports it is estimated that up to 130 000[22] people were displaced as a result of the conflict and that those

---

14 Anton La Guardia, *Holy Land Unholy War: Israelis and Palestinians* (London: John Murray, 2001) 126; Jimmy Carter, *Palestine: Peace Not Apartheid* (London: Pocket Books, 2007) 34.

15 'Regions and Territories: The Golan Heights' *BBC News*, 15 January 2008, available online at: http://news.bbc.co.uk/2/hi/middle_east/country_profiles/3393813.stm.

16 La Guardia (n14) 129.

17 Lesch (n7) 22. The UN Disengagement Observer Force (UNDOF) was established in 1974 in order to supervise the Agreement between Israel and Syria – see http://www.un.org/Depts/dpko/missions/undof/.

18 Bard (n11).

19 Eyal Zisser, 'June 1967: Israel's Capture of the Golan Heights' (2002) 7(1) *Israel Studies* 168, 170.

20 Abu Fakhr (n5) 5–6. Prior to its capture, 153 000 people lived in the Syrian Golan. During the 1967 War, Israel successfully captured 70 per cent of the area that contained approximately 139 villages and 61 farms. Before 1967, only 6 per cent of the Golan population was Druze.

21 Al-Marsad, United Nations Periodic Report to the Committee on the Elimination of Racial Discrimination, available online at: http://www.golan-marsad.org/pdfs/Periodicreport.pdf.

22 *Syria: Forty Years On, People Displaced From The Golan Remain in Waiting* (2007) IDMC Internal Displaced Monitoring Centre, available online at: http://www.internal-displacement.org/8025708F004BE3B1/(httpInfoFiles)/11354A1A3BE82407C12573850037B6C6/$file/Syria_IDPs_Overview_Oct07.pdf.

displaced and their descendents now number in the region of 500 000.[23] Most of those expelled in 1967 were unable to return.

Today approximately 18 000 indigenous Syrian people remain in the Occupied Syrian Golan, mostly members of the Islamic Druze sect who have retained Syrian nationality.[24] The Occupied Golan also contains a community of about 17 000 Israeli-Jewish settlers.[25] Another report suggests that the number is somewhere between 18 000 and 20 000, while the number of illegal Israeli settlements constructed since 1967 is approximately 37.[26]

Following the capture of the region in 1967, the Israeli government handed all necessary power to its military commanders to control and administer the occupied territory. In 1981, Israel ended military rule with the enactment of the Golan Heights Law.[27] This legislation purported to annex the occupied territory to the state of Israel, a move comprehensively denounced by the international community.[28]

2. ISRAELI ACTIONS IN THE OCCUPIED SYRIAN GOLAN

Since Israel began its occupation in 1967, it has carried out numerous actions that have violated a number of the basic norms of international law. These actions have deliberately and negatively impacted on the local Syrian population. The depopulation of the native inhabitants was the first major abuse perpetrated in the Golan. Prior to the occupation, the Syrian Golan contained approximately 153 000 inhabitants; following the capture of 70 per cent of the territory by Israel, approximately 130 000 were forcibly transferred or displaced to Syria proper[29] and forbidden

---

23 See the Permanent Mission of the Syrian Arab Republic to the UN (n1).

24 International Labour Conference, Report of the Director-General, *The Situation of Workers of the Occupied Arab Territories*, 97th session (Geneva: ILO, 2008) para 86.

25 *Ibid.*, para 19.

26 See UN Security Council, *Report of the Secretary-General on the Middle East* (2006) UN Doc S/2006/956, 11 December 2006, para 39; see also 'Facts about Golan Heights, Disputed Between Israel and Syria', *International Herald Tribune* (21 May 2008) available online at: http://www.iht.com/articles/ap/2008/05/21/africa/ME-GEN-Israel-Syria-Glance.php.

27 Golan Heights Law (n3).

28 Eyal Benvenisti, *The International Law of Occupation* (Princeton, NJ: Princeton University Press 2004) 114.

29 IDMC, Internal Displaced Monitoring Centre (n22).

from returning. The remaining Syrian population was located in six villages situated at the far north of the Golan. These villages were Majdal Shams, Masa'da, Bqa'atha, 'Ein Qinyeh, Al Ghajar and Su'heita. In 1967 Su'heita was partially destroyed and a military post built in its place. It was completely destroyed in 1971–2 and its population forcibly transferred to the neighbouring town of Masa'da.[30]

Israel succeeded in depopulating the Golan through a number of measures, including a regime of Military Orders that were introduced to administer the newly occupied territory. For example, Military Order 39, 27 August 1967 ordered that 101 villages in the Occupied Golan be declared closed military zones. No one was allowed to enter the villages listed without special permission and those who violated this order were subject to punishment of five years' imprisonment or a fine of 5000 Israeli Liras, or both.[31] This framework of military orders provided a mechanism to enforce the depopulation by prohibiting those who had been forcibly transferred, displaced or who had fled the conflict, from returning to their place of residence.

The focus of this article is on one village, 'Jubata Ez-Zeit', which had a population of between 1500 and 2000 prior to the 1967 War. At the end of June 1967, the Israeli occupying forces forcibly transferred the entire population of the village. Hammood Maray, a resident of the neighbouring town of Majdal Shams, recalls what happened:

> *Hammood Maray from Majdal Shams, Occupied Syrian Golan*
> *Al-Marsad Affidavit*
> *Extract 1.3*
> During the war in 1967 roughly about half the people from Jubata Ez-Zeit left their village and came to Majdal Shams to hide because it was perceived to be a safe place, because it was high in the mountain. They had left Jubata because they were afraid of the war. After the war the Israeli military occupied the village of Jubata and began to forcibly transfer the people who had remained in Jubata, the people who had left Jubata and tried to return once they thought it was safe were also transferred. The Israeli army began shooting in the air and towards the people, all the time, to frighten the people of Jubata, to transfer the people from the village. After the transfer Jubata became a closed military area; nobody could return.

---

30 Appendix: 'Testimonies from the Occupied Golan Heights' (1979) 8(3) *Journal of Palestine Studies* 128. The original inhabitants of Su'heita are still fighting for the right to return to their village.

31 Israel Defence Forces and Defence Ministry Archive (IDFA) Military Organisation Orders, Military Order No. 39, 27 August 1967. See appendix for unofficial English translation of Military Order No. 39.

2.1 The Destruction of Villages and Farms

With thousands of people forced to leave the Occupied Golan and unable to return (an estimated 130 000 people), the Israeli military were, for the most part, unopposed in their administration of the newly occupied territory and began a widespread campaign that destroyed numerous villages and farms. Israeli settlements were then built in a number of places over destroyed Arab villages and farms, and in so doing control was taken of the land and resources.

Hayel Abu Jabal from neighbouring Majdal Shams, describes what happened.

> *Hayel Abu Jabal – Al-Marsad Affidavit*
> *Extract 1.5*
> The people from Jubata Ez-Zeit were afraid, some of the people came to Majdal Shams to hide. The Israeli army came to Majdal Shams and found the people from Jubata hiding here. The army than began ordering the people to return to Jubata, those who didn't return and remained in Majdal Shams were eventually transferred from Majdal Shams, out of the Golan, to other parts of Syria. The people who returned to Jubata that were hiding in Majdal Shams were also transferred on their return; they were tricked by the Israeli army into thinking they could return to their villages. After some days after the conclusion of the war, a week or two weeks, the village of Jubata Ez-Zeit was destroyed by the Israeli army.

2.2 Transfer of Israeli Population into Occupied Territory

Illegal settlements have become a means used by the Israeli government to establish physical and demographic obstacles to a withdrawal from occupied territory by creating 'facts on the ground'.[32] As early as 1969, Moshe Dayan spoke of his belief in developing Israeli possessions in the Occupied Territories:

> Israel should establish Jewish and Israeli possessions in the administered areas throughout, not just the Golan, and not just with the intention of withdrawing there. These should not be tent camps which are set up and taken down. With this in mind, we should establish possession in areas from which we will not withdraw in accord with our view of the map.[33]

---

[32] UN Security Council, *Report of the Secretary-General on the Middle East* (n26) para 6.

[33] Moshe Dayan, former Israeli Chief of Staff and later Defence Minister, cited in Martin Gilbert, *Israel: A History* (London: Black Swan, 1999) 405.

One of the largest of the approximately 37 Israeli settlements in the Golan is Katsrin, with a population of 5000 people. These settlements, and the use and exploitation of Syrian land and resources, would appear to amount to what has been described as:

> [a] form of colonialism of the kind declared to be a denial of fundamental human rights and contrary to the Charter of the United Nations as recalled in the General Assembly's Declaration on the Granting of Independence to Colonial Countries and Peoples.[34]

The presence of Israeli settlements and their continued expansion inside occupied territory, including that of the Syrian Golan, represents a major obstacle to lasting peace in the Middle East. Settlements further represent a clear violation of international humanitarian law and international human rights law.

Taiseer Maray explains the Israeli settlement programme in the Occupied Golan and in particular the settlement of Neve Ativ, which is built on the destroyed Arab village of Jubata Ez-Zeit.

> *Taiseer Maray from Majdal Shams, Occupied Syrian Golan*
> *Al-Marsad Affidavit*
> *Extract 1.7*
> The settlement of Merom Golan was the first Israeli settlement in the Occupied Syrian Golan . . . The Israeli Jewish settlements have confiscated all the land of the Arab villages and they now use this land and exploit all the resources such as water. Another thing is that they limit the development of the remaining Arab villages; I'm speaking about physically, because the settler land is very close to my village and we cannot expand or build out because the settler land is blocking us. Another thing, the Israeli government gives them a lot of support in agriculture and now they are competing with us. They produce the same apples like ours, the Israeli government gives them lots of support, financial and scientific support, we are completely left behind . . .

3. THE STATUS OF THE SYRIAN GOLAN UNDER INTERNATIONAL LAW

Under the laws of occupation, occupation is considered a temporary condition, and the law places an obligation on the Occupying Power to act in a manner which has been described as 'fiduciary', that is to say, as

---

[34] John Dugard, 'Report of the Special Rapporteur on the situation of human rights in the Palestinian territories occupied since 1967', UN Doc A/HRC/4/17, 29 January 2007, para 60.

administrator of public property and natural resources, and of the existing laws and form of government and penal system in the occupied region.[35] In keeping with the principle that occupation is intended to be temporary, customary international law prohibits unilateral annexation of territory, particularly where a conflict is continuous, and even where the government of the occupied territory does not participate actively in military operations.[36]

The relevant question in determining the applicability of the laws of occupation is one of fact. When a situation exists that factually amounts to an occupation, i.e., when territory comes under the effective control of the Occupying Power, the laws of occupation are applicable.[37] These laws are motivated primarily by humanitarian considerations. The Fourth Geneva Convention provides that persons who are in occupied territory and protected under the Convention's provisions 'may not be deprived, in any case or in any manner whatsoever' of the protections of the Convention, notwithstanding any changes to the government of the territory, any agreement between the authorities of the occupied territory and the occupier, or by annexation.[38] Thus, independent of the legality of the occupation, the 1907 Hague Regulations and Fourth Geneva Convention are meant to apply and to protect humanitarian principles.

Despite the clear factual grounds for the application of the laws of occupation, Israel has thwarted these laws in two particular ways: first, by failing to recognize the *de jure* application of the Hague Regulations and Fourth Geneva Convention in the Syrian Golan, and secondly, by its *de facto* annexation of the Syrian Golan in 1981.[39]

---

[35] Nicholas F. Lancaster, 'Occupation Law, Sovereignty, and Political Transformation: Should the Hague Regulations and the Fourth Geneva Convention Still Be Considered Customary International Law?' (2006) 189 *Military L. Rev.* 51 at 54 and see Christopher Greenwood, 'The Administration of Occupied Territory in International Law', in Emma Playfair (ed.) *International Law and the Administration of Occupied Territories* (Oxford: OUP, 1992) 241 and Kathleen Cavanaugh, 'The Israeli Military Court System in the West Bank and Gaza' (2007) 12(2) *Journal of Conflict and Security Law* 197.

[36] Adam Roberts, 'Transformative Military Occupation: Applying the Laws of War and Human Rights' (2006) 100 *AJIL*, 580, 583.

[37] *Case Concerning Armed Activities on the Territory of the Congo (Democratic Republic of the Congo v. Uganda)* Judgment, 19 December 2005 (2005) ICJ Reports 168, paras 167–80.

[38] Geneva Convention Relative to the Protection of Civilian Persons in Time of War (12 August 1949, entered into force 21 October 1950) 75 UNTS 287, Art. 47.

[39] See Benvenisti (n28) 107–48 and UN Security Council Resolution 497(1981) (n4). Thomas Davenport, 'A Study of Israel's Occupation of the Golan Heights'

Article 42 of the 1907 Hague Regulations (hereinafter Hague Regulations) defines occupation as follows:

> Territory is considered occupied when it is actually placed under the authority of the hostile army. The occupation extends only to territory where such authority has been established and can be exercised.[40]

The International Criminal Tribunal for the Former Yugoslavia (ICTY) adopted guidelines to determine whether the authority of the Occupying Power has actually been established.[41] Applying these guidelines to the situation in the Syrian Golan since 1967, this territory may be considered occupied for the following reasons:

- Israel had effective control over the territory in the Golan it was occupying, Syrian authority was ineffective and Israel was in a position to substitute its authority for that of Syria.
- Syrian forces in the Golan were defeated during the 1967 War and the Israeli army did not encounter any significant military resistance to the occupation until the 1973 so-called Yom Kippur War (when Syrian forces were again defeated).[42]
- Israel maintains a substantial military presence in the region (many Israeli training facilities and camps are located in the Occupied Golan) fulfilling the requirement to have troops present or the capacity to send troops within a reasonable time to the Occupied Territory to enforce the authority of the Occupying Power.
- Israel provided its military commanders in the Golan with legislative authority to administer the occupied territory; this regime was subsequently replaced by the Golan Heights Law which purported to annex the territory into the state of Israel.[43]
- Israel began issuing directions to the local population in the early days of the occupation by means of Military Orders. These Orders

---

(Unpublished LL.M. thesis) Irish Centre for Human Rights, National University of Ireland, Galway, 2008. For analysis of the jurisprudence of the Israeli Supreme Court relating to the occupied territories, see David Kretzmer, *The Occupation of Justice –The Supreme Court of Israel and the Occupied Territories* (New York: State University of New York Press, 2002).

[40] Convention (IV) Respecting the Laws and Customs of War by Land [1910] UKTS 9, annex (hereinafter, 'Hague Regulations') Art. 42.

[41] *Prosecutor v. Naletilić and Martinović*, Judgment, Case No. IT-98-34-T, 31 March 2003, para 217.

[42] Herzog (n13) 285–306.

[43] Golan Heights Law (n3).

were replaced by Israeli civil laws in 1981 when Israel purported to annex the Occupied Golan, thus fulfilling the final indicator adopted by the ICTY for determining whether the authority of the Occupying Power has actually been established.

Israel rejects the notion that the Syrian Golan is still an occupied territory, basing its claims to sovereignty on its purported annexation pursuant to the 1981 legislative act – the Golan Heights Law.[44] This law placed the Occupied Golan under Israeli civilian law, effectively extending Israel's laws and jurisdiction to the Occupied Golan, and granting the people residing there status as permanent residents of Israel. Israel outlined its position to the ILO in the following terms:

> The ILO mission is meant to collect material for the Director-General's Report on the occupied Arab territories. It is the position of the Government of Israel that the Golan, to which Israeli law, jurisdiction and administration have been applied, is not now such an area. In view of this consideration, approval for a visit of the ILO mission to the Golan was given as a gesture of goodwill and without prejudice. The decision to facilitate such an informal visit shall not serve as a precedent and does not contravene the Israeli Government's position.[45]

On 17 December 1981, the UN Security Council declared the Israeli decision to impose its laws, jurisdiction and administration in the occupied Syrian Golan Heights as 'null and void' in Resolution 497.[46]

Since 1981, the UN has refused to recognize Israel's claim to the Golan and has adopted a series of resolutions to this effect. In January 2008, the General Assembly adopted Resolution 62/85.[47] This reaffirmed the 'fundamental principle of the inadmissibility of the acquisition of territory by force' and the applicability of the Fourth Geneva Convention to the Occupied Golan.

The UN General Assembly also declared that 'Israel has failed to comply with Security Council resolution 497' and that Israel's decision to impose its laws on the Syrian Golan 'is null and void and has no validity whatsoever.'[48] A number of other bodies also condemned Israel's occupation and annexation of the Syrian Golan. The League of Arab States

---

44 *Ibid.*

45 International Labour Conference, Report of the Director-General, 2008 (n24) 1.

46 UN Security Council Resolution 497 (1981) (n4).

47 UN UN GA Res 62/85 (2008) UN Doc A/Res/62/85, 21 January 2008.

48 *Ibid.*

has on numerous occasions expressed its disapproval of Israel's efforts to change the legal, physical and demographic character of the Occupied Syrian Golan.[49] In a recent resolution, the UN Human Rights Council took a similar position. The Council stated that Israel's annexation of the territory was illegal and called on Israel to refrain from 'changing the physical character, demographic composition, institutional structure and legal status of the Occupied Syrian Golan'.[50] In another resolution the Council called for all the displaced population to be allowed return to their homes and reclaim their properties.[51]

Israel's purported annexation of the Syrian Golan is illegal and a violation of Article 2(4) of the UN Charter[52] and the principle of customary international law prohibiting the acquisition of territory by threat or use of force. The customary status of this principle was recently confirmed by the International Court of Justice in its *Advisory Opinion on the Legal Consequences of the Construction of a Wall in Occupied Palestinian Territory*.[53] The commentary on the Fourth Geneva Convention also confirms this line of reasoning and offers the opinion that the occupation of territory during wartime is:

> . . . essentially a temporary *de facto* situation, which deprives the Occupied Power of neither its statehood nor its sovereignty; it merely interferes with its powers to exercise its rights. That is what distinguishes occupation from annexation, whereby the Occupying Power acquires all or part of the occupied territory and incorporates it in its own territory.[54]

As occupied territory, the Syrian Golan enjoys a specific legal status in international law, governed by the law of belligerent occupation. The relevant provisions are enshrined in the Hague Regulations, the Fourth Geneva Convention and certain provisions of the Protocol 1 of 1977

---

49 Arab League Resolution, March 2006, as cited in IDMC Internal Displaced Monitoring Centre (n22) 8.

50 UN General Assembly (2007) UN Doc A/HRC/Res/2/3 – A/HRC/2/9, 22 March 2007.

51 *Ibid.*

52 Art. 2(4) of the UN Charter states: 'All Members shall refrain in their international relations from the threat or use of force against the territorial integrity or political independence of any state, or in any manner inconsistent with the Purposes of the UN.'

53 *Legal Consequences of the Construction of a Wall in the Occupied Palestinian Territory* Advisory Opinion, 2004 ICJ Reports 136, para 87.

54 Jean Pictet (ed.) *International Committee for the Red Cross (ICRC) Commentary: Geneva Convention IV Relative to the Protection of Civilian Persons in Time of War (*Geneva: ICRC, 1958) 275.

Additional to the Geneva Conventions of 1949.[55] Israel has recognized the application of the Hague Regulations to some of the territories it occupies, but has never fully acquiesced to their application in the Syrian Golan, which it has effectively annexed.[56] Nor has Israel recognized the application of the Fourth Geneva Convention there.[57] With regard to the Hague Regulations, Israel's primary justification for its position is that the Hague Regulations are part of customary international law. According to the Israeli Supreme Court, if the Hague Regulations are part of customary international law, they apply to the occupied territories, but only insofar as they comport with Israeli law. Israel's position seems to be, then, that it is in compliance with the Hague Regulations as part of customary international law, even though the Hague Regulations do not apply *de jure* in the Syrian Golan, and only when they do not conflict with Israeli law.[58]

Israel has rejected the *de jure* application of the Fourth Geneva Convention in the Syrian Golan. It has, however, indicated that it will abide by the 'humanitarian provisions' of the Convention and some scholars argue that the Fourth Geneva Convention's formal applicability is of little relevance, given Israel's willingness to abide by its 'humanitarian provisions.'[59] This position is unsatisfactory; without formal application of the Convention or definition of what it considers 'humanitarian provisions', Israel's accountability under the Convention's standards is tenuous at best.

In contrast to Israel's position, there is agreement amongst the international community regarding the applicability of the Fourth Geneva Convention in territory occupied by Israel since 1967. The International Court of Justice confirmed that it considered the Convention applicable

---

55 Hague Regulations (n40); Geneva Convention IV Relative to the Protection of Civilian Persons in Time of War (adopted 12 August 1948, entered into force 21 October 1950) 75 UNTS 287 (hereinafter, 'Fourth Geneva Convention'); Protocol 1 Additional to the Geneva Conventions of the 12 August 1949, and Relating to the Victims of International Armed Conflict (adopted 8 June 1977, entered into force 7 December 1978) 1125 UNTS 3 (hereinafter, 'Additional Protocol 1').

56 Adam Roberts, 'Prolonged Military Occupation: The Israeli-Occupied Territories Since 1967' (1990) 84 *AJIL* 44, 53.

57 Lancaster (n35) 72.

58 See *Jama'iat Iscan v. Commander of the IDF in Judea and Samaria* 37 (4) PD 785, 792 (1983); *Suleyman Tawfiq Oyyeb and ors v. The Minister of Defence and others*, High Court of Justice (HCJ) 606, 610/78, 15 March 1979, reprinted in (1985) 2 *Palestine Yearbook of International Law* 134–50, esp. 141–2; *Bassil Abu Aita v. The Regional Commander of Judea and Samaria*, HCJ. 69/81, 4 April 1983, sections 10 and 11.

59 Roberts (n56) 62.

in *any* territory occupied in the event of an armed conflict between two or more High Contracting Parties.[60] Both Syria and Israel were parties to the Convention when the armed conflict broke out in 1967. Consequently, Israel has certain legal obligations as the Occupying Power that it must uphold and respect, while the peoples occupied (the indigenous Syrian population) are afforded the rights of protected persons according to the provisions enshrined in the Fourth Geneva Convention. This is highlighted in Article 4(1) of the Fourth Geneva Convention.[61]

International human rights law is also applicable to the Occupied Syrian Golan. In principle, international human rights law applies at all times, both during peacetime and in situations of armed conflict. Both international human rights law and international humanitarian law are complementary branches of law. However, some human rights treaties permit governments to derogate from certain rights provisions in times of extreme public emergency where the perceived life of the nation might be in danger. Such derogation, however, is guided by strict guidelines, which includes that a state must act proportionally to the crisis. The derogation cannot be enforced on a discriminatory basis and it must not contravene other rules of international law. Accordingly, there are a number of principles of international human rights law that a state may never derogate from, regardless of the situation.[62]

4. VIOLATIONS OF INTERNATIONAL LAW IN THE OCCUPIED SYRIAN GOLAN

4.1 Forcible Transfer and Deportation

Following the 1967 war and Israel's capture and subsequent occupation of the Syrian Golan, approximately 130000 people were forced to leave their place of residence and were prohibited from returning. It is not surprising that the deportation and transfer prohibitions under international

---

60 *ICJ Advisory Opinion on the Construction of a Wall in Occupied Territory* (n53) para 101.

61 See *ICRC Commentary to the Fourth Geneva Convention* (n54) 46. Art. 27 sets out some of the basic protections afforded to the occupied civilian population while Art. 32 of the Convention goes on to elaborate upon those protections.

62 These include the right to life and the prohibition of torture or cruel, inhuman or degrading treatment or punishment, to name but a few. See Marco Sassòli and Antoine Bouvier, *How Does Law Protect in War* (2nd edn, Geneva: ICRC, 2006) 341–53.

humanitarian law are primarily relevant to occupied territory. These are foremost concerned with prohibiting the forcible movement of protected persons within the territory (transfer) or their forcible expulsion from the territory (deportation).[63] However, both transfer and deportation are equally prohibited and each entails the same potential criminal responsibility for the perpetrators of such crimes.

According to David Kretzmer, it is the near-universal opinion of experts in international law that Article 49 of the Fourth Geneva Convention places an absolute prohibition on deportations of residents of occupied territory.[64]

Article 49 reads:

> Individual or mass forcible transfers, as well as deportation, of protected persons from occupied territory to the territory of the Occupying Power or to that of any other country, occupied or not, are prohibited regardless of their motive.[65]

It is interesting to note that before the Rome Statute of the International Criminal Court (hereinafter the Rome Statute) came into force in 2002, the distinction between deportation (the forced removal of people from one country to another) and forcible transfer of a population (compulsory movement of people from one area to another within the same state)[66] was not obvious in any of the major international criminal instruments such as the Nuremberg Charter, the Tokyo Charter, and the statutes of the international criminal tribunals for both Rwanda and the former Yugoslavia.[67]

The jurisprudence of the ICTY makes a clear distinction between deportation and forcible transfer.[68]

---

63 Knut Dörmann, in Otto Triffterer (ed.) *Commentary on the Rome Statute of the International Criminal Court* (2nd edn, Berlin: Nomos Verlagsgesellschaft, 2008) 316.

64 Kretzmer (n39) 45 and 167.

65 See *ICRC Commentary to the Fourth Geneva Convention* (n54) 277.

66 See M. Cherif Bassiouni, *Crimes Against Humanity in International Law* (The Hague: Kluwer Law International, 1999) 312.

67 See Roy S. Lee (ed.) *The International Criminal Court: Elements of Crimes and Rules of Procedure and Evidence* (Ardsley, NY: Transnational Publishers, 2001) 86; M. Cherif Bassiouni and Peter Manikas, *The Law of the International Criminal Tribunal for the Former Yugoslavia* (Ardsley, NY: Transnational Publishers, 1996) 627–8.

68 *Prosecutor v. Krnojelac*, Judgment, Case No. IT-97-25, 15 March 2002, para 474 and *Prosecutor v. Stakić*, Judgment, Case No. IT-97-24-T, 31 July 2003, para 671.

The ICTY decided in *Prosecutor v. Kvocka* that the physical act or material element (*actus reus*) for committing a crime is:

> That the accused participated, physically or otherwise directly, in the material elements of a crime under the tribunal's statute, through positive acts or omissions, whether individually or jointly with others.[69]

Regarding the material element of forcible transfer, the Trial Chamber in *Prosecutor v. Brđanin* was satisfied that the forced displacement of individuals from the area where they are lawfully present to an area within the boundaries of the state constituted the *actus reus* of forcible transfer. The Chamber highlighted the fact that it was essential the forcible transfer be carried out under coercive measures and that such displacement was unlawful.[70] This is what occurred in the forced displacement of the people from Jubata Ez-Zeit village.

The term 'force', when used in the context of forcible transfer should be interpreted broadly.[71] The Appeals Chamber in *Prosecutor v. Stakic* highlighted this point stating:

> The term 'forced', when used in reference to the crime of deportation, is not to be limited to physical force but includes the threat of force or coercion, such as that caused by fear of violence, duress, detention, psychological oppression or abuse of power against such persons or persons of another person, or by taking advantage of a coercive environment.[72]

The terms, 'forcible' and 'forced', should be interpreted to include any form of coercion, which leads to the departure of people from the area where they are located.[73]

Article 49(2) of the Convention does provide for two exceptions to the prohibition on forcible transfer of protected persons. Article 49(2) states that:

---

69 *Prosecutor v. Kvočka*, Judgment, Case No. IT-98-30/1, 2 November 2001, para 251.

70 *Prosecutor v. Brđanin*, Judgment, Case No. IT-99-36-T, 1 September 2004, paras 540–4.

71 *Prosecutor v. Krnojelac* (n68) para 475.

72 *Prosecutor v. Stakić,* Judgment, Case No. IT-97-24-A, 22 March 2006, para 281.

73 See Christopher K. Hall, in Otto Triffterer (ed.) *Commentary on the Rome Statute of the International Criminal Court* (n63) 199. See also *Prosecutor v. Simić*, Judgment, Case No. IT-95-9-T, 17 October 2003, para 125.

> The Occupying Power may undertake total or partial evacuation of a given area if the security of the population or imperative military reasons so demand.[74]

Evacuation should be distinguished from forcible transfer or deportation. It is a provisional or temporary measure taken in the interests of those being evacuated. The International Committee of the Red Cross (ICRC) commentary to the Convention indicates that if either of the exceptions is invoked to evacuate a protected person, the evacuation must be carried out under strict criteria. First, those evacuated would have to be placed in a 'place of refuge'.[75] Secondly, the 'evacuation must not involve movement of protected persons to places outside the occupied territory, unless physically impossible to do otherwise'.[76] Thirdly, 'protected persons who have been evacuated are to be brought back to their home as soon as the hostilities in the area have ended.'[77]

Israel, as the Occupying Power, has met none of the above criteria. At the time of the forcible transfer of the inhabitants of Jubata Ez-Zeit, the Israeli military were in effective control of the region, and there was no military operation or intense bombing that was placing the occupying force or the local population at risk. The protected people were driven from their homes at gunpoint,[78] and not moved to a place of refuge.

The issue revolves around the question as to whether the persons concerned exercised a genuine choice in the matter.[79] The evidence demonstrates that those deported or transferred had no option. In summary, according to Knut Dörmann, to constitute a war crime, it must be determined that:

a. the deportation was carried out unlawfully in violation of international conventions; or
b. generally recognized standards of decency and humanity were disregarded (the provisions of the Convention can be an indication in this respect).[80]

---

74 See *ICRC Commentary to the Fourth Geneva Convention* (n54) 280.
75 *Ibid.*
76 *Ibid.*
77 *Ibid.*
78 See Extract 1.3, Hammood Maray, Al-Marsad Affidavit.
79 *Prosecutor v. Krstić,* Judgment, Case No. IT-98-33-T, 2 August 2001, para 530.
80 Knut Dörmann, *Elements of War Crimes under the Rome Statute of the International Criminal Court* (Cambridge: CUP/ICRC, 2002) 111.

Israeli policy has violated both of these conditions. The unlawfulness of the Israeli action is of paramount importance. The protected persons were driven out of the occupied territory into Syria proper when a more suitable area of refuge inside the occupied territory may have been available.[81] Furthermore, the people of Jubata were not permitted to return to their village after the perceived danger had passed; instead, the Israel military razed Jubata to the ground.[82] Israel's forcible transfer of the people from Jubata Ez-Zeit village was a clear violation of Article 49 of the Fourth Convention. The nature of the crime is so serious that it also constitutes a 'grave breach' of Article 147 of the Convention.[83]

Initially, the Israeli forces informed the people from Jubata that had taken refuge in nearby villages, such as Majdal Shams, that it was safe to return to their own village. However, this information was misleading. On their return to Jubata the Israeli forces began to shoot over their heads to frighten them. The people were too frightened to enter Jubata and were unable to go back to the villages where they had initially sought refuge. They were then forced to flee into other parts of Syria, most taking refuge around Damascus.[84] Once all people had been removed, the village became a closed military zone. This ensured that no one could return, thus making the displacement a permanent feature.[85]

4.2 Destruction of Property

Following Israel's occupation of the Syrian Golan, the Israeli military forces began a widespread campaign of destruction, demolishing numerous villages and farms. In the course of the 53rd session of the UN Commission on Human Rights, a Syrian official claimed that during its settlement occupation of the Golan, Israel had destroyed 244 villages and farms, and today, only 5 Arab villages remain.[86] Most of this activity

---

81 See Extract 1.1, Taiseer Maray, Al-Marsad Affidavit.

82 See Extract 1.5, Hayel Abu Jabal, Al-Marsad Affidavit.

83 'Article 147', *ICRC Commentary to the Fourth Geneva Convention* (n54) 599.

84 See Extract 1.1, Taiseer Maray, Al-Marsad Affidavit and Extract 1.5, Hayel Abu Jabel, Al-Marsad Affidavit.

85 See Extract 1.3, Hammood Maray, Al-Marsad Affidavit.

86 Mission of the Syrian Arab Republic to the UN in Geneva, 11 March 1997, Statement by Mr Taher Al-Hussami, Permanent Representative of the Syrian Arab Republic, at the 53rd session of UNCHR under agenda item (4) as cited in International Displacement Monitoring Centre, *Little hope for the displaced to recover property in the Golan Heights*, available online at: http://www.internal-displacement.org/8025708F004CE90B/(httpEnvelopes)/48B59EFD9DF0AA7980 2570B8005AA9B4?OpenDocument.

occurred during the occupation and not when the actual fighting took place. Furthermore, the testimonies above give first-hand accounts of the village Jubata Ez-Zeit being destroyed after the cessation of hostilities.[87] The largest of the centres of population was Qunaytra, which had a population of approximately 53 000[88] and was partly regained by Syria following the 1974 armistice agreement. A large part of Qunaytra was levelled during the 1967 War; however, Syria claims that the Israeli occupying forces completely destroyed the remainder as they withdrew in 1974.[89]

There are a number of references to the protection of property in the Hague Regulations, most notably Article 23(g) which states that it is forbidden:

> To destroy or seize the enemy's property, unless such destruction or seizure be imperatively demanded by the necessities of war.[90]

The Hague Regulations go further and in Article 56 provide that:

> The property of municipalities, that of institutions dedicated to religion, charity and education, the arts and sciences, even when State property, shall be treated as private property.
>
> All seizure of, destruction or wilful damage done to institutions of this character, historic monuments, works of art and science, is forbidden, and should be made the subject of legal proceedings.[91]

The Geneva Conventions further reinforce the protection of property and various articles establish different degrees of protection for distinct categories.[92] However, the property in question must be 'protected property' under one or more of the Geneva Conventions. According to Article 53 of the Fourth Convention:

---

87 See Extract 1.5, Hayel Abu Jabel, Al-Marsad Affidavit and Extract 1.6, Hammood Maray, Al-Marsad Affidavit.

88 Jo Marie Fecci, 'A View from Damascus: Internal Refugees from the Golan's 244 Destroyed Villages', *Washington Report on Middle East Affairs*, June 2000, available online at: http://web.archive.org/web/20011112045101/www.washington-report.org/backissues/062000/0006010.html.

89 Neil MacFaquhar, 'Syria Talks of Rebuilding City Crushed by War', *International Herald Tribunal*, 23 October, 2004. Available online at: http://www.iht.com/articles/2004/10/22/news/syria.php.

90 Hague Regulations (n40) Art. 23(g).

91 *Ibid*. Art. 56.

92 *ICRC Commentary to the Fourth Geneva Convention* (n54) 601.

> Any destruction by the Occupying Power of real or personal property belonging individually or collectively to private persons, or to the State, or to other public authorities, or to social or cooperative organisations, is prohibited, except where such destruction is rendered absolutely necessary by military operations.[93]

The report by the International Committee of the Red Cross (ICRC) on customary international humanitarian law also states that 'private property must be respected and not be confiscated'.[94] However, international humanitarian law provides an exception to the prohibition of the destruction or confiscation of property, if such destruction is justified by absolute military necessity. This exception has consistently been interpreted in a restrictive manner. In the Trial Chamber judgment in *Prosecutor v. Tihomir Blaskic*, the Chamber held that the destruction of moveable and non-moveable property was prohibited unless military operations made the destruction absolutely necessary.[95] This followed a similar line of reasoning in the post-Second World War *Hostage Trial* which established that '[t]he destruction of property to be lawful must be imperatively demanded by the necessities of war'.[96]

Again taking the example of Jubata Ez-Zeit village, the Israeli forces had total control/effective control in the region;[97] there was little or no fighting taking place, and the village did not pose a security threat to the Israeli occupying forces.[98] There were also no major military operations taking place that could have made the destruction of the village an absolute military necessity.[99]

Israel's action in destroying Jubata Ez-Zeit while under its effective control, without justification on the basis of absolute military necessity, violated Article 23(g) of the Hague Regulations and Article 53 of the Fourth Geneva Convention. The 'extensive destruction and appropriation of property, not justified by military necessity and carried out unlawfully

---

93 *Ibid.* 300

94 See Jean-Marie Henckaerts and Louise Doswald-Beck, *Customary International Humanitarian Law – Volume 1: Rules* (Cambridge: CUP, 2005) 178.

95 See *Prosecutor v. Blaškić*, Judgment, Case No. IT-95-14-T, 3 March 2000, para 157.

96 *Trial of Wilhelm List and Others*, UN War Crime Commission, Law Reports of Trials of War Criminals, Volume VIII, 1949, 66.

97 See Extract 1.6, Hammood Maray, Al-Marsad Affidavit.

98 *Ibid.*

99 See Extract 1.5, Hayel Abu Jabal, and Extract 1.6, Hammood Maray, Occupied Syrian Golan, Al-Marsad Affidavits.

and wantonly' was also a violation of Article 147 and a 'grave breach' of the Fourth Convention.[100]

The way the destruction of Jubata was carried out indicted that the perpetrators acted with a premeditated intent to destroy the village, and they had the knowledge or were aware of the likelihood that the village would be destroyed when they began bombing it.[101] It must also be noted that all the residential areas that were destroyed in the Occupied Golan followed the same pattern.[102] Residents were displaced from their homes and the residential area became a closed military zone before being destroyed by the Israeli military. Such a systematic pattern indicates that Israeli officials had a premeditated plan in place which included the forcible transfer of the local inhabitants and the destruction of their villages and farms.

4.3 Transfer of Israeli Population into Occupied Territory

Almost immediately after the conclusion of the 1967 Middle East war and the beginning of Israel's occupation of Arab territory, Israeli settlers began arriving in the Occupied Golan. Merom Golan was the first Israeli settlement established there. Today, according to various reports, the number of Israeli settlers in the Occupied Golan is anything between 17000 and 20000.[103]

According to Article 55 of the Hague Regulations, an Occupying Power has an obligation not to make permanent changes in occupied territory.[104] Article 49(6) of the Fourth Geneva Convention states that:

> The Occupying Power shall not deport or transfer parts of its own civilian population into the territory it occupies.[105]

---

[100] *ICRC Commentary to the Fourth Geneva Convention* (n54) 596. See also *Naletilić and Martinović* Judgment (n41) para 577, and *Prosecutor v. Brđanin* (Judgment) IT-99-36-T (1 September 2004) para 589.

[101] See Extract 1.5, Hayel Abu Jabal, Al-Marsad Affidavit.

[102] *Ibid.*

[103] See International Labour Conference, Report of the Director-General (n24) para 19; see UN Security Council, *Report of the Secretary-General on the Middle East* (2006) (n26) para 39 and 'Facts about Golan Heights, Disputed between Israel and Syria' *International Herald Tribune*, 21 May 2008, available online at http://www.iht.com/articles/ap/2008/05/21/africa/ME-GEN-Israel-Syria-Glance.php.

[104] Hague Regulations (n40) Art. 55.

[105] *ICRC Commentary to the Fourth Geneva Convention* (n54) 283.

Israeli settlements such as Neve Ativ, built on the destroyed village of Jubata Ez-Zeit, constitute a violation of both of these provisions.

Unlike the crimes highlighted above (forcible transfer and the destruction of property), there is no exception that would give legitimacy to Israel transferring parts of its own population into the territory of the Occupied Golan. An argument put forward by Israel for the legitimacy of settlements in occupied territory resides around the terminology of Article 49(6) of the Fourth Geneva Convention.[106] Israel claims that Article 49(6) only prohibits the forcible transfer of the population of the Occupying Power into the occupied territory and hence is not concerned with the voluntary movement of people into occupied territory.[107] This argument is flawed in that the provision simply does not restrict itself to forced population movement.[108] The provision specifically uses the term 'transfer', and hence the transfer of population can thus be carried out forcibly or voluntarily. The UN Security Council also condemned Israel's settlement policy in occupied Arab territory, highlighting that Israeli settlements were a violation of the Fourth Geneva Convention and an obstacle to a lasting peace in the Middle East.[109]

4.4 Forcible Transfer and Destruction of Protected Property as Grave Breaches of International Humanitarian Law

The crimes of forcible transfer and the destruction of protected property are regarded as so egregious that the drafters of the Convention considered it necessary to include both in Article 147 governing grave breaches of the Fourth Geneva Convention. Article 147 includes the unlawful deportation or transfer and extensive destruction of property, not justified by military necessity and carried out unlawfully and wantonly. However, Article 147 must be read in conjunction with Article 49 which deals with deportations, transfers and evacuations, and Article 53 which deals with prohibited destruction. Both Articles 49 and 53 provide exceptions whereby certain

---

106 See *ibid.* 283. Art. 85(4)(a) Additional Protocol I explicitly criminalizes as a grave breach 'the transfer by the Occupying Power of parts of its own civilian population into the territory it occupies, . . . in violation of Article 49 of the Fourth [Geneva] Convention'.

107 Israeli Ministry of Foreign Affairs, *Israel's Settlements – Conformity with International Law*, 1 December 1996 at http://www.mfa.gov.il/MFA/Government/Law/Legal+Issues+and+Rulings.

108 See generally *ICJ Advisory Opinion on the Construction of a Wall in Occupied Territory* (n53) para 120.

109 UN Security Council Resolution 465 (1980) 1 March 1980.

action otherwise unlawful may be deemed legitimate. However, Israel's action in forcibly transferring the people of Jubata Ez-Zeit village before destroying their homes met neither of the exceptions set out in Articles 49 or 53. Grave breaches of the Fourth Convention are considered the most heinous category of war crimes and invoke a special legal regime.

In order to make the perpetrators of the grave breaches of forcible transfer and destruction of protected property criminally responsible, it is necessary to establish that the crimes were committed in a certain context.

Both the jurisprudence of the ICTY and the *Elements of Crimes* document[110] (adopted by the Assembly of States Parties to the Rome Statute) identified a number of conditions that must be satisfied for the commission of a grave breach. They are:

- an armed conflict must exist and be international in scope and there must be a link or nexus between this conflict and the crimes alleged;
- the persons or property subject to grave breaches must be defined as 'protected' under the Geneva Conventions.[111]

Israel's occupation constitutes an armed conflict that is international in character because it involves the intervention of Israeli armed forces into the territory of the Syrian Golan.[112] In this way the crimes were committed in the context of an international armed conflict. To constitute a war crime, there must be a sufficient link between the criminal act and the armed conflict.[113] The existence of a link or nexus to an armed conflict is established if the alleged crimes were closely related to the hostilities.[114] In this case there is a direct link between the violations outlined and the Israeli occupation.

The people of Jubata Ez-Zeit village qualified as 'protected persons' according to the guidelines set out in both Article 4 of the Fourth Convention and the ICRC commentary.[115] They were nationals of Syria

---

110 Assembly of States Parties to the Rome Statute of the International Criminal Court 'Elements of Crimes' in *First Session, New York, 2002,* ICC-ASP/1/3, 3–10 September 2002, 108–55.

111 *Naletilić and Martinović* Judgment (n41) para 176.

112 See Art. 2 Common to the Geneva Conventions and *ICRC Commentary to the Fourth Geneva Convention* (n54) 17. See also *Prosecutor v. Tadić,* Decision, Case No. IT-94-1, 2 October, 1995, para 70.

113 Dörmann (n80) 27.

114 *Naletilić and Martinović* Judgment (n41) para 177 citing the *Tadić* Jurisdiction Decision, para 70, as authority. See also *Prosecutor v. Blaškić*, Judgment, Case No. IT-95-14-T, 3 March 2000, para 69.

115 See *ICRC Commentary to the Fourth Geneva Convention* (n54) 46.

and under the occupation of Israel, which was engaged in armed conflict with Syria. As such they were not nationals of the Occupying Power; hence, the people of Jubata had protected status under international humanitarian law. It is also clear from the definition set out in Article 53[116] of the Fourth Convention that the property destroyed by Israel in Jubata had also gained protected status once Israel became the Occupying Power of the territory.

5. CONCLUSION

The Israeli settlement policy and its consequences remain major obstacles to finding a just and sustainable resolution to the conflict in the Middle East. An Israeli expert in international law has described the settlement policy thus:

> According to the international law of belligerent occupation, the political *status quo* of the occupied territories must be maintained so that their ultimate fate can be determined by political negotiation. In contrast, the political aim of settlements is to create facts that will predetermine the outcome of any negotiations by making Israeli withdrawal from settled part of the Territories politically unfeasible. Furthermore, the existence in the Territories of a large number of settlers, who enjoy the full democratic right of Israeli citizens and for whose benefit scarce land and resources have been harnessed, has made the regime there much closer to a colonial regime than one of belligerent occupation.[117]

Common Article 1 of the Geneva Conventions imposes a general obligation on every High Contracting Party to respect and ensure respect for the Convention.[118] Common Article 1 can be viewed as one of the principal legal imperatives in the Fourth Convention for the protection of the civilian population. The International Committee of the Red Cross commentary on the Convention reaffirms this point by declaring that a state must not only be concerned about its own performance regarding the application of the provisions of the Convention, but also urges the High Contracting Parties to ensure compliance by other states.[119]

In light of Israel's failure to recognize the applicability of the Convention in the Occupied Syrian Golan, there is an added dimension to the responsibility of the other High Contracting Parties, who are obliged to act, in

116 *Ibid.*, 300.
117 Kretzmer (n39) 75.
118 *ICRC Commentary to the Fourth Geneva Convention* (n54) 15.
119 *Ibid.*, 288.

accordance with the UN Charter and international law, to ensure that Israel complies with its obligations and that the protected persons under Israel's occupation receive the rights afforded them by the Convention.

The International Court of Justice has also confirmed that High Contracting Parties to the Convention have an obligation to ensure that Israel implements and respects the provisions of the Convention in the occupied territory, including that of the Occupied Syrian Golan.[120] Despite Israel's purported annexation of the Syrian Golan in 1981 with the introduction of the Golan Heights Law, it remains occupied territory to which the laws of belligerent occupation apply. In the course of its period as an Occupying Power, Israel has committed numerous war crimes, notably the forcible transfer of much of the Syrian population from the Occupied Golan, the destruction of protected property and the transfer of Israeli-Jewish settlers into the occupied territory. The most obvious consequence of these crimes is the change in the physical and demographic landscape of the Occupied Golan.

While all of these acts constitute war crimes, two have attained the magnitude of grave breaches of the Fourth Geneva Convention, namely, the forcible transfer of the population and destruction of property. Grave breaches are considered the most serious of crimes that invoke a special legal regime. As a High Contracting Party to the Convention, Israel is obligated to investigate and prosecute those responsible for grave breaches; however, such proceedings are rare and very unlikely to happen. Hence, the responsibility must shift to other High Contracting Parties to the Convention. It is the responsibility of other High Contracting Parties, in accordance with Article 146 of the Fourth Geneva Convention, to search for individuals alleged to have committed or to have ordered to be committed, grave breaches of the Convention, and initiate extradition proceedings to bring these suspects before a court of law.[121] Regarding other war crimes committed by Israel such as the transfer of Israeli-Jewish settlers into the Occupied Golan, the High Contracting Parties to the Convention must also act with more authority to end this continuing violation of the Convention and disregard for the rule of law.[122] This is the

---

120 *ICJ Advisory Opinion on the Construction of the Wall in Occupied Territory* (n53) para 158.

121 *ICRC Commentary to the Fourth Geneva Convention* (n54) 589.

122 See generally Human Rights Watch, *Universal Jurisdiction in Europe: The State of Art, 2006,* available online at: http://www.hrw.org/reports/2006/ij0606/. Luc Reydams, *Universal Jurisdiction – International and Municipal Legal Perspectives* (Oxford: OUP, 2003); Antonio Cassese, 'Is the Bell Tolling for Universality: A Plea for a Sensible Notion of Universal Jurisdiction' (2003) 1(3)

minimum responsibility of High Contracting Parties to the Convention. Under customary international law, states have a duty not to recognize and not to assist a situation arising from or giving rise to violations of international law.[123] Pressure must be brought to bear on Israel to ensure it respects its obligation as a State Party to the Convention and end settlement building in all occupied territory, including that of the Occupied Syrian Golan. There are no circumstances where the acquisition of territory by force can be recognized or accepted. Such action poses an ongoing serious threat to regional and international peace and security.

JICJ 589, and George P. Fletcher, 'Against Universal Jurisdiction' (2003) 1(3) *JICJ* 580.

[123] See also UN Security Council Resolution 465, UN Doc S/Res/465 (1980) 1 March 1980, preambular para 7, which '[*c*]*alls upon* all states not to provide Israel with any assistance to be used specifically in connection with settlements in the occupied territories'. The Resolution was adopted unanimously at the 2203rd meeting of the Security Council, and was reaffirmed in UN Security Council Resolution 471, UN Doc S/RES/471 (1980) 5 June 1980.

8. Forging a convention for crimes against humanity

Leila Nadya Sadat

During the trials of the German and Japanese leaders by the Allies following World War II, crimes against humanity emerged as an independent basis of individual criminal liability in international law. Although the so-called 'Martens Clause' of the 1907 Hague Convention Respecting the Laws and Customs of War on Land referenced the 'laws of humanity, and . . . the dictates of the public conscience'[1] as protections available under the law of nations to human beings caught in the ravages of war, this language was too uncertain to provide a clear basis for either state responsibility or criminal liability under international law.[2] Subsequently, crimes against humanity were specifically included in the Charters of the International Military Tribunals at Nuremberg[3] and Tokyo[4] to address depredations directed by the State against civilian populations – including those within their own borders. Indeed it was in many ways the most revolutionary of the charges upon which the accused were convicted, given that its foundations in international law were so fragile.[5] Following the trials, the Nuremberg Principles embodied in the IMT Charter and Judgment were adopted by the General Assembly in 1946,[6] and codified by the

---

1 Convention (IV) Respecting the Laws and Customs of War by Land [1910] UKTS 9, annex, preamble.

2 See, for example, Leila Nadya Sadat, 'The Interpretation of the Nuremberg Principles by the French Court of Cassation: From Touvier to Barbie and Back Again' (1994) 32 *Columbia J. Transnat'l L.* 296.

3 Agreement for the Prosecution and Punishment of Major War Criminals of the European Axis, and Establishing the Charter of the International Military Tribunal (IMT) – Annex (8 August 1945) 82 UNTS 280.

4 Charter of the International Military Tribunal for the Far East (19 January 1946, amended 26 April 1946) TIAS No. 1589.

5 The other was the crime of waging an aggressive war.

6 *Affirmation of the Principles of International Law Recognized by the Charter of the Nuremberg Tribunal: Report of the Sixth Committee*, UN GAOR, 1st Sess.,

International Law Commission in 1950.[7] Thus, 'crimes against humanity', whatever their uncertain legal origin, had apparently found a firm place in international law as a category of offences condemned by international law for which individuals could be tried and punished. The codification of the crime of genocide, itself a crime against humanity, lent some truth to this assumption; however, the important achievement of the Genocide Convention's adoption and entry into force in 1951[8] was overshadowed by Cold War politics. Indeed, no trials for genocide took place until 1998, when Jean-Paul Akayesu, mayor (*bourgmestre*) of the town of Taba, was convicted by the International Criminal Tribunal for Rwanda (ICTR) for his role in the slaughter that had engulfed Rwanda in 1994.[9] Crimes against humanity percolated into the legal systems of a handful of countries that had domesticated the crime, such as France, and certain elements of their prohibition could be found in new international instruments prohibiting torture and apartheid.[10] Scholarly articles periodically appeared as well.[11] But the promise of 'never again', as many have observed before me, was repeatedly dishonoured as the mass atrocities committed in the second half of the twentieth century unfolded before the eyes of the world, bloody in their carnage and the human toll they exacted, and shocking in their cruelty and barbarism.[12] There was little accountability of any kind

---

pt. 2, 55th plenary meeting at 1144, UN Doc. A/236 (1946) (also appears as GA Res. 95(I) UN Doc. A/64/Add.1, at 188 (1946)).

7 Documents of the second session including the Report of the Commission to the General Assembly, [1950] 2 *Yearbook of the Int'l L. Comm'n* 374, UN Doc. A/CN.4.SER.A/1950/Add.I.

8 Convention on the Prevention and Punishment of the Crime of Genocide (adopted 9 December 1948, entered into force 12 January 1951) 78 UNTS 277 [hereinafter 'Genocide Convention'].

9 *Prosecutor v. Akayesu*, Judgment, Case No. ICTR-96-4-T, 2 September 1998, para 494.

10 See International Convention on the Suppression and Punishment of the Crime of Apartheid (adopted 30 November 1973, entered into force 18 July 1976) 1015 UNTS 243; Convention against Torture and Other Cruel, Inhuman or Degrading Treatment or Punishment (adopted 10 December 1984, entered into force 26 June 1987) 1465 UNTS 85; Organization of American States, Inter-American Convention to Prevent and Punish Torture (adopted 9 December 1985, entered into force 28 February 1987) OASTS 67; Council of Europe, European Convention for the Prevention of Torture and Inhuman or Degrading Treatment or Punishment (adopted 26 November 1987, entered into force 1 February 1989) ETS 126.

11 See, e.g., M. Cherif Bassiouni, '"Crimes Against Humanity": The Need for a Specialized Convention' 31 *Columbia J. Transnat'l L.* 457; Egon Schwelb, 'Crimes Against Humanity', 23 *British Yearbook Int'l L.* 178.

12 M. Cherif Bassiouni has suggested that between 1945 and 2008, between

exacted from those responsible for these crimes against humanity – *ces crimes contre l'esprit* – whether committed by government officials or military leaders, rebels, insurgents or low-level perpetrators. The Nuremberg promise remained unfulfilled.[13]

One of the most horrific examples of post-World War II crimes against humanity was the Cambodian 'genocide', discussed by Gareth Evans in the lecture he gave on the occasion of the Experts' Meeting of the Crimes Against Humanity Initiative in June 2009.[14] From 1975 to 1979, the Khmer Rouge regime killed an estimated 1.7 to 2.5 million Cambodians, out of a total population of 7 million.[15] Although the atrocities of the Khmer Rouge regime are now popularly referred to as a 'genocide', legally that is a difficult case to make. Indeed, there has been a great deal of criticism and worry generated by the decision of the co-prosecutors of the Extraordinary Chambers for Cambodia to bring charges of genocide against several former high-ranking leaders of the Khmer Rouge regime, for fear that the charges will not be legally possible to prove.[16] For the

---

92 and 101 million persons were killed in 313 different conflicts, the majority of whom were civilians. In addition to those killed directly in these events, others died as a consequence, or had their lives shattered in other ways – through the loss of property, through victimization by sexual violence, through disappearances, slavery and slavery-related practices, deportations and forced displacements and torture (M. Cherif Bassiouni, 'Assessing Conflict Outcomes: Accountability and Impunity', in M. Cherif Bassiouni (ed.) *The Pursuit of International Criminal Justice: A World Study on Conflicts, Victimization, and Post-conflict Justice* (Antwerp: Intersentia, 2010) 6).

[13] In 1989, the Cold War ended with the fall of the Berlin Wall and this began to change. The International Criminal Court project, which had lain fallow, was restarted with the introduction of a resolution into the General Assembly by Trinidad and Tobago, leading a coalition of 16 Caribbean nations, and work on the Draft Code of Crimes continued at the International Law Commission. See Report of the Commission to the General Assembly on the work of its Forty-Eighth Session, [1996] 2 *Yearbook of the Int'l L. Comm'n* 15–42, UN Doc. A/CN.4/SER.A/1996/Add.1; see also Leila Nadya Sadat, *The International Criminal Court and the Transformation of International Law: Justice for the New Millennium* (Leiden: Hotei Publishing, 2002).

[14] Gareth Evans, 'Crimes Against Humanity and the Responsibility to Protect', in Leila Nadya Sadat (ed.) *Forging a Convention for Crimes Against Humanity* (Cambridge: CUP, 2011).

[15] Compare Craig Etcheson, *After the Killing Fields: Lessons from the Cambodian Genocide* (Westport, CT: Praeger, 2005) 118–20.

[16] Order on Request for Investigative Action on the Applicability of the Crime of Genocide at the ECCC, Case No. 002/19-09-2007-ECCC-OCIJ, 28 December 2009. See further, Peter Maguire, 'Cambodia's Troubled Tribunal', *New York Times*, 28 July 2010, available online at: http://www.nytimes.com/2010/07/29/opinion/29iht-edmaguire.html, and William A. Schabas, 'Problems of International

most part, individuals were killed, tortured, starved or worked to death by the Khmer Rouge not because of their appurtenance to a particular racial, ethnic, religious or national group – the four categories to which the Genocide Convention applies – but because of their political or social classes, or the fact that they could be identified as intellectuals.[17] While theories have been advanced suggesting ways that the Genocide Convention applied to these atrocities[18] and an argument can certainly be made that some groups were exterminated *qua* groups – such as Buddhist monks, whose numbers were reportedly reduced from 60 000 to 1000[19] – most experts agree with Evans' chilling assessment that:

> [F]or all its compelling general moral authority the Genocide Convention had absolutely no legal application to the killing fields of Cambodia, which nearly everyone still thinks of as the worst genocide of modern times. Because those doing the killing and beating and expelling were of exactly the same nationality, ethnicity, race and religion as those they were victimizing – and their motives were political, ideological and class-based . . . the necessary elements of specific intent required for its application were simply not there.[20]

Once again, the international community had failed both to prevent the commission of mass atrocities and to provide the legal tools necessary to react to their occurrence.[21] As war broke out in the former Yugoslavia, and the Rwandan genocide took place with the world watching in horror, the international community reached for the Nuremberg precedent only to find that it had failed to finish it. This made the task of using law as an antidote to barbarism a difficult and complex endeavour. The uncertainty in the law was evidenced by the texts of the Statutes for the International

---

Codification – Were the Atrocities in Cambodia and Kosovo Genocide?' (2001) 35 *New England L. Rev*. 287.

[17] Compare Samantha Power, *'A Problem From Hell'. America and the Age of Genocide* (New York: Harper Collins, 2002) 87–154.

[18] See Hurst Hannum, 'International Law and Cambodian Genocide: The Sounds of Silence' (1989) 11(1) *HRQ* 82, describing the mass atrocities in Cambodia as an 'auto genocide'.

[19] Power (n17) 143.

[20] Evans (n14).

[21] The international community eventually negotiated an agreement with the Cambodian government to establish a court known as the Extraordinary Chambers in the Court of Cambodia for the trial of a handful of former Khmer Rouge leaders in 2003. Agreements between the United Nations and The Royal Government of Cambodia Concerning the Prosecution Under Cambodian Law of Crimes Committed during the Period of Democratic Kampuchea, 43 UNTS 2329, 6 June 2003.

Criminal Tribunal for the former Yugoslavia (ICTY) and the International Criminal Tribunal for Rwanda (ICTR), which contained different and arguably contradictory definitions of crimes against humanity. The ICTY Statute, for example, included a link to armed conflict whereas the ICTR Statute did not. Conversely, the ICTR Statute required a persecutory or discriminatory element in its *chapeau* requirements, which the ICTY Statute did not. These substantive and potentially important variations in the definition of the crime were difficult to square with the idea of universal international crimes.[22] Cherif Bassiouni underscored this problem in an important but little-noticed article, in which he lamented the 'existence of a significant gap in the international normative proscriptive scheme, one which is regrettably met by political decision makers with shocking complacency'.[23]

With the adoption of the International Criminal Court (ICC) Statute in 1998, crimes against humanity were finally defined and ensconced in an international convention. The ICC definition is similar to earlier versions, but differs in important respects, such as the requirement that crimes against humanity be committed 'pursuant to a State or organizational policy'.[24] However it was a convention that *by its own terms* did not purport to represent customary law, but only law defined for the purposes of the Statute itself.[25] Moreover, even if the ICC definition ultimately represents customary international law, it applies only to cases to be tried before the ICC. While presumably ICC Party States can and will adopt the ICC definition as domestic law (and are encouraged to do so pursuant

---

22 See Statute of the International Criminal Tribunal for the former Yugoslavia, UN Doc S/RES/827, UN Security Council, 1993, and Statute of the International Criminal Tribunal for Rwanda, UN Doc S/RES/955, UN Security Council, 1994. The IMT Statutes for Tokyo (n4) and Control Council Law No. 10, Punishment of Persons Guilty of War Crimes, Crimes against Peace and Humanity, 20 December 1945, *Official Gazette of the Control Council for Germany*, No. 3, 31 January 1946, also differed slightly from the Nuremberg definition.

23 Bassiouni, '"Crimes Against Humanity": The Need for a Specialized Convention' (n11).

24 Rome Statute of the International Criminal Court (adopted 17 July 1998, entered into force 1 July 2002) 2187 UNTS 90 [hereinafter 'ICC Statute'], Art. 7(2)(a).

25 See, for example, ICC Statute, Art. 7(1) ('for the purpose of this Statute, "crime against humanity" means. . .'). Whether it has *subsequently* come to represent customary international law is the subject of some debate: see Guénaël Mettraux, 'The Definition of Crimes Against Humanity and the Question of a "Policy" Element' and Kai Ambos, 'Crimes Against Humanity and the International Criminal Court', both in Leila Nadya Sadat (ed.) *Forging a Convention for Crimes Against Humanity* (n14).

to the principle of complementarity), the ICC Statute provides no vehicle for inter-state cooperation. Putting it more simply, the adoption of the Rome Statute advanced the normative work of defining crimes against humanity considerably, but did not obviate the need to fill the *lacunae* in the legal framework as regards the commission of atrocity crimes, most of which are crimes against humanity, and not genocide, and many of which are crimes against humanity, and not war crimes. As the *ad hoc* Tribunals begin to close down, shoring up the capacity for national legal systems to pick up cases involving crimes against humanity appears imperative if the small gains achieved during the past two decades of international criminal justice are not to be reversed. This is particularly true as regards crimes against humanity, for recent experience demonstrates that crimes against humanity have been committed and charged in all situations currently under examination before the international criminal tribunals (and the ICC) to date.

The case of *Bosnia v. Serbia*[26] before the International Court of Justice again evidenced the difficulty this normative gap engenders.[27] For the debate in that case, centring upon whether the mass atrocities in Bosnia committed during the 1990s constituted genocide, missed the point. Although the Court recognized that many serious violations of the laws of armed conflict and crimes against humanity had been committed by Bosnian Serb troops, these other crimes were not before them as the Court's jurisdiction was limited to genocide[28] and they thereby 'slipped off the table'.[29] Of the nearly 200000 deaths, 50000 rapes estimated to have occurred, and the 2.2 million forcibly displaced as a result of the Serb ethnic cleansing campaign,[30] genocide was held to have been proven only in the massacre of some 8000 Muslim men and boys in Srebrenica in July of 1995.[31] Had a Convention on Crimes against Humanity been available

---

26 *Case Concerning the Application of the Convention on the Prevention and Punishment of the Crime of Genocide* (*Bosnia & Herzegovina v. Serbia & Montenegro*) 2007 ICJ Reports 91, 26 February 2007 (hereinafter, '*Bosnia & Herzegovina v. Serbia & Montenegro* Genocide Case').

27 Richard J. Goldstone, 'Foreword', in Leila Nadya Sadat (ed.) *Forging a Convention for Crimes Against Humanity* (n14).

28 Genocide Convention (n8) Art. IX.

29 Goldstone (n27).

30 These are estimates of the number of deaths, rapes and forcibly displaced as a result of the armed conflict in Bosnia; see, e.g., Amnesty International, *Whose Justice? The Women of Bosnia and Herzegovina Are Still Waiting*, 29 September 2009, 5. Some critics claim that these numbers are overestimates and have been politicized.

31 *Bosnia & Herzegovina v. Serbia & Montenegro* Genocide Case (n26) para

and given the International Court of Justice jurisdiction, the Court would have been adequately equipped to address some of the horrors of the Balkans in the early 1990s.[32]

Thus, in 2008, the Whitney R. Harris World Law Institute, under my direction, launched the Crimes Against Humanity Initiative. As the Commentary to the Proposed Convention explains, the Initiative had three primary objectives: (1) to study the current state of the law and sociological reality as regards the commission of crimes against humanity; (2) to combat the indifference generated by an assessment that a particular crime is 'only' a crime against humanity (rather than a 'genocide'); and (3) to address the gap in the current law by elaborating the first-ever comprehensive, specialized convention on crimes against humanity.[33]

The Initiative has progressed in phases, each building upon the work of the last. The forthcoming publication of a book,[34] including the expert papers commissioned by the project and the Proposed Convention in English and in French, represents the culmination of the first three phases of the Initiative: *preparation* of the project and methodological development (I); *private study* of the project through the commissioning of the papers, the convening of expert meetings and collaborative discussion of draft treaty language (II); and *public discussion* of the project with relevant constituencies and the publication of the Proposed Convention (III). Ambitious in scope and conceptual design, the project is directed by a Steering Committee of renowned experts, and has drawn upon the Harris Institute's connections, particularly overseas, to assemble a truly extraordinary international effort on the elaboration of a Proposed Convention on crimes against humanity.

---

297. In its recent June 2010 judgment, the ICTY found that there is enough DNA evidence to identify at least 5336 individuals but evidence continues to be discovered, so the numbers could be as high as 7826. *Prosecutor v. Popović*, Judgment, Case No. IT-05-88-T, 10 June 2010, para 664.

[32] Art. 26 of the Proposed Convention grants such jurisdiction. See Proposed International Convention on the Prevention of Crimes Against Humanity, documented as Appendix 1 in Leila Nadya Sadat (ed.) *Forging a Convention for Crimes Against Humanity* (n14). Of course, the same can be said for the actions brought to the Court by Croatia and Serbia, as well. See *Case Concerning the Application of the Convention on the Prevention and Punishment of the Crime of Genocide (Croatia v. Serbia)* 2008 ICJ Reports 118 (18 November 2008).

[33] Leila Nadya Sadat, 'A Comprehensive History of the Proposed International Convention on the Prevention and Punishment of Crimes Against Humanity', in Leila Nadya Sadat (ed.) *Forging a Convention for Crimes Against Humanity* (n14).

[34] *Ibid.*

During Phase II of the Initiative, papers written by leading experts were presented and discussed at a conference held at the Washington University School of Law on 13–14 April 2009, and then revised for publication.[35] They addressed the legal regulation of crimes against humanity and examined the broader social and historical context within which these occur. Each chapter was commissioned not only to examine the topic's relationship to the elaboration of a future treaty, but to serve as an important contribution to the literature on crimes against humanity in and of itself.

The papers ranged from technical discussions of specific legal issues such as modes of responsibility, immunities and amnesties, enforcement and gender crimes to broader conceptual treatments of earlier codification efforts, the definition of the crime in the Rome Statute and customary international law, and the phenomenon of ethnic cleansing. Several of the papers contrasted the ICC and *ad hoc* Tribunal definitions of crimes against humanity and were very helpful to the discussions as the drafting effort progressed; the same can be said for the many other contributions which addressed specific topics such as crimes against humanity and terrorism, universal jurisdiction, and the Responsibility to Protect. David Crane's contribution outlining 'Operation Justice' in Sierra Leone represents an outstanding case study of 'peace and justice' in action; likewise, Cherif Bassiouni's exposé of 'revisiting the architecture of crimes against humanity' is a magisterial account of the crime's development during the past century.

In discussing the scholarly work more questions were raised than answered. What was the social harm any convention would protect against? Atrocities committed by the state, or a broader concept that would include non-state actors? Would a new legal instrument prove useful in combating atrocity crimes? How would any new instrument interact with the Rome Statute for the International Criminal Court? The lengthy discussions that transpired are memorialized in the comprehensive history included in the volume and will no doubt continue after this book has been published, but it should be emphasized that the discussion and elaboration of the Convention's provisions are deeply intertwined with the academic work accomplished at the same time.

As the initial scholarly work was undertaken, a preliminary draft

---

[35] One paper was commissioned subsequent to the April meeting based upon the emphasis in that meeting on inter-state cooperation as a principal need to adopt the Convention: Laura M. Olson, 'Re-enforcing Enforcement in a Specialized Convention on Crimes Against Humanity: Inter-State Cooperation, Mutual Legal Assistance, and the *Aut Dedere Aut Judicare* Obligation', in Leila Nadya Sadat (ed.) *Forging a Convention for Crimes Against Humanity* (n14).

text of the Convention, prepared by Cherif Bassiouni, was circulated to participants at the April meeting to begin the drafting process. As the Initiative progressed, nearly 250 experts were consulted, many of whom submitted detailed comments (orally or in writing) on the various drafts of the Proposed Convention circulated, or attended meetings convened by the Initiative either in the United States or abroad. Between formal meetings, technical advisory sessions were held during which every comment received – whether in writing or communicated verbally – was discussed as the Convention was refined. The Proposed Convention went through seven major revisions (and innumerable minor ones) and was approved by the members of the Steering Committee in August 2010 in English.

It is to be hoped that the Proposed Convention will begin, not end, debate. Elaborated by experts without the constraints of government instructions (although deeply cognizant of political realities), it is, in the view of the Initiative's Steering Committee, an excellent platform for discussion by states with a view to the eventual adoption of a United Nations Convention on the Prevention and Punishment of Crimes Against Humanity. The Proposed Convention builds upon and complements the ICC Statute by retaining the Rome Statute definition of crimes against humanity but has added robust inter-state cooperation, extradition and mutual legal assistance provisions in Annexes 2–6. Universal jurisdiction was retained (but is not mandatory), and the Rome Statute served as a model for several additional provisions, including Articles 4–7 (Responsibility, Official Capacity, Non-Applicability of Statute of Limitations) and with respect to final clauses. Other provisions draw upon international criminal law and human rights instruments more broadly, such as the recently negotiated Enforced Disappearance Convention, the Terrorist Bombing Convention, the Convention Against Torture, the United Nations Conventions on Corruption and Organized Crime, The European Transfer of Proceedings Convention, and the Inter-American Criminal Sentences Convention, to name a few.[36]

Yet although the drafting process benefited from the existence of current international criminal law instruments, the creative work of the Initiative was to meld these and our own ideas into a single, coherent international convention that establishes the principle of state responsibility as well as individual criminal responsibility (including the possibility of responsibility for the criminal acts of legal persons) for the commission of crimes against humanity. The Proposed Convention innovates in many respects

[36] A complete list can be found in the table at the back of the Proposed Convention, reproduced in Appendices I and II of the volume: see Sadat (n33).

by attempting to bring prevention into the instrument in a much more explicit way than predecessor instruments, by including the possibility of responsibility for the criminal acts of legal persons, by excluding defences of immunities and statutory limitations, by prohibiting reservations, and by establishing a unique institutional mechanism for supervision of the Convention. Echoing its 1907 forebear, it also contains its own 'Martens Clause' in paragraph 13 of the Preamble.[37] Elaborating the 27 articles and six annexes of the treaty was a daunting challenge, and one that could not have been accomplished without the dedication and enthusiasm of many individuals.[38]

At the end of the day, however, it is perhaps to Whitney R. Harris, former Nuremberg Prosecutor, that we are most indebted. For it was Whitney who, along with his fellow trial counsel, first prosecuted crimes against humanity at Nuremberg; Whitney who endowed the Institute bearing his name, providing it with the means to carry on his life's work; and Whitney who served as our counsellor, advisor and friend on this

---

[37] This clause provides: 'Declaring that in cases not covered by the present Convention or by other international agreements, the human person remains under the protection and authority of the principles of international law derived from established customs, from the laws of humanity, and from the dictates of the public conscience, and continues to enjoy the fundamental rights that are recognized by international law. . .'.

[38] I am particularly grateful to Cherif Bassiouni for his extraordinary efforts in leading the drafting effort and his service as a member of the Initiative's Steering Committee, and equally grateful to Hans Corell, Richard Goldstone, Juan Mendez, William A. Schabas and Christine Van den Wyngaert – the other members of the Steering Committee – for their leadership. Each member brought tremendous energy and expertise to the project, guiding its methodological development and conceptual design, and carefully reading, commenting upon and debating each interim draft of the Proposed Convention extensively. The collegial spirit with which our discussions were carried out and our work engaged helped enormously in keeping us on track, and the collective wisdom and experience of my colleagues made working on this project both delightful and inspiring. As with all such projects, many supported the effort without being on the front pages of it, so to speak. Of special note are the experts who gave generously of their time and talent, particularly Morten Bergsmo, Robert Cryer, Larry Johnson, Guénaël Mettraux, Laura Olson, Göran Sluiter and Elies van Sliedgredt, who attended one or more technical advisory sessions and contributed extensively to the elaboration of the Convention's text, and the Harris Institute's staff which has kept the project on track. We could of course not have undertaken this effort at all without the extraordinary support provided by Steven Cash Nickerson, Washington University alumnus, who gave generously to support the first three phases of the Initiative, as well as the United States Institute of Peace, Humanity United and the Brookings-Washington University Academic Venture Fund for additional, critical, financial support.

project, as with so many before it. I am sorry that he did not live to see it bear fruit.

One cannot embark upon an endeavour such as this without being keenly aware of the currents of history. Here in the heartland of America, calling for the elaboration of an international convention, embodying international legal principles for the settlement of international problems, is not new. The Resolution responsible for the convening of the Second Hague Peace Conference – from which emanated the 1907 Hague Convention – issued from the Inter-Parliamentary Union meeting in St Louis, Missouri, upon the occasion of the 1904 World's Fair.[39] Indeed, the participants in the first meeting of the Initiative, in April 2009, gathered in historic Ridgeley Hall on the Washington University campus for a photograph, which was taken in the same room in which, 105 years earlier, the Inter-Parliamentary Union had issued its call for peace. Nor is it unheard of for a group of experts[40] or an academic institution to spearhead an effort such as this. Witness, for example, the Harvard Research project in international law, which produced three draft conventions, published in 1935.[41] The authors of that project cautioned that the 'drafts [were] completed within the limits of a rigorous time-schedule, by men already burdened with exacting duties; and these facts should be borne in mind in any appraisal of the work done'.[42] We hope that our work fares somewhat better, although the men – *and women* – who contributed to it, of course, were under the same constraints of busy schedules and deadlines.

What will become of the *Proposed International Convention on the Prevention and Punishment of Crimes Against Humanity*? Phase IV of the Initiative contemplates a global awareness campaign to help make the Convention a reality. But will states embrace this 'academic offering' and take up the challenge to negotiate a convention for the suppression of crimes against humanity? Or will indifference continue to be the hallmark of international policy?

As Whitney R. Harris admonished us, shortly before his death:

---

39 Editorial Comment, 'The Second Peace Conference of the Hague' (1907) 1 *AJIL* 431. The hopes of that second Peace Conference, however, and the 1907 Convention it produced, were soon dashed as European leaders led their countries into the terrible war that followed.

40 The International Law Association, for example, elaborated a draft statute for an international criminal court in 1926; see International Law Association, *Report of the Thirty-Fourth Conference* (London: Sweet and Maxwell, 1927).

41 Philip Marshall Brown, 'The Codification of International Law' (1935) 29 *AJIL (Supp)*.

42 *Ibid.*, 8.

> The challenge to humanity is to establish and maintain the foundations of peace and justice upon the Earth for the centuries to come. We must learn to end war and protect life, to seek justice and find mercy, to help others and embrace compassion. Each person must respect every other person and honor the God who made this incredible mystery of human life a reality.[43]

I hope that this Initiative, undertaken by the Institute that bears his name, will contribute to the realization of these goals.

[43] Whitney R. Harris, *This I Believe*, written and recorded for National Public Radio, 12 June 2006.

9. Doublespeak and double standards: Does the jurisprudence on retrial following acquittal under international criminal law spell the end of the double jeopardy rule?

Yvonne McDermott*

The rule against double jeopardy, which stipulates that no person may be tried twice for the same offence, is an integral component of the criminal justice system and constitution of most countries,[1] as well as being a general principle of both human rights and international criminal law. The broad idea behind the principle and the values it seeks to protect are relatively straightforward: the powerful state, with its abundance of resources, should not be permitted to make repeated attempts to convict a person, thereby subjecting him or her to restrictions on his right to liberty, as well as to personal expense and anguish.[2] The principle of finality also serves to ensure effective prosecutions at first instance, and saves witnesses from the emotional burden of having to testify more than once.[3]

* The author wishes to thank William A. Schabas, Middlesex University and Megan A. Fairlie, Florida International University, for their comments on an earlier draft.

1 The term 'double jeopardy', as is common to adversarial legal traditions, is used interchangeably with the term '*ne bis in idem*', as the principle is called in most civil legal codes, throughout. There is a difference between the terms, insofar as the first refers to repeat prosecutions in the one jurisdiction, while *ne bis in idem* generally covers the rule that no-one should be prosecuted twice for the same conduct, regardless of where that prosecution takes place. This chapter covers subsequent prosecution in the same jurisdiction, so the distinction is of little relevance.

2 These principles were established in *inter alia*, *Green v. United States* (1957) 355 US 184, 187–188 and *Cullen v. The King* [1949] SCR 658.

3 Paul Roberts, 'Justice for All – Two Bad Arguments (and Several Good Suggestions) for Resisting Double Jeopardy Reform' (2002) 6 *Int'l J. Evidence & Proof* 197, 206; see also, Ian Dennis, 'Rethinking Double Jeopardy: Justice and Finality in Criminal Process' [2000] *Crim. L. R.* 933.

On the other hand, many would rightly be uncomfortable with the idea that a serious offender could be acquitted after intimidating prosecution witnesses, or on the basis of a mere technicality at trial, such as a remark made in error by one of the jurors,[4] and that such an error would result in the accused's release and a prevention of the state from ever pursuing a course of action against him for that crime again.[5] A number of cases appear to suggest that, in any event, no more than one retrial ought to be held, particularly if the errors which caused the original trial to end and retrial to be ordered were no fault of the accused's own.[6] The topic of retrial following an overturned conviction on appeal has been the subject of much scholarly and judicial debate,[7] as have issues such as the meaning of the 'same charges' requirement.[8]

This chapter examines a somewhat distinct strand of practice in criminal law as it relates to the double jeopardy rule – that is, when the public prosecutor appeals an acquittal and seeks a retrial or reopening of the case. Part 1 discusses the circumstances under which retrial or the reopening of a case following acquittal may be allowed under human rights law and domestic criminal law standards, and the permissible scope of such a retrial. Part 2 compares international criminal law and practice with these established standards and posits that international criminal law has

---

[4] Andrew Ashworth, *Human Rights, Serious Crime and Criminal Procedure* (London: Sweet & Maxwell, 2002) 37; Jo Stigen, *The Relationship between the International Criminal Court and National Jurisdictions: The Principle of Complementarity* (Leiden: Brill, 2008) 210.

[5] Chris Corns, 'Retrial of Acquitted Persons: Time for Reform of the Double Jeopardy Rule?' (2003) 27 *Crim L. J.* 80.

[6] See the various authorities for this position cited by M. Cohen, 'Retrial after a Hung Jury' (1983) 12(3) *Anglo-Am. L. Rev.* 174, 177. A third retrial was held to be a breach of the applicant's right to trial without undue delay in *Graasser v. Germany*, App. No. 66491/01 [2006] ECtHR 827 (5 October 2006) and *Rokhlina* v. *Russia*, App. No. 54071/00 [2005] ECtHR 227 (7 April 2005); *cf. McPhelim v. HM Advocate (No 2)* (1997) SLT 1281, where a third retrial was permitted when the second trial had to be abandoned owing to remarks made by the accused himself (cited in James Chalmers and Fiona Leverick, 'When Should a Retrial be Permitted after a Conviction is Quashed on Appeal?' (2011) 74(5) *Modern L. R.* 721, 743).

[7] E.g. Chris Corns, 'Proven Miscarriages of Justice: Retrial or Acquittal? The Discretionary Power of Courts of Appeal in Hong Kong and Australia' (2007) 37(1) *Hong Kong Law Journal* 41; Roy A. Nakano, 'The Case of Elmer "Geronimo" Pratt: A Long and Winding Road to Retrial' (1984–86) 9 *Black L. J.* 189; Chalmers and Leverick (n6).

[8] *Gradinger v. Austria*, App. No. 15963/90, Judgment, 23 October 1995. See also *Heaney and McGuinness v. Ireland*, App. No. 34720/97, Judgment, 21 December 2000, paras 44–6.

stretched the limits of when a retrial is permissible far beyond the confines of the concept under international human rights law or the criminal law in any domestic jurisdiction, and moreover, has allowed the scope of a retrial to reach the standard of trial *de novo*, in clear breach of the double jeopardy rule. Part 3 concludes that the International Criminal Tribunal for the former Yugoslavia (hereafter, ICTY) has lowered the standard of review for retrial following acquittal to such an extent as to be a fundamental breach of the right not to be placed in double jeopardy, and discusses some of the consequences of the dilution of the concept in this regard.

1. RETRIALS FOLLOWING ACQUITTAL UNDER HUMAN RIGHTS AND DOMESTIC CRIMINAL LAW

1.1 International Human Rights Law

The principle of *ne bis in idem* is contained in most instruments of human rights law,[9] and prohibits a subsequent trial where the accused has been *finally* convicted or acquitted.[10] The finality clause is taken to mean the stage at which the original trial has been held and any permissible appeals have been made to the national appellate jurisdiction, or the time limit for lodging appeals has passed. To those from jurisdictions where the prosecu-

---

[9] Art. 14(7) International Covenant on Civil and Political Rights (adopted 16 December 1966, entered into force 23 March 1976) 999 UNTS 171 (ICCPR); Art. 8(4) American Convention on Human Rights, 1144 UNTS 123, 22 November 1969 (ACHR); Art. 50 Charter of Fundamental Rights of the European Union, 7 December 2000, *Official Journal of the European Communities*, 18 December 2000 (2000/C 364/01). Interestingly, there is no parallel provision in the African Charter on Human and Peoples' Rights, 1520 UNTS 217, 27 June 1981, although there is a term that no *state* can be found in violation twice for the same conduct against a complainant (Art. 56(7); see further, Frans Viljoen, 'Admissibility under the African Charter', in Malcolm D. Evans and Rachael Murray (eds) *The African Charter on Human and Peoples' Rights: The System in Practice, 1986–2000* (Cambridge: CUP, 2002) 61, 92). That is not to say that a protection against double jeopardy could not be creatively read into the Charter by future decisions of the Court *per* Christof Heyns, 'Civil and Political Rights in the African Charter' in Evans and Murray, *ibid.*, 137, 155.

[10] Art. 14(7) ICCPR (n9) and Art. 50 Charter of Fundamental Rights (n9) (emphasis added); Art. 8(4) ACHR (n9) states that, 'an accused person acquitted by a *nonappealable judgment* shall not be subjected to a new trial for the same cause' (emphasis added).

tor is not permitted to appeal acquittals at first instance, it might appear to be in breach of an accused's rights to allow a prosecutorial appeal from acquittal which can result in a final conviction, but this possibility is expressly envisaged by Protocol 7 to the ECHR.[11] There has been no jurisprudence on this provision of Protocol 7 thus far, but we can presume from its terms that where a prosecutor appeals an acquittal on a point of fact or law, the preferred approach is to impose a conviction at the appellate stage rather than to order a retrial.

This position is copper-fastened by the fact that retrials are strictly prohibited under human rights law, while cases may be 'reopened' under extremely limited conditions. Article 4 of Protocol 7 to the ECHR illustrates this point: Article 4(1) includes a strict prohibition on a second prosecution or trial, while Article 4(2) expressly envisages that an individual may have his or her case reopened, in accordance with domestic law, and may have to accept prosecution on the same charges as a result of new evidence which came to light (including evidence obtained as a result of new technologies),[12] or the discovery of a 'fundamental defect' in the original proceedings.[13] The types of serious procedural defects which can allow the case to be reopened in this manner are to be determined by applicable domestic legislation. However, the fact that the term 'fundamental' is included implies that the Court could find a violation if the domestic legislation allowed for cases to be reopened in situations of relatively insignificant defects at trial. In *Bujnita v. Moldova*, a violation of the Convention was found where the basis for reopening the case was neither one of new evidence or serious procedural defects at trial, but the Deputy Prosecutor General's disagreement with the judges' assessment of the facts at trial.[14]

On the scope of retrial following an appeal, the Convention is very clear, insofar as it differentiates between a 'reopening' of the case and a trial *de novo*.[15] In perhaps its best-known ruling on the subject, *Nikitin v. Russia*,[16] the Court concluded that the reopening of a judgment on the grounds of serious procedural defects had the effect of annulling the final decision at trial and constituted a continuation of the previous proceedings, and

[11] Art. 2, Protocol No. 7 to the Convention for the Protection of Human Rights and Fundamental Freedoms, adopted 22 November 1984 (ECHR).

[12] Pieter van Dijk and G.J.H. van Hoof, *Theory and Practice of the European Convention on Human Rights* (3rd edn, The Hague: Kluwer Law, 1998) 691.

[13] Art. 4, Protocol 7, ECHR (n11).

[14] App. No. 36492/02, Judgment, 16 January 2007.

[15] See further, *Xheraj v. Albania*, App. No. 37959/02, Judgment, 29 July 2008, paras 72–74.

[16] App. No. 50178/99, Judgment, 24 July 2004.

thereby was not in breach of the *ne bis in idem* proviso.[17] This means that the court is to continue with the trial from the position it was in before the final judgment was handed down, and evidence which was not impugned by the procedural defect will continue to stand. This is important, as one of the major theoretical bases for the double jeopardy rule is that evidence and witness's memories may fade over time, and so neither party should be placed in a less privileged position than it was in before as a result of the retrial order. The prosecution, in particular, should not be allowed to benefit from the experience gained from the former trial and to change its prosecutorial strategy as a result.[18]

In General Comment 13 on Article 14(7) of the ICCPR, the Human Rights Committee noted that States Parties were permitted to reopen a completed case in 'exceptional circumstances', and differentiated a resumption of a completed trial from a retrial, the latter of which was strictly prohibited.[19] The Committee's objective in making this point was to bridge the gap that appeared in a number of countries' reservations to Article 14(7), where they pointed out that final acquittals or convictions could be reopened in accordance with domestic legal regulations, and to encourage those states to withdraw such reservations.[20] The only state to do so was the Republic of Korea on 19 January 1993.[21] As with the ECHR,

---

[17] *Ibid.*, para 46. See also, *Makhmudov v. Russia*, App. No. 35082/04, Judgment, 26 July 2007, para 39.

[18] Annabelle James, Nick Taylor and Clive Walker, 'The Reform of Double Jeopardy' [2000] 5 *Web JCLI*, citing Law Commission Consultation Paper No. 156, *Double Jeopardy*, December 1999, para 4.16; Janet E. Findlater, 'Retrial after a Hung Jury: The Double Jeopardy Problem' (1981) 129(3) *U. Penn. L. Rev.* 701, 726.

[19] UN Human Rights Committee, *CCPR General Comment No. 13: Article 14 (Administration of Justice) Equality before the Courts and the Right to a Fair and Public Hearing by an Independent Court Established by Law*, 13 April 1984, para 19.

[20] Luke McNamara, *Human Rights Controversies: The Impact of Legal Form* (Oxford: Routledge-Cavendish, 2007) 41. See, for example, Austria's reservation to the ICCPR, para 4(c); para 4 of the Belgian government's reservation; para 2 of the Danish reservation; para 2 of Finland's reservation; Iceland's reservation, para 4; para 6 of the Netherlands' reservation, and the reservations of Norway and Sweden, all of which are available online at: http://treaties.un.org/Pages/ViewDetails.aspx?src=TREATY&mtdsg_no=IV-4&chapter=4&lang=en. Similar reservations were made to equivalent provisions in Protocol I Additional to the Geneva Conventions, 1125 UNTS 3, 8 June 1977: see ICRC, *Study on Customary International Humanitarian Law*, Guide to Practice, Rule 100, Section N (*ne bis in idem*) available online at: http://www.icrc.org/customary-ihl/eng/docs/v2_rul_rule100_sectionn.

[21] See http://treaties.un.org/Pages/ViewDetails.aspx?src=TREATY&mtdsg_no=IV-4&chapter=4&lang=en, endnote 34.

no guidance on the circumstances which could be considered 'exceptional' enough to warrant the reopening of a case has been given by the Human Rights Committee, although the discovery of new evidence was used as an example of such circumstances in General Comment 32 of 2007.[22] The Special Rapporteur on the Independence of Judges and Lawyers censured Kyrgyzstan's practice of allowing high-level prosecutors to take so-called 'supervisory reviews', which were essentially a unilateral form of appeal following a final judgment, and recommended that 'reopening of closed cases should be made subject to an exhaustive list of preconditions, such as the existence of new evidence on behalf of the person convicted.'[23]

From the above, we can conclude that, while human rights law contains a strict prohibition on retrials following a final acquittal or conviction, cases may be reopened in exceptional circumstances. Such circumstances include the emergence of new evidence that was not available at trial, and the existence of serious procedural defects, in accordance with the domestic law of the State Party; these domestic provisions shall be discussed in part 1.2 below. The imposition of a conviction when the accused was originally acquitted is only permitted where there has been an error of fact or of law, in accordance with domestic standards of review. The strict distinction between a 'retrial' and a 'reopening' of the case means that the case put to the accused upon reopening is limited, and the exceptions to the double jeopardy rule may not be used to give the prosecution a second chance to prosecute, being aware of the accused's defence, following the reopening of an acquittal.

1.2 Domestic Law

This section examines the practice of a number of domestic criminal jurisdictions, of both inquisitorial and adversarial legal traditions, on the issue of appeal of acquittals, the possibility of retrial as an appropriate remedy, and the scope of such a retrial where applicable. It will be shown that the grounds on which a retrial can be granted following an acquittal are almost universal and extremely limited.

At the outset, it should be noted that previously, the prosecution's right to appeal acquittals was a precept of inquisitorial systems alone, but over time, the prosecutor in adversarial criminal law systems has been awarded

---

[22] UN Human Rights Committee, *General comment no. 32, Article 14, Right to Equality before Courts and Tribunals and to a Fair Trial*, 23 August 2007, CCPR/C/GC/32, para 56.

[23] ECOSOC, Commission on Human Rights, Sixty-second Session, UN Doc. E/CN.4/2006/52/Add.3, 30 December 2005, para 83.

the ability to appeal in certain circumstances.[24] In the United States, quite uniquely, it remains the case that a 'not guilty' verdict is a final disposition and cannot be appealed, even if the acquittal is later shown to have been made in error.[25] In certain countries, the public prosecutor has the right to appeal acquittals only on a question of law,[26] while others allow both questions of law and of fact to be raised.[27] Questions of law in criminal appeals refer to the interpretation applied to existing components of criminal liability, such as the mode of commission, while questions of fact 'generally respond to inquiries about who, what, when and where.'[28] Appellate jurisdictions are generally loath to contradict a lower court's assessment of the evidence, as the trial judges had the opportunity to observe the demeanour of the witness and other factors, unless a palpable and overriding error of fact has occurred.[29] New evidence introduced at appeal can occasionally demonstrate a finding of fact to have been incorrect, and to this end the appellate jurisdictions generally have the discretion to admit new evidence,[30] but this evidence must be limited to issues raised at trial.[31]

---

24 E.g. in England and Wales until recently, the issue of post-sentence review was governed solely by the Criminal Appeal Act 1995, under which the Criminal Cases Review Commission was permitted to refer suspected mistaken convictions (but not acquittals) to the Court of Appeal for re-assessment.

25 Findlater (n18) 727, notes that three states – Connecticut, Vermont and Wisconsin – once had provisions in their federal law which allowed prosecutors to appeal acquittals on the grounds of an error of law. This legislation was overturned following the case of *Benton v. Maryland* (1969) 395 US 784, which interpreted a strict principle of *autrefois acquit* in the fifth amendment of the US Constitution.

26 E.g. s. 676(1)(a) of the Canadian Criminal Code. Applications to review convictions which were possible miscarriages of justice can be made pursuant to s. 696 of the Canadian Criminal Code, but there is no parallel provision for acquittals. Danish law allows for appeal from the High Court to the Supreme Court on a point of law or procedure only, with the higher court prohibited from assessing any further evidence. However, there is the possibility of referring an acquittal to the Court of Revision (*Den Særlige Klageret*) – see n41 below.

27 Code of Criminal Procedure (StPO) in the version published on 7 April 1987 (Bundesgesetzblatt (Federal Law Gazette) I, page 1074, 1319) as last amended by Art. 3 of the Act of 30 July 2009 (Federal Law Gazette I, page 2437) s. 312; the French Criminal Code (s. 543) allows 'all subjects' to appeal, unless otherwise provided in law.

28 Henry P. Monaghan, 'Constitutional Fact Review' (1985) 85 *Colum. L. Rev.* 229, 235.

29 E.g. *Coghlan v. Cumberland*, [1898] 1 Ch. D. 704, 705; *Housen v. Nikolaisen*, [2002] 2 SCR 235, para 23.

30 StPO, s. 323; Swedish Criminal Code, s. 330; Ghanaian Criminal Code, s. 333.

31 *S v. Ndweni & Ors.*, 1999 (4) SA 877 (A) at 880 (South Africa).

A number of countries espouse diverging remedies for successful prosecutorial appeals. Under the Albanian Criminal Code, the Court of Appeal may enter a more serious legal qualification, may sentence a person who was acquitted at first instance and/or extend precautionary measures or lengthen the sentence imposed at trial.[32] In Germany, if the appeal on law or fact is well-founded, the appellate jurisdiction is to decide on the merits; the case will only be referred back to a lower court if the original court wrongly assumed jurisdiction.[33] In deciding on the merits, the matter shall be referred back to another division or chamber of the court whose judgment was quashed or to another court of the same rank located in the same *Land*.[34]

A separate strand of law in the United States, falling outside the scope of the appeal process, is that of 'mistrials' – where the jury was unable to reach a decision. In such circumstances, the issue of whether it is in the interests of justice to order a retrial or to release the accused shall be assessed on a case-by-case basis, with the court assessing whether the mistrial was caused by a 'manifest necessity'. Interestingly, for reasons that shall be discussed in Part 2 below, in a number of cases where a key prosecution witness has failed to show, even following a subpoena being issued for their appearance, the US Supreme Court[35] and State Supreme Courts[36] have held that this does not meet the 'manifest necessity' requirement, and retrials have been barred on the grounds that they would constitute a breach of the double jeopardy guarantee.

An acquittal becomes final when all appeals are exhausted, or when the time limit for lodging an appeal has expired.[37] However, most states now allow a final acquittal to be revisited when fresh and compelling evidence has emerged. This is a relatively new provision in many jurisdictions, and has been inspired by advances in DNA testing and other forensic science over the years,[38] but it can also apply to confessions by the accused

---

32 Albanian Criminal Code, s. 425(2).

33 StPO, s. 328.

34 StPO, s. 354.

35 *Downum v. United States* (1963) 372 US 734, 738.

36 *State of Maine v. David Nielsen*, Docket No. Cum-99-589, Supreme Judicial Court of Maine, 16 November 2000, para 2.

37 Swedish Criminal Code, s. 310.

38 In England and Wales, the changes to the law in this regard were introduced in Part 10 of the Criminal Justice Act 2003 following a recommendation by the Law Commission (*Double Jeopardy and Prosecution Appeals* (2001) Law Com. No. 267). For a case on this legislation, see *R v. Dobson (Gary)* [2011] EWCA Crim 1256, 18 May 2011, where the case was reopened on the basis of new scientific evidence. In Ireland, the law was changed in 2010 (s. 8, Criminal Procedure Act,

post-acquittal.[39] The 'new evidence' proviso remains the only circumstance under which acquittals can be revisited in a number of jurisdictions, including the UK[40] and Denmark,[41] and many jurisdictions reserve the reopening of a case only for the most serious offences.[42] Breaching the double jeopardy rule can be justified on a public interest basis when the individual is conclusively shown to be guilty.[43] However, state authorities must bear in mind that DNA evidence is not necessarily infallible,[44] and thus the presumption of innocence must continue to permeate any later review of the acquittal. Moreover, the argument in *Green v. US*,[45] that the former accused person must be able to move on with his life following trial without a fear of further prosecutions, continues to stand, regardless of technological advances in the law of evidence.

In Australia, even though there was no statutory authority for reopening a case following acquittal if new evidence emerged, the Victorian Court of Appeal made an exception for a former defendant who had been acquitted of terrorism charges and who gave interviews after his acquittal which suggested that he had, indeed, committed the offences.[46]

In other jurisdictions, a conviction of an offence against the administration of justice which has been shown to have perverted the course of justice in the original trial – such as the intimidation of witnesses – will itself be grounds for reopening an acquittal.[47]

2010; Act No. 27 of 2010) to take account of circumstances where there is 'new and compelling evidence' against an acquitted person; ss 975 and 976 of the Danish Code of Criminal Procedure allow an acquittal to be reopened when new evidence of weight ('nye beviser af vægt') comes to light.

39 German Code of Penal Procedure, s. 362.

40 Criminal Justice Act 2003, s. 78 (UK).

41 Danish Code of Criminal Procedure, s. 976. A decision to reopen a case in this manner was discussed in detail in *Pedersen and Baadsgaard v. Denmark*, Application No. 49017/99, Judgment, ECtHR, 19 June 2003, para 21.

42 Part 10, Criminal Justice Act 2003 (UK); Criminal Procedure Act, 2010 (Ireland) Schedule; Crimes (Appeal and Review) Amendment (Double Jeopardy) Act, 2006, s. 3, Division 2 (NSW, Australia); Queensland Consolidated Criminal Code 1899, s. 678C; French Code of Criminal Procedure, Art. 622.

43 Ashworth (n4) 52.

44 See, e.g., Janet C. Hoeffel, 'The Dark Side of DNA Profiling: Unreliable Scientific Evidence Meets the Criminal Defendant' (1990) 42 *Stanford L. Rev.* 465; Beatrice Schiffer and Christophe Champod, 'Judicial Error and Forensic Science: Pondering the Contribution of DNA Evidence', in C. Ronald Huff and Martin Killias (eds) *Wrongful Conviction: International Perspectives on Miscarriages of Justice* (Philadelphia: Temple University Press, 2008) 33.

45 *Green v. US* (n2).

46 *R v. Thomas (No 3)* [2006] VSCA 300.

47 In 2010, a suggestion to this effect was made by the Law Reform Commission

Aside from the 'new evidence' and the less common witness interference exceptions, some jurisdictions allow a retrial to take place where a judge or jury has acted with gross misconduct. One example would be when a judge directed a jury to disregard a piece of evidence and enter an acquittal, where that evidence should not have been disregarded and was instrumental to the case against the accused.[48] In New Zealand, for example, the Court of Appeal was faced with an appeal against a case where the accused had been indicted for the intention to smuggle *either* Class A or Class B drugs, as the prosecution was unclear as to which applied.[49] As the sentence was different for each class of drug, the trial judge dismissed the jury and entered an acquittal – this was the incorrect course of action, as he should instead have directed the jury towards a finding on the least serious offence,[50] and as a result, the Court of Appeal quashed the conviction. Bearing in mind that the case charged the accused with serious offences, the Court of Appeal held that justice required that a new trial be held, and if no further evidence was available to the Crown, that the new indictment should be confined to the least serious offence.[51] A number of jurisdictions also allow retrial where the original acquittal was based on a piece of evidence that was forged, or if an expert witness knowingly and wrongfully gave a false statement.[52]

---

of Hong Kong (Double Jeopardy Sub-Committee, *Consultation Paper on Double Jeopardy*, available online at www.hkreform.gov.hk/en/docs/doublejeopardy_se.doc, para 30) but the provision has not yet been incorporated into law. Under s. 9(1)(b) of the Criminal Procedure Act 2010 (Ireland) a retrial can be ordered where the acquitted person, or another person, 'has been convicted of an offence against the administration of justice relating to the proceedings which resulted in the acquittal'. S. 678E of the Queensland Consolidated Criminal Code 1899 and s. 3, Division 2 of the Crimes (Appeal and Review) Amendment (Double Jeopardy) Act 2006, Act No. 69 of 2006 (New South Wales, Australia) also reserve an exception to the double jeopardy rule in the case of 'tainted acquittals', where the accused person or another person has been convicted of an administration of justice offence in connection with the proceedings in which the accused person was acquitted, and that it is likely that, were it not for that offence, the accused would have been convicted.

48 In this regard, the United Kingdom Law Commission has recommended reform by allowing prosecution appeals against so-called 'terminating rulings', but this proposed reform has not yet been adopted. (See further, Corns (n5) 97; Rosemary Pattenden, 'Prosecution Appeals Against Judges' Rulings' (2000) *Crim. L. R.* 971).

49 *The Queen v. Rokas Karpavicius* [2001] NZCA 171, 24 May 2001.

50 *Gilson v. R* (1991) 172 CLR 353, 20 June 1991, para 13.

51 *The Queen v. Rokas Karpavicius* (n49) paras 36–37.

52 German Code of Penal Procedure, s. 362(2) (the phrase 'was guilty of wilful or negligent violation of the duty imposed by the oath' is used, implying

From the above, we can adduce a number of themes on the subject of retrials following acquittal in domestic legal proceedings: first, prosecutors are permitted to appeal acquittals on questions of law and, in certain jurisdictions, on questions of fact occasioning a miscarriage of justice. Second, when an acquittal is overturned on these narrow grounds, the appellate courts of most jurisdictions will simply enter a conviction and sentence. The fairness of this approach to the accused may be questioned, as no further avenue of appeal is open after this appellate conviction. This author posits that there is a moral argument in favour of this practice, as judgments need to become final at some point – if the accused were allowed to appeal the later conviction, surely the prosecutor would seek to appeal this appeal, and so on, to the financial and temporal burden of the state. Furthermore, the limited grounds on which an appeal can be granted and the standard of proof for appeals safeguard this possibility to the narrowest of circumstances. Third, new evidence can be introduced at the appeal stage of proceedings, but this is almost universally limited to evidence of import that was not available at trial. Last, final acquittals can be reopened without prejudice to the double jeopardy rule, in a number of extremely limited circumstances, namely:

- where fresh and compelling evidence has come to light;
- where the acquittal was tainted by gross judicial misconduct or proven juror or witness interference, of which the accused or another person was convicted; or
- where the accused has later confessed to the crime he was acquitted of.

Where an acquittal is reopened under any of these circumstances, the renewed trial should be limited in scope to ensure that it does not fall within the definition of a retrial, which is strictly prohibited by human rights law.

2. INTERNATIONAL CRIMINAL LAW

In general, where cases have already been tried in a domestic jurisdiction, the ICTY, International Criminal Tribunal for Rwanda (ICTR) and

---

that a separate trial for false testimony would need to be concluded, and the witness found guilty, before this provision could apply); Danish Code of Criminal Procedure, s. 976.

International Criminal Court (ICC) allow an exception to the double jeopardy rule where the national trial was held with the purpose of shielding the accused from the reach of the law, or where the trial was not conducted impartially, independently or in accordance with international norms of due process.[53] Aside from that exception, the statutes of the international criminal tribunals contain a strict prohibition on *ne bis in idem*.[54]

The Rules of Procedure of the ICTY and ICTR both allow for a retrial to be held 'according to law' following an appeal[55] and in 2010, the ICTY ordered its first retrial, following a prosecutorial appeal of acquittals.[56] This section examines that decision and discusses whether the remedy of retrial should have been granted in part 2.1. Part 2.2 analyses later decisions on the scope of the retrial, concluding that the ICTY has stretched the retrial remedy to an extent which could render it in breach of the *ne bis in idem* rule.

2.1 *Prosecutor* v. *Haradinaj et al.*: Granting the Appeal

Under the ICTR and ICTY Statutes, both the Prosecutor and convicted persons may appeal, on the grounds of an error of law invalidating the decision or an error of fact 'which has occasioned a miscarriage of justice'.[57] Article 81 of the ICC Statute allows both Prosecutor and convicted person to appeal on errors of law, errors of fact or 'procedural error'.[58] Appeals must be strictly limited to the confines of errors of law or fact, and the appeal stage should not be seen by parties as offering an opportunity to reargue their case.[59] However, new evidence can be admitted at appeal provided that it is additional to evidence adduced at trial,

---

53 Art. 9(2) ICTR Statute; Art. 10(2) ICTY Statute; Art. 20(3) ICC Statute.

54 Art. 20(1) ICC Statute; Art. 9(1) ICTR Statute; Art. 10(1) ICTY Statute.

55 Rule 117 ICTY Rules of Procedure and Evidence; Rule 118 ICTR Rules of Procedure and Evidence.

56 *Prosecutor v. Haradinaj et al.*, Appeal Judgment, Case No. IT-04-84-A, ICTY, 19 July 2010.

57 Art. 24 ICTR Statute; Art. 25 ICTY Statute. *Prosecutor v. Tadić*, Appeals Judgment, Case No. IT-94-1-A, 15 July 1999, para 315 added a third possible ground of appeal, which is not found in the Statute: 'matters of general importance' which affect the conduct of trials before the Tribunal.

58 The convicted person can also appeal on grounds relating to the fairness of proceedings – Art. 81(1)(b).

59 *Prosecutor v. Kupreškić et al.*, Appeal Judgment, Case No. IT-95-16-A, 23 October 2001, para 22. See also *Prosecutor v. Erdemović*, Case No. IT-96-22-A, Appeals Judgment, 7 October 1997, para 15.

that it was not available at trial, and is relevant and credible and could have played a decisive role in reaching the decision at trial.[60]

In *Bagilishema*, the ICTR reasoned that the standard of proof was higher for the Prosecutor when appealing an acquittal on the basis of errors of fact, because the Prosecutor bears the burden of proof:

> The Prosecution . . . must show that, when account is taken of the errors of fact committed by the Trial Chamber, all reasonable doubt of the accused's guilt has been eliminated.[61]

Following an appeal by the Prosecutor or an accused, the Appeals Chamber may 'affirm, reverse or revise' the impugned decision[62] or it may order a retrial 'according to law'.[63] In this author's view, the terminology 'according to law' should be taken to mean that a retrial ought to be carried out in accordance with applicable provisions of human rights law and of domestic criminal procedure, which were outlined in Section 1 above.

The *Haradinaj* retrial decision issued by the ICTY Appeals Chamber in 2010 contained a surprising lack of analysis on the meaning and applicability of the 'according to law' condition.[64] The facts of the case are thus: at trial, there were some difficulties in obtaining prosecution witnesses' testimony due to alleged witness interference.[65] The Trial Chamber largely overcame these difficulties by issuing subpoenas, ordering protective measures and arranging for testimony to be given via video-link.[66] Two witnesses, however, remained unavailable – one for reasons of ill-health[67] and another, Shefqet Kabashi, continued to refuse to testify despite the initiation of contempt proceedings against him.[68] The Trial Chamber

---

60 Rule 115 ICTY RPE; Rule 115, ICTR RPE.

61 *Prosecutor v. Bagilishema*, Appeal Judgment, Case No. ICTR-95-1A-A, 3 July 2002, para 14.

62 Art. 25 ICTY Statute; Art. 24 ICTR Statute.

63 Rule 117 ICTY RPE; Rule 118 ICTR RPE; Art. 84(2) ICC Statute allows the Appeals Chamber to reconvene the Trial Chamber, convene a new Trial Chamber or decide itself whether the judgment should be revised.

64 *Haradinaj* Appeals Decision (n56).

65 *Prosecutor v. Haradinaj et al.*, Judgment, Case No. IT-04-84-T, 3 April 2008, para 6.

66 *Ibid.* para 22; Appendix A, 'Procedural History', para 24.

67 *Haradinaj* Trial Judgment (n65) para 22.

68 I cannot talk about the things you are asking me . . . If you want to force me, to take me to prison, I will go to prison.' *Prosecutor v. Haradinaj et al.*, Transcript, T. 5441-3, 5 June 2007. Kabashi was arrested in August 2011 and was in fact sentenced to two months' imprisonment for contempt of court in September

issued a number of extensions of time to obtain the testimony of these two witnesses, and expressed that it would remain open to issuing a further extension or extensions, should a change of circumstances indicate that such an extension would facilitate the testimony of these two.[69] No less than three extensions were granted for the ill witness and on 26 November 2007, the prosecution informed the Trial Chamber that it would be another seven to ten days before an assessment could be made as to his condition and fitness to testify. The Trial Chamber issued a scheduling order on 30 November 2007, considering that the prosecution case had closed and that defence teams had informed the Chamber that no defence witnesses would be called, nor would defence submissions be made,[70] scheduling final trial briefs and closing arguments.[71]

One of the accused was found guilty on only two counts, while the other two defendants were acquitted on all counts. In appealing the acquittal on a question of law: namely, that the Trial Chamber had 'violated the Prosecution's right to a fair trial',[72] the Appeals Chamber found that the Trial Chamber had placed expedience over fairness of proceedings and had not taken adequate steps to ensure the testimony of the two crucial witnesses.[73] On the basis of this error, a retrial on six of the counts for which the accused were acquitted was ordered.[74]

The present author has argued elsewhere that the finding of an error of law in this regard was extremely misguided.[75] The prosecutor's 'right to a fair trial' is based on a misreading of the Statutes, which demand both that the Chamber shall ensure that proceedings are fair and expeditious

---

2011 (*Prosecutor v. Kabashi*, Sentencing Judgment, Case No. IT-04-84-R77.1, 16 September 2011).

69 *Haradinaj* Trial Judgment (n65) Appendix A, paras 20–24; *Haradinaj* Appeals Decision (n56) Dissenting Opinion of Judge Robinson, paras 24–28.

70 This procedure leaves the Trial Chamber to make a determination as to whether the evidence put forward by the prosecution was sufficient to sustain a conviction and derives from the fact that the burden of proof rests with the Prosecutor.

71 *Prosecutor v. Haradinaj et al.*, Scheduling Order, Case No. IT-04-84-T, 28 March 2008.

72 *Prosecutor v. Haradinaj et al.*, Prosecutor's Appeal Brief, Case No. IT-04-84-A, 16 July 2008, para 5.

73 *Haradinaj* Appeals Decision (n56) para 40. Compare Dissenting Opinion of Judge Robinson (n69) para 32.

74 *Haradinaj* Appeals Decision (n56) para 377.

75 Yvonne McDermott, 'Rights in Reverse: A Critical Analysis of Fair Trial Rights under International Criminal Law' in William A. Schabas, Yvonne McDermott and Niamh Hayes (eds), *The Ashgate Research Companion to International Criminal Law: Critical Perspectives* (Aldershot: Ashgate, 2012).

and that 'all persons' shall be equal before the tribunal.[76] The former should be taken as a provision which places responsibility for the fairness of proceedings squarely in the hands of the Chambers, while the latter was intended to mean equality between persons as opposed to parties, as it falls under the *chapeau* of 'rights of the accused'.

Furthermore, the standard of proof for errors of law is extremely high, regardless of which party brought the appeal: it must be shown that the error on a question of law invalidates the decision.[77] The Appeals Chamber recognized that standard of proof at the outset of the decision, noting that it would have to determine whether the Trial Chamber 'abused its discretion by closing the Prosecution case before Kabashi and the other witness had testified' and, if so, whether the prejudice caused amounted to an error of law, invalidating the trial judgment.[78] However, the Appeals Chamber's analysis is notably devoid of reasoning as to how the Trial Chamber's decision to issue a scheduling order on 30 November, resulting in the loss of two potential witness's testimonies had the effect of invalidating the acquittal decision reached based on the testimony of a total of 97 prosecution witnesses, with no defence evidence to the contrary.[79]

Lastly, as pointed out by Judge Robinson in his dissent, the issue was really one of trial management – i.e. how many extensions of time were enough – and an appellate jurisdiction should not seek to override the trial management function with its own discretion, absent a manifest abuse of process.[80] When issues of trial management have been raised by the accused at appeal in other cases, the Appeals Chamber has almost universally deferred to the Trial Chamber's judgment on adequate time and facilities for the defence, setting a trial date and so on.[81] The *Haradinaj* Appeals Chamber espoused double standards of the highest order in

---

[76] Arts 19(1) and 20(1) ICTR Statute; Arts 20(1) and 21(1) ICTY Statute; Arts 64(2) and 67(1) ICC Statute.

[77] *Bagilishema* Appeal Decision (n61) para 9.

[78] *Haradinaj* Appeals Decision (n56) para 17.

[79] *Haradinaj* Trial Judgment (n65) para 6.

[80] Dissenting Opinion of Judge Robinson (n69) para 7.

[81] To give but a couple of examples: *Prosecutor v. Karadžić*, Decision on Appeal from Decision on Motion for Further Postponement of Trial, Case No. IT-95-5/18-AR73.7, 31 March 2010, para 21; *Prosecutor v. Katanga, Situation in the DRC*, Judgment on the Appeal of Mr. Katanga against the Decision of Trial Chamber II of 20 November 2009 Entitled 'Decision on the Motion of the Defence for Germain Katanga for a Declaration on Unlawful Detention and Stay of Proceedings', Case No. ICC-01/04-01/07-2259, 12 July 2010, para 34.

taking it upon itself to review an issue which fell firmly within the Trial Chamber's discretion and was not a clear error of law or of fact.

In spite of these factors and assuming, for the sake of argument, that there was an error of law, was the retrial 'in accordance with law'? It was ascertained in Part 1 that human rights standards strictly proscribe retrials, and in cases where an acquittal is overturned on appeal on a point of fact or law which invalidated the decision, the imposition of a conviction is the preferred course of action. The difference between a retrial and reopening a case is discussed in Part 2.2 below, pertaining to the scope of the retrial in *Haradinaj*, but the limited grounds for reopening under both human rights and general principles of domestic criminal procedure warrant a brief mention. The first is the discovery of new evidence – this was not the case in *Haradinaj*, nor, indeed, did the prosecution indicate that either of the 'crucial' witnesses had become available in the 18 months since the trial ended.[82]

The second such instance is where the accused or any other person was convicted of witness or juror intimidation, or where there is evidence of fraud or falsification of documents, in certain jurisdictions. The 'intimidation' exception is far less universal than the 'new evidence' exception, but in countries which do allow cases to be reopened on this ground, one component is universal – there must be an actual conviction of a person for intimidation or interference with the course of justice, and it must be shown that, were it not for the offence, the accused would have been convicted. The existence of witness intimidation at trial is implicitly given as a justification by the Appeals Chamber, which contextualizes its ruling by reference to 'the unprecedented atmosphere of widespread and serious witness intimidation that surrounded the trial.'[83] No reference is made to either of the completed cases on contempt of court,[84] nor is any prosecution argument on the intimidation of witnesses raised, outside of the limited 'failure to grant an extension of time' ground of appeal. It is submitted that the prosecution would have been on much sturdier legal ground had it pursued and secured convictions of those allegedly involved

---

82 If the witnesses had become available, the prosecution would have been allowed to proffer their testimony under Rule 115 ICTY RPE ('Additional Evidence').

83 *Haradinaj* Appeals Decision (n56) para 34.

84 In *Prosecutor v. Haraqija and Morina*, Case No. IT-04-84-R77.4, 17 December 2008, both accused were convicted and sentenced to terms of imprisonment of five and three months, respectively for intimidating 'Witness 2', whose testimony was not of issue to the present appeal. *Prosecutor v. Haxhiu*, Case No. IT-04-84-R77.5, 24 July 2008, related to the unlawful publication of a protected witness's name by a journalist; he was fined €7000.

in the intimidation of prosecution witnesses, and applied for a review of the judgment later under Article 26 of the ICTY Statute. This course of action would have avoided much of the 'doublespeak' surrounding the Appeals Chamber decision, and the consequent violation of the rights of the accused individuals.

2.2 Scope of the Retrial

One might point to the fact that over 90 witnesses with no defence evidence put forward to counter their testimony had been insufficient to uphold the prosecution case, and ask how two further witnesses could make a difference to this finding on retrial. Given the limited scope of the prosecution's motion for appeal of the Trial Chamber's decision, and the remedy authorized on the foot of this motion, it ought to be obvious that the reopening of the case should be limited to allowing the prosecution team to question the two crucial witnesses and the defence response thereto. The evidence already introduced at trial on the six counts of the retrial, including transcripts of the prior testimony of witnesses, should have been introduced into the record with the proviso that if further questioning was needed of any of the earlier witnesses, they should be available to appear before the court for such questioning. This would have saved the retrial from falling under the rubric of the strictly forbidden trial *de novo*.[85]

Instead, the Trial Chamber has allowed the prosecution to include the testimony of six new witnesses, of whom the defence knew nothing at the original trial, along with the testimony of the two 'crucial' witnesses which was the subject of the appeal, in its pre-trial brief.[86] This clearly allows the Prosecutor to address some of the original weaknesses of his original case and therefore goes against one of the fundamental principles of a retrial – that it should not serve as a 'second-chance saloon' for failed cases.[87] Furthermore, the prosecution even moved to introduce evidence which was denied admissibility at trial on the grounds of its irrelevance

---

85 See section 1 above.

86 *Prosecutor v. Haradinaj et al.*, Appeal Brief on Behalf of Ramush Haradinaj on Scope of Partial Retrial, Case No. IT-04-84*bis*-AR73.1, 10 February 2011, para 20; *Prosecutor v. Haradinaj et al.*, Decision on Haradinaj's Appeal on Scope of Partial Retrial, Case No. IT -04-84*bis*-AR 73.1, 31 May 2011, para 26.

87 In *Prosecutor v. Muvunyi*, Decision on the Prosecutor's Appeal Concerning the Scope of Evidence to be Adduced in the Retrial, Case No. ICTR-2000-55A-AR73, 24 March 1999, the Appeals Chamber said that new evidence could be introduced at retrial, with a determination to be made at the Trial Chamber's discretion, 'which is guided by the same criteria governing the admission of evidence at trial' (para. 13).

and unreliability.[88] Even more bizarrely, this motion was accepted by the newly constituted Chamber, rendering previously inadmissible evidence admissible,[89] despite the fact that no change in circumstance had warranted deeming the evidence somehow more relevant or reliable at appeal. In a final blow to the defendants, even though the Appeals Chamber had strictly limited the counts of the indictment to which the retrial should refer,[90] the new Trial Chamber declined to strike allegations unrelated to the retrial from the original indictment,[91] which do encompass, as the prosecution had asserted, broad factual allegations,[92] but some paragraphs also concern crimes of which the accused have already been acquitted.[93]

3. CONCLUSION

Section 2 posited that the ICTY's 2010 decision in the *Haradinaj* trial, and the scope of that retrial as delineated by later decisions, have stretched the limits of retrial on appeal to such an extent as to find cause for reopening the case when the prosecution is merely unhappy with the outcome. This stands in stark contrast to the *lex lata* under human rights and domestic criminal law standards, as laid out in Section 1, and sets a very dangerous precedent, as international criminal tribunals are supposed to be beacons of the highest fair trial standards. The dilution of the concept of double jeopardy by the ICTY could provoke even more derogations from the double jeopardy rule, to add to the remarkable sea change on rules regarding the reopening of acquittals that we have witnessed in domestic jurisdictions over the past ten years. One hopes that international prosecutors will not be encouraged by the *Haradinaj* precedent, which opens wide the door to appeal of acquittals, and might, in turn, lead to less than thorough prosecutions at first instance in the future.

---

88 *Prosecutor v. Haradinaj et al.*, Prosecution's Motion for Admission of Transcripts of Evidence in Lieu of Viva Voce Testimony Pursuant to Rule 92bis with Confidential Annex A, Case No. IT -04-84bis-AR 73.1, 27 June 2011.

89 *Prosecutor v. Haradinaj et al.*, Decision on Prosecution's Motion for Admission of Transcripts of Evidence in Lieu of Viva Voce Testimony Pursuant to Rule 92bis with Confidential Annex A, Case No. IT -04-84bis-AR 73.1, 22 July 2011, para 60.

90 *Haradinaj* Appeals Decision (n56) para 377.

91 *Prosecutor v. Haradinaj et al.*, Decision on Shortened Form of the Fourth Amended Indictment, Case No. IT-04-84bis-PT, 14 January 2011, para 42.

92 *Haradinaj* Scope of Partial Retrial Appeal Decision (n86) Partially Dissenting Opinion of Judge Robinson, para 9.

93 *Ibid.*, para 8.

10. Third world approaches to international law and the ghosts of apartheid

John Reynolds

The concept and practice of apartheid was central to the post-war evolution of international law as a site of contestation between imperial interests and anti-imperial discourse, and as a rallying call for the international human rights movement and global solidarity action. This essay glances back at the recent history of international law through the looking glass of apartheid, and argues for the continuing relevance of its prohibition. The prohibition of apartheid serves both as a reminder of the role played by former colonized nations in the development of legal doctrine, and as a potentially valuable normative and analytical framework in situations where segregation and institutionalized racial discrimination persist or re-emerge.

1. INTERNATIONAL LEGAL IMPERIALISM

When we as historians, legal scholars or statesmen/women cast our minds back to the beginning of the United Nations era and the new dawn of human rights protection that it aspired to, our accounts tend to be tinged with nostalgia and awe. Nostalgia for the hope and potential of a new and improved global order emerging from the ashes of almighty death and destruction; awe of the visionaries and paragons who would lead us out of the shadows of war and totalitarianism, towards the twin beacons of peace and human rights.

The occasions on which we have lost sight of those beacons in the decades that have followed – and there have been many – are put down to various structural obstacles and procedural flaws that festered within: the political permafrost that kept the two dominant post-war powers cool on cooperation; the wrong choice of mandate for peacekeeping troops in a given situation; the obstinate refusal of unilateralist neo-conservatives to follow the course that had been plotted for them by their infinitely wiser and more progressive predecessors. We have tended to maintain a retrospective blind spot for the shortcomings and contradictions that tainted the post-war international legal order itself, not just in its effectiveness in practice but in its very conception and ideology. Was the utopian rhetoric of universal rights and freedoms that we narrate into the story of the formation of the UN actually of such central concern to the organization's imperious, war-victorious founders? We celebrate Réné Cassin, Eleanor Roosevelt and Charles Malik for their role in crafting the Universal Declaration of Human Rights, but what of the UN's original founding Charter, and what of the participation of the world's colonized peoples in the formation of this purportedly universal body? As it transpires, the main African actor in the process was an architect of white settler nationalism; at once Afrikaner political leader and member of the British Imperial War Cabinet. Mark Mazower's questions and observations are prescient:

> What to make of the fact that Jan Smuts, the South African statesman, helped draft the UN's stirring preamble? How could the new world body's commitment to universal rights owe more than a little to the participation of a man whose segregation policies back home paved the way for an apartheid state? Smuts, exponent of racial superiority, believer in white rule over the African continent, casts an enigmatic shadow over the founding of the new United Nations Organization at the end of the Second World War. Yet it was not a shadow many people at the time gave any sign of noticing.[1]

Mazower's *No Enchanted Palace* is a timely appraisal of the future role of the UN in the international order which necessarily draws on an understanding of its history; a history awash with contradictions, not least that between the utopianism attached to the UN's founders and founding principles and the central role played by an actor like Smuts. On this basis, the warning-bells remind us that 'it is surely necessary to be cautious about making our own hopes and dreams too dependent on the stories we tell about the past.'[2] Many left the UN's inaugurating conference in San Francisco in 1945 unconvinced by what they saw as a universalizing rhetoric of freedom and rights that were in reality partial at best, and riddled with double-standards; 'a veil masking the consolidation of a great power directorate' that retained a regressive imperial attitude to how

---

[1] Mark Mazower, *No Enchanted Palace: The End of Empire and the Ideological Origin of the United Nations* (Princeton, NJ: Princeton University Press, 2009) 19.

[2] *Ibid.*, 9.

the weak and the poor of the world should be governed.[3] This is not the historical narrative we generally receive, however. Human rights scholar Peter Bailey refers glowingly to the reference to human rights contained in the preamble to the UN Charter, as 'inspired by the great South African pre-apartheid leader Field-Marshal Smuts'.[4]

Jan Smuts is one of the most significant figures in South African political history. Having commanded Boer forces in the second Boer War (1899–1902), Smuts was the leading force behind the unification of South Africa in 1909, formed the South African Defence Force in 1914 and led the South African conquests of German colonies in South-West Africa (Namibia) and East Africa (Rwanda, Burundi, Tanganyika) during the First World War. He subsequently served as a British army field marshal in the Second World War, and was a member of the British Imperial War Cabinet during both wars. He was Prime Minister of the Union of South Africa from 1919–1924 and from 1939–1948, holding a host of other ministerial positions in between.

Smuts was a staunch believer in, and advocate of, racial segregation. In a seminal speech entitled 'The White Man's Task'[5] given at a reception held in his honour in London in 1917, Smuts set out his vision for the future of South Africa. He spoke eloquently of national unity in South Africa: 'The ideal of national unity means a continuous effort towards better relations, towards mutual respect and forbearance, towards co-operation, and that breadth of view and character, which will be the most potent instrument for dealing with our other problems.' The national unity envisaged here was a selective one, however, excluding the majority of the nation's population and referring only to conciliation between the 'allied racial stock' of British and Boer settlers.

Foremost among common English and Dutch concerns was what Smuts described as 'our immense native problem'. Where there may once have been traces of 'attempts at civilization' on the African continent,

---

[3] *Ibid.*, 7. Mazower cites British civil servant Gladwyn Jebb who 'cynically praised the ability of his American colleagues to "delude" human rights activists at San Francisco into believing "that their objectives had been achieved in the present Charter"'.

[4] Peter Bailey, 'The Creation of the Universal Declaration of Human Rights', *Universal Rights Network*, available online at http://www.universalrights.net/main/creation.htm.

[5] All quotes in the ensuing paragraph are taken from Smuts' speech, 'The White Man's Task', delivered at the Savoy Hotel in London on 22 May 1917 and reproduced in Jan C. Smuts, *Plans For A Better World: Speeches of Field-Marshal the Right Honourable J.C. Smuts, P.C., C.H., K.C., D.T.D* (London: Hodder & Stoughton, 1942).

'barbarism once more rules over the land and makes the thoughtful man nervous about the white man's future in Southern Africa.' The axiom presented to govern relations between white and black was simple: 'no intermixture of blood between the two colours.' According to Smuts, 'earlier civilisations have largely failed because that principle was never recognised, civilising races being rapidly submerged in the quicksands of the African blood.' Black Africans and white Europeans 'are different not only in colour but in minds and in political capacity, and their political institutions should be different'. Smuts' tone and language was marked by a racial supremacy that was characteristic of colonial attitudes at the time:

> Natives have the simplest minds, understand only the simplest ideas or ideals, and are almost animal-like in the simplicity of their minds and ways . . . Instead of mixing up black and white in the old haphazard way, which instead of lifting up the black degraded the white, we are now trying to lay down a policy of keeping them apart as much as possible in our institutions. In land ownership, settlement and forms of government we are trying to keep them apart, and in that way laying down in outline a general policy which it may take a hundred years to work out, but which in the end may be the solution of our native problem.

On this basis, Smuts endorsed the structures suggested in the appendix to the 1909 Act of Union 'that the native territories in South Africa should be governed apart from the Parliamentary institutions of the Union and on different lines which would achieve the principle of native self-government.' He also conveyed imperial aspirations for the spread of 'civilization' in the African continent from the south up, extolling the potential created in central Africa, 'those other enormous territories farther north, which our troops from South Africa and other parts of the Empire have conquered and occupied.' The objectification and dehumanization of the indigenous population comes through in Smuts' discussion of the strategic significance of central Africa in particular, with the all-conquering General confessing that '[w]e were not aware of the great military value of the natives until this war.'

In academia, Smuts developed the influential concept of 'holism', which described the natural tendency to form wholes greater than the collective sum of individual parts through a form of creative evolution.[6] His work in this regard can be seen as complementing his political and military activities and his advocacy of white racial supremacy. In 1929 Smuts restated in

---

6 Jan Christiaan Smuts, *Holism and Evolution* (London: Macmillan & Co, 1926).

further detail his earlier calls for segregation and separate development on the basis of racial denomination:

> The old practice mixed up black with white in the same institutions, and nothing else was possible after the native institutions and traditions had been carelessly or deliberately destroyed. But in the new plan there will be what is called in South Africa 'segregation' – separate institutions for the two elements of the population living in their own separate areas. Separate institutions involve territorial segregation of the white and black. If they live mixed together it is not practicable to sort them out under separate institutions of their own. Institutional segregation carries with it territorial segregation.[7]

This vision is the essence of the 'Bantustan' policy that would later be formalized by the apartheid regime as the solution to South Africa's 'native problem'. During the period of Smuts' premiership between 1919 and 1924, crucial foundations for apartheid had been laid by the erosion of the last remnants of native suffrage and the introduction of segregation policies and settlement restrictions. Most notably, the 1923 Native (Urban Areas) Act was enacted to divide South Africa into 'prescribed' (urban) and 'non-prescribed' (rural) areas, and provided for strict controls to be placed by local authorities on the movement of black males between the two. Advisory boards were set up to limit the inflow of black workers into urban areas, and to order the removal of 'surplus' unemployed Africans. The aim and effect was to render South African towns almost exclusively white zones, with the passage of native labourers tightly regulated, and only domestic workers allowed to live in the towns.

And yet, although the world's most acute race problem fermented under his policies at home, Smuts remains exalted as an outstanding statesman of the late British Empire and a central figure in the history of internationalism and the idea of international organization. It may appear in retrospect that a curious myopia developed around Smuts, blinding many to the contradictions between the racial divisions that he championed domestically, and the cooperation that he fostered internationally. In fact, Smuts' belief in white superiority informed much of his thinking on how to make settler-colonial nationalism compatible with broader international imperial interests, and his theorizing on international order.

With a view to keeping South Africa and other colonies within the British Empire, Smuts embraced the concept of commonwealth as a way

---

7 O.F. Cook, 'Race Segregation in South Africa: New Policies and Factors in Race Problems' (1930) 21(5) *Journal of Heredity* 225, quoting a lecture delivered at the University of Oxford by Jan Smuts, entitled 'The Native Policy of South Africa'.

to imagine the coalescing of nations for the common cause of (white) democracy.[8] He saw the international organization as a natural extension of the idea of empire and commonwealth, and therefore as the choice vehicle to ensure the continuation of white leadership in an evolving world order. It would provide the means to consolidate the economic and security interests of the imperial powers, as well as facilitating the continuation of the civilizing mission.

Mazower traces an unbroken chain from the constitutional reconfiguration of the British Empire in the early twentieth century through to the formation of the UN. Jan Smuts was central to each of the major links in that chain: from the debates over internationalism in the aftermath of the Boer War, to the reframing of the empire under Smuts' preferred rubric of the 'British Commonwealth of Nations',[9] to the emergence of the League of Nations following the First World War and its evolution into the UN in the wake of the Second World War. The influence of British colonial structures on Smuts' conception of the international organization is manifest in his thinking:

> the elements of the future World Government, which will no longer rest on the Imperial Ideas adopted from Roman law, are already in operation in our Commonwealth of Nations . . . As the Roman ideas guided European civilisation for almost two thousand years, so the newer ideas embedded in the British constitutional and Colonial system may, when carried to their full development, guide the future civilisation for ages to come.[10]

Smuts hailed the British Empire as 'the only successful experiment in international government' and as the 'only embryo league of nations.'[11] He was central to the creation of the post-war League of Nations. After the German surrender in 1918, Smuts circulated an influential memorandum that outlined the framework for an international league of nations[12] and would eventually garner both British and American support. The idea of Mandate territories turned out to be the perfect method of bridging the gap between the British Dominions' aspirations of annexing conquered German colonies, and Woodrow Wilson's stated ideal of self-determination for all nations. For Smuts, this was the ideal way to bring

---

8 Mazower (n1) 20.

9 W.K. Hancock, *Smuts: The Sanguine Years, 1870–1919* (Cambridge: CUP, 1962) 198.

10 Quoted in Mazower (n1) 37.

11 *Ibid.*, 37–8.

12 Jan Christiaan Smuts, *The League of Nations: A Practical Suggestion* (London: Hodder and Stoughton, 1918).

the Americans into an 'Anglo-American colonial alliance',[13] and yielded the desired result: further expansion of the British Empire, now to a scale larger than it or any other empire had been at any point in history.

By the time the next post-war discussion on international cooperation came around in the 1940s, the League of Nations had been subject to such criticism – not least for acting as an international proxy for elite imperial interests and as a vehicle for the continuation of the racially inflected civilizing mission – that a new model was needed. Ultimately, however, the UN did not amount to any radical departure from the League template of an association of states that Smuts had formulated. Along with a number of technical experts and think-tanks who had been involved in the earlier experiment, Smuts' role in the shaping of the UN underscores a continuity, rather than rupture, between the League and the UN.[14]

He was satisfied that the UN represented a sufficiently improved democratic imperial order by virtue of having the Soviet Union on board, yet would continue to facilitate the civilizing mission in Africa and the extension of white rule through international cooperation. Recognizing the need to distinguish the new organization from its hegemonic predecessor in the face of a changing tide of public opinion, however, Smuts drafted the inspirational preamble with its reference to human rights as a way of 'attracting public support' for what otherwise would have been 'all too obviously a great power stitch up'.[15] The status quo as far as the global South was concerned, however, was preserved.

The initial talks at Dumbarton Oaks in 1944 made no mention of liberation for colonial territories. When the Philippines delegation proposed that a commitment to independence be written into the UN Charter, they were leaned on by the Americans (the Wilsonian ideal of self-determination by now having ceded ground to an acute realization of the strategic value for the US of holding territories in the Pacific and elsewhere); an Ecuadorian attempt to allow a vote by two-thirds of UN members to bring about a colony's independence was similarly quashed; and 'wartime American drafts of a declaration of independence of colonial peoples were archived as were thoughts of making a declaration of human rights an integral part of the Charter.'[16] Mandates became trusteeships, and colonies became dependent territories, but little of substance changed. As British diplomat Charles Webster admitted in his diaries, the UN Charter simply

---

[13] Mazower (n1) 45.

[14] Smuts was in fact the only person to sign the charters of both the League of Nations and the UN.

[15] Mazower (n1) 60–1.

[16] *Ibid.*, 62–3.

established another 'Alliance of the Great Powers embedded in a universal organization.'[17]

2. THE DECOLONIZATION OF INTERNATIONAL LAW

This was the context in which the new post-war international law was born. On this basis, the seamless shift from elite club of states to utopia of human rights protection that many of our history books and human rights texts portray appears somewhat specious. Indeed, prominent scholars have suggested that the modern human rights movement dates back to the 1970s at the earliest.[18] With the establishment of the UN, however, a blueprint had been drawn up for a site that could potentially evolve into a forum for rights-based claims by those who had historically borne the brunt of European conquest and subjugation. This happened faster than Jan Smuts could ever have envisaged, and it was the apartheid policies then in incubation in his own South Africa that would provide the rallying call around which the nations of the global South would unite to make their presence felt.

The prologue to this contestation came as early as the first session of the UN General Assembly in 1946, before apartheid had been formalized as official policy following Smuts' electoral defeat by the National Party in 1948, and before the emancipation from colonial rule of the majority of third world nations had been attained. The protagonist, Jawaharlal Nehru's pre-independence Indian government, chose to contest the official discrimination to which Indians in South Africa were subjected by the Smuts administration under the 1946 Asiatic Land Tenure and Indian Representation Act.[19] Strategically bypassing the traditional channels of the British colonial apparatus, Nehru brought the issue directly to the General Assembly, making a formal complaint against South Africa.

---

[17] Philip A. Reynolds and E.J. Hughes, *The Historian as Diplomat: Charles Kingsley Webster and the United Nations, 1939–1946* (London: Martin Robertson, 1977) 59.

[18] Samuel Moyn, *The Last Utopia: Human Rights in History* (Cambridge, MA: Harvard University Press, 2010).

[19] Notably, in his first political position of note in the early 1900s, as Colonial Secretary in the Transvaal self-government before South African unification, Smuts had forcefully opposed Mohandas Gandhi's equal rights movement for South Asian workers. Later, in his first period as Prime Minister, during the imperial conferences of 1921–1923, Smuts rejected Indian government demands that Indians be given citizenship rights in South Africa.

Smuts appeared in person to defend his administration's racial policies and to dispute the Indian argument that South Africa should abide by the Charter whose formulation he himself had been central to. It was a matter of domestic jurisdiction, he claimed, not of concern to the UN. To Smuts' dismay, the General Assembly sided with India and requested that South Africa bring the treatment of its Indian population into line with the basic principles of the UN Charter.[20]

The resulting General Assembly resolution can be seen as the first act of assertion at the UN by the colonized world against racial hierarchy and European domination, suggesting that 'the new world organization contained within it – however embryonically – the potential to become a very different organization from that envisaged by the wartime great powers.'[21] Britain and the United States were not in favour of any criticism of South Africa but were unable to prevent it in the face of competing opinion in the Assembly. The dictates of *Realpolitik* that had been embedded in the structure of the UN soon revealed their worth, however. Lacking the support of the Security Council, the General Assembly resolution did little to improve the situation of South Africa's Indian-origin population, or to deter the subsequent institutionalization of racism by the apartheid regime. It can nonetheless be seen as a watershed moment for the utilization of international law and institutions by the 'Third World'.

Disempowered and dispossessed by the doctrines and structures of international law ever since its sixteenth-century formation in the context of Spanish colonial expeditions in South America,[22] the non-European world would have been forgiven for resisting incorporation into the established legal order. Instead, as African and Asian nations rode the wave of decolonization in the 1950s, 60s and 70s, they bullishly entered the arena of international law and its institutions in the hope of asserting the historically neglected claims of their peoples and challenging the imperial status quo. They were supported by third world jurists and scholars with a reform agenda, who offered an anti-hegemonic critique of the prevailing system and from whose ranks the first generation of the 'Third World Approaches to International Law' (TWAIL) movement emerged.[23]

---

20 United Nations UN GA Res A/RES/44(I) 8 December 1946.

21 Mazower (n1) 26; Hugh McKinnon Wood, 'Notes on the Question of Domestic Jurisdiction under the Charter of the United Nations' (1946) IV:M:2 *British Documents on Foreign Affairs* (Washington, DC: University Publications of America, 2002) 281–3.

22 See generally Antony Anghie, *Imperialism, Sovereignty and the Making of International Law* (Cambridge: CUP, 2005).

23 For a succinct overview of TWAIL, see Antony Anghie and Bhupinder

While indicting colonial international law for legitimizing the subjugation and oppression of Third World peoples, this movement believed that international law could be transformed to incorporate the needs and aspirations of the newly independent states, and as such adopted a non-rejectionist stance towards modern international law.[24] Reform was to be achieved primarily through the UN system. Now that the decolonized states had an equal voice and vote in the General Assembly, it was hoped that a more democratic international legal order could be attained so as to redress the imbalance and exclusion that had long underwritten North–South relations. The aim was thus not simply to repudiate the existing international legal order but to produce a truly universal and participatory international law.

Leading contemporary TWAIL scholars Antony Anghie and Bhupinder Chimni explain that third world international legal scholarship at the time 'was closely aligned with the diplomatic initiatives undertaken by newly-independent Third World states, and . . . placed immense faith in the UN to bring about the changes necessary to usher in a just world order.'[25] Attempts were made 'to formulate a new approach to sources doctrine by arguing that General Assembly resolutions passed by vast majorities had some binding legal effect.'[26] The crucial accompaniment to political independence, that of structural reform of the global economy, was to be the product of a 'new international economic order'.[27]

Chimni, 'Third World Approaches to International Law and Individual Responsibility in Internal Conflicts' (2003) 2 *Chinese JIL* 77, 79–87.

[24] *Ibid.*, 80–1.

[25] *Ibid.*, 81.

[26] *Ibid.*, 81, citing: Georges Abi-Saab, 'The Development of International Law by the United Nations', in Frederick Snyder and Surakiart Sathirathai (eds) *Third World Attitudes to International Law: An Introduction* (Leiden: Nijhoff, 1987); V.S. Mani, *Basic Principles of Modern International Law: A Study of the United Nations Declaration on the Principles of International Law Concerning Friendly Relations and Co-operation Among States* (New Delhi: Lancers Books, 1993); O.Y. Asamoah, *The Legal Significance of the Declarations of the General Assembly of the United Nations* (Leiden: Nijhoff, 1966). See also Richard A. Falk, 'On the Quasi-Legislative Competence of the General Assembly' (1966) 60 *AJIL* 782, arguing that: 'The expansion of international society to include the active participation of the Afro-Asian states and the growth of a global consciousness has produced a situation that calls for a more sociologically grounded re-interpretation of the basis of obligation in international law. One way to attempt this re-interpretation is to complicate the relationship between state sovereignty and the growth of international law by examining the argument that the General Assembly is endowed with, and actually exercises, a limited legislative competence.'

[27] UN GA Res 3201 (S-VI) 'Declaration on the Establishment of a New

While discrete advances were made, as with the consolidation of the doctrine of permanent sovereignty over natural resources,[28] attempts to democratize the international legal system and empower the General Assembly were generally stilted by positivist arguments relating to sources and consent. The much-touted new world economic order, meanwhile, failed to materialize in the face of powerful Western financial interests and the hegemony of the Bretton Woods institutions. In the midst of such adversity, apartheid in South Africa emerged as perhaps the most tangible issue that the nations of the global South felt could and must be addressed by the UN, irrespective of dominant imperial interests and Security Council resistance.

Following the General Assembly's censure of the Smuts government in 1946 over its discriminatory policy towards Indians, the status quo at the UN maintained a relatively conservative stance on South Africa. The necessary two-thirds majority was not attained for a follow-up resolution on the situation of the Indian population by the General Assembly in 1947, and even with the institutionalization of apartheid in 1948, condemnation was initially not forthcoming. The General Assembly remained mute on the situation of black South Africans and limited its focus to the 'Treatment of People of Indian Origin in the Union of South Africa', with resolutions not going further than proposing a round-table conference between South Africa, India and Pakistan.[29]

It was 1952 before the General Assembly added 'The Question of Race Conflict resulting from the policies of apartheid of the Government of the Union of South Africa' to its agenda at the urging of a group of thirteen Arab and Asian states.[30] A number of resolutions were thence passed,[31]

International Economic Order', 1 May 1974. See Mohammed Bedjaoui, *Towards a New International Economic Order* (New York/London: UNESCO, 1979); Jagdish N. Bhagwati (ed.) *New International Economic Order: North–South Debate* (Cambridge, MA: MIT Press, 1977).

28 UN GA Res 1803 (XVII) 'Permanent sovereignty over natural resources', 14 December 1962; Common Art. 1(2) of the International Covenant on Civil and Political Rights (adopted 16 December 1966, entered into force 23 March 1976) 999 UNTS 171 (ICCPR) and the International Covenant on Economic, Social and Cultural Rights (adopted 16 December 1966, entered into force 3 January 1976) 993 UNTS 3 (ICESCR); and the 1974 Charter of Economic Rights and Duties of States, UN GA Res 3281 (XXIX) 12 December 1974. The doctrine is recognized as part of customary international law.

29 UN GA Res 265 (III) 14 May 1949; UN GA Res 395 (V) 2 December 1950.

30 See UN Doc A/2183 (1952).

31 See, for example, UN GA Res 616 (VII) 5 December 1952; UN GA Res 820 (IX) 14 December 1954.

prompting South Africa to announce in 1956 that, on the basis that it was being singled out for undue criticism, it would henceforth maintain only token representations at the UN headquarters in New York and the meetings of the General Assembly. Britain, France, Belgium and Australia were among the minority of states that routinely voted against resolutions condemning apartheid and supported draft resolutions tabled by South Africa claiming that the General Assembly had no competence to interfere in its domestic affairs. The policy adopted by states such as the USA, Canada and the Netherlands was to abstain from voting on resolutions concerning South Africa, and in plenary debates to question the propriety of retaining the issue on the General Assembly's agenda.

In 1958, South Africa restored its full participation in the UN due to a softening of the approach taken by the Assembly during its 1957 session. Resolutions on apartheid in 1958 and 1959 were couched in quite general terms, containing only a single paragraph apiece referring directly to South Africa that expressed regret and concern that it had not reconsidered its racial policies.[32] 1960, however, marked a notable shift towards a tougher stance on apartheid. The March 1960 killing of 69 peaceful demonstrators in Sharpeville by the South African police came at a time when the 'Third World' bloc was consolidating a solid majority at the UN as a result of a substantial spate of decolonization in the late 1950s and early 1960s. At the General Assembly's 1961 session, African and Asian delegations pressed for sanctions against South Africa, and a resolution tabled by five Asian countries asking states 'to consider taking such separate and collective action as is open to them' to bring about the abandonment of apartheid was adopted by 96 votes to 1.[33]

The following year, the General Assembly went further again by requesting its members to take specific measures aimed at bringing about the abandonment of apartheid, including the breaking of diplomatic, economic and transport relations with South Africa.[34] It subsequently requested all states and organizations 'to suspend cultural, educational, sporting and other exchanges with the racist régime and with organisations or institutions in South Africa which practise apartheid', and to

[32] UN GA Res 1248 (XIII) 30 October 1958; UN GA Res 1375 (XIV) 17 November 1959.

[33] UN GA Res 1598 (XV) 13 April 1961. The single dissenting vote in this instance was cast by Portugal.

[34] UN GA Res 1761 (XVII) 6 November 1962. The resolution also established the Special Committee against Apartheid which would report to the General Assembly and the Security Council.

'intensify the dissemination of information on the evils of apartheid'.[35] Resolutions pertaining to South Africa also began to employ the language of self-determination and emphasized apartheid as an inherent violation thereof, equating the rights of those subject to a regime of racial domination with those subject to colonialism and foreign occupation.

In 1970, for example, the General Assembly affirmed 'the legitimacy of the struggle of peoples under colonial and alien domination recognized as being entitled to the right of self-determination to restore to them that right by any means at their disposal', and condemned 'those Governments that deny the right to self-determination of peoples recognized as being entitled to it, especially of the peoples of southern Africa and Palestine.'[36] Such coupling of the Palestinian and anti-apartheid causes became commonplace in resolutions through the 1970s[37] as the non-aligned movement continued to build on seminal resolutions[38] regarding the three particular regimes it saw as inimical to human rights: colonialism, apartheid and foreign military occupation.

1973 saw the International Convention on the Suppression and Punishment of the Crime of Apartheid approved by the General Assembly.[39] This deepened the engagement of international law with apartheid beyond its prohibition – which had already been enshrined under Article 3 of the 1965 International Convention for the Elimination of All Forms of Racial Discrimination – by rendering it a criminal offence. Apartheid was defined as a crime against humanity[40] subject to universal jurisdiction, with States Parties to the Convention accordingly obliged to adopt legislative measures to suppress, discourage and punish the crime of apartheid. The General Assembly's concerted campaign against apartheid continued through the 1970s and 1980s with, *inter alia*, recognition of the liberation movements, rather than the apartheid regime, as

---

35 UN GA Res 2396 (XXIII) 2 December 1968.

36 UN GA Res 2649 (XXV) 30 November 1970.

37 See, for example, UN GA Res A/3070 (XXVIII) 30 November 1973.

38 UN GA Res 1514 (XV) 14 December 1960, UN GA Res 2625 (XXV) 24 October 1970.

39 UN GA Res 3068 (XXVIII) 30 November 1973.

40 The codification of the crime in the Apartheid Convention followed references to apartheid as a crime against humanity in soft law instruments from the mid-1960s onwards. See, for example, UN GA Res 2202 (XXI) 16 December 1966, para 1; 'Proclamation of Teheran, Final Act of the International Conference on Human Rights', UN Doc A/CONF.32/41, 13 May 1968, para 7. See also the 1968 Convention on the Non-Applicability of Statutory Limitations to War Crimes and Crimes against Humanity, Art. 1 of which considers crimes against humanity to include 'inhuman acts resulting from the policy of apartheid'.

'the authentic representatives of the overwhelming majority of the South African people';[41] proclamation of International Anti-Apartheid Year[42] and the International Year of Mobilisation for Sanctions against South Africa;[43] repeated calls for the release of Nelson Mandela and all political prisoners as well as condemnation of repressive 'anti-terrorism' legislation 'designed to suppress the legitimate struggle of the South African people for freedom and self-determination';[44] and the adoption of the International Convention against Apartheid in Sports.[45] The Assembly was particularly forceful in its condemnation of South Africa's Bantustan policy as invalid; denouncing the Bantustans as designed 'to consolidate and perpetuate domination by a white minority and the dispossession and exploitation of the African and other non-white people of South Africa as well as of Namibia.'[46]

The Security Council, for its part, had a more fitful and equivocal engagement with apartheid. Having avoided the issue for over a decade, the Council succumbed in March 1960 to the demands of 29 African and Asian states[47] and determined that the Sharpeville massacre and the broader problems of apartheid ought to be given due consideration.[48] The result was a Security Council resolution deploring the disturbances and loss of life in South Africa and recognizing that the situation had been brought about by the government's racial policies and disregard of General Assembly resolutions.[49] This was followed by resolutions acknowledging the situation in South Africa as a disturbance to international peace and security. No enforcement measures were pursued by the

---

41 UN GA Res 3151 (XXVIII) 14 December 1973.

42 UN GA Res 32/105 14 December 1977.

43 UN GA Res 36/172 17 December 1981.

44 UN GA Res 3411 (XXX) 28 November 1975.

45 UN GA Res 40/64 10 December 1985.

46 UN GA Res 2775 (XXVI) 29 November 1971. Two days after the granting of so-called independence to Transkei in 1976, a resolution was adopted by 130 votes to nil denouncing 'the establishment of Bantustans as designed to consolidate the inhuman policies of apartheid, to destroy the territorial integrity of the country, to perpetuate white minority domination and to dispossess the African people of South Africa of their inalienable rights.' See UN GA Res 31/6A (1976) 26 October 1976.

47 UN Doc S/4279 (1960).

48 The Security Council began consideration of the situation in South Africa for the first time on 30 March 1960 under an agenda item entitled 'The situation arising out of the large-scale killings of unarmed and peaceful demonstrators against racial discrimination and segregation in the Union of South Africa'.

49 Security Council Resolution 134, 1 April 1960 (with Britain and France abstaining).

Security Council, however, which limited itself to requests that the South African government cease its discriminatory practices, and called upon third states to voluntarily cease the sale of arms and military equipment to South Africa.[50]

The weight that may have been felt by South Africa as a result of these resolutions was also diluted somewhat by frequent abstentions by Britain and France. From 1964 to 1972, as the noose of apartheid continued to tighten in South Africa, the Security Council fell silent on the matter,[51] and draft resolutions for the imposition of economic sanctions against South Africa were vetoed by the three Western permanent members. In 1974, in response to a near-unanimous General Assembly resolution calling on the Security Council 'to review the relationship between the United Nations and South Africa in the light of the constant violation by South Africa of the principles of the Charter and the Universal Declaration of Human Rights',[52] a proposal to expel South Africa from the organization received ten votes of support at the Security Council, but was vetoed by Britain, France and the United States.

By the time of its endorsements of the General Assembly's call for non-recognition of the independence of the Transkei Bantustan[53] and its condemnation of South Africa's violent response to the Soweto uprising in 1976,[54] the Security Council's language had sharpened, now 'strongly condemning the South African racist régime for its resort to massive violence and repression', and issuing 'demands' that it abolish the policy of bantustanization and abandon apartheid.[55] Notably, its resolutions were now being adopted unanimously.

In November 1977, the Security Council took another unanimous

---

[50] See, for example, Security Council Resolution 181, 7 August 1963; Security Council Resolution 182, 4 December 1963; Security Council Resolution 191, 18 June 1964.

[51] The Security Council did address the situation in Namibia during this period, condemning South Africa's continuing occupation as illegal and criticizing the extension of apartheid policies beyond South Africa's borders. See Security Council Resolution 264, 20 March 1969; Security Council Resolution 276, 30 January 1970; Security Council Resolution 282, 23 July 1970 (with Britain, France and the USA abstaining).

[52] UN GA Res 3207 (XXIX) 30 December 1974.

[53] Security Council Resolution 402, 22 December 1976; Security Council Resolution 407, 25 May 1977. Similar denunciations came from the UN in response to subsequent denationalization of Bophuthatswana in 1977, Venda in 1979 and Ciskei in 1981.

[54] Security Council Resolution 392, 19 June 1976.

[55] Security Council Resolution 417, 31 October 1977.

decision under Chapter VII of the UN Charter to impose a mandatory arms embargo on South Africa,[56] the first and only enforcement measure in response to apartheid. This was followed up and recalled by subsequent resolutions in the years that followed,[57] and when the South African government imposed a state of emergency in large parts of the country in 1985, the Security Council urged the adoption of sectoral economic boycotts and the suspension of sports and cultural relations. This resolution, however, encouraged voluntary boycotts rather than binding member states to do so, and was not supported by the British or American governments.[58] On 8 March 1988, the Thatcher and Reagan administrations also vetoed a draft Security Council resolution for selective mandatory sanctions.

During the crucial period between 1986 and 1992, as South Africa careered through a turbulent and violent climactic chapter in its apartheid era, the Security Council was again conspicuously silent. The General Assembly stepped into the breach, and its 1989 'Declaration on Apartheid and its Destructive Consequences in Southern Africa'[59] – the culmination of an initiative from below that began with an African National Congress draft and made its way through the Organisation of African Unity and the Movement of Non-aligned Countries – would prove to be a landmark document, forming the basis for negotiations and transition to a non-racial democracy.

3. THE GHOSTS OF APARTHEID IN INTERNATIONAL LAW

Apartheid has been a largely forgotten and neglected concept in international law since the collapse of the regime in South Africa and establishment of formal democracy in 1994. Despite the comprehensive treatment of apartheid by the international legal system, there remains a sense among many international lawyers that it was a *sui generis* regime, specific to South Africa, and has now been confined to the annals of legal history. Alexander Zahar, for instance, calls the existence of the 'so-called crime of

---

56 Security Council Resolution 418, 4 November 1977.

57 See, *inter alia*, Security Council Resolution 421, 9 December 1977; Security Council Resolution 473, 13 June 1980; Security Council Resolution 558, 13 December 1984.

58 Security Council Resolution 569, 26 July 1985 (with Britain and the USA abstaining).

59 UN GA Res S-16/1, 4 December 1989.

apartheid' into question, partly on the basis of apartheid having been eliminated in South Africa.[60] Zahar concludes that 'politics rather than legal engineering' is behind the placement of apartheid in the Rome Statute of the International Criminal Court,[61] without providing an explanation of what – or whose – politics he is hinting at. It can only be assumed that he is suggesting that apartheid was retained in the Rome Statute merely as a token measure to placate the nations of the global South.

Western powers such as Canada, France, Germany, Italy, the Netherlands, Britain and the United States never ratified the Apartheid Convention, which could have exposed their own citizens to prosecution for aiding and abetting apartheid. Only five State Parties have acceded since 1994,[62] and post-apartheid South Africa itself has not ratified the Convention, opting to focus its internal transition on truth and reconciliation rather than accountability for apartheid-era crimes and human rights violations.[63] From the demise of the apartheid system in South Africa flowed the suspension of the UN treaty-monitoring body for the Apartheid Convention (the 'Group of Three') in 1995,[64] as well as the dissolution of the Special Committee against Apartheid and the UN Centre against Apartheid.[65] On these grounds the relevance of the international legal prohibition on apartheid beyond South African history is disputed from certain quarters.

That universally applicable norms of international law often materialize in response to a specific experience is no revelation. The historical triggers for the formulation of the prohibitions of slavery and genocide do not require citation. While the prohibition of apartheid may have been inscribed in international law with the prevailing circumstances in South Africa in mind, there is little to suggest that it was intended to be confined to those circumstances. Apartheid is described as policies of racial segregation and discrimination *similar* to those practised in *southern* Africa, which both reflects the fact that the history of apartheid relates to a larger swathe

---

60 Alexander Zahar, 'Apartheid as International Crime', in Antonio Cassese (ed.) *The Oxford Companion to International Criminal Justice* (Oxford: OUP, 2009) 246.

61 *Ibid.*

62 These are Serbia, Guatemala, Honduras, Moldova and Montenegro.

63 See Truth and Reconciliation Commission of South Africa Report (Cape Town: 2003).

64 UN Economic and Social Council, *Implementation of the International Convention on the Suppression and Punishment of the Crime of Apartheid: Report of the Group of Three established under the Convention*, UN Doc E/CN.4/1995/76, 25 January 1995, para 20.

65 *Ibid.*, para 12.

of the southern part of the African continent than only South Africa itself, and indicates that its prohibition is applicable beyond that region. Roger Clark correctly observes that 'the Convention is drafted in such a way as not to apply solely to the South African case, although South Africa is mentioned as an example'.[66]

The prohibition of apartheid is also more widely embedded in international law than solely with reference to the Apartheid Convention. The Committee on the Elimination of Racial Discrimination has confirmed the universal application of Article 3 of the International Convention on the Elimination of all forms of Racial Discrimination, which 'prohibits all forms of racial segregation in all countries.'[67] The International Law Commission views the prohibition of apartheid as a peremptory norm of general international law and emphasizes that the practice of apartheid amounts to 'a serious breach on a widespread scale of an international obligation of essential importance for safeguarding the human being.'[68]

---

66 Roger S. Clark, 'Apartheid', in M. Cherif Bassiouni, *International Criminal Law, Volume 1: Crimes* (Ardsley, NY: Transnational, 1999) 643–4. See also, for example, Ilias Bantekas and Susan Nash, *International Criminal Law* (2nd edn., New York: Routledge-Cavendish, 2003) 121–2; and Jeffrey S. Morton, *The International Law Commission of the United Nations* (Columbia, SC: University of South Carolina Press, 2000) 27: 'apartheid was declared to be a crime against humanity, with a scope that went far beyond South Africa. While the crime of apartheid is most often associated with the racist policies of South Africa after 1947, the term more generally refers to racially based policies in any state.' Such an interpretation can also be supported by reference to the Convention's *travaux préparatoires*. During the drafting process, state representatives envisaged that the terms of the Apartheid Convention would apply beyond the geographical limits of southern Africa. The delegate of Cyprus, for example, stated that: 'When drafting and adopting such an international convention, it must be remembered that it would become part of the body of international law and might last beyond the time when *apartheid* was being practiced in South Africa.' Statement by Mr. Papademas (Cyprus) UN General Assembly, Official Records, 28th Session, 1973, 3rd and 4th Committees, 2003rd meeting, 22 October 1973, Agenda Item 53, Draft Convention on the Suppression and Punishment of the Crime of *Apartheid*, UN Docs. A/9003 and Corr.1, chaps XXIII, sect. A.2; A/9095 and Add.1, 142-143, para 39. See also statement by Mr. Wiggins (United States of America) at 142, para 36: 'Article I would be open to very broad interpretations going beyond both the intentions of its drafters and the geographical limits of southern Africa'; statement by Mr. Petherbridge (Australia) at 143, para 4: 'the concept of apartheid was being widened to such an extent that it could be applicable to areas other than South Africa.'

67 UN Committee on the Elimination of Racial Discrimination, 'General Recommendation XIX: Racial segregation and apartheid (Art. 3)', UN Doc A/50/18, 18 August 1995, para 1.

68 International Law Commission, 'Draft Articles on Responsibility of States

The Commission notes that 'widespread agreement' is shared by states as to the peremptory character of the prohibition on apartheid, and that apartheid is 'prohibited in widely ratified international treaties and conventions admitting of no exception.'[69]

Contrary to Zahar's claim, the retention of apartheid as an international crime in the Rome Statute of the International Criminal Court, negotiated and adopted subsequent to the fall of apartheid in South Africa, can itself be seen as further evidence of the continuing applicability of the prohibition 'to other situations in which discriminatory racial practices entailing a dual structure of rights and duties are imposed by prevailing law on a subordinated people.'[70]

Although the general trend since the Second World War and the delegitimization of colonialism has been a slow but discernible move away from formal racialized state policies, such dual structures retain the potential to arise as long as consolidated settler-colonial populations and large-scale migration patterns persist. Where state-imposed discrimination and segregation between competing ethnic or racial groups exist, a system of apartheid can evolve if the domination over the subjugated group becomes sufficiently pervasive and institutionalized. In a situation of settler colonialism, this will most likely occur at the expense of the native population, as was the case in South Africa.

The situation may also materialize in reverse, however, if a settler community is discriminated against by an indigenous population seeking to preserve its own domination, as has been suggested in relation to 'the *de facto* separation of the two major ethnic groups in Fiji',[71] particularly following the coups in 1987 and the adoption of a new Constitution in 1990. The racially contingent system of governance discriminated between indigenous Fijians and indo-Fijians, prompting claims of 'apartheid, Fiji-style'[72] and 'Pacific apartheid'.[73] Although separate institutions were developed, however, it has been argued that the purpose was not to

---

for Internationally Wrongful Acts, with commentaries' (2001) II(2) *Yearbook of the Int'l L. Comm'n* 113.

[69] *Ibid.*, 112.

[70] 'Report of the Special Rapporteur on the situation of human rights in the Palestinian territories occupied since 1967', Richard Falk, UN Doc. A/65/331, 30 August 2010, para 5.

[71] Joshua Castellino and David Keane, *Minority Rights in the Pacific Region: A Comparative Legal Analysis* (Oxford: OUP, 2009) 198.

[72] William Sutherland, *Beyond the Politics of Race: An Alternative History of Fiji to 1992* (Canberra: Research School of Pacific Studies, 1992) 184.

[73] Then Australian Foreign Minister Alexander Downer, quoted in 'Fiji Prime Minister Sacked', *BBC News*, 27 May 2000.

establish a system of racial domination and subordination, but rather to protect native Fijians against domination and to preserve indigenous cultural values and autonomy.[74] In any event, Fiji's discriminatory 1990 Constitution was subsequently revoked, but the temporary manifestation of a form of institutionalized separateness – and the continuing fragility of an ethnically divided country that remains prone to routine coups d'état – suggests that the legal prohibition of apartheid cannot be discarded as obsolete.

Domination and segregation of migrant communities, particularly in the context of exploitative labour conditions, may also evoke undertones of apartheid. In its review of the United Arab Emirates, for example, members of the Committee on the Elimination of Racial Discrimination expressed concern in the context of Article 3 of the Convention over the separation between Emirati nationals and south Asian migrant workers, and warned of the dangers of a condition of racial segregation ensuing.[75]

As with any legal concept that possesses evocative and profound connotations, however, apartheid is liable to misuse for rhetorical and sensationalist purposes, and care must be exercised in this regard. While the apartheid terminology is used loosely in non-legal contexts to underscore the gravity of various inequalities, be they those labelled as 'gender apartheid', 'economic apartheid' or 'global apartheid', those engaged in legal advocacy have been guilty on occasion of unsupported reference to apartheid. In 2007, for example, Human Rights Watch launched a campaign describing systematic caste-based discrimination and segregation in India as 'Asia's hidden apartheid'. The organization published a lengthy report on caste-based discrimination and entitled it *Hidden Apartheid*, yet its 118 pages contained no substantive reference to or engagement with apartheid or the applicability of its prohibition to the situation of the Dalits.[76] While I do not intend to suggest that the prohibition of apartheid cannot be considered in this context, it has a specific meaning under international law that must be central to any such consideration.

Where sufficiently comprehensive evidence and analysis may not be available to support claims that the presently prevailing situations in Fiji, the United Arab Emirates or India meet the threshold of systematic

---

[74] Joseph Carens, 'Democracy and Respect for Difference: The Case of Fiji' (1992) 25 *U. Mich. J.L. Reform* 547, 594.

[75] Committee on the Elimination of Racial Discrimination, Seventy-fifth session, Summary Record of the 1936th Meeting, UN Doc CERD/C/SR.1936, 7 August 2009, para 41.

[76] Human Rights Watch, *Hidden Apartheid: Caste Discrimination against India's 'Untouchables'* (New York, February 2007).

and institutionalized racial domination required for the determination of an apartheid system, the debate regarding the circumstances of the Palestinians is more evolved. An increasingly expansive body of social science scholarship has used the apartheid paradigm to expound the situation that has developed since the formation of an ethnic-Jewish state in part of historic Palestine and its subsequent belligerent occupation of the remaining Palestinian territory, to the extent that some scholars have suggested that 'the notion of apartheid is gaining a specific meaning in the context of Israel/Palestine, where explicit comparisons with South Africa pale in importance.'[77]

Patterns of colonization and racialization feeding into systematic legal differentiation by the Israeli state in the realms of nationality, citizenship, land and rights certainly demand consideration of whether an institutionalized architecture of apartheid has been built, subjecting the Palestinians to Jewish-Israeli domination. Significantly, from the perspective of international law, detailed empirical study and legal analysis has found this to be the case with specific regard to the situation in the occupied Palestinian territory.[78] Such a conclusion has been echoed by consecutive UN Special Rapporteurs on Palestine.[79] In March 2012, the UN Committee on the Elimination of Racial Discrimination took the unprecedented step of censuring Israel under the rubric of apartheid. Having reiterated previous concerns about the general segregation of Jewish and non-Jewish sectors of Israeli society,[80] the Committee declared itself 'particularly appalled at the hermetic character of the separation' between Jewish and Palestinian populations in the Occupied Palestinian Territory (specifically citing separate legal systems and institutions, physical infrastructure, access to

---

[77] Abigail B. Bakan and Yasmeen Abu-Laban, 'Israel/Palestine, South Africa and the "One-State Solution": The Case for an Apartheid Analysis' (2010) 37(2) *Politikon* 331, 337.

[78] Human Sciences Research Council, *Occupation, Colonialism, Apartheid?: A Re-assessment of Israel's Practices in the Occupied Palestinian Territories under International Law* (HSRC 2009). A revised and updated version of this 300-page study is forthcoming as Virginia Tilley (ed.), *Beyond Occupation: Apartheid, Colonialism & International Law in the Occupied Palestinian Territories* (London: Pluto, 2012).

[79] John Dugard, 'Report of the Special Rapporteur on the situation of human rights in the Palestinian territories occupied since 1967', UN Doc A/HRC/4/17, 29 January 2007, paras 49–50, 61; Richard Falk, 'Report of the Special Rapporteur on the situation of human rights in the Palestinian territories occupied since 1967', UN Doc A/65/331, 30 August 2010, paras 3, 5.

[80] Committee on the Elimination of Racial Discrimination, 'Concluding observations: Israel', UN Doc CERD/C/ISR/CO/14–16, 9 March 2012, para 11.

services and resources, and entitlements to freedoms and rights) and urged Israel to prohibit and eradicate policies or practices of racial segregation and apartheid that 'severely and disproportionately affect the Palestinian population'.[81] While the evidence of a breach of the international legal prohibition of apartheid is strongest in respect of the West Bank and Gaza Strip, legal arguments have also been advanced regarding the situation inside Israel,[82] where even Palestinians holding Israeli citizenship are subject to discrimination in law on the basis that they are not of 'Jewish nationality'. With Israeli law applying extra-territorially to Jews and Palestinians through a number of funnels, there are also grounds for consideration of a comprehensive regime of domination over the Palestinian people as a whole, encompassing its three constituencies: citizens of Israel, residents of the occupied territories, and refugees who remain displaced outside historic Palestine.[83]

Despite this, a range of diplomatic and geo-political factors allow Israel to operate as an exceptional case, rendering otherwise unlawful practices beyond normative challenge and exempting Israel from mainstream political and academic discussions of racialization. The perpetual state of emergency that Israel has constructed for itself enables a temporally boundless process of population management. Pervasive Foucauldian security apparatuses in the context of a militarized society allow repression and discrimination to continue unchecked beneath the guise of security, with separate legal and institutional structures for the two racial groups entrenched and normalized. In this context, the prohibition of apartheid provides a valuable normative framework through which to unpack the racial elements of Israeli law and policy. It also carries significant strategic weight for the mobilization of international solidarity.

The question of Palestine remains a central issue to the anti-hegemonic struggle in international law, evidenced not just through what Israel and its supporters project as an agenda-driven singling out of one state by its counterparts in the General Assembly and the Human Rights Council – the credentials of some of whom is undoubtedly tainted by their own tendencies toward violence and repression – but also through the campaigning of civil society. In the context of the 'Arab Spring', Palestine has

---

81 *Ibid.*, para 24.

82 John Quigley, 'Apartheid Outside Africa: The Case of Israel' (1991) 2 *Indiana Int'l & Comp L. Rev.* 221.

83 For some reflections on the potential benefits of such a holistic approach, see John Reynolds, 'The Spectre of South Africa', *Jadaliyya*, 29 October 2011, available online at: http://www.jadaliyya.com/pages/index/3006/the-spectre-of-south-africa

been a far more central element of the protest movements in Egypt and beyond than the narratives of the Western media would suggest.[84]

The spectre of apartheid also permeates the favourable and widespread response of global civil society to a Palestinian call for boycott, divestment and sanctions against Israeli state institutions and agents. Issued in 2005 by a broad collective of Palestinian political parties, unions and civil society organizations, the 'BDS' call is modelled to a certain extent on the South African precedent, and cites Israel's 'entrenched system of racial discrimination' against the Palestinians among its core concerns.[85] The boycott campaign gained significant momentum on the back of Israel's 'Operation Cast Lead' offensive in the Gaza Strip in 2008–2009 and its attack in international waters on the 'Gaza Freedom Flotilla' in May 2010, and has been supported by Jewish groups in Israel and abroad.[86] In a manifesto citing the three pre-eminent issues to be addressed by progressive emancipatory politics in the twenty-first century, Richard Falk places 'support for the Palestinian Solidarity Movement, including its BDS campaign as both a creative form of resistance to oppressive circumstances' at the centre of the agenda, alongside the struggle against unjust and unsustainable forms of globalized neo-liberal capitalism and the need to urgently address the perils of man-made climate change.[87]

The international campaign against apartheid in South Africa was emblematic of the struggle of third world peoples and, with the workings of international law rarely favouring the people and nations of the global South, represents one of the few major success stories of the human rights movement that post-colonial nations can claim ownership of. In this sense, apartheid provides a useful lens through which to understand the engagement of the post-independence third world with international law. By the 1970s, the battle lines between lingering imperial interests and anti-imperial discourse were clearly drawn, evidenced by the General

---

84 See, for example, Matthew Duss, 'The Arab Spring and the Palestine Reality', *Middle East Progress*, 26 April 2011; Rami G. Khouri, 'The Arab Spring and Israel-Palestine', *Daily News Egypt*, 8 May 2011.

85 Palestinian BDS National Committee, 'Palestinian Civil Society Call for Boycott, Divestment and Sanctions', 9 July 2005, available online at: http://www.bdsmovement.net/call.

86 Groups such as Boycott from Within, Not in Our Name: Jews Opposing Zionism, and the International Jewish Anti-Zionist Network.

87 Richard Falk, 'A Few Notes on What is Left (or Toward a Manifesto for Revolutionary Emancipation)', 19 June 2011, available online at: http://richardfalk.wordpress.com/2011/06/19/a-few-notes-on-what-is-left-or-toward-a-manifesto-for-revolutionary-emancipation/.

Assembly's condemnation of 'the unholy alliance between Portuguese colonialism, South African racism, zionism and Israeli imperialism.'[88]

The connections between apartheid South Africa and Israel are well known, not least in respect of collaboration on nuclear weaponry[89] and Israel's support for the Bantustan policy,[90] but the historical ties long predate the official beginnings of the Israeli state and the apartheid regime in 1948. Their common settler-colonial roots and entwinement in the British imperial web are salient; Jan Smuts was an ardent advocate of Zionism, personally raising funds for a number of Zionist organizations while he was Prime Minister of South Africa,[91] and a prominent supporter of the 1917 Balfour Declaration which pledged British support to Jewish colonization of Palestine. During the Mandate period, the British cabinet offered Smuts the post of High Commissioner of Palestine 'so that he could civilize the Arabs as well as the Africans.'[92]

That notion of the civilizing mission – spawned by the European colonial project and percolating through the League of Nations – persists, now finding purchase in more subtle forms of racial patronization emanating from Western liberal discourse and its international institutions. The Palestinians are subject to a system of institutionalized discrimination bearing certain resemblances to the apartheid system in South Africa that the world came to outlaw as unbefitting humanity and civilization. Yet like the 'Communists' and 'terrorists' of black South Africa before them,[93] it is the Palestinians who must be civilized; schooled in the ways of Americanized national security and compelled to embrace Western conceptions of 'good governance' and socio-economic development.

International legal doctrine and practice is in many ways implicated

---

88 UN GA Res 3151 (XXVIII) 14 December 1973.

89 See, for example, Sasha Polakow-Suransky, *The Unspoken Alliance: Israel's Secret Alliance with Apartheid South Africa* (New York: Pantheon Books, 2010); Chris McGreal, 'Revealed: how Israel offered to sell South Africa nuclear weapons', *The Observer*, 23 May 2010.

90 See, for example, Jane Hunter, 'Israel and the Bantustans' (1986) 15(3) *Journal of Palestinian Studies* 53. Israel was the only UN member state – apart from apartheid South Africa – to afford diplomatic recognition of any kind to the Bantustans, and engaged in military and economic cooperation with Bophuthatswana and Ciskei.

91 Jane Hunter, *Israeli Foreign Policy: South Africa and Central America* (Boston, MA: South End Press, 1987) 21–2.

92 Mazower (n1) 53.

93 It bears noting that, as late as 1988, the United States government designated the African National Congress as a foreign terrorist organization, with Nelson Mandela only removed from Washington's terrorist watch list in 2008.

in such an anomaly. The history of apartheid in South Africa provides a stark reminder of how vested interests can cause the global hegemonic powers to maintain their support or mute their criticism of an unjust regime long past the point of that regime's illegitimacy becoming apparent to the world. The prohibition of apartheid provides an important normative tool to challenge such hegemonic interests where they persist or re-emerge, as well as a framework for a post-racial transformation, and thus should not be left forgotten.

11. Exploitation rebranded: How international law sold slavery as forced labour

Nicholas McGeehan

The prohibition of slavery was arguably the first human right which prompted action from a global community of states. This paper posits that the European colonial powers of the time were less concerned with abolishing slavery than they were with maintaining and developing their economic interests in Africa, a situation which led to a normative and institutional fracturing of slavery, as first forced labour and then servitude appeared in international law as practices related to, but somehow distinct from, slavery. It furthermore considers that the failure of human rights law to question the integrity of a framework it adopted, rather than designed, is to a large extent responsible for slavery's marginalization in the human rights discourse.

Part 1 addresses the human rights law framework on slavery, servitude and forced labour and highlights the extent of the confusion over the exact nature of those practices, with reference to recent case law from the European Court of Human Rights and the International Criminal Tribunal for the Former Yugoslavia (henceforth ECtHR and ICTY). Part 2 examines the position that slavery relates exclusively to ownership, a position which to a large extent justifies the separate existence of forced labour and servitude. Part three explores the background to the drafting of the international treaties which facilitated the separation of slavery and forced labour. Essentially, this is a study of how personalities and politics combined to shape the international lawmaking process which in turn influenced the treatment of slavery within human rights law.

1. SLAVERY, SERVITUDE AND FORCED LABOUR IN HUMAN RIGHTS LAW

Article 4 of the European Convention on Human Rights[1] proscribes slavery, servitude and forced labour in an almost identical manner to Article 8 of the International Covenant on Civil and Political Rights.[2] Article 4 of the European Convention reads as follows:

> 1. No one shall be held in slavery or servitude.
> 2. No one shall be required to perform forced or compulsory labour.
> 3. For the purpose of this article the term 'forced or compulsory labour' shall not include:
> a. any work required to be done in the ordinary course of detention imposed according to the provisions of Article 5 of this Convention or during conditional release from such detention;
> b. any service of a military character or, in case of conscientious objectors in countries where they are recognised, service exacted instead of compulsory military service;
> c. any service exacted in case of an emergency or calamity threatening the life or well-being of the community;
> d. any work or service which forms part of normal civic obligations.

The corresponding provision in the Inter-American Convention on Human Rights is similarly worded and constructed.[3] The pre-eminent instruments of human rights law therefore employ a substantively identical framework to proscribe this family of three similar, yet apparently distinct, practices.[4] Absent from all of these human rights instruments are definitions of the practices they individually and collectively proscribe. The definitions of slavery and forced labour are found in the Slavery Convention adopted by the League of Nations in 1926 and the International Labour Organization's 1930 Forced Labour Convention

---

1 Council of Europe, European Convention for the Protection of Human Rights and Fundamental Freedoms, 4 November 1950, ETS 5.

2 Convention for the Protection of Human Rights and Fundamental Freedoms, 213 UNTS 222, entered into force 3 September 1953; International Covenant on Civil and Political Rights (adopted 16 December 1966, entered into force 23 March 1976) 999 UNTS 171 (ICCPR).

3 Art. 6, American Convention on Human Rights, 1144 UNTS 123, 22 November 1969, entered into force 18 July 1978.

4 The African Charter of Human Rights makes no reference to forced labour, and considers slavery and the slave trade to be a degradation of man in the same Art. as the prohibition of torture. Art. 5, African Charter on Human and Peoples' Rights, OAU Doc CAB/LEG/67/3, entered into force 21 October 1986.

respectively,[5] instruments which pre-date the birth of the contemporary instruments and mechanisms of human rights law. However, despite the widespread acceptance of these definitions,[6] and a consistent instrumental framework, the legal discourse is characterized by disagreement. Slavery, servitude and forced labour clearly belong to the same family, but, to draw a taxonomic analogy, what exactly is that genus and within it, how are these species distinct from one another, if at all? Scholars, intergovernmental agencies and NGOs appear unable to agree on this fundamental issue, and in January 2010 the European Court of Human Rights delivered jurisprudence on Article 4, which not only contradicts an earlier Article 4 judgment of the Court, but appears to challenge the normative worth of the human rights law framework on slavery, servitude and forced labour.

1.1 Confusion in the Discourse

The relatively recent rise to prominence of trafficking in the human rights discourse, with the Palermo Protocol and the Council of Europe Convention Against Trafficking in Human Beings reflecting an international scramble for credibility on the issue,[7] has stimulated much-needed scholarly debate on the value of framing the modern abolitionist movement as an anti-trafficking movement, and on the nature of the exploitative practices which it seeks to tackle. James Hathaway is highly critical of the anti-trafficking movement, arguing that 'the decision to take action against "human trafficking," rather than against slavery in all of its contemporary forms, has given comfort to those who prefer not to tackle the claims of the majority of enslaved persons.'[8] Anne Gallagher disputes

---

[5] 1926 Slavery Convention or the Convention to Suppress the Slave Trade and Slavery, 60 LNTS 253, entered into force 9 March 1927. International Labour Organization Convention concerning Forced or Compulsory Labour, entered into force 1 May 1932.

[6] Servitude has no accepted definition in international law, although Art. 1 of the 1956 Supplementary Slavery Convention did enumerate practices and institutions which confer servile status on victims. Supplementary Convention on the Abolition of Slavery, the Slave Trade, and Institutions and Practices Similar to Slavery, 226 UNTS 3, entered into force 30 April 1957.

[7] Protocol to Prevent, Suppress and Punish Trafficking in Persons, Especially Women and Children, Supplementing the United Nations Convention Against Transnational Organized Crime, 60, UN Doc A/45/49 (Vol. I) (2001) entered into force 9 September 2003. Council of Europe Convention on Action against Trafficking in Human Beings, CETS No. 197, entered into force 1 February 2008.

[8] James Hathaway, 'The Human Rights Quagmire of "Human Trafficking"' (2008–2009) 49 *Va. J. Int'l L.* 1, 5.

Hathaway's claims in a direct rebuttal, and argues that his argument is fundamentally undermined by its reliance on the statistics of Kevin Bales.[9] According to Bales, an expert in modern-day slavery, there are 27 million slaves in the world today,[10] a figure which Gallagher considers to be inflated. In arriving at this conclusion, Bales – a sociologist – applies his own definition of slavery as 'a state marked by the loss of free will where a person is forced though violence or the threat of violence to give up the ability to sell freely his or her own labor power.'[11] Bales argues that no definition of slavery exists which is sufficiently dynamic to be applicable to historical, contemporary and future models of slavery.[12] Jean Allain, the most prolific legal scholar writing on slavery, argues that the issue is one of interpretation. He has accused Bales of 'riding roughshod over the law',[13] and raised questions over Bales' competence to appraise international law. The criticism is tempered with a recognition that Bales' approach 'does not diverge significantly'[14] from his own consideration of the legal definition of slavery. Bales deserves credit for raising the global profile of slavery, and if he has indeed attempted to ride roughshod over the law, it is surely in part because legal scholars have ignored the issue for so long – that Allain's study of the *travaux préparatoires* of the 1926 and 1956 Slavery Conventions, conducted in 2009, was the first ever of its kind is remarkable, and indicative of the dearth of academic research on the issue.[15] One wonders what Gallagher would make of Anne Yasmine Rassam's assertion that an estimated 200 million people worldwide are subject to contemporary forms of slavery.[16] M Cherif Bassiouni, for his

---

[9] Anne T. Gallagher, 'Human Rights and Human Trafficking: Quagmire or Firm Ground? A Response to James Hathaway' (2008–2009) 49 *Va. J. Int'l L.* 789, 802.

[10] Kevin Bales and Peter T. Robbins, '"No-one Shall Be Held in Slavery or Servitude": A Critical Analysis of International Slavery Agreements and Concepts of Slavery' (2001) 2 *Hum. Rts Rev.* 18, 38. See generally Kevin Bales, *Understanding Global Slavery: A Reader* (Berkeley: University of California Press, 2007).

[11] *Ibid.*, 32.

[12] *Ibid.*, 41.

[13] Jean Allain, 'Book Review' (2008) 20 *Int'l J. Refugee L.* 228, 228, reviewing Bales, *Understanding Global Slavery* (n10).

[14] Jean Allain, *The Definition of 'Slavery' in General International Law and the Crime of Enslavement within the Rome Statute*, ICC-CPI Guest Lecture Series of the Office of the Prosecutor, International Criminal Court, The Hague, 26 April 2007, 3.

[15] Jean Allain, *The Slavery Conventions: The* Travaux Préparatoires *of the 1926 League of Nations Convention and the 1956 United Nations Convention* (Leiden: Nijhoff, 2008).

[16] A. Yasmine Rassam, 'Contemporary Forms of Slavery and the Evolution

part, states that 'slavery is unique in that it has almost been totally eradicated since the beginning of the 1900s without reliance on an international enforcement machinery',[17] by which it is assumed that he is referring to chattel slavery since he goes on to criticize the 1926 Convention definition as being 'too limited' to apply to new forms of slavery.[18]

Modern-day models of slavery were, until recently, dealt with at UN level by the now-defunct Working Group on Contemporary Forms of Slavery. Allain has described its work as 'meaningless hyperbole',[19] Hathaway has concurred, arguing that it did 'little beyond periodically revising a catalog of the causes of slavery that is so vague and all encompassing that it is a meaningless standard around which to design real action.'[20] Suzanne Miers was so disheartened by the experience of attending a 1980 meeting of the Working Group that she felt compelled to write a book on international attempts to abolish slavery from the turn of the twentieth century.[21] The Working Group on Contemporary Forms of Slavery was disbanded in 2006 and replaced by the special mandate of the Special Rapporteur on Contemporary Forms of Slavery.[22] In the Resolution which set up that mandate, the Human Rights Council estimated that the number of people in slavery was over 12 million and increasing.[23] It does not state where this figure comes from, but the figure corresponds with the ILO's 2005 estimate of 12.3 million people worldwide in a condition of forced labour, a figure which has gained widespread acceptance.[24] Thus, the UN appears to believe that 12 million people are held in slavery, while the ILO, its specialized labour agency, believes that 12 million people worldwide are held in conditions of forced labour. The ILO conceptualization of slavery and forced labour is noteworthy:

> It is the view of the ILO that the definition of forced labour is sufficiently broad to encompass most forms of slavery, with the possible exception of a form of

---

of the Prohibition of Slavery and the Slave Trade Under Customary International Law' (1998–1999) 39 *Va. J. Int'l L.* 303, 305.

17 M. Cherif Bassiouni, 'Enslavement as an International Crime' (1990–1991) 23 *NYU J. Int'l L & P.* 445, 453.

18 *Ibid.*, 468.

19 Allain (n14) 3.

20 Hathaway (n8) 20.

21 Suzanne Miers, *Slavery in the Twentieth Century: The Evolution of a Global Problem* (Walnut Creek, CA: AltaMira Press, 2003) xii.

22 Human Rights Council Resolution 6/14, 28 September 2007.

23 *Ibid.*

24 Anti-Slavery International, the world's oldest and most prominent slavery NGO, refer to the ILO figure in their literature.

slavery consisting of ownership in which the slave is not under any obligation to perform work or services.[25]

The ILO therefore views slavery as part of the wider family of forced labour and there is an implied equation of slavery with ownership.

1.2 The European Court of Human Rights and Article 4

Two recent cases from the European Court of Human Rights illustrate the extent of the confusion over the precise legal character of slavery, servitude and forced labour. *Siliadin v. France* related to the treatment of a Togolese national, Ms Siwa-Akofa Siliadin, who arrived in France on a tourist visa at the age of 15, and was forced to work as a domestic servant for a period of several years before escaping.[26] Ms Siliadin's application to the European Court claimed that the French national authorities had failed to comply with their positive Article 4 obligation to secure tangible and effective protection against the practices prohibited therein.[27] The Court first assessed whether or not the applicant's treatment did indeed constitute any or all of the three practices proscribed by Article 4. The Court substantiated charges of forced labour and servitude,[28] but in relation to slavery, the Court concluded that Ms Siliadin's treatment did not constitute slavery: '[T]he evidence does not suggest that she was held in slavery in the proper sense, in other words, that Mr and Mrs B. exercised a genuine legal right of legal ownership over her, thus reducing her to the status of an "object".'[29] In arriving at its decision the Court referred to the definition provided in the 1926 Slavery Convention: 'slavery is the status or condition of a person over whom any or all of the powers attaching to ownership are exercised.' It stated that the 1926 definition 'corresponds to the "classic" meaning of slavery as it was practiced for centuries.'[30]

The ECtHR's 2010 decision in *Rantsev v. Cyprus and Russia* delivered timely and important jurisprudence on trafficking and the positive Article 4 obligations which flow therefrom, but of greatest interest here is its thinly

---

25 ILO Special Action Programme to Combat Forced Labour and Human Trafficking, *Casebook of Court Decisions* (Geneva: International Labour Organization, 2009) 9.

26 *Siliadin v. France*, Application No. 73316/01, Judgment, 26 July 2005.

27 *Ibid.*, para 58.

28 *Ibid.*, paras 118–120 (forced labour) paras 126–128 (servitude).

29 *Ibid.*, para 122.

30 *Ibid.*, para 122.

veiled criticism of the *Siliadin* judgment and its support for jurisprudence from international criminal law which takes an entirely different stance on the character of slavery and its relationship to servitude and forced labour.[31] The *Rantsev* case related to the death of a young Russian woman who had been working as a cabaret artiste in Cyprus. According to an *ex officio* report of the Cypriot Ombudsman, the word 'artiste' had become synonymous with prostitute in Cyprus.[32] The case gave the Court its first opportunity to develop jurisprudence on trafficking as it pertained to Article 4, and to outline the concomitant procedural obligations, not only for states in whose territorial jurisdictions alleged violations took place, but also for the home states of applicants or their families. The Court stated that it 'considers it unnecessary to identify whether the treatment about which the applicant complains constitutes "slavery", "servitude", or "forced and compulsory labour"',[33] but there are clear indications that it disagreed with the *Siliadin* judgment, in particular its interpretation of slavery and the distinctions it drew between slavery, servitude and forced labour. In *Rantsev*, the Court referred to, but did not state any support for, the *Siliadin* judgment's assertion that slavery requires the 'genuine' legal right of ownership.[34] The Court was less equivocal on the issue of evolutive and effective interpretation,[35] the importance of which was asserted and then affirmed by reference to case law from the International Criminal Tribunal for the Former Yugoslavia.

The Court observed that the ICTY concluded that the traditional concept of 'slavery' has evolved to encompass various contemporary forms of slavery based on the exercise of any or all of the powers attaching to the right of ownership.[36] The true value of the European Court's *Rantsev* judgment lies not in its explicit assertion of the applicability of trafficking to Article 4, but rather its implicit criticism of its own Article 4 case law in *Siliadin*. A brief study of the ICTY *Kunarac* judgment highlights the fundamental nature of that criticism.

---

[31] *Rantsev v. Cyprus and Russia*, Application No. 25965/04, Judgment, 7 January 2010.

[32] *Ibid*, para 83.

[33] *Ibid*, para 282.

[34] *Ibid*, para 276.

[35] *Ibid*, paras 274–275. *Loizidou v. Turkey (Preliminary Objections)* Application No. 15318/89, Judgment, 23 March 1995, para 71: 'That the Convention is a living instrument which must be interpreted in the light of present day conditions is firmly rooted in the Court's case law [. . .] It follows that these provisions cannot be interpreted solely in accordance with the intentions of their authors as expressed more than forty years ago.'

[36] *Rantsev* (n31), para 280.

The *Kunarac* Appeals Chamber laid down the gauntlet to human rights law on three key points: the need for precise, evolutive interpretation of the definition of slavery; the impracticality of an enumerative approach to slavery; and the legal justification for the existing distinctions between slavery, servitude and forced labour. Firstly, it asserted that, today, *de jure* slavery has evolved to the point where it relates exclusively to a condition, not a legal status:

> . . . the law does not know of a 'right of ownership over a person'. Article 1(1) of the 1926 Slavery Convention speaks more guardedly 'of a person over whom any or all of the powers attaching to the right of ownership are exercised.' That language is to be preferred.[37]

Thus, according to the Appeals Chamber, to assert that slavery relates to a genuine right of ownership is not simply a restrictive interpretation and a failure to treat the 1926 Slavery Convention as a living instrument, it amounts to a literal misreading of the definition of slavery provided in that Convention, which refers not to the alleged right of ownership, but to powers attaching to the right of ownership. Secondly, on account of slavery's multifarious character, it rejected the adoption of an enumerative approach to slavery:

> . . . the traditional concept of slavery, as defined in the 1926 Slavery Convention and often referred to as 'chattel slavery', has evolved to encompass various contemporary forms of slavery which are also based on the exercise of any or all of the powers attaching to the right of ownership. In the case of these various contemporary forms of slavery, the victim is not subject to the exercise of the more extreme rights of ownership associated with 'chattel slavery', but in all cases, as a result of the exercise of any or all of the powers attaching to the right of ownership, there is some destruction of the juridical personality; the destruction is greater in the case of 'chattel slavery' but the difference is one of degree.
> 38. . . [T]he question whether a particular phenomenon is a form of enslavement will depend on the operation of the factors or indicia of enslavement identified by the Trial Chamber . . . Consequently, it is not possible exhaustively to enumerate all of the contemporary forms of slavery which are comprehended in the expansion of the original idea . . .[39]

Thirdly, in the most striking section of the judgment, the Appeals Chamber characterized enslavement as an umbrella term covering the

---

[37] *Prosecutor v. Kunarac et al.,* Appeal Judgment, Cases No. IT-96-23-T and IT-96-23/1-T, 12 June 2002, para 118.

[38] *Ibid.,* para 117.

[39] *Ibid.,* para 119.

three practices of slavery, servitude and forced labour. It first defined enslavement in customary international law:

> . . . at the time relevant to the indictment, enslavement as a crime against humanity in customary international law consisted of the exercise of any or all of the powers attaching to the right of ownership over a person . . . This definition definition [sic] may be broader than the traditional and sometimes apparently distinct definitions of either slavery, the slave trade and servitude or forced or compulsory labour found in other areas of international law. This is evidenced in particular by the various cases from the Second World War . . . which have included forced or compulsory labour under enslavement as a crime against humanity. The work of the ILC . . . further supports this conclusion.[40]

The work of the ILC to which the Appeals Chamber refers is the 1996 International Law Commission's Draft Code of Crimes against the Peace and Security of Mankind, in which the ILC characterized enslavement as:

> . . . establishing or maintaining over persons a status of slavery, servitude or forced labour contrary to well-established and widely-recognized standards of international law, such as: the 1926 Slavery Convention (slavery); the 1956 [Supplementary Slavery Convention] (slavery and servitude); the [ICCPR] (slavery and servitude); and the 1957 [Forced Labour Convention] (forced labour).[41]

In this characterization, enslavement is as an umbrella term, which can be applied to slavery, servitude and forced labour. Implicitly, this seems to suggest that while three separate practices do exist in international law, any distinction between the three is irrelevant in the *lex specialis* of international criminal law.

It is beyond the scope of this paper to analyse in detail the three normative issues raised by the *Kunarac* judgment i.e. slavery's relationship to ownership, the legal impossibility of adopting an enumerative approach to slavery, and the necessity to normatively distinguish between slavery, forced labour and servitude. However, it is possible to briefly disprove the assertion that slavery has ever been related exclusively to ownership in international law, and to raise questions over the dubious foundations of the introduction of forced labour, as distinct from slavery, into international law. If they are substantively identical (and this paper makes no claim that they are), what factors could

---

40 *Ibid.*, para 539.

41 Report of the International Law Commission on the work of its forty-eighth session, 6 May–26 July 1996, GA, Supp. No 10 (A/51/10) 93, Art. 18 of the Draft Code ('Crimes against Humanity').

explain the normative and institutional separation of slavery and forced labour in the 1920s? With regard to the enumeration of slavery, it suffices to say that slavery is a complex socio-economic concept and any attempt to comprehensively enumerate its various forms will only serve to quasi-legitimize new forms of slavery which develop in response. It is to just such an approach that we owe the unwelcome existence of servitude in international law.[42]

2. SLAVERY AND OWNERSHIP

According to Article 1(1) of the1926 Slavery Convention, 'slavery is the status or condition of a person over whom any or all of the powers attaching to the right of ownership are exercised'. The 1926 Slavery Convention does not refer simply to the legal status of a slave flowing from rights of ownership – what might have been termed *de jure* slavery – but also to the condition of a slave resulting from the exercising of powers attaching to ownership. Reference to the *travaux préparatoires* as a supplementary source of interpretation,[43] confirms that the drafters intended both status and condition to be prohibited. The definition of slavery first proposed in the British Draft Protocol, the first text in the drafting process, read as follows: 'Slavery is the status in which one person exercises a right of property over another.'[44] After some debate, the definition which remains the accepted definition of slavery in international law was proposed by Viscount Cecil of Chelwood, who acted as Rapporteur: '[S]lavery is the status or condition of a person over whom any or all of the powers attaching to the right of ownership are exercised.' The initial definition related exclusively to the legal status associated with the exercising of a legal right whereas the accepted definition extends its scope to include a condition associated with the exercise of power. The text therefore proscribed what, at the time, could legitimately be termed *de facto* slavery as well as *de jure* slavery.

In 1950, the United Nations Secretary-General suggested that an ad hoc Committee revisit the 1926 definition with a view to assessing whether

---

42 Art. 1 1956 Supplementary Slavery Convention enumerated practices which conferred servile status on victims. Supplementary Convention on the Abolition of Slavery, the Slave Trade, and Institutions and Practices Similar to Slavery, 226 UNTS 3, entered into force 30 April 1957.

43 Art. 32 Vienna Convention on the Law of Treaties, 115 UNTS 331, entered into force 27 January 1980.

44 Art. 1(2) British Draft Protocol.

or not it 'might be improved in the light of modern thinking.'[45] The ad hoc Committee concluded that 'there is not sufficient reason for discarding or amending the definition of slavery contained in Article 1 of the International Slavery Convention of 1926'.[46] The League of Nations archives shed little light on the evolution of the definition,[47] but it is possible to draw a clear conclusion from the evolution alone. The drafters did not intend that slavery be associated exclusively with legal ownership. The claim that slavery does relate exclusively to ownership cannot be substantiated by reference either to the text of the 1926 Slavery Convention, the drafting history of the definition in the *travaux préparatoires*, or by revisiting the drafting process used by the UN ad hoc Committee in the drafting of the 1956 Supplementary Convention. Nonetheless, the European Court in *Siliadin* stated that slavery relates to a genuine right of legal ownership, and the International Labour Organization – the spearhead of the contemporary abolitionist movement – continues to conflate slavery with ownership.

In trying to make sense of the confusing normative framework on slavery, servitude and forced labour, it is essential to examine the drafting history of the first Slavery and Forced Labour Conventions, but for the purposes of this paper, it is perhaps more interesting to look at the background to their drafting. These instruments – drafted well before the birth of human rights law and its espousal of the equality of man – were shaped by individuals, not by states, and they were adopted by colonial powers at the height of the colonial era.

3. THE DUBIOUS FOUNDATIONS OF FORCED LABOUR

The British abolitionist movement remained the key player in the global drive for abolition at the start of the twentieth century, and it played a central role in the push for international cooperation in the aftermath of World War Two. Figures such as Sir John Harris and E.D. Morel took on the mantle of the renowned nineteenth-century abolitionists William Wilberforce and Thomas Clarkson.[48] Harris, with his 'boundless

---

45 Economic and Social Council, Report of the Ad Hoc Committee on Slavery (Second Session) UN Doc E/1988, E/AC.33/13, 4 May 1951, 5–7.

46 *Ibid.*

47 Allain (n15) 57.

48 The work of the British nineteenth-century abolitionist movement is detailed in Adam Hochschild, *Bury the Chains: the British Struggle to Abolish Slavery*

enthusiasm and single-mindedness',[49] was secretary of the Anti-Slavery and Aborigines Protection Society, and a key player behind the scenes in the drafting of the first Slavery and Forced Labour Conventions. It was largely on account of Harris's persistent lobbying that the Assembly of the League of Nations put slavery on its agenda for 1923. This led to the setting up of the Temporary Slavery Commission in 1924, a body which 'was to change fundamentally the emphasis of the League's work in the area of slavery from being one of monitoring, to one of legislating the international suppression of slavery, the slave trade and forced labour.'[50] Harris had close working relationships with two members of the Temporary Slavery Commission: Frederick Lugard, a British former colonial official with whom he kept up 'voluminous correspondence'[51] and Harold Grimshaw, chief of section in the Diplomatic Division in the International Labour Organization. Also on the Committee were Maurice Delafosse from France, Alfredo Freire d'Andrade from Portugal, Albrecht Gohr from Belgium (Director of Justice in King Leopold's administration), Commandant Roncagli from Italy, Van Rees from the Netherlands, (who was vice-President of the Permanent Mandates Commission, a body on which Lugard, Grimshaw and Freire d'Andrade also served), and Louis Dante Bellagarde, who was the only non-white member. Van Rees, Lugard, Grimshaw and Freire d'Andrade had also sat on the Permanent Mandates Commission.[52] On 25 July 1925, Gohr presented the Temporary Slavery Commission's findings to the Council of the League of Nations. It recommended that the League should negotiate a treaty, the League accepted the proposal, and a British draft protocol was drawn up, the document which was to form the basis of the 1926 League of Nations Slavery Convention.[53]

Harris and Grimshaw were also instrumental in securing the remit for forced labour for the International Labour Organization.[54] It was at Grimshaw's suggestion that an ILO Committee of Experts on Native Labour was convened to examine the issue of forced labour, four of whose

---

(London: Macmillan Press, 2005). See also Adam Hochschild, *King Leopold's Ghost: A Story of Greed, Terror and Heroism in Colonial Africa* (New York: Mariner Books, 1999).

49 Miers (n21) 63.

50 Allain (n15) 32.

51 Miers (n21) 103.

52 *Ibid.*, 100–16.

53 *Ibid.*, 121.

54 Gertrude E. Newbury and Colin W. Newbury, 'Labor Charters and Labor Markets: The ILO and Africa in the Interwar Period' (1976) 3 *Journal of African Studies* 311, 314.

members – Lugard, Gohr, Freire d'Andrade and Van Rees – also sat on the Temporary Slavery Commission. The findings of this Committee formed the basis of the 1930 ILO Forced Labour Convention.[55] Ostensibly, the 1926 Slavery Convention and the 1930 Forced Labour Convention were entirely separate instruments, regulated by separate agencies, but in reality they were designed to complement one another. Furthermore, their creation was not down to the actions of states, but rather the ambition of a core group of idealistic figures – Allain compares the atmosphere during the drafting of the 1926 Convention to that of 'a gentleman's club'[56] – who quickly appreciated the potential offered by the institutions and mechanisms of the new League of Nations in the fight to abolish slavery and raise labour standards in the colonies. The process, from conception to adoption, pitted idealistic individuals such as John Harris, Frederick Lugard, Viscount Cecil and Harold Grimshaw, against the political, strategic and economic prerogatives of the European colonial powers. However, the two parties arguably shared a common goal, which was not the abolition of slavery, but the facilitation and continuation of a more benevolent slavery, which could provide all the perceived economic benefits of slavery but would be free of the abuses which had characterized previous models. To achieve this, slavery would have to be simultaneously abolished and repackaged.

The 1926 Slavery Convention defined and proscribed slavery, but an examination of the text and drafting history of the 1930 Forced Labour Convention shows that it was, in effect and purpose, facilitative, not proscriptive. Provisions on exploitative contract labour, trade unions and complaints mechanisms were omitted from the text,[57] and colonial military labour was exempt from the scope of the Convention.[58] Forced labour was only to be used in exceptional circumstances,[59] according to certain conditions,[60] but full discretion as to what might constitute exceptional circumstances was granted to the colonial authorities by the terms of Article 8(1): '[T]he responsibility for every decision to have recourse to

---

55 Miers (n21) 134.

56 Allain (n15) Introduction.

57 International Labour Conference, Twelfth Session, Geneva 1929. International Labour Office. Appendix VII. Third Item on the Agenda: Forced Labour. 15 June 1929, 968 (contract labour) and 980 (trade unions and complaints mechanisms).

58 Art. 2(2)(a) Convention concerning Forced or Compulsory Labour, ILO Convention C029, 28 June 1930, entered into force 1 May 1932 (hereinafter, 'Forced Labour Convention').

59 Art. 1(2) Forced Labour Convention.

60 Arts 5–24, Forced Labour Convention.

forced or compulsory labor shall rest with the highest civil authority in the territory concerned.' This provision, combined with absence of any procedural reporting, supervisory or enforcement mechanisms render the 1930 Forced Labour Convention closer in character to a set of self-regulated best practices than a human rights treaty, which it manifestly was not. The humanitarian lobby's support was based on its belief that theoretically at least, it would be slavery without the abuses and the horrors of the most egregious models of slavery, such as the Atlantic slave trade. However, they were also aware that chattel slavery was not the greatest problem facing the abolitionist movement. As early as 1909, the amalgamation of the British and Foreign Anti-Slavery Society and the Aborigines Protection Society was justified in terms of the dangers posed by non-chattel forms of slavery.

> Now that slavery is so commonly found under a disguise, and the great evil which has to be fought is the exploitation and coercion of natives in order to secure their labour for the white man . . . one strong society, representing the cause of the native races of mankind, could more effectively serve their interests.[61]

The ILO's representative on the Temporary Slavery Commission, Harold Grimshaw, made a similar point in a 1924 letter to John Harris.

> I have no need to explain at length to you that 'slavery' in the old sense, is not the worst problem facing humanity, but that under other names and rather different conditions a state of virtual slavery is devastating large populations.[62]

This prompts the question as to why, in such circumstances, the humanitarian lobby chose not only to support but to lobby for a separate convention on forced labour. The timing of the drafting of the 1926 Slavery and 1930 Forced Labour Conventions is key to understanding their combined purpose in this regard. They were drafted well before the birth of human rights law and its assertion of the equality of man, at a time when racist ideology prevailed. In the drafters, this tended to manifest itself as paternalism. As Miers points out, 'the attitude of the Temporary Slavery Commission to indigenous peoples left much to be desired. They were regarded as children to be protected and brought up to be consumers

---

[61] *Anti-Slavery Reporter, XXIX*, no. 2, series 4, March–May 1909, cited in Miers (n21) 63.

[62] Grimshaw to Harris ('Private') 4 February 1924, cited in Newbury and Newbury (n54) 314.

working for wages and producing crops like the workers of the Western world.'[63] A report of the Temporary Slavery Commission states that 'to propose labour legislation for backward peoples would be to undertake a task which lies entirely outside the competence of the Temporary Slavery Commission'.[64] Frederick Lugard 'tended to dismiss non-Muslim peoples as savages'[65] and Freire d'Andrade 'believed firmly that Africans would not work unless forced to do so.'[66] States, for their part, expressed racist views unabashedly. Portugal disputed the inclusion of a forced labour provision in the 1926 Convention on the grounds that it would suggest 'to the native races that its prohibition implies for them a right to idleness' and that it was counter to their 'well-being and development.'[67] The British Draft Protocol made specific reference to 'the less advanced races'[68] and in 1930, the Government of India proposed to allow an exception in the Forced Labour Convention for 'any work or service which in India may be exacted in virtue of measures taken by the competent authority for the regeneration of certain tribes or social groups whose members are addicted to the systematic commission of crimes'.[69] It was only defeated by a ratio of two votes to one. A deputy to the French parliament from Senegal, speaking in support of the need for military labour, stated:

> I speak as an African ... on behalf of my race and of my people and my country, and I say that we are by nature indolent and so incapable that we really require force and compulsion; that even under stress and famine we are not capable of finding food in the forest unless someone compels us to do it.[70]

---

63 Miers (n21) 115.

64 League of Nations, Note Submitted to the First Sub-Committee of the Sixth Committee by the Portuguese Delegate, General Freire d'Andrade, A.VI/S.C.1/2.1925, 11 September 1925, as found in Folder R.67.D.46214 entitled 'La question de l'esclavage: Discussions, y relatives, de la Vie Assembleé', 4.

65 Miers (n21) 103.

66 Personal correspondence between G.A. Morton and the Anti-Slavery and Aboriginal Protection Society from October 1924, as forwarded by Grimshaw to Rappard, 27 January 1925, in LON 1/41255/23252, cited in Miers (n21) 104.

67 Note Submitted to the First Sub-Committee of the Sixth Committee by the Portuguese Delegate (n64) 3.

68 League of Nations, Annex 1: Slavery: Draft Resolution and Protocol, Official Journal: Record of the Sixth Assembly, Meetings of the Committees, Minutes of the Sixth Committee (Political Questions) Special Supplement No. 39, 14 September 1925, 41.

69 International Labour Conference, Fourteenth Session, Geneva 1930, Appendix V, First Item on the Agenda: Forced Labour, 693.

70 Speech by Vernon to the 8th Colonial Office Conference, 8 July 1930, COCP 885/32 Miscellaneous no. 416 confidential and FO 371/15036 W 8250/34/52, 128–44. Cited in Miers (n21) 146. The deployment of racist ideology to excuse

The Workers' Group supported the text on the basis that, for all its shortcomings, it was a step in the right direction,[71] but its unease was palpable:

> There are two ways of regarding the proposed Draft Convention so far as it affects forced labour for public purposes (no-one having undertaken to defend publicly forced labour for the profit of private persons): It may be really intended either to prepare the way for its final disappearance in the shortest possible period; or else to cover this aspect of forced labour, to legitimize it, and to perpetuate by regulations. The Workers' Group is obliged to declare that, in spite of the declarations of principle which have been made, it is not convinced that in the text which has been submitted to us the former of these two ideas has prevailed.[72]

The Workers' Group had good reason to be sceptical, in view of the importance of African resources to European colonial powers. Writing in 1930, Benson outlined the extent of colonial involvement in Africa, a process which, he argued, had 'not yet reached its maximum velocity.'[73] He stated:

> British Africa, however, is perhaps not the most striking example during the year of the harnessing of European capital to African resources. In France loans have been authorised amounting to nearly five thousand million francs for French West Africa, Madagascar, Cameroons, Togoland, French Equatorial Africa, and also Indo-China. With this money, the execution is being planned of far-reaching schemes for the creation of the pre-conditions of modern production: railways, roads, navigable rivers, mechanical transport. The Portuguese Government, although in the end it appears to have rejected the proposal for political reasons, seriously considered the settlement of a thousand Poles in Angola. The Belgian Congo is continuing its advance, no longer content with the production of raw materials. Congo-grown cotton is being spun and woven in the Congo, where mills have been established and African mill-workers trained by Belgians.[74]

---

forced servitude was not the preserve of the white European. Writing of the justification of slavery in the former Abyssinia, Lord Buxton wrote, 'The excuse which the Abyssinians make is that these people [the slave class] would otherwise be savages running naked in the forest and it is good for them to come into touch with civilization.' Lord Noel Buxton, 'Slavery In Abyssinia: Address Given at Chatham House on May 23rd 1932' (1932) 11(4) *International Affairs* 512, 514.

71 International Labour Conference (n69) 725.

72 *Ibid.*. 727.

73 W. Benson, 'African Labour in 1930' (1931) 30 *J. of the Royal African Society* 119, 142.

74 *Ibid.*

The new League of Nations system empowered the humanitarian lobby to push for reform, but only up to a point which would not overly compromise the interests of states. Thus, slavery was abolished, and a system of self-regulation was imposed on the use of forced labour. Slavery as a business was simply repackaged and rebranded as forced labour, but in order to achieve this, a normative and institutional separation was required, and that separation still exists, unchallenged, in international law today.

4. CONCLUSION

Human rights law has done little to challenge the prevailing normative framework on slavery, servitude and forced labour. This trinity rests, to a large extent, on the argument that slavery is related exclusively to a legal right of ownership, a position which has no legal basis. The thesis that racist ideology provided an ideological basis for the fragmentation of slavery does not necessarily preclude the contemporary efficacy of individual components of the slavery and forced labour conventions. However, the confusion in the legal discourse, which reached a nadir with the European Court of Human Rights' *Siliadin* judgment, does warrant an examination of an alternative normative framework in the fight against modern-day slavery. The approach taken by international criminal law, most notably in the ICTY's *Kunarac* judgment, discussed previously in brief, is arguably more insightful and practical. The *Rantsev* judgment's implicit support for this approach can be interpreted as a suggestion that human rights law should reconceptualize and reframe its approach to slavery. An important step in this regard, is a recognition that slavery, despite its legal abolition, did not disappear. It was simply more convenient to call it something else for a while.

12. Between the wars – the Refugee Convention of 1933: A contemporary analysis

Peter Fitzmaurice

The modern study of the law of refugee protection conventionally commences in the years following the Second World War. The immediate post-war period saw the creation of the United Nations and the emergence of the modern international human rights regime, with which refugee protection is closely entwined.[1] The mass displacements caused by the war led to the setting up of the United Nations Relief and Rehabilitation Agency in 1943, which by the war's end was tasked with refugee protection. In the years following the war, European refugees were repatriated or resettled under the aegis of the International Refugee Organization, which was succeeded by the United Nations High Commissioner for Refugees as the principal UN agency concerned with refugees.[2]

Finally, the Convention Relating to the Status of Refugees[3] was drafted and adopted in 1951. Although the definition of a refugee in the 1951 Convention was initially limited temporally to events occurring before 1 January 1951, and contracting states to the Convention could limit their obligations geographically, to events occurring in Europe before that date, these limitations were removed by the 1967 Protocol relating to the Status of Refugees.[4] The 1951 Convention and the 1967 Protocol taken together are now universally considered the cornerstone of international refugee

[1] 'Everyone has the right to seek and enjoy in other countries asylum from persecution' Art. 14 (1), Universal Declaration of Human Rights, UNGA Res 217 A(III) UN Doc A/810 91, UN General Assembly, 10 December 1948.

[2] See Louise W. Holborn, *The International Refugee Organization: A Specialized Agency of the United Nations, its History and Work 1946–1952* (London: OUP, 1956).

[3] Convention Related to the Status of Refugees (adopted 28 July 1951, entered into force 22 April 1954) 189 UNTS 2545 (1951 Refugee Convention).

[4] Art. 1(B), 1951 Refugee Convention.

protection and the 1951 Convention has been termed 'the *Magna Carta* for refugees'.[5]

Modern readers of the 1951 Convention rightly tend to focus on the refugee definition in Article 1(A)(2) of the 1951 Convention. It is often forgotten, however, that the 1951 Convention actually resurrected a series of earlier international commitments to protect refugees. The preceding article states:

> For the purposes of the present Convention , the term 'refugee' shall apply to any person who: Has been considered a refugee under the Arrangements of 12 May 1926 and 30 June 1928 or under the Conventions of 28 October 1933 and 10 February 1938, the Protocol of 14 September 1939 or the Constitution of the International Refugee Organisation . . .

The 1933 Convention Relating to the International Status of Refugees[6] was the first attempt to create a comprehensive legal framework for refugees. It was the first international multilateral treaty to offer refugees legal protection and guarantee their basic civil and economic rights, and was second only to the 1926 Slavery Convention in establishing a voluntary system of international supervision of human rights.[7] The 1933 Convention, which itself drew on earlier precedents of the law of responsibility for injuries to aliens and international protection of national minorities,[8] was a milestone in the protection of refugees. Crucially, it was the first international agreement to guarantee the right to non-*refoulement* which, in broad terms, now proscribes the forced direct or indirect removal of a refugee to a country or territory where he or she runs a risk of being exposed to persecution.[9] The right to non-*refoulement* is considered fundamental to modern international refugee law.[10]

---

[5] James M. Read, *Magna Carta for Refugees* (New York: United Nations Information Services, 1953).

[6] Convention Relating to the International Status of Refugees (adopted 28 October 1933, entered into force 13 June 1935) 159 LNTS 3663 (1933 Refugee Convention).

[7] Convention to Suppress the Slave Trade and Slavery (adopted 25 September 1926, entered into force 9 March 1927) 60 LNTS 25.

[8] James Hathaway, *The Rights of Refugees Under International Law*, (Cambridge: CUP, 2005) 75.

[9] The term derives from the French *refouler*, which means to drive back or repel. The prohibition on non-*refoulement* in international law is usually described in relation to three key areas: refugee law, human rights law and customary law.

[10] For a modern examination and analysis of the prohibition in a variety of international and regional instruments see Kees Wouters, *International Legal Standards for the Protection from* Refoulement (Antwerp: Intersentia, 2009).

Tragically, the 1933 Convention in many ways marked the high watermark of refugee protection between the wars. The 1933 Convention was severely limited in its scope to those groups already considered refugees under the protection of the League of Nations,[11] and ultimately, it was ratified by only eight countries, many of whom had a variety of reservations to its provisions.[12] Egypt signed but did not ratify, and a further eight countries were not signatories but applied the provisions of the 1933 Convention in practice.[13] As the refugee crisis in Europe came to be increasingly defined in terms of German Jews fleeing the Third Reich, further potential ratifications by states of the Convention were constrained by the dire economic events of the mid-1930s and the outbreak of the Second World War. Nonetheless, given the challenges of the inter-war period, even modest adherence to the provisions of the Convention by a number of states can be seen as a substantial achievement. This is particularly true considering the low numbers ratifying the subsequent League of Nations agreements concerning those fleeing the National Socialist regime in Germany.[14]

Despite these deficiencies, the 1933 Convention served as a basis for the 1951 Convention. The dominant narrative of the inter-war period with regard to refugee protection has traditionally concentrated on the failure of the international system to assist Jewish refugees fleeing the Third Reich up to the outbreak of war. However, as Skran argues, this inter-war period should be seen as a time of great creativity and innovation, when much was accomplished with minimal resources and when millions of refugees were helped to begin new lives.[15] This short essay seeks to examine the

---

[11] The Convention protected Russian, Armenian, and assimilated refugees who were Assyrian, Assyro-Chaldean and a small number of Turks from the former Ottoman Empire.

[12] Belgium, Bulgaria, Czechoslovakia, Denmark, France, Italy, Norway and the United Kingdom.

[13] Estonia, Finland, Iraq, Greece, Latvia, Sweden, Switzerland and the United States.

[14] The Provisional Agreement concerning the Status of Refugees coming from Germany (signed 4 July 1936) 3952 LNTS 77 (the 1936 Provisional Agreement) and the Convention concerning the Status of Refugees coming from Germany (signed 10 February 1938, entered into force 26 October 1938) 4461 LNTS 61 (the 1938 Convention) could only muster seven signatories. In addition there was also the Arrangement of 24 May 1935 Relating to Refugees from the Saar which extended the Nansen passport scheme to those fleeing the reincorporation of the Saar into the German Reich.

[15] Claudena Skran, *Refugees in Inter-war Europe – The Emergence of a Regime* (Oxford: Clarendon Press, 1995) 9.

background of the refugees in Europe in the inter-war years and the legal response to them in the form of the 1933 Convention.

1. ORIGINS OF THE REFUGEE PROBLEM IN INTER-WAR EUROPE

Throughout human history, people have been forced to flee their homes and states of origin in search of protection and safety elsewhere. The term 'refugee' has been used in a general way to describe these people for centuries.[16] The more than 10 000 French Protestants (Huguenots) who settled in Ireland following the revocation of the Edict of Nantes in 1695 are archetypical examples of exiles seeking sanctuary from persecution in their homelands. They are representative of the large numbers of religious refugees found on the European continent during the period of religious wars in Europe. Indeed the word 'refugee' is believed to have originated with the Huguenots.[17]

During the middle of the nineteenth century, Europe was relatively free of such large population movements. Revolutionary refugees, numbering in the thousands, were more typical of the period and tended to be relatively affluent.[18] Given the dominant *laissez-faire* political ideology of the time and the inadequacy of practical immigration administration, those who wished to flee from their own state generally had little difficulty entering the liberal states of Western Europe. On a practical level and, before the modern passport and visa system was instituted, the tiny bureaucracies of Western Europe would have found it impossible to prevent refugees crossing frontiers and living unmolested. For example, in England during the nineteenth century from 1823 onwards not a single refugee was blocked at a port of entry or ordered to leave the country.[19] Simply put, those who had the financial means to do so were able to settle in London, Paris, Geneva and other major cities despite many professing strong socialist

---

16 For a thorough examination see Atle Grahl-Madsen, 'The European Tradition of Asylum and the Development of Refugee Law' (1966) 3 *Journal of Peace Research* 278–89.

17 See Frederick A. Norwood, *Strangers and Exiles: A History of Religious Refugees* (Nashville: Abingdon Press 1969) on religious refugees throughout history.

18 Michael R. Marrus, *The Unwanted – European Refugees in the Twentieth Century* (Oxford: OUP, 1985) 19–26.

19 Bernard Porter, *The Refugee Question in Mid Victorian Politics* (Cambridge: CUP, 1979) 1.

and anarchist politics.[20] At the same time, large numbers of migrants of all kinds were emigrating to the New World, and as long as countries in the Americas continued to accept practically everyone, European governments did not have to deal with large numbers of refugees.[21] As long as refugees remained few in number and appeared benign in the handful of countries that were prepared to accept them, nothing changed.

Towards the last third of the nineteenth century, attitudes began to change even in the liberal countries with a tradition of political refugees. The wars of German reunification and the Franco-Prussian war led to an increase in nationalistic sentiment and mobilization of populations on a previously unprecedented scale. Pogroms in Tsarist Russia against the Jews in the 1880s caused millions to flee. In addition, after the assassination of Tsar Alexander II in 1881, Tsarist exiles were much more numerous throughout Europe and potentially dangerous.[22]

However it was the First World War, its preceding conflicts (the Balkan wars of 1912–1913) and its aftermath in the Near East (the wars in the Caucasus from 1918–1921 and the Greco–Turkish War of 1919–1922) and the events of the Russian Revolution and Civil War which necessitated and ushered in the inter-war era of refugee protection. The war sent the four dynastic Empires that had dominated Eastern Europe – the Romanov; the Ottoman; the Hapsburg; and the Hohenzollern – into ruin. As these old Empires collapsed and gave way to the formation of their successor states, the transformation from the imperial order to new states bound on national, linguistic, ethnic and religious grounds was accompanied by conflict, persecution and mass displacement.

In addition, the existence of huge masses of refugees following the war coincided with the rise of modern systems of social organization and economic and political nationalism throughout Europe. Many of the refugees were victims of the new-style nation states and the consolidation of their existence in the post-war world. The governments of these new states began to regulate more closely their economic and social affairs and consequently, to limit the entitlement of these benefits to their own citizens. This, in turn, led all states to reassert the distinction between citizens and non-citizens and to reinforce border controls and the visa regimes which,

---

20 Karl Marx for example left France for London after he was ordered to leave Paris for the Département of Morbihan in Brittany following a confrontation with the French government in July 1849 despite writing to the Ministry of the Interior complaining that there had been an 'misunderstanding' about his activities. Marrus (n18) 18.

21 *Ibid*. chapter 1.

22 *Ibid*. 26.

having been introduced during the war, became permanent aspects of immigration control at this time.

The magnitude and scale of refugee movements in inter-war Europe dwarfed all previous experiences. By 1926, more than 20 million people were estimated to be displaced within states, while the refugee population was estimated at 9.5 million.[23] This state of affairs, however, was neither perceived nor acknowledged amongst policy makers as a refugee crisis demanding a coordinated, international legal intervention. The legal responses were piecemeal at first. For the most part, refugees were left to fend for themselves. The general response from states worldwide was the adoption of more guarded immigration policies in general and more restrictive policies for refugees in particular. The development of immigration restrictions beginning in the United States and leading there to the Immigration Acts of 1921 and 1924, and the extension of immigration barriers worldwide, constructed a formidable obstacle to the resolution of refugee problems in inter-war Europe.

2. THE INTERNATIONAL LEGAL RESPONSE AND FIRST REFUGEE AGREEMENTS

The refugee problem of inter-war Europe arose in the absence of any clearly defined rules for the treatment of refugees. In the classic state-centric understanding of international law, the concept of asylum was understood to be the right of states to accord protection to refugees and to refuse to return them to their state of origin.[24] As Simpson stated in 1939, 'Asylum is a privilege conferred by the State. It is not a condition inherent in the individual.'[25]

A potential source of rights for refugees was international aliens' law, which had developed in the preceding centuries as a means by which trading states were able to guarantee a minimum of civil and economic rights for their nationals working abroad. Like aliens, refugees, by definition, are outside the boundaries of their own state. However, the rights considered in international aliens' law were the rights of the national state

---

23 Marrus (n18) 52. This number was made up of 1.5 million forcibly exchanged between Greece and Turkey, 280 000 exchanged between Greece and Bulgaria, two million Poles awaiting repatriation, two million Russian and Ukrainians, 250 000 Hungarians, and one million Germans.

24 Louise W. Holborn, 'The Legal Status of Political Refugees, 1920–1933' [1938] *AJIL* 681.

25 John H. Simpson, 'The Refugee Problem' [1939] *International Affairs* 230.

usually agreed by bilateral agreement.[26] These would vary depending on the terms of the bilateral agreement between the states. For the nationals of the contracting state these agreements could guarantee access to many of the same benefits as citizens of the host state while in the host state. The most generous terms would be guaranteed for the nationals of a 'most favoured nation.' Reciprocity between the two states was the essential precondition; the nationals of one state could only expect benefits in the cooperating state if their own government in turn ensured the rights of nationals of the cooperating state. It was this reciprocity requirement which refugees, who had lost the protection of their former state, were unable to fulfil.[27]

Refugees were, thus, uniquely disadvantaged in the absence of any legal framework as they did not become the holders of particular rights in their host countries. Furthermore, unlike aliens, they were at the mercy of the foreign states without the traditional remedy of diplomatic protection from their country of origin. The League of Nations system for the protection of national minorities was a further body of law which influenced the birth and development of the international refugee regime. The Minorities Treaties were designed to advance the interest of states following the First World War in limiting future conflicts by requiring the defeated states to respect the human rights of ethnic and religious minorities.[28] By doing so they established the legitimacy of international legal oversight to the human rights of minorities of sovereign states and in addition provided the context for the collective supervision of human rights by the international community.[29]

The beginnings of more restrictive policies of admittance among the emerging states of Europe and the traditional immigrant states of the New World coincided with the migration of nearly two million people following the events of the Russian Revolution of 1917–1918, and the subsequent civil war. The Russians, initially, made up the largest post-war group of refugees. These multi-ethnic and multi-confessional populations consisted of individuals, families and even entire armies.[30] The situation of these refugees was desperate and called for immediate relief measures. They were without employment or travel documents, and the value of any roubles they had deteriorated quickly. There was little possibility of repatriation by the new Soviet authorities, and their situation was wors-

26 Hathaway (n8) 75–80.
27 *Ibid.* 84.
28 *Ibid.* 81–83.
29 *Ibid.* 83.
30 Marrus (n18) 53–61.

ened by the decree of the All Russian Central Executive Committee and the Council of All People's Commissars, which effectively rendered those Russians who had fled the Revolution as stateless. In addition, their position was further complicated by their host countries' relationships with the new Soviet government. Countries which still recognized the consuls of the Tsarist government gave the refugees the status of other foreigners so that they enjoyed the full rights of aliens under domestic law.[31] Other states such as Poland, which had recognized the Soviet government by the Treaty of Riga, treated the refugees according to the treaty provisions or a conventional right to asylum. Given the now effectively stateless position of most of the Russian refugees, the simplest solution would have been for their host countries to naturalize them *en masse.* The host governments rejected this as a solution, and, in addition, many of the Russian refugees rejected this as an option as they believed their exile was temporary.[32]

In February 1921, the International Committee of the Red Cross appealed to the Council of the League of Nations to take action on behalf of the 'Russian refugees scattered throughout Europe without legal protection or representation'.[33] This combination of events triggered a critical legal response and forced the international community to consider the issue of refugees within a more global framework. It was clear that the Covenant of the League of Nations contained no explicit reference to the protection of refugees.[34] However, one of the stated purposes of the League was considered to be applicable; that is, 'to promote international co-operation and to achieve international peace and security.' Thus, in June 1921 the Council of the League decided that the refugee problem should be the subject of further investigation. In August of that year, the League also appointed a Norwegian, Dr. Fridtjof Nansen, to the newly created post of High Commissioner for Refugees to address the problems of the Russian refugees in Europe. He was assigned a tripartite task: arranging the coordination of relief work; securing a definition for the legal status of refugees; and considering a solution through repatriation to Russia, employment in the country in which they were residing, or emigration to other countries.

The response of the League of Nations was the convening of a conference in Geneva in July 1922 which drafted the Arrangement with

---

31 Holborn (n24) 682.
32 *Ibid.* 682.
33 (1921) 2 (2) League of Nations OJ 227.
34 Grahl-Madsen (n16) 281.

Regard to the Issue of Certificates of Identity to Russian Refugees.[35] The Arrangement was not a treaty and was not legally binding. It recommended a standard of conduct for signatory states. Under the terms of the 1922 Arrangement, governments could issue the identity certificates, but this did not confer citizenship rights upon the bearer. However it did allow travel over international boundaries. The documents, notably, did not offer a clear definition of the term 'refugee' but stated that the bearer was a Russian national by origin. The certificate was valid for one year and became invalid if the holder, of Russian origin, adopted another nationality. The document was subject to a fee, and governments readily agreed to issue them precisely because this did not impact dramatically on their sovereignty. It was this document that was later to be known more commonly as the 'Nansen passport'.

These Nansen passports, although only a partial solution to the refugee problem, did mark an important first step in the request for refugee protection. They had a profound effect on the lives of refugees carrying them and allowed them to legally cross international boundaries. Over time, the Nansen passport system served as the foundation for a clearly defined legal status for refugees, and some consider its establishment as the beginning of international refugee law.[36] States quickly adopted the Nansen system. By September 1923, 31 states had signed the arrangement; and by 1925 this had increased to over 40.[37] In September 1923, there was a call to the Council of the League of Nations for Nansen passports to be extended to refugees from Armenia.[38] Armenians had long been a Christian minority of around two million people in the Ottoman Empire. However, their position became more precarious as the Turkish nation state consolidated, with violence against them reaching genocidal proportions during the First World War. Around two-thirds of the total Ottoman Armenian population is thought to have died while a mass exodus from Turkey ensued during 1921 and 1922. In June 1924, Nansen prepared a report on the situation and estimated that 320 000 Armenians were in need of identity certificates.[39] The League of Nations responded favourably to Nansen's report by adopting a Resolution to extend to the Armenian

---

[35] Arrangement with regard to the issue of Certificates of Identity to Russian Refugees (5 July 1922) 355 LNTS 238 (1922 Arrangement).

[36] Skran (n15) 104.

[37] *Ibid.* 105.

[38] (1924) 5 (7) League of Nations OJ 967 cited in James Hathaway, 'The Evolution of Refugee Status in International Law: 1920–1950' (1984) 33 *ICLQ* 348, 352.

[39] *Ibid.*

refugees an emergency certificate essentially the same as that issued to Russian refugees.[40]

The system of Nansen passports for Russian and Armenian refugees was generally well received with the eventual recognition of the scheme by 54 and 38 states respectively. The system also helped host governments to calculate the number of refugees in their territory. However, difficulties arose in administration of the schemes because the eligible groups were simply referred to as 'Russian refugees' and 'Armenian refugees', with no clear definition of these terms agreed. Issuing governments were also not uniform in their practice in relation to fees and the right of return to the issuing country.

In light of the shortcomings of the 1922 arrangement, an Intergovernmental Conference was convened in Geneva in May 1926 to discuss its improvement. Nansen proposed the following definitions to the member governments of the League of Nations:

> Russian refugee: Any person of Russian origin who does not enjoy the protection of the Government of the Union of Soviet Socialist Republics and who has not acquired any other nationality.
> Armenian refugee: Any person of Armenian origin, formerly a subject of the Ottoman Empire, who does not enjoy the protection of the Government of the Turkish Republic and who has not acquired any other nationality.

These definitions were adopted in this form on 12 May 1926, in the Arrangement relating to the Legal Status of Russian and Armenian Refugees.[41] The definition is by country of origin or ethnic group, and the central element in both is for the refugee claimant to have been deprived of the 'protection' of their former government or successor state and to not have acquired a further nationality. The 1926 Arrangement marks the first formal definition of a refugee in international law. Unfortunately, however, the number of states agreeing to be bound to the 1926 Arrangement fell to 23.

At the end of 1926 the Council of the League of Nations began the process of extending the provisions in the 1926 Arrangement to other groups that were in the same position as the Russian and Armenian refugees. The High Commissioner produced a list of 7 groups, encompassing approximately 155 000 persons. However, this report met with disapproval when considered by the League of Nations Council in September

---

40 *Ibid.*

41 Arrangement relating to the Issue of Identity Certificates to Russian and Armenian Refugees, 12 May 1926, 2004 LNTS 48 (The 1926 Arrangement).

1927. Nansen revised his report and the question of extending League of Nations protection was placed on the agenda of the June 1928 Inter-Governmental Conference which had been called to discuss all elements of the refugee question.

The Conference resulted in the Arrangement concerning the Extension to Other Categories of Refugee of Certain Measures taken in favour of Russian and Armenian Refugees.[42] The 1928 Arrangement differed markedly from the previous 1922 and 1926 Arrangements in a key way. First, it extended the previous coverage to Assyrian, Assyro-Chaldean persons of Syrian or Kurdish origin as well as some persons of Turkish origin who were former subjects of the Ottoman Empire, and the mandate of the High Commissioner was also extended to cover these groups. In the absence of diplomatic protection, refugees were entitled to benefit from actions taken on their behalf by a succession of League of Nations High Commissioners.[43]

Second, and more fundamentally, although again in the form of non-binding recommendations,[44] the 1928 Arrangement set standards for the recognition of personal status and addressed issues such as the right to work, access to court, protection against expulsion, equality in taxation and the state's responsibility to honour identity certificates. The 1928 Arrangement also highlighted the inadequacy of the reciprocity principle with regard to refugees and signified the League of Nations first attempt to standardize the rights to be extended to refugees.

These first refugee agreements illustrate the perception that the refugee problem was of a temporary nature and would resolve itself. The Agreements were not treaties and did not set specific responsibilities for states other than cooperation in the recognition of League of Nations documentation. As most European states granted generous benefits to the nationals of 'most-favoured nations', a group with which refugees were effectively assimilated, further precision was not considered necessary.

[42] Arrangement concerning the Extension to other Categories of Refugee of Certain Measures taken in favour of Russian and Armenian Refugees, 30 June 1928, 2006 LNTS 65 (The 1928 Arrangement).

[43] The mandate of the High Commissioner was gradually expanded throughout the 1920s, and in 1930 following the death of Nansen it was replaced with the Nansen International Refugee Office.

[44] The meeting in 1928 rejected the idea of concluding formal obligations on behalf of refugees which had been proposed in 1927 by Jacques Rubinstein, a Russian refugee with international expertise. See Jacques J. Rubenstei, 'The Refugee Problem' [1936] 15 *International Affairs* 727.

3. THE 1933 CONVENTION

3.1 Drafting the 1933 Convention

The response to the 1928 Arrangement was not satisfactory to the League of Nations. As the 'temporary' refugee problem refused to disappear and economic and political instability rose, states increasingly refused to assimilate refugees as most-favoured foreigners, instead focusing resources on their own citizens. Many governments adopted legislation prohibiting the employment of foreigners.[45] Even France, which had been the major country of immigration in Europe and was home to many of the Russian and Armenian refugees, was convulsed with anti-alien feeling.[46]

In August 1931, the Inter-governmental Advisory Commission for Refugees convened in Geneva for the work of its fourth session. This body had been set up by the League of Nations Council in 1928 to conduct a general assessment of the League's refugee operations and it continued to advise the League's refugee agencies after it had completed its May 1929 report. The report of the fourth session referred to the comparative inefficacy of the 1928 recommendations.[47] The Commission now proposed to establish a formal convention which would 'stabilise the situation' of refugees with the anticipation of the liquidation of the Nansen International Office at the end of 1938.[48] This recommendation was considered by the Twelfth Assembly of the League of Nations, which recognized the need for a more permanent system to protect refugees and agreed requests that the Nansen Office, in consultation with the Commission, consider the advisability of preparing such a refugee treaty.[49] A Committee of Experts was set up by the Nansen Office which in their report concluded that a convention was necessary and endorsed a simplified procedure for the conclusion of the convention.[50] This report and the need for a convention was adopted by the Intergovernmental Advisory Commission at its

---

[45] For example in 1930–31 Albania, Belgium, Brazil, Germany, Malaya, Poland, Portugal, Switzerland and Tunisia enacted restrictions on the employment of foreign workers. International Labour Office, *Annual Review 1930*, cited Skran (n15) 122.

[46] France enacted the Law for the Protection of Foreign Labour in 1932: Skran (n15) 122–3.

[47] 12 (2) LN OJ 2118 (1931), at 2119 cited in Hathaway (n8).

[48] A.24.1932 cited in Robert J. Beck, 'Britain and the 1933 Refugee Convention: National or State Sovereignty?' (1999) 11 *IJRL* 604.

[49] A.24.1932 and 1931 League of Nations, *Official Journal*, Special Supplement 92, 38, cited in Beck (n48) 605.

[50] GAC 2/1933 – Geneva, January 9, 1933, cited in Beck (n48) 607.

fifth session which went on to request preparation of a draft treaty and endorse the simplified procedure. The Advisory Commission's recommendations were in turn endorsed by the Nansen Office's governing body in its seventh session in April 1933. The governing body's President, Professor Georges Werner, in turn appeared before the Council of the League of Nations 73rd session presenting the reports from the governing body and the Inter-governmental Advisory Commission and urging the adoption of the proposals contained in the reports which the Council did.[51] Crucially, the draft convention which followed would impose a series of obligations upon signatory states rather than the non-binding recommendations system of the previous agreements.

The Intergovernmental Conference met in October 1933 to attempt to find this more secure grounding for refugee protection.[52] Government representatives from 15 states attended the three-day meeting in October of 1933: Austria, Belgium, Bulgaria, China, Czechoslovakia, Egypt, Estonia, Finland, France, Greece, Latvia, Poland, Romania, Switzerland and Yugoslavia. Great Britain, Germany and Lithuanian representatives were absent. Two members of the Committee of Experts, Nolde and Rubinstein, were present, as were several prominent refugees representing the Central Committee for Armenian refugees.[53]

There was agreement that the 1926 and 1928 Arrangements, although limited in their application, were appropriate for incorporation into the new Convention despite the strong objection of the delegates from Czechoslovakia and Poland that the definitions were too imprecise.[54] After three days, agreement was eventually reached on a text and the Convention relating to the International Status of Refugees[55] was adopted. The 'simplified procedure' that had been proposed rapidly produced a treaty.

3.2 Provisions of the 1933 Convention

Article 1 stated that the Convention was applicable to those refugees as defined by the 1926 and 1928 Arrangements – that is Russians, Armenians,

---

51 League of Nations *Official Journal*, July 1933, 806–7, cited in Beck (n48), 608.

52 Intergovernmental Conference for Refugees, LSC/1/1933 – LSC/15/1933, cited in Skran (n15).

53 Beck (n48) 609.

54 Hathaway (n38) 357.

55 159 LNTS 3663, entry into force 13 June 1935. The Convention had just eight State Parties.

and assimilated refugees who were Assyrian, Assyro-Chaldean and a small number of Turks from the former Ottoman Empire – although each Contracting Party could introduce modifications or amplifications at the moment of signature or accession.[56] From a contemporary perspective this definition of a refugee in Article 1 of the 1933 Convention is the most striking difference. The approach in the early refugee agreements which the 1933 Convention follows is a group definition or category approach, and stands in stark contrast to the individual definition in the 1951 Convention which defines a refugee as any person who,

> As a result of events occurring before 1 January 1951 and owing to a well-founded fear of being persecuted for reasons of race, religion, nationality, membership of a particular social group or political opinion, is outside the country of his nationality, membership of a particular social group or political opinion, is outside the country of his nationality and is unable or owing to such a fear is unwilling to avail himself of the protection of that country; or who, not having a nationality and being outside the country of his former residence as a result of such events, is unable or owing to such a fear, is unwilling to return to it.[57]

This group approach required that the refugee be outside their country of origin and be without the protection of the government of that state. This approach does not require that the refugee be in danger of persecution, which is so crucial to the modern understanding of the definition of a refugee. The refugees defined under the 1933 Convention were stateless in modern terms. Hathaway has characterized three distinct approaches to refugee definition in the period of 1920–1950, being juridical, social and individual.[58] The refugee definition in the 1933 Convention is characterized in juridical terms which means that refugees were treated as refugees because of their membership of a group of persons effectively deprived of the formal protection of their country of origin. As we have seen these first refugee definitions were formulated because of the dilemma in international law caused by the denial of state protection. The group definition attempted to correct this anomaly in the international legal order. The refugee definition in the 1933 Convention has no potential for exclusion from the definition in contrast to the modern refugee definition which obliges the denial of the benefits of refugee status to certain persons who would otherwise qualify as refugees.[59]

---

[56] No Contracting Parties attempted to amplify the definition with the Bulgaria maintaining its reservation made to the 1928 Arrangement.

[57] 1951 Refugee Convention (n3).

[58] See Hathaway (n38).

[59] Arts 1(D), (E) and (F) of the 1951 Refugee Convention read as follows:

The 1933 Convention also built on the success of the Nansen passport system requiring a text of authorization of exit and return on the certificates and allowing those with valid certificates exit and re-entry without any authorization on exit or visa for return. The consuls of the Contracting Parties were empowered to extend the certificates for a period of up to six months. There was provision for the cost of visas for Nansen certificates to be standardized as free to the indigent and the lowest tariff applied to the visas of foreign passports for others. The modern equivalent of the Nansen passport scheme is the Convention travel document which is authorized under Article 28 of the 1951 Convention and which requires that Contracting States shall issue to refugees lawfully staying in their territory travel documents for the purpose of travel outside their territory, unless compelling reasons of national security or public order otherwise require. There is direct continuity with the Nansen passport scheme in that under Article 28(2) of the 1951 Convention travel documents under previous schemes are to be honoured by the Contracting States to the 1951 Convention.

The most important addition to the recommendations in the 1928 Arrangement was Article 3 which introduced the critical right to non-*refoulement* which states:

> Each of the Contracting Parties undertakes not to remove or keep from its territory by application of police measures, such as expulsions or non-admittance

---

'(D) This Convention shall not apply to persons who are at present receiving from organs or agencies of the United Nations other than the United Nations High Commissioner for Refugees protection or assistance. When such protection or assistance has ceased for any reason, without the position of such persons being definitively settled in accordance with the relevant resolutions adopted by the General Assembly of the United Nations, these persons shall *ipso facto* be entitled to the benefits of this Convention.

(E) This Convention shall not apply to a person who is recognized by the competent authorities of the country in which he has taken residence as having the rights and obligations which are attached to the possession of the nationality of that country.

(F) The provisions of this Convention shall not apply to any person with respect to whom there are serious reasons for considering that:

(a) He has committed a crime against peace, a war crime, or a crime against humanity, as defined in the international instruments drawn up to make provision in respect of such crimes;

(b) He has committed a serious non-political crime outside the country of refuge prior to his admission to that country as a refugee;

(c) He has been guilty of acts contrary to the purposes and principles of the United Nations.'

> at the frontier (*refoulement*), refugees who have been authorised to reside there regularly, unless the said measures are dictated by reasons of national security or public order.
>
> It undertakes in any case not to refuse entry to refugees at the frontiers of their countries of origin.
>
> It reserves the right to apply such internal measures as it may deem necessary to refugees who, having been expelled for reasons of national security or public order, are unable to leave its territory because they have not received, at their request or through the intervention of institutions dealing with them, the necessary authorisations and visas permitting them to proceed to another country.

This was the first explicit obligation of states in treaty law not to expel authorized refugees, and to avoid *refoulement* which was defined to include 'non-admittance at the frontier.' The modern prohibition on *refoulement* in international refugee law is contained in Article 33 of the 1951 Convention which states:

> No Contracting State shall expel or return (*'refouler'*) a refugee in any manner whatsoever to the frontiers of territories where his life or freedom would be threatened on account of his race, religion, nationality, membership of a particular social group or political opinion.
>
> The benefit of the present provision may not, however, be claimed by a refugee whom there are reasonable grounds for regarding as a danger to the security of the country in which he is, or who, having been convicted by a final judgement of a particularly serious crime, constitutes a danger to the community of that country.

The prohibition of *refoulement* under international and regional human rights instruments has developed greatly in the years following the 1951 Convention[60] and has now arguably developed the status of a *jus cogens* norm in international law.[61] However the right to non-*refoulement* in the 1933 Convention could be claimed only by refugees who had been authorized to reside regularly. The other limit to the right to non-*refoulement* was the right of Contracting Parties to adopt police measures resulting in *refoulement* if those measures were dictated by reasons of national security or public order. The limit on the prohibition of *refoulement* in the 1951 Convention contained in Article 33 provides a similar provision preventing its application to those refugees that there are reasonable grounds for regarding as posing a danger to the security of the country. In addition, the 1951 Convention provided the Contracting States with an exception

---

60 See Wouters (n10).

61 See Jean Allain, 'The *jus cogens* nature of *non-refoulement*' (2002) *IJRL* 533-538.

to the general prohibition on expulsion under Article 31. Refugees can be expelled on the grounds of national security or public order, where a decision has been made in accordance with law. Refugees have a right of appeal except where compelling reasons of national security prevent this.[62]

The 1933 Convention also contained important provisions in relation to labour conditions (Chapter IV), industrial accidents (Chapter V), welfare and relief (Chapter VI) and education (Chapter VII). Some of these replicated the provisions of the 1928 Arrangement. However three key socio-economic rights, although limited, were added to those rights from the 1928 Arrangement, the right to work, to social welfare and education.[63] With regard to the right to work, refugees were to be protected from the harshness of the restrictions on foreign labour and limitations of any kind were proscribed in the following circumstances: where a refugee had three years' residence; where a refugee was married to or the parent of a national; and finally where a refugee was an ex-combatant of the First World War.[64] The right to social welfare granted refugees access to the host state's welfare and relief system, including medical care and workers' compensation. The right to education allowed access to education, including the remission of fees in some circumstances.

Chapter III provided for the right of access to the courts and recognition of legal status which were guaranteed absolutely. Refugees were to enjoy the benefit of legal assistance as if they were nationals of the host state and they were to be exempt from *cautio judicatum solvi*.[65]

The structure of the 1933 Convention drew on the precedent of aliens' law to establish a mix of absolute rights and contingent rights. It was more common for the contingent rights formula to be used. The Convention states that governments should provide refugees with the 'most favourable treatment' that it accords to nationals of a foreign country in relation to industrial accidents (Art. 8), medical care and hospital treatment (Art. 9), social insurance (Art. 10), admission to relief associations (Art. 11) and education (Art. 12). With liability for taxation (Art 13), exceptionally, refugees were assimilated to citizens of the host state.

Crucially, the Convention also contained an important provision on reciprocity: Article 14 states that 'the enjoyment of certain right[s] and the benefit of certain favours accorded to foreigners subject to reciprocity shall not be refused to refugees in the absence of reciprocity.' This is an

62 Art. 32, 1951 Refugee Convention (n3).
63 Hathaway (n8) 88.
64 Art. 7, 1933 Refugee Convention (n6).
65 The requirement to post security for costs in legal actions.

attempt to ameliorate the fact that refugees do not have a home government to provide reciprocity and without such a provision, that refugees could easily be deprived of basic rights such as the right to inherit, to be a trustee, to obtain a patent, to appear as a plaintiff in court and others.[66]

The rights contained in the 1933 Convention had further application because of its impact on refugee life in the countries that adhered to it whether formally or not. Despite many of the Contracting States making reservations to key articles, ratifying countries gradually moved to bring their domestic law in line with the provisions of the 1933 Convention. This was most noticeable in relation to social services.[67]

3.3 State Cooperation and the 1933 Convention

Unfortunately, in reality the 1933 Convention did not significantly expand refugee rights. Only eight states ratified the treaty, several with serious reservations. Although further states were bound by its provisions, the worsening economic and political crises that were convulsing Europe meant that the assimilation of refugees' status with that of most favoured foreigners was not a guarantee of reasonable treatment, as the effect of the great depression on unemployment meant that states denied critical social benefits, including the right to work, to all foreigners. The strategy of assimilating refugee rights into aliens' protection, rather than providing equality of treatment as nationals or through naturalization, now led to great hardship for refugees.

The issue of refugees in Europe as with the fate of the League of Nations became increasingly bound up with the rise of Fascism and especially, the rise of National Socialism in Germany, with large numbers of persons beginning to leave the state. A High Commissioner for Refugees Coming from Germany was appointed to address the issue in 1933,[68] and the Nansen passport scheme was extended to refugees from the Saar after the reoccupation by Germany. The League of Nations responded to the exodus from Germany by concluding a Provisional Arrangement concerning the Status of Refugees coming from Germany[69] and the 1938

---

66 Rubinstein (n44) 726.

67 See Skran (n15) 129–130 for details.

68 UN GA Res of 11 October 1933, *LNOJ* 1933 Special Supplement 114, 11–14.

69 Provisional Arrangement concerning the Status of Refugees Coming from Germany (signed 4 August 1936, entered into force 20 August 1948) 77 LNTS 3952 (1936 Provisional Agreement).

Convention concerning the Status of Refugees coming from Germany.[70] However, this was a rearguard action. These agreements adopted what Hathaway characterized as a social approach to refugee definition in that they are concerned with ensuring the refugee's well-being rather than correcting an anomaly in the international legal system.[71] The extent of this retreat from protection can be seen by the 1936 Provisional Agreement, which guaranteed only identity certificates, protection from expulsion, recognition of personal status, and access to the courts. Only seven states were signatories. The 1938 Convention even provided for return to Germany if the refugee did not move to a third country, without just cause.

4. CONCLUSION

The 1933 Convention established the standard that refugees should be accorded the same treatment as that given to aliens in the host country. It guaranteed all refugees rights, either absolutely or on terms of equivalency or on terms with citizens of most favoured states. It did not go as far as to institute equality of treatment for both refugees and nationals. Nevertheless the 1933 Convention is noteworthy because it set the first universal standard on the treatment of refugees which in the vast majority of cases accorded refugees better treatment than they received in their host countries. The prohibition on *refoulement* was arguably stronger than in the 1951 Convention and the refugee definition termed in a group manner meant that there was no individual status determination process to endure for refugees. In addition there was no express provision for expulsion in the 1933 Convention. Indeed, the structure of the 1933 Convention with pattern of variant levels of obligation lives on in the 1951 Convention and subsequent regional refugee arrangements. The 1951 Convention built on the rights structure of the 1933 Convention and expanded the socio-economic and civil rights contained therein.

After the Second World War, the group definitions of refugees under the League of Nations system were criticized for misconceiving the essence of refugee-hood. Atle Grahl-Madsen writing in 1966 stated that the definition of refugees which stressed the lack of diplomatic protection as the distinguishing feature was incorrect as 'the lack of protection is not

---

70 Convention on the Status of Refugees coming from Germany (signed 10 February 1938, entered into force 26 October 1938) (1938 Refugee Convention).

71 Hathaway (n38).

relevant unless it is caused by a deep rooted political controversy between the authorities and the individual.'[72] Skran sees this as a consequence of refugees becoming synonymous with the victims of Nazi persecution in the years after the Second World War. She argues that the true purposes of the legal definitions put forward by the League of Nations were on the one hand to formalize the political consensus on the groups that should be given status, and on the other hand to aid governments and international organisations to determine who qualified in refugee groups.[73]

Hathaway argues that the 1933 Convention and the other inter-war refugee agreements' importance stems from introducing two concepts which have proven central to the modern system of refugee protection.[74] The first is the states consenting to national human rights standards being subject to international supervision. This was a fundamental shift in the collective supervision to a means of states advancing shared objectives rather than a penalty to be paid. Secondly, from the 1928 arrangement and most clearly in the 1933 Convention developed the substantive law guaranteed to aliens. States developed general principles to meet the needs of refugees rather than using the existing alien's law regime. As Hathaway states:

> The consequential decisions to waive reciprocity, and to guarantee basic civil and economic rights in law, served as a direct precedent for both the modern refugee rights regime and a variety of international human rights mechanisms.[75]

As one of the earliest examples of the codification of human rights under binding international law the 1933 Convention should not be forgotten.

---

[72] Atle Grahl-Madsen, *The Status of Refugees in International Law* (Leiden: A.W. Sijthoff, 1966) i.

[73] Skran (n15).

[74] Hathaway (n8), 88–91.

[75] *Ibid.*, 91.

13. Drafter decision-making in international human rights treaties

Daragh McGreal

This chapter looks at the drafting process of international human rights treaties using the discipline of law and economics, giving particular emphasis to how drafters might most efficiently structure such treaties.

Combining the disciplines of law and economics and human rights law might initially seem a peculiar concept. The roots of the former in promoting efficiency and using economic tools to analyse laws could appear anathema to the human rights ideal of advancing the security and liberty of individuals. The two might at first glance seem uncomfortable bedfellows, arguing endlessly about efficiency, costs, contractual obligations, or the primacy of law, but this does not preclude the application of economic tools to the analysis of human rights law or international treaties. In fact, the absence of any previous work in this area, as evidenced by Sykes when he states that 'despite its importance within the legal academy, virtually nothing has been written from a theoretical perspective by economically oriented scholars on international human rights law',[1] suggests that the aim of the current project is very pertinent. In following through with this approach, the present chapter intends to suggest where law and economics can aid the more traditional analysis of international human rights treaties. It does not purport to answer all the questions, given the infancy of the concept, but the chapter does express some novel ideas about how the drafting of treaties can impact upon ratification. The chapter proceeds by firstly introducing the field of law and economics and briefly explaining some basic concepts; thereafter it uses basic economic tools to assess how drafting decisions and ratification decisions are intrinsically linked.

1 Alan O. Sykes, 'International Law', in A. Mitchell Polinsky and Steven Shavell (eds) *Handbook of Law and Economics: Volume 1* (Amsterdam: North-Holland, 2007) 757, 815.

1. LAW AND ECONOMICS

In order to properly understand the intentions of the present project, it is firstly important to outline the fundamentals of law and economics, which includes a wide variety of economic approaches. The discipline itself grew during the twentieth century and can be traced back to Guido Calabresi and Ronald Coase.[2] They suggested that traditional legal analysis had failed to account for the hidden and potential costs of legal rules and norms. Their approaches, and the field that consequently grew, makes suggestions that are often quite counterintuitive to lawyers trained to apply the law strictly. The positive application of law and economics aims to predict which legal rules will result in certain effects, while normative law and economics argues that laws might be structured so as to allocate property rights to those that value them the most. In that respect, there could be a conflict between the economic analysis of law's emphasis on efficiency and human rights law's emphasis on fairness. This chapter does not address these theoretical issues but rather applies basic tools of economics to the drafting process of human rights treaties and aims to avoid the potentially problematic issue as to whether efficiency and fairness conflict. Instead, I utilize three important principles in law and economics: externalities, rationality, and cost–benefit analyses.

2. EXTERNALITIES

The starting point in applying law and economics to international human rights law is to suggest why human rights law comes about. The formation of international treaties in the twentieth century has been suggested as having emanated from the catastrophe of the Second World War.[3] Thereafter, the later treaties were more deliberate in their structure and outlined in greater detail the human rights that would be respected and

---

[2] Some important contributions include: Guido Calabresi, *The Cost of Accidents: A Legal and Economic Analysis* (New Haven: Yale University Press, 1970); Guido Calabresi and A. Douglas Melamed, 'Property Rules, Liability Rules and Inalienability' [1972] 85(6) *Harv. L. Rev.* 1089; Ronald Coase, 'The Nature of the Firm' [1932] 4(16) *Economica* 385; Ronald Coase, 'The Problem of Social Cost' [1960] 3 *Journal of Law and Economics* 1.

[3] Mary Ann Glendon, *A World Made New: Eleanor Roosevelt and the Universal Declaration of Human Rights* (New York: Random House, 2002) 176, citing the UN Human Rights Commission's Third Committee, Summary Records, UN Doc A/C.3/257383.

how they should be protected. In contrast to the more traditional explanation for the shift toward codifying human rights in the international setting, I suggest that these treaties were promulgated because states wished to reduce the externalities of human rights violations and wanted each state to internalize these externalities. When states provide what I term 'substandard human rights', either through legislation or in their constitutions, or through more direct and intentional violations, they impose costs on states that provide better quality human rights. In such instances, when a state changes its constitution or introduces legislation contrary to human rights norms, law and economics suggests that the state is externalizing costs onto other states. In order to rectify this situation and to regulate these states, international human rights law emerges. Such law intends to encourage states both to provide human rights to all individuals and also to reduce the costs imposed on other states.

This approach, I contend, is simple and intuitive. Equally, it applies a simple economic principle to the development of international human rights law and suggests an alternative explanation as to why this law emerges. Further, it does not conflict with the traditional rationale, but rather complements it. Secondly, the paradigm suggests that it is cheaper to encourage states to align domestic law with international expectations *ex ante* than to leave the situation to an *ex post* costly war. By outlining the human rights standards to which states are expected to adhere, an attempt is made to reduce the externalities of human rights violations.

3. RATIONALISM AND COST–BENEFIT ANALYSES

My contention in this approach is that the extent of the internalization of the externalities of poor human rights standards stems from how international treaties are structured. These treaties are suggested as being akin to contract law in the domestic setting. We assume that states are rational and will only sign and ratify treaties when the gains to be had from contracting outweigh the losses of not contracting. This suggests that international human rights law, argued here as being a contract between states to provide high quality human rights, is formed because the benefits of making the treaty outweigh the costs of not having the treaty at all. In other words, states will only sign and ratify treaties after having done a cost–benefit analysis.

States, for instance, with poor domestic human rights provisions should be less likely to accept treaties which express human rights standards that diverge in scope from those existing on the domestic level. Importantly, though, some research has suggested that countries with poor human rights standards are often quite likely to sign and ratify treaties outlining radically different human rights standards.[4] The decision to do so, I suggest, is that states gain more from accepting the treaties than not doing so and that they are in a position to ratify because the oversight mechanisms in international human rights law are weak.[5] From an economic viewpoint, and since we argue that such law develops because of a desire of states to reduce externalities, it becomes clear that the ability of states to sign treaties to which they have no intention of adhering is an obvious form of regulatory failure. Regulation of domestic law is a function of each particular treaty, indicating that the structure of treaties can have a direct causal impact on the extent of the internalization of human rights violations.

Economic theory therefore suggests that in order to understand the degree to which states align their domestic laws with international standards, we must recognize that the structure of the treaties must also be examined. Considerable previous research has investigated whether human rights treaties are successful in effecting change to human rights standards on the domestic level.[6] I contend that the principal failure of international human rights treaties is their inability to encourage internalization of externalities and the ability of states to ratify treaties at low cost. Low cost ratification comes about because states, having done a cost–benefit assessment of the gains and losses of ratification, can ratify treaties without having to deal with the consequences. There is a reputational gain to be had from ratifying, as it seems to indicate both a willingness by the state to improve its domestic standards and an acceptance that a regulator – a human rights committee – can assess those standards, but unless the oversight mechanisms are strong then states will be able to ratify at low cost. Oona Hathaway argues that while human rights treaties therefore hold an 'expressive' function, in that they can act as indicators of a state's position on human rights issues, the genuineness of that expression

---

[4] Oona A. Hathaway, 'Do Human Rights Treaties Make a Difference?' [2002] 111 *Yale Law Journal* 1935, 1992.

[5] Oona A. Hathaway, 'Testing Conventional Wisdom' [2003] 14 *EJIL* 185, 188.

[6] Oona A. Hathaway, 'Why Do Countries Commit to Human Rights Treaties?' [2007] 51(4) *JCR* 588; Christof Heyns and Frans Viljoen, 'The Impact of the United Nations Human Rights Treaties on the Domestic Level' [2001] 23(3) *HRQ* 483–535; Linda Camp Keith, 'The United Nations International Covenant on Civil and Political Rights: Does It Make a Difference in Human Rights Behavior?' [1999] 36 *J. Peace Res.* 95; Beth A. Simmons, *Mobilizing for Human Rights: International Law in Domestic Politics* (Cambridge: CUP, 2009).

can depend on the strength of the oversight mechanism.[7] I contend that rational states will always ratify treaties when the reputational benefit from doing so outweighs the losses that result from increased monitoring of domestic human rights provisions. This forms the central thesis behind the discussion elaborated in this chapter. In applying such a theory to the decision of states on the question as to whether treaties should be signed or ratified, this approach argues that states will accept international treaties until the marginal gain no longer justifies it. This point is the point at which the benefits of ratifying begin to be outweighed by the costs. Depending on the characteristics of the state, this margin will fall differently. As a result of this, the specificity of human rights treaties should therefore be reliant upon the marginal level of ratification deterrence, in order that as many states as possible are encouraged to ratify.

This background explanation of the potential applicability of law and economics to the analysis of human rights treaties suggests that if human rights violations are externalities and if states are rational then the structure and specificity of treaties will determine the balance of a state's cost–benefit analysis.

4. TREATY SPECIFICITY

With the basic theory elaborated, the contention follows that when international treaties are being written, some important considerations must be taken into account: which rights should be included? How specifically should these rights be written? Should the rights be actionable in an international court or committee? In making these decisions, however, treaty drafters should consider the potential impact of the treaty's degree of detail. Treaty drafters face a simple and logical dilemma: detailed treaties take longer to write, more clearly outline the human rights standards expected of ratifying states, but result in less ratification by states with poor standards,[8] while less detailed treaties take less time to write and are less specific in their outline of the standards expected of ratifying states, but result in a higher level of ratification by all states.[9]

---

[7] Hathaway (n6) 2007.

[8] See, for example: United Nations Convention on the Protection of the Rights of All Migrant Workers and Members of Their Families, 2220 UNTS 93, 18 December 1990, entered into force 1 July 2003.

[9] See, for example: International Covenant on Economic, Social and Cultural Rights (adopted 16 December 1966, entered into force 3 January 1976) 993 UNTS 3 (ICESCR).

All treaty drafters must be aware of this incongruity during the drafting process. More detailed treaties will deter ratification by states with domestic provisions of human rights which do not fit the proposed international treaty's express standards because the greater detail increases the costs of compliance for those states. The cost of compliance can involve a number of issues, including the potential obligation to change domestic law, the increased level of investigation by the treaty body, or a greater level of pressure by other states for that state to comply with the treaty. These costs, we suggest, are balanced against the benefits to be gained from ratifying a more detailed treaty, with the most obvious benefit being the reputational gain.

Behind this, however, Hathaway points out that unless such treaties include an oversight mechanism then the credibility of the commitment is brought into question.[10] The existence of an oversight mechanism, which is analogized as a regulator, is therefore assumed to determine both treaty effectiveness and the level of treaty ratification. The costs and benefits of ratifying treaties are intrinsically linked to the existence and ambit of a monitoring body. Treaty drafters will be aware, nonetheless, that the inclusion of such a mechanism will alter ratification levels, meaning they will also measure the costs and benefits of more or less detailed treaties.

In order to achieve more detail, however, drafters face the problem of transaction costs, a core issue in law and economics. Detailed treaties become a function of transaction costs, in that it is more difficult to attain consensus on greater detail. At the drafting stage, the drafting committee, aware of the effects of the detail on the decisions of states to ratify, must decide to what extent the treaties are detailed. Firstly, drafters face negotiation costs: some parties to the negotiation – those that are most eager to offer to states a treaty with clear and strict human rights pronouncements – are likely to drive a hard bargain, while other parties – those that are more concerned with getting a greater uptake of treaty ratification by all states – will seek more vague treaties. This game, in which the drafting committee bargains over how to write and structure the treaty, takes time. Each party takes strategic positions pursuant to its own outlook. Each party will hold out at the relevant stage, thereby delaying potential negotiation.

From law and economics, Ronald Coase pointed out that in a world absent transaction costs, parties will bargain to an efficient outcome, where when transaction costs do exist, as they inevitably do in the real

---

10 Hathaway (n6) 2007.

world, bargaining efficiently becomes more difficult.[11] This reflects the situation of the drafting committee during the drafting process. It must decide a number of things and should take into account not only the costs of actually making those decisions, but also the likely future costs of those decisions. Ergo, treaty drafters decide to what extent a human right is explicit and how might it be actionable. This asks, for instance, whether rights enshrined in treaties can be called upon by individuals in future periods, either in the domestic setting or in the international setting. States will consider the actionability of rights when deciding whether to ratify treaties, conscious of course that the rights in the treaties might not conform with the rights in the state's own constitution. More explicitly outlined human rights have the obvious benefit that states cannot question them, whereas more vaguely outlined human rights might be subject to judicial interpretation at the domestic level.

In deciding the level of detail, therefore, I follow Robert Cooter and Thomas Ulen, who suggest that contracts are left with gaps when the transaction costs of filling those gaps outweigh the *ex post* costs of allocating loss by the likelihood of loss.[12] Joel Trachtman elaborated this for international law, suggesting that sometimes treaties may be left vague.[13] Treaty specificity is therefore a function of the likelihood the treaty will be breached and the costs of determining the loss of that. In applying this to human rights treaties, this suggests that when there is a strong possibility that states will breach their treaty obligations and when loss from breach is acute, then the rights should be framed specifically. By contrast, gaps may be left in treaties when filling those gaps involves higher costs than the danger the treaty will be breached ex post.

The economic analysis of contract law can therefore aid us in understanding how best to address human rights treaties. When treaty drafters expect that it will be difficult to agree on a treaty's structure, and when they anticipate that it will be cheaper for human rights committees to adjudicate on treaty provisions at a lower cost in the future, it is more efficient to leave the treaty vague. To many human rights lawyers this may seem anathema. However, the purpose of the present chapter is to suggest how human rights treaties can be most efficiently formed both ex ante and ex post. If it is cheaper for courts and committees to interpret treaties than it

---

11 Coase, 'The Problem of Social Cost' (n2) 15.

12 Robert B. Cooter and Thomas Ulen, *Law and Economics* (2nd edn, Reading, MA: Addison-Wesley, 1997) 181.

13 Joel P. Trachtman, *The Economic Structure of International Law* (Cambridge, MA: Harvard University Press, 2008) 49.

is for the drafting committee to do likewise at the time the treaty is being drafted, then framers should leave treaties vague.

This assumes, however, that a court or committee is in place in order to make determinations as to treaty violation. In most instances in relation to human rights treaties, no such court or committee is initially in place, although the conventions might call for their establishment.[14] In fact, as is widely known, courts or committees are generally formed pursuant to optional protocols to the initial treaty, although it is never known whether or when those optional protocols will actually be drafted in subsequent periods.[15] This leads to a situation where treaty drafters are in limbo with regard to the extent of the provisions in the initial treaties. Not knowing whether a regulator, either a court or a committee, will be in a position to adjudicate on treaty issues ex post affects the decision set of the treaty drafters. Instead of being able to opt for either more or less detail, the balance is tilted toward treaties with more detail. This increases the costs of drafting a treaty and reduces the likely uptake of that treaty by the varying states.

By having treaty formation and optional protocol formation as two separate games, an inefficiency results: treaties are drafted with greater detail when it might have been more efficient to leave gaps in the treaty. This point, then, that treaties might be left with gaps, is important: gaps or uncertainties are left when filling them is unjustifiable.

In putting this in practical terms, I posit a hypothetical treaty in which the drafter must decide between the right to food and the right to nutrition with these rights being subject to the obligation that they be respected, protected, and fulfilled. When respect is the issue we assume that the right will be negative, and that respect refers to the state allowing access to the right, whether that is food or nutrition. We assume that non-interference with access to food is more costly for that state than non-interference with access to nutrition: given that food is a broader definition it is more likely that a state's domestic actions might infringe the citizens' access to food. Secondly, with regard to both the obligation to protect and fulfil, we assume they impose positive obligations: the state must act proactively.

---

[14] See, for example, Art. 34, Convention on the Rights of Persons with Disabilities, 993 UNTS 3, 30 March 2007, entered into force 3 May 2008; Art. 43, Convention on the Rights of the Child, 1577 UNTS 3, 20 November 1989, entered into force 2 September 1990.

[15] A notable exception is Art. 14 of the International Convention on the Elimination of All Forms of Racial Discrimination, 660 UNTS 195, 21 December 1965, entered into force 4 January 1969, which includes the individual complaints mechanism, thereby removing the need for an optional protocol.

In that respect, the right to nutrition will be more costly than the right to food because ensuring access to nutrition imposes greater obligations on the state. From this viewpoint, the inclusion of the right to nutrition in the treaty will increase the costs of ratification more than will the inclusion of the right to food. This holds even though frustrating access to food is more likely than frustrating access to nutrition. This is outweighed, however, by the greater cost of protecting and fulfilling a right to nutrition.

In that vein, then, we should consider another situation: rights that impose largely positive obligations. Ergo, we consider a situation in which drafters may choose between a human right guaranteeing freedom from hunger, a right guaranteeing freedom from malnutrition, and a right guaranteeing freedom from starvation. A very basic argument assumes hunger relates to a lack of basic foodstuffs meaning hunger is a function of food. We assume, secondly, that malnutrition does not necessarily stem from a lack of food, although it may, but rather a poor, unbalanced diet. Thirdly, we assume that starvation is a function of both a lack of food and a lack of nutrition.

In this light, I contend that costs graduate as the right moves from freedom from hunger to freedom from malnutrition to freedom from starvation. We expect that states are required to ensure that these rights are fully provided for, meaning that resources will be spent when infringement of the rights becomes more pronounced. Ergo, a state will have to expend more to prevent starvation than it will to prevent hunger or malnutrition. Treaty drafters should consider this in their decision set. The inclusion of the more specific right (i.e. the right to nutrition or the right to be free from starvation) will increase the costs for states considering ratification. When this takes place, or when the drafting committee is facing high bargaining costs, we would expect less specificity and the determining of specificity to be allocated to the ex post regulator. When bargaining costs are low and when deterrence from greater specificity is low, we assume the right will be framed in greater detail. Resultantly, the specificity of the human rights enshrined in the treaty is a function of the costs of bargaining for more specificity at the drafting stage plus the costs more specificity places on potential ratifying states (through deterring ratification) minus the costs of adjudicating on the relevant right ex post (as adjudication will be easier).

As mentioned, however, unless such drafters are aware that a court or committee will be present ex post then the costs of more specific human rights are higher. With this in mind, a clear picture emerges from this analysis: unless treaties are drafted contemporaneously with the formation of an ex post adjudicator, rights will be more specific. By drafting treaties and creating adjudicatory bodies at the same time, treaty drafters are in a position to choose the most efficient means of creating international human rights law.

In reality, though, this is not the case: optional protocols creating regulators are drafted later. There is, of course, a rational explanation for this: to indicate during the drafting of the treaty that an adjudicator will be present may deter states from ratifying the treaty. Equally, though, as discussed, doing so enables treaties to be written at a cheaper cost. Further, if rights are less specific states may be more likely to ratify, since they might undercalculate the costs of ex post adjudication. The impact on ratification decisions of less specific rights plus an adjudicator might be lower than the impact of more specific rights but no adjudicator.

If this holds, then the traditional approach has followed an inefficient path. Treaties with less specific rights but with an adjudicator in place that can determine specificity at a cheaper cost ex post might experience a higher level of ratification than traditionally constituted treaties. This, I argue, is rooted in the state's assessment of the treaty and its calculation of the costs and benefits of ratifying the treaty. States compare their provision of human rights against the extent of the human rights enshrined in the treaty. When rights are specific, and when states provide similar rights, they will ratify the treaty, irrespective of the existence of a court or committee.

Given the linearity between the state's provision of human rights and the expectations of the treaty, the adjudicator becomes irrelevant. When, however, a state's provision of human rights does not meet with the expectations of the treaty, the specificity of the rights matter. More specific rights may deter ratification because the reputational benefits of ratifying the treaty are more muted than if division between the state and the treaty's rights were not so evident. By contrast, treaties with less specific rights are likely to see greater ratification from states with a substandard provision of human rights. Such states ratify because doing so affords them a reputational benefit, although the vagueness of the rights stifles that benefit.

Now consider the relevance of an adjudicator. I have assumed that vague treaties come with courts or committees because the drafters were unable to agree upon specificity and so they elected to leave the specificity to ex post adjudication. I also assume that treaties that specifically outline human rights in great detail do not include a regulatory body.

Consequently, we might contend that states with poor human rights standards might be deterred from ratifying the more vague treaties, given the adjudicator's existence. However, my central assertion is that such states might ratify those treaties to gain a reputational benefit but will fail to fully internalize the costs of ex post regulation. This they do because, although they are aware that their own human rights provisions are substandard, they measure substandard in relation to the phrasing of the human rights in the treaty. In reality, they should be measuring substandard in relation to what the treaty drafters would have agreed upon had there been no transaction costs during the drafting stage.

Therefore, by leaving treaties vague drafters push states with substandard human rights provisions toward using the treaty as the fulcrum around which those states measure substandard. These states thereby carry out a skewed cost–benefit analysis and ratify treaties with vague human rights provisions but with adjudication ex post. Vagueness coupled with a regulatory body may therefore induce ratification by states with poor human rights standards as these states cannot know the optimal standard.

5. CONCLUSION

I argue that this approach suggests some interesting policy conclusions. It points out, for instance, that if we are eager to gain ratification from states with poor human rights standards, and if the transaction costs of negotiating treaty terms more specifically are high, then we should draft treaties with 'gaps' and leave the gap-filling to ex post adjudication. This approach flows from the economic approach to contract law and is, I suggest, an interesting contribution to the human rights literature. In some respects, it goes against the traditional understanding in the human rights community, in which treaties must outline the expected human rights standards as clearly as possible. I do not disagree, but in situations when the costs of negotiating a treaty are high, economic theory indicates it is more efficient to take an alternative approach.

It is important to stress that this approach is general and stylized. Its firm assumption that states sign and ratify treaties in order to gain reputation follows a rationalist approach, contrary to the theories of liberalism and idealism. In addition, it assumes that the core intention of drafters of human rights treaties is to achieve maximum ratification, rather than achieving an effective treaty system. The two, from the perspective of the present approach, do not necessarily exist separately however. Instead, I have contended that the problem of achieving both goals lies in the fact that human rights treaties are drafted separately to the formation of monitoring committees. Specificity of treaty expectations but lack of clarity regarding future regulation can deter states with poor human rights standards from ratifying, with these states viewing ratification, given the uncertainty of the future, as too costly. By contrast, more vague treaties should see greater ratification, as the states will fail to internalize the future costs of the contemporaneously constituted monitoring mechanism, focusing instead on the gains from ratifying a treaty at all.

All of this points in one direction: if maximum ratification of human rights treaties is the normative goal and if drafters find it difficult to draft a treaty with specific rights, then ex post regulators should be allocated the role of determining optimal human rights standards.

14. Free and fair elections for some? The potential for voting rights for under-18s

Aoife Daly

> Well, I called my congressman
> And he said, quote,
> 'I'd like to help you, son
> But you're too young to vote'
>
> Eddie Cochran, *Summertime Blues*, 1958

In a democracy, the right to vote is the ultimate characteristic of citizenship. Even where its practical value is arguable, it is a symbolic confirmation of one's status as citizen. Yet a number of exclusions from enfranchisement have existed in various places and times. These have included women, slaves, those without property, and particular ethnic groups. Similarly, age limits persist; setting the age of 18 as the voting age is common practice[1] and it is confirmed to an extent within international human rights law. The right to vote is not included explicitly in the UN Convention on the Rights of the Child for example, although Article 12 goes some way towards addressing the traditional invisibility of under-18s in the political sphere. Article 12 enshrines the 'right to be heard' of children, stipulating that states 'shall assure' that right to a child once he or she is capable of forming his or her own views. Children must be able to express those views freely in all matters affecting them, and crucially those views must be given due weight 'in accordance with the age and maturity of the child'.

It is no longer sufficient, therefore, to assume that under-18s are incapable of contributing to decision-making processes. Article 12 reflects increasing acceptance at both domestic and international level that chil-

---

1 André Blais *et al.* found near consensus across democracies on a minimum voting age of 18. André Blais *et al.*, 'Deciding who has the Right to Vote: A Comparative Analysis of Election Laws' (2001) 20 *Electoral Studies* 41.

dren can and should contribute to matters affecting them. Nevertheless, voting rights – and therefore the right to be heard directly through elections – are granted to only a tiny minority of the 2.2 billion of the world's population who are under 18 years old. Those who are accorded the right are those aged 16 and 17 years who live in Austria, Brazil, Cuba, Indonesia and Nicaragua,[2] and those of 17 years in East Timor, Indonesia, Sudan and North Korea.[3]

Under-18s are excluded from political decision-making processes because this group are so excluded from mainstream life generally, at least in the 'Northern'/'Western' world.[4] As part of this phenomenon of exclusion, they are kept from involvement in political decision-making processes which are vital to the exercise of citizenship rights. Our instinct to protect children and young people from the everyday world means that the experiences and knowledge of this group about their own lives are consequently segregated and excluded from the mainstream – the arena of politics included. Children's experiences are rendered invisible, and as a group, children are unable to contribute to decision-making concerning them.

Kohn points out that '[s]elective disenfranchisement of distinct groups of citizens with shared interests reduces the likelihood that elected officials and democratically enacted initiatives will reflect the will of the people.'[5] As 'non-voters',[6] children cannot exert influence on policy-making to further their interests as a group. Their interests are inevitably less likely to feature on the agendas of those formulating law and policy.[7] To illustrate this point, Pantell and Shannon note the fact that changes in social policy over the past four decades in the US context have resulted in the provision of health insurance for all those over the age of 65, yet 10 million children remained uninsured in 2009. The authors cite many more examples (i.e. low levels of investment in children's needs in other areas) and opine that this intergenerational inequity reflects the lack of children's voices in

---

2 See Joerg Chet Tremmel, 'Editorial' (2009) 9 *Intergenerational Justice Rev.* 127. The Isle of Man, Guernsey and Jersey have also adopted 16 as the voting age.

3 Robert Pantell and Maureen Shannon, 'Improving Public Policy for Children: A Vote for Each Child' (2009) 9 *Intergenerational Justice Rev.* 139, 141.

4 See further below.

5 Nina Kohn, 'Cognitive Impairment and the Right to Vote: Rethinking the Meaning of Accessible Elections' 1 *Canadian Elder L.J.* 29, 44.

6 Aoife Nolan, 'The Child as "Democratic Citizen": Challenging the "Participation Gap"' (2010) *Public Law* 767, 2.

7 *Ibid.*

political decision-making.[8] Indeed it is a well-known fact that older people typically vote in high numbers.[9] It is very likely that if the same could be said about children and young people as a group, their issues would take a higher position on the political agenda.

This is a dilemma which seems strikingly obvious, and yet there has arguably been very little attention to date accorded to the fact that there exists a vast group of disenfranchised people in every democracy. It seems to be accepted as legitimate almost without question. Yet the widespread acceptance of 18 as the age at which one gains voting rights belies some striking inconsistencies. Lecce opines that '[u]ltimately, there is a deep tension between the egalitarian presuppositions of democracy and our apparent unwillingness to grant children voting rights.'[10] Children and young people are often taught lessons about citizenship and democracy in schools and yet will not have the right to vote until long after they have developed the capacity to understand such concepts. Considering the vital nature of the right to vote,[11] it must be recognized that restrictions placed on children and young people in this regard should only be those deemed necessary and proportionate in accordance with children's minor status.

Most democratic states are subject to the obligations of non-discrimination legislation whether at domestic[12] or international[13] level. Such legislation enshrines the principle of proportionality which determines that distinctions in legal rights should have a 'reasonable relationship of proportionality between the means employed and the aim sought

---

8 Pantell and Shannon (n3) 139. The authors conclude that 'children's issues are no match for the political agendas of groups with voting power.'

9 See e.g. Organisation for Economic Cooperation and Development (OECD), *Society at a Glance: OECD Social Indicators 103* (2006) available at: http://dx.doi.org/10.1787/58-368180314, which reports on voter participation in 23 countries by age; and House of Commons Library, *UK Election Statistics 1918–2004*, 28.

10 Steven Lecce, 'Should Democracy Grow Up?' (2009) 9 *Intergenerational Justice Rev.* 133.

11 See, for example, Armand Derfner, 'Racial Discrimination and the Right to Vote' (1973) 26 *Vand. L. Rev.* 523 and Pantell and Shannon (n3).

12 See e.g. the UK Equality Act 2010 and the Equal Status Act 2000 in the Republic of Ireland. EU anti-discrimination legislation also exists. See e.g. the Charter of Fundamental Rights of the European Union (2006) Chapter III.

13 See e.g. Arts 2(1) and 26 of the International Covenant on Civil and Political Rights (adopted 16 December 1966, entered into force 23 March 1976) 999 UNTS 171 (ICCPR), and at regional level, Art. 14, European Convention for the Protection of Human Rights and Fundamental Freedoms (4 November 1950, entered into force 3 September 1953) 213 UNTS 222.

to be reali[s]ed.'[14] Research concerning the decision-making capacities of children and young people indicates that this group has been traditionally hugely underestimated. Therefore it is, in fact, difficult to justify the age of 18 as a blanket cut-off point between childhood and adulthood for many purposes, including in the area of voting rights. There has consequently developed a more modern conceptualization, in international law and elsewhere, of under-18s as potentially active agents who may have a high level of capacity to influence their environment. It must be asked, therefore, whether a continuation of the exclusion of under-18s from voting systems is justified.[15]

It will be argued in this paper that a somewhat false dichotomy has been created between adults and under-18s regarding the notion of capacity to vote. It will be emphasized that the time has come for revisiting the current consensus of a voting age of 18 years both within international human rights law and at domestic level. Changes to voting ages must be made in order to recognize the new understanding of childhood and the capacities of children and young people, and consequently to accord children with much-needed (and deserved) political strength.

Empirical research within developmental psychology will be drawn upon to argue that the right to vote should be accorded to children, at least from the age of 12 years. The traditional denial of the right to vote to under-18s, and the potential for an evolution in practice towards recognition of this basic human right for this group, will be examined. The treatment by legal systems (including international legal systems) of the factor of age will be considered. The denial of voting rights to other repressed groups will be highlighted. Contemporary thinking about the voting rights of adults with 'relative capability deficits'[16] will be analysed in order to further illustrate the argument that the blanket categorization of under-18s as incompetent for voting purposes is both illogical and unfair. Current state practice and recent developments will be considered and the conclusion will be drawn that, despite little progress in the area so far, there is potential for, and positive aspects to, according the right to vote to under-18s.

---

14 *Belgian Linguistic* Case (No. 2) Series A, No.6 (1979–80) 1 EHRR 252, 23 July 1968, para 10.

15 The matter of the exclusion of children from running for political positions is also a worthy issue; however the scope of this chapter will be confined to the matter of voting. As Tremmel opines, it is important to consider voting rights in particular 'because they are the most important step for increasing youth influence in politics and to make children's interests more visible' (n2) 127.

16 Lecce (n10) 137.

1. THE CONVENTION ON THE RIGHTS OF THE CHILD AND PARTICIPATION

In 1924, the League of Nations adopted the Declaration on the Rights of the Child,[17] which enshrined protection and provision rights for children. The notion at that time of children as primarily helpless beings was reflected in the Declaration. However the drafting of the Convention on the Rights of the Child heralded a change in how children were conceptualized in international law,[18] by including for the first time in an international human rights text what are now known as 'participation rights'. This category of rights includes those provisions which relate to the participation of children in decision-making affecting them and other aspects of their lives.[19] This is a theme which is also included and reflected in other provisions in the Convention,[20] for example the right to freedom of information[21] and the right to freedom of expression.[22] Article 12, which enshrines the right of children to be heard, is the most prominent provision in this regard, as it explicitly affords to children the right to be heard in matters affecting them. Lansdown writes of participation rights that:

> At the core is Article 12, which insists on the 'visibility' of children in their own right. Its implementation, alongside the other civil rights, involves a profound and radical reconsideration of the status of children in most societies and the nature of adult/child relationships. It requires us to begin to listen to what children say and to take them seriously. It requires that we recognise the value of their own experience, views and concerns.[23]

The participation rights enshrined within the Convention on the Rights of the Child, and Article 12 in particular, have acted to some extent as an

---

[17] The Declaration on the Rights of the Child was followed by the 1959 Declaration on the Rights of the Child which contained a number of additional rights such as the right to play. See Geraldine Van Beuren, *The International Law on the Rights of the Child* (The Hague [etc.]: Nijhoff, 1998).

[18] The Convention opened for signature on 20 November 1989 and came into force on 2 September 1990.

[19] It is currently a term which is widely used in relation to Art. 12 and other relevant articles of the Convention. See Committee on the Rights of the Child, *General Comment on Article 12*, UN Doc CRC/C/GC/12, 1 July 2009, para 3.

[20] See further Gerison Lansdown, *Children's Participation in Democratic Decision-Making* (Florence: UNICEF Innocenti Research Centre, 2001) 12.

[21] Art. 17, Convention on the Rights of the Child.

[22] Art. 13, Convention on the Rights of the Child.

[23] Lansdown (n20) 1.

influence on thinking around children's rights and abilities. The provision has furthered the notion of children as active agents who can provide valuable information about their own experiences, and should participate to some degree in decision-making affecting them.[24] However participation rights are controversial for those who want to keep power solely in adult hands. Article 12 is also often misunderstood and there is the belief in some circles that the provision seeks to hand decision-making powers to children.[25] In fact the provision simply states that children should have some level of input into decision-making, and the specifics are unclear, which could explain the slow progress for under-18s in areas such as voting rights.[26] The participation of children as a concept has, however, been the subject of scholarly research in recent years, and has been explicitly linked to greater democratic involvement for children. Roger Hart's definition of participation demonstrates the notion of democracy inherent in that category of rights:

> [T]he fact of being involved in the decision-making that concerns oneself and that concerns the life of the community in which one lives. It is the corner stone of democracy on the looks of which democracies should be evaluated.[27]

Other theorists also make a strong link between participation and social inclusion.[28] Cattrijsse and Delens-Ravier argue that the phenomenon of participation increases generally a sense of community and that it 'facilitates the acceptance of decisions, even if a decision does not bring into

---

24 Bren Neale, 'Dialogues with Children: Children, Divorce and Citizenship' (2002) 9 *Childhood* 455.

25 See e.g. Christopher Klicka and William Estrada, *The UN Convention on the Rights of the Child: The Most Dangerous Attack on Parents' Rights in the History of the United States* (Home School Legal Defense Association, 2007) 4; and Bruce Hafen and Jonathan Hafen, 'Abandoning Children to their Autonomy: The United Nations Convention on the Rights of the Child' (1995) 55 *First Things* 18 refer to the CRC's right to freedom of information as being of an 'unrestrained spirit'.

26 See Rachel Hodgkin and Peter Newell, *Implementation Handbook for the UN Convention on the Rights of the Child* (Florence: UNICEF, 2002) 163, which points to state reports highlighting that Art. 12 is difficult to implement.

27 Roger Hart, *Children's Participation: From Tokenism to Citizen* (Florence: UNICEF, 1992) 5.

28 Fiona Ang *et al.*, 'Introduction', in Fiona Ang *et al.* (eds) *Participation Rights of Children* (Antwerp: Intersentia, 2006) 3; Bruce Winck, 'The Side Effects of Incompetency Labelling and the Implications for Mental Health' (1995) 1 *Psychology, Public Policy and Law* 6, 22; Iris Marion Young, *Justice and the Politics of Difference* (Princeton, NJ: Princeton University Press, 1990) 58.

account everybody's concern. It secures social rest'.[29] Just as with any group, exclusion of children and young people could well lead to resentment towards the oppressors (i.e. adults) and consequently the wider community. It is quite possible that denying voting rights to under-18s is a cause of a sense of exclusion and isolation from society for this group, particularly amongst teenagers.

There are a number of other arguments which can be made in favour of according participation rights, including the right to vote for under-18s. Potential benefits in terms of greater levels of social cohesion are notable. Moreover, as noted above, conceptualizations of childhood are rapidly evolving. It is increasingly recognized that children are experts on their own experiences, and that even very young children may have perspectives to bring to decision-making about their own lives.[30] And indeed it is undeniable that children are not simply passive recipients of adult care throughout childhood. The experience of childhood is just not that straightforward.

Children make decisions regularly, ranging from the simple to the complex. Children with more average backgrounds in the 'Northern'/'Western' world make many such decisions such as with whom they will play and associate. Children from complex, difficult backgrounds will have to make more challenging decisions. Those from families in which domestic violence exists, for example, may be faced with such decisions on a regular basis. It has been shown, for example, that they can utilize astute judgement on the matter of whether to intervene in a violent attack on a parent.[31] Another group which takes on huge responsibility is that of child carers. A large percentage of the child population in any country are carers for someone else close to them (usually a parent or grandparent) – in Northern Ireland, for example, 10 per cent of 16 year olds have taken on such a role.[32] These responsible, brave and somewhat

---

[29] Lieve Cattrijsse and Isabelle Delens-Ravier, 'Reflections on the Concept of Participation', in Fiona Ang *et al.* (eds) *Participation Rights of Children* (Antwerp: Intersentia, 2006) 32.

[30] E.g. Neale (n24); Allison James, Chris Jenks and Alan Prout, *Theorizing Childhood* (Oxford: Polity Press, 1998) and Allison James and Alan Prout, *Constructing and Reconstructing Childhood: Contemporary Issues in the Sociological Study of Childhood* (London: Falmer Press, 1990).

[31] See Liz Kelly, *Surviving Sexual Violence* (Oxford: Polity, 1988) who documented the reports of victims of domestic violence that the timing of the intervention of a child had, they believed, saved their lives.

[32] Paula Devine and Katrina Lloyd, 'Young Carers Too' in (2011) 76 *Economic and Social Research Council: Research Update* 1 available online at: http://www.ark.ac.uk/publications/updates/update76.pdf, accessed 22 July 2011.

altruistic actions of children and young people remain largely hidden from the public sphere, with the media preferring to focus instead on negative stories, portraying teenagers as irresponsible and threatening.[33] The discourse in the 2011 London riots for example, has very much involved condemnation and demonization of children,[34] though over 77 per cent of those charged with offences in hearings relating to the riots were over 18.[35]

In the 'Global South'/'Developing World' children take, on average, even more responsibility for themselves and their families. Children often make contributions without which their families could not survive.[36] The matter of child carers is even more pertinent in this part of the world – recent research highlights South African children of parents with HIV/AIDs taking huge responsibility for their families, and the medical treatment of their parents in particular.[37] There has also developed a

---

The definition of a young carer in this research was 'a 16 year old whose life is significantly affected by caring for a family member who has an illness or disability or has a problematic use of drugs or alcohol' (*Ibid.,* 1).

[33] See e.g. Committee on the Rights of the Child, *Concluding Observations: United Kingdom of Great Britain and Northern Ireland* UN Doc CRC/C/GBR/CO/4, 20 October 2008, para 24, in which the Committee expresses concern 'at the general climate of intolerance and negative public attitudes towards children, especially adolescents, which appears to exist in the State party, including in the media, and may be often the underlying cause of further infringements of their rights'. See also initiatives to tackle such negative reporting, e.g. at the website of the National Youth Council of Ireland, *Initiative to Challenge Negative Stereotyping of Young People*, available online at: www.youth.ie and Children and Young People Now, *Northern Ireland: Youth Charity Takes on Negative Media*, 16 March 2005, available online at: www.cypnow.co.uk.

[34] See, amongst the numerous examples, Tom Newton Dunne, 'Boris: Send Riot Kids to Borstal' *The Sun*, 15 August 2011, available online at: http://www.thesun.co.uk/sol/homepage/news/3752123/Boris-Johnson-Send-riot-kids-to-Borstal.html?OTC-RSS&ATTR=News. David Cameron stated that 'children without fathers' were amongst those to blame. See Janaki Mahadevan, 'Riots Blamed on Absent Fathers and Poor School Discipline' *Children and Young People Now*, 15 August 2011, available online at: http://www.cypnow.co.uk/Education/article/1084793/riots-blamed-absent-fathers-poor-school-discipline.

[35] Guardian, 'UK Riots: The List of Magistrate Cases and Convictions so Far' *The Guardian*, 15 August 2011, available online at: http://www.guardian.co.uk/news/datablog/2011/aug/11/uk-riots-magistrates-court-list.

[36] See e.g. Stuart Aiken *et al.*, 'Reproducing Life and Labor: Global Processes and Working Children in Tijuana, Mexico' (2006) 13 *Childhood* 365.

[37] Lucy Tobin, 'South Africa's Children Caring for Parents with AIDS' *The Guardian*, 22 June 2010, available online at: http://www.guardian.co.uk/education/2010/jun/22/hiv-aids-child-carers-south-africa.

phenomenon of child workers forming their own organizations, highlighting the potential for children to become involved in politics.[38]

Children take decisions and contribute to the survival of families, and therefore societies, every day. So why, then, do we see fit to exclude them from political processes? Some commentators argue that to include children in 'adult' arenas, such as politics, would be to burden them unfairly with adult concerns; however many children are already clearly bearing many of those burdens.

2. CHILDREN'S CAPACITIES AND THE LEGAL DISABILITY OF CHILDHOOD

While it is important to recognize the decisions and activities undertaken by children on a daily basis, it is also necessary to acknowledge the reality that under-18s may have what Lecce refers to as 'relative capability deficits.'[39] Very young children will certainly fall into this category. Research in the area of developmental psychology is useful in this regard to examine whether the exclusion from voting of those under the age of 18 is proportionate. Developmental psychologist Jean Piaget devised what he referred to as 'Stage Theory'– conceptualizing the cognitive development of children as a process of maturation whereby children generally reach particular developmental milestones at particular ages.[40] Although Stage Theory has been criticized for underestimating children and for defining them by capacities which they lack at certain stages (as opposed to what children *have* and can do),[41] Stage Theory remains a useful rough gauge of the abilities of the 'average' child.

According to Piaget, childhood consists of four main stages. Piaget theorized that, in the first two stages (from birth to seven years and from age three to seven years) children acquire basic reasoning, and in the final two stages abstract thought becomes sophisticated. I will not focus here on how to tackle the matter of the lack of voting rights for children

---

[38] See Manfred Liebel, 'Working Children as Social Subjects: The Contribution of Working Children's Organizations to Social Transformations' (2003) 10 *Childhood* 265.

[39] Lecce uses the term in relation to adults with 'intellectual' or 'learning' disabilities. Lecce (n10) 137.

[40] Jean Piaget, *The Origins of Intelligence in Children* (London: Routledge and Kegan Paul Ltd., 1953).

[41] See, for example, Margaret Donaldson, *Children's Minds* (London: William Collins Sons and Co. Ltd, 1978).

without some capacity to understand voting, as I am arguing for the right to vote for 'older' children, i.e. those who have the capacity to form views. However it is noteworthy that some interesting (and controversial) suggestions have been put forward in this regard. In Hungary, for example, it has been suggested that mothers will be permitted to vote on behalf of their children.[42] This, of course, retains to a large extent the paternalistic approach to children's interests.[43] Furthermore, it is possibly unfair to dismiss the capacity of even young children to contribute personally to the voting process. Nevertheless, I focus herein on the argument that the abilities of older children are such that it is unacceptable to exclude them from voting.

Piaget wrote that, at approximately age seven, children generally begin to develop the capacity for logical and objective thought. They will increasingly have the capacity to logically consider outcomes relating to concrete events, gaining a better understanding of cause and effect relationships and of the viewpoints of others. Piaget then highlighted the milestone of age 11/12 years as a particular turning point in children's thinking. The capacity for abstract thought becomes increasingly sophisticated, Piaget argued. Children at this stage are capable of reasoning logically, thinking in terms of hypotheticals and capable of considering various possibilities from various perspectives. They have reached, according to Piaget, the ultimate stage of development, although the knowledge base will yet further develop. Santrock highlights in particular the increased social awareness of children at this stage of development.[44] Recent research indicates that young people aged from 14 to 17 years possess 'the reasoning skills to face even complex questions of justice and moral issues.'[45] Assumptions exist about greater risk-taking behaviour by

---

42 See Pantell and Shannon (n3) 141, who also propose proxy voting rights for parents, arguing that 'there is a long legal (and moral) tradition that allows parents to make proxy decisions for their child'.

43 The idea has faced much criticism with one commentator suggesting '. . .the Hungarian government might want to ask the children whether they agree with the politics of their parents, who it's assumed will be voting on their behalf, and if children themselves had the vote, what – not only who – they would vote for.' Selma James, 'This Hungarian Children's Vote is Grossly Dishonest' *The Guardian*, 18 April 2011, available online at: http://www.guardian.co.uk/commentisfree/2011/apr/18/hungary-childrens-vote-mothers-democracy.

44 John Santrock, *A Topical Approach to Lifespan Development* (3rd edn, Boston: McGraw-Hill, 2008) 221.

45 Roberta Bosisio, '"Right" and "Not Right": Representations of Justice in Young People' (2008) 15 *Childhood* 290. See also Charles Lewis, 'Decision-Making related to Health: When Could/Should Children Behave Responsibly?', in Gary

adolescents. Available research on this matter, however, is not conclusive on this point.[46]

Young adolescents will, of course, still lack experience compared to those over the age of 18. However education can be argued to account for this, and to assist children to understand political matters.[47] There is little doubt, considering the reasoning skills of children aged 11/12 and over, that the majority of this group will have the capacity to understand the nature and consequences of voting, and to form voting preferences.

The age of majority is set at 18 years in most countries, and this minimum age usually correlates with the right to vote. However, as much as the law seeks to create convenient categorizations, an assumption that children are totally incapable until the age of 18 is to underestimate children and to ignore empirical research on the decision-making capacities of this group. The notion of the evolving capacities of the child, enshrined in Article 5 of the Convention on the Rights of the Child, attempts to account for this dilemma. Responsible adults are to guide children in the exercise of their rights 'in a manner consistent with the evolving capacities of the child'– this acknowledges that children experience different levels of capacity depending on age, experiences, etc.

Domestic law goes some way towards accounting for the notion of evolving capacities by establishing a number of minimum ages which determine when children are considered to be capable of making decisions for themselves. Many of these restrictions do not correlate with the age of majority, and upon close inspection often appear as arbitrary as the age of majority itself. The most troubling and contentious area is probably that of criminal responsibility. The age of criminal responsibility varies from seven (e.g. India) right up to the age of 18 (e.g. Belgium),[48] highlighting lack of understanding of and consensus on the point at which to hold children responsible for criminal behaviour. In Ireland and the UK,

---

Melton *et al.* (eds) *Children's Competence to Consent* (New York: Plenum Press 1998) cited in Gerison Lansdown, *The Evolving Capacities of the Child* (Florence: UNICEF Innocenti Research Centre, 2005) 24.

46 Fortin cites research by Alicia Benthin *et al.*, 'A Psychometric Study of Adolescent Risk Perception' (1993) 16 *Journal of Adolescence* 153, as demonstrating greater risk-taking behaviour in adolescents, and research by Susan Millstein, 'Perceptual, Attributional and Affective Processes in Perceptions of Vulnerability Through the Lifespan', in Nancy Bell and Robert Bell (eds) *Adolescent Risk Taking* (Thousand Oaks: Sage Publications, 1993) which refutes this. Jane Fortin, *Children's Rights and the Developing Law* (3rd edn, Cambridge: CUP, 2009) 85.

47 See further below.

48 See John Gillen, 'The Age of Criminal Responsibility: "The Frontier between Care and Justice"' 12 *Child Care in Practice* 129, 136.

children as young as ten years can potentially be held fully responsible for violent actions, yet will not be considered competent for voting purposes for another eight years. The area of medical consent is another which highlights inconsistencies in thinking about children and their capacities. The notion of the '*Gillick*-competent'[49] child has emerged in the UK in recent years to account for the perceived importance of autonomy over one's own body. The judgment in the *Gillick* case determined that, if a person under the age of majority was deemed to be of a certain level of competence, the need for parental permission would be obviated for consent to medical treatment. By this logic a young girl could be deemed competent to terminate a pregnancy, but not be considered to have the capacity to vote for a number of years. If children are competent to make medical decisions which have potentially lifelong consequences, then how is it logical to exclude them from the voting process?

There are a number of minimum ages in place for various purposes, often contradictory and indeed sometimes seemingly arbitrary. In the absence of mechanisms to provide assessments of every child in every context, minimum ages seem a necessary evil. Yet the establishment of the age of 18 in relation to voting seems seriously flawed. Considering the research findings above, in particular in relation to Piaget's Stage Theory which sets the age of 11/12 as the vital point around which abstract thought and logical reasoning become sophisticated, it seems appropriate to consider extending the right to vote to children aged approximately 12 years and over.

Children usually enter second-level schooling at approximately age 12 years, a transition which also recognizes the significant milestone of this age. Considering the fact that politics are not generally geared towards children, it would be desirable (and possibly essential) if schools provided impartial, non-partisan information to children from this age to encourage their thinking and decision-making. Kohn advocates for 'cognitively accessible voting'[50] (i.e. keeping the voting process straightforward to avoid errors and to decrease the need for assistance from others) to assist adults with 'relative capability deficits' to vote, and there should be a similar approach to young people.

The outcome of research with under-18s indicates that it is difficult to generalize about their decision-making abilities compared to adults, although on an anecdotal level one may assume that the thinking of many

---

[49] *Gillick v. West Norfolk and Wisbech Area Health Authority* [1986] AC 112; [1985] 3 WLR 830.

[50] Kohn (n5) 31.

young people from age 12 to 17 operates somewhat differently to that of most adults. I would argue that the thinking and decision-making of children is not necessarily deficient, but simply different to that of older persons. At the very least society generally and the law in particular has constructed a dichotomy between under-18s and over-18s which encourages simplistic thinking about a rather complex matter.

Undoubtedly some would argue that there is a risk that children may be subjected to exploitation and undue influence in terms of their voting choices. However it is simplistic to claim that children– particularly older children– do not know their own minds, whilst those over 18 do. Even if a child's views have been influenced by, for example, an adult such as a parent, who is to say that the view of the child is not her own? Are not all of us influenced every day by family, friends and others in the culture in which we live? Does that make our views less our own? There are no straightforward answers; however it is illogical to impose unrealistic expectations (which we could not apply to ourselves) and consequently limitations on children.

3. GROUPS TRADITIONALLY DENIED THE RIGHT TO VOTE

There are a variety of arguments employed by theorists against the notion of according rights to children as individuals. Some have argued against making political something that should remain a private family matter, although feminist theorists have already triumphed against that claim.[51] Others have claimed that, because children are not yet fully developed, adults should exercise their rights on their behalf, and the focus should be on adult duties as opposed to children's rights.[52] It has also been argued that children's freedom should be limited in order for them to acquire the qualities desirable in 'fully developed' citizens.[53] There are, of course,

---

[51] See, for example, Nancy Fraser, *Rethinking the Public Sphere: A Contribution to the Critique of Actually Existing Democracy* (Durham, NC: Duke University Press, 1992) and Shazia Choudhry and Jonathan Herring, 'Righting Domestic Violence' (2006) 20 *IJLPF* 95.

[52] Onora O'Neill, 'Children's Rights and Children's Lives', in Philip Alston *et al.* (eds) *Children, Rights and the Law* (Oxford: OUP, 1992).

[53] See further Laura Purdy, *In Their Best Interest?: The Case Against Equal Rights for Children* (New York: Cornell University Press, 1992). I qualify 'fully developed' as I resist the implication that children are not 'full' people, because they have yet to reach adulthood, or 'full' citizens because they do not work, or because they are different to the average adult in other ways.

those who maintain that children should enjoy the innocence and ignorance which childhood supposedly involves. Arguments are also made that children are ignorant of the area of politics, that children could be easily swayed by others, and that consequently the political balance could be affected detrimentally.[54] However, these particular points against the possibility of enfranchisement of a particular group are not new.

Kulynych highlights similarities between many of the arguments against the provision of voting rights to under-18s and those used in relation to other marginalized groups in the US. The language used in relation to previously disenfranchised groups is both revealing and familiar. Kulynych points to the US case *Cherokee Nation v. Georgia*[55] of 1831 in which Chief Justice Marshall stated that Indian tribes had a relationship to their government which 'resembles that of a ward to his guardian'[56] and the court, therefore, did not have jurisdiction to hear the merits of a claim relating to the removal of Cherokee rights. In other words, the dependent nature of that group stripped them of legal standing and, conveniently for the government 'guardian', the ability to assert independent interests in court. Kulynych also cites Fitzhugh, who argued in 1857 against the emancipation of slaves on the basis that emancipation was not in their interests, claiming that slaves were the 'happiest and in some sense the freest people in the world . . . the balance of their time is spent in perfect abandon . . . they luxuriate in corporeal and mental repose.'[57] The Fifteenth Amendment to the US Constitution ultimately prohibited states from denying votes on the basis of race.[58]

Perhaps the most illuminative of exclusions from suffrage for the

---

[54] See e.g. John Mitchell, 'Why 16-year-olds Cannot Serve as Rational and Informed Voters in a Democratic Society' (2001) submitted to Alberta Queens' Bench and Court of Appeal in *Fitzgerald (Next Friend of) v. Alberta* [2002] AJ No 1544, 2002 ABQB 1086 (Alta QB) and see further Jessica Kulynych, 'No Playing in the Public Sphere: Democratic Theory and the Exclusion of Children' (2001) 27 *Social Theory and Practice* 231, 234.

[55] 30 US 1 (1831). Cited in Kulynych, *ibid.* See also the case of *Porter v. Hall* 271 P 411 (Ariz 1928) in which the Arizona court concluded that Native Americans were barred from voting. See further Henry Watkins, *The Right to Vote of Persons under Guardianship – Limited and Otherwise* (Phoenix, AZ: Arizona Center for Disability Law, 2006).

[56] See further Watkins, *ibid.*

[57] George Fitzhugh, 'Cannibals All!' (1857), in Kenneth Dolbeare (ed.) *American Political Thought* (New York: Chatham House Publishers, 1998) 273. Cited in Kulynych (n54).

[58] Amendment XV, ratified on 3 February 1870. It reads 'Section 1. The right of citizens of the United States to vote shall not be denied or abridged by the United States or by any State on account of race, color, or previous condition

purposes of the current argument was that imposed on women. Women were traditionally denied full civil and political rights in common law countries, as the legal personality of a woman was considered to be incorporated into that of her husbands'. Blackstone in his *Commentaries on the Laws of England* in 1765[59] noted that:

> By marriage, the husband and wife are one person in law; that is, the very being or legal existence of the woman is suspended during the marriage, or at least is incorporated and consolidated into that of the husband: under whose wing, protection, and cover, she performs everything . . . These are the chief legal effects of marriage during the coverture; upon which we may observe, that even the disabilities, which the wife lies under, are for the most part intended for her protection and benefit. So great a favourite is the female sex of the laws of England.

The denial of women's suffrage in the early part of the twentieth century was constructed as a caring, paternalistic measure. Arguments included claims that it would be burdensome for women, and that it was the matter of husband's duties, and not women's rights, which was at issue.[60] Of course, democratic countries now accord women the right to vote, as they do citizens from ethnic minorities. This is because the social discourse transformed to one which recognized the inconsistencies in the supposed moral basis for subsuming the rights of one person into those of another. There are various arguments against this which now seem very obvious. The 'responsible' person can (and often will) have competing interests. It is demeaning where the 'dependent' person has her own views. And so on. When one thinks of an individual who is under the age of 18 and holds her own views, obvious comparisons can be made. Adults can have competing interests to children, and children can have well-formed views of their own.

However it is not solely the categories of race and sex which have undergone a transformation in terms of enfranchisement in relatively recent times. The fact that the age of majority, and consequently the age of suffrage, was previously 21 in the UK and Ireland (and

---

of servitude. Section 2. The Congress shall have power to enforce this article by appropriate legislation.'

59 William Blackstone, *Commentaries on the Laws of England* (Oxford: Clarendon Press, first published 1765) 122.

60 See generally Susan Kingsley Kent, *Sex and Suffrage In Britain 1860–1914* (London: Routledge, 1990). Winston Churchill once stated that women's suffrage would lead to a breakdown in society and that women did not require the vote as they were 'well represented by their fathers, brothers, and husbands'.

elsewhere)[61] seems to highlight the potential fluidity of the approach of states to minimum ages in relation to the right of young people to vote, as well as the minimum age in relation to other matters. O'Neill has argued in favour of a focus on the obligations of adults as opposed to the rights of children, because, she opines, children's dependence on others is not comparable to that of other groups which have been traditionally oppressed.[62] However this belies the complexity of the social conceptualization of 'childhood'[63] and the blanket assumption of incapacity which is, for the most part, applied to those under age 18.[64] Social understandings and interpretations of age and capacity are in transition.

It is easy to initially dismiss the notion of children as voters. Very small children, for example, will simply not understand the matter of voting. However, for older children, the logic becomes quite difficult to sustain, particularly when one compares their situation to that of groups which were previously disenfranchised because of prejudice against them. Older children (particularly those over the age of 11/12, as outlined below) generally operate at a very advanced level of decision-making, and some reach levels of abstract thought which will never be attained by some adults. The differences in thought processes between older children and adults are overestimated to a large extent, and for this reason their exclusion from the voting process should be seen in light of the experiences of other groups who were previously disenfranchised.

4. ADULTS WITH 'RELATIVE CAPABILITY DEFICITS'

As outlined above, there is a clearly contradictory approach taken by the law to the abilities of children at various stages, and this is certainly relevant to arguments in favour of votes for under-18s. Another fascinating perspective is that relating to the matter of the right to vote of people with

---

61 Indeed, in the UK the voting age for women was in fact originally (i.e. in 1918) set at the age of 30, and limited to particular groups of women.

62 O'Neill (n52).

63 The social conceptualization/construction of childhood refers to the assumptions that we have in the 'Western'/'Northern' modern world about children. We hold assumptions that all children are helpless and in need of care and always have been, whereas in reality many children provide care to others, and outside of the 'Western'/'Northern' modern world many children undertake paid work to ensure the survival of their families.

64 There are, of course, exceptions to this where under-18s attain majority earlier for particular purposes, such as sexual or medical consent.

disabilities. Some adults have disabilities which lead to 'relative capability deficits' in terms of decision-making.[65] Lecce compares the situation of the exclusion of children from voting to the situation of this particular group. He argues that invoking children's less developed capacities as a reason for denying them the right to vote does not suffice:

> [B]ecause, beyond the legal age of majority, disabilities of those kinds typically do *not* disqualify adults above the threshold. In Canada, for example, neither the insane nor convicted criminals are barred from voting. In short, the common intuition about the absurdity of granting voting rights to children is, in fact, quite hard to sustain in light of both the best arguments for democracy and existing electoral practices.[66]

Indeed, the approach of democratic countries to the voting rights of adults with 'relative capability deficits' is possibly the most striking matter in this debate. Some states do not have any system for disenfranchising adults with 'relative capability deficits'.[67] Many states do, and a system operates whereby the courts may determine where an adult with 'relative capability deficits' will not have the right to vote. In the US, for example, the case of *Doe v. Rowe* determined that a person will not be considered to have the capacity to vote if they 'lack the capacity to understand the nature and effect of voting such that they cannot make an individual choice'.[68] Kohn points to the use of 'informal screening' in some contexts, whereby carers determine whether the individual will vote (often with no expertise or guidelines).[69] It would, therefore, be inaccurate to assert that this group does not still experience obstacles to vindication of the right to vote.[70] However there is an increasing trend towards recognizing that it is unacceptable to apply blanket discrimination to individuals on the basis of 'relative capability deficits'.

---

[65] Adults can have 'relative capability deficits' through learning disability (e.g. due to autism) through acquired brain injury, or through mental health problems (e.g. schizophrenia). The terminology in respect of adults with 'decreased' capacities varies between countries and organizations. It is contentious because terms such as 'decreased', 'intellectual disability', 'cognitive impairment', 'learning disability' etc. suggest inferior abilities, when one could see the capacities of such individuals as simply different to those of the average adult. Lecce uses the term 'relative capability deficits' which is useful as it qualifies the assumption of deficiency. Lecce (n10) 137.

[66] Lecce (n10) 133.

[67] E.g. Canada, Ireland, Italy, and Sweden. See Kohn (n5) 36.

[68] *Doe v. Rowe*, 156 F Supp 2d 35 (D Me 2001).

[69] Kohn (n5) 43.

[70] See e.g. Andrew Ward *et al.*, 'Ensuring the Enfranchisement of People with Disabilities' (2009) 20 *Journal of Disability Policy Studies* 79.

It is not just those who can be clearly identified as having relevant disabilities who may be affected in their ability to vote – there exist a variety of further obstacles, such as literacy problems. The 'Every Vote Counts' project in England, which advocates for votes for those with learning disability in England emphasizes that:

> As well as around a million adults with a learning disability there are estimated to be as many as 1 in 5 people with low literacy levels in England. This means that a highly significant amount of people rely on others to ensure they can access important information and activities.[71]

Literacy problems could clearly affect the ability to vote because of potential difficulties with accessing information about candidates, and with reading ballot papers and other relevant documents. Kanter highlights the fact that there are many groups who require assistance to access their right to vote, for example '[t]he right to political participation means nothing to an elderly person with limited vision who wishes to vote but is unable to see the ballot.'[72] Yet the law seeks to assist those with such issues to vote, not to exclude them completely. While the situation of obstacles for children is not identical to these latter comparisons, these examples at least serve to highlight the need to reconsider assumptions about excluding children.

The inconsistencies between the approach to children and adults with disabilities at the level of international human rights law are also quite striking. Article 29 of the Convention on the Rights of People with Disabilities applies to the right of people with disabilities to fully participate in political and public life on an equal basis with others. It stipulates that states undertake to ensure that people with disabilities are afforded the opportunity to vote, *inter alia*, by '[e]nsuring that voting procedures, facilities and materials are appropriate, accessible and easy to understand and use'. The provision for the right of people with disabilities to vote (and generally participate in public life) is in clear contrast to the lack of such provisions in the Convention on the Rights of the Child. Nolan highlights the lack of initiative taken by the Committee on the Rights of the Child in terms of taking a stance on how Article 12 should apply to the matter of voting ages.[73] The difference between the two instruments can be

---

71 See http://www.everyvotecounts.org.uk/mda/learning-disability.php.

72 Arlene Kanter, 'The UN Convention on the Rights of Persons with Disabilities and its Implications for the Rights of Elderly People under International Law' (2009) 25 *Georgia State Uni. L. Rev.* 527, 573.

73 Nolan (n6) 6.

explained perhaps at least in part by the fact that it was most likely drafted with adult interests in mind, and the right to vote is seen as a key 'adult' right. Many of the adults whom the Convention on the Rights of People with Disabilities seeks to encompass will have 'relative capability deficits' as regards decision-making capacities, however, as do many under-18s.

The Convention on the Rights of the Child has not proven to be an effective vehicle for progressing voting rights for under-18s. Other international law instruments have likewise failed to facilitate gains for children in this area. Although the International Covenant on Civil and Political Rights holds that '[e]veryone shall have the recognition everywhere as a person before the law', the active exercise of some of these rights may be restricted, Nowak opines, 'for minority-aged persons or the mentally ill.'[74] Nowak specifically provides *inter alia* the example of Article 25 – the right to take part in public affairs and to vote – which permits reasonable restrictions by states.[75] However it is clear that the restrictions for adults considered to be 'mentally ill' (as Nowak puts it) or in some other way incapacitated, are rapidly changing both at domestic and international level. Law and practice in relation to children has not yet progressed significantly.

Although neither the International Covenant on Civil and Political Rights nor the Convention on the Rights of the Child have proven particularly useful to date as regards the right to vote for under-18s, there is an argument to be made in favour of the voting rights of under-18s because of the principle of evolutive interpretation, i.e. that 'the meaning of a concept can change over time'.[76] It could be argued that modern standards, for example those stemming from research on children's capacities, as well as progress for people with disabilities, necessitate a more progressive interpretation of the right to vote. It is hoped that either the Committee on the Rights of the Child or the Human Rights Committee (preferably both) adopt this stance in the future.

---

[74] Manfred Nowak, *UN Covenant on Civil and Political Rights: CPPR Commentary* (Kehl, Germany; Arlington, VA: N.P. Engel, 1993) 286.

[75] *Ibid.* Moreover, the Human Rights Committee has stipulated that the right to vote must be subject 'only to reasonable restrictions, such as setting a minimum age limit for the right to vote'. Human Rights Committee, *General Comment No. 25: The Right to Participate in Public Affairs, Voting Rights and the Right of Equal Access to Public Service*, UN Doc CCPR/C/21/Rev.1/Add.7, 12 July 1996, para 10.

[76] Eva Brems, *Human Rights: Universality and Diversity* (The Hague: Nijhoff, 2001) 396.

5. UNDER-18S AND VOTING PRACTICE

It is clear that younger people – that is, those under the age of 30 – are currently marginalized from the political arena. Between the late 1970s and the last decade, seven of the EU member states have experienced substantial falls in voter turnout in national elections. In the EU generally, voter turnout has dropped by over 8 per cent.[77] Moreover, there is evidence that this level of marginalization will become increasingly worse. A recent motion to the Parliamentary Assembly of the Council of Europe noted the fact that children and young people in Europe are increasingly outnumbered[78] and this could further alienate young people from a political process which caters for their needs to a lesser and lesser extent.[79] There is a strong argument that affording children the right to vote, and indeed encouraging them to do so through formal education, will benefit the democratic process.

It seems necessary to consider the possibility that younger people vote less than older people because they are not encouraged to do so from an early age. This seems a shame, since under-18s consistently express interest in greater participation in political matters, including voting. Some years before Austria extended the vote to those of 16 years of age, in one Austrian study children expressed significant desire for greater involvement in local matters. When 13–17 year olds were asked whether they wanted political information and participation, 93 per cent wanted to be informed on any new projects planned in their area, and 65 per cent wanted youth-specific consulting hours with local politicians.[80] In more recent times, the UK Youth Parliament voted overwhelmingly in favour of a campaign on votes from the age of 16 years.[81] In Ireland, research by

---

[77] International Institute for Democracy and Electoral Assistance, *Voter Turnout* (Franklin, 2001).

[78] EUROSTAT statistics indicate that there will be a 44.5% increase in the number of 65–79 year olds and a 24.3% decline in 15–24 year olds by year 2050.

[79] See 'Expansion of Democracy by Lowering the Voting Age to 16: Motion for a Resolution Presented by Mr Jensen and Others', available online at: http://assembly.coe.int/Documents/WorkingDocs/Doc09/EDOC11895.pdf, 4 May 2009.

[80] 'Jugendliche Reden Mit', Unpublished report, Riepl and Riegler, *Graz: Kommunale Beratungsstelle fur Kinder and Jugendinitiativen* (1997). Cited in Lansdown (n20) 5.

[81] *Parliament Debate*, 2009. Transcript available online at: http://www.publications.parliament.uk/pa/cm200809/cmhansrd/youth/debtext/91030.htm. The Youth Parliament elects members aged 11–18 on an annual basis. The members organize projects and campaigns on issues affecting young people and lobby decision-makers on such issues.

the National Youth Federation found that 68 per cent of 16 year olds and 71 per cent of 15 year olds felt that the voting age should be lowered to 16.[82] Unfortunately adults are not as enthusiastic. As noted earlier, only a handful of countries have accorded the right to vote to children of 16 and 17 years.[83]

Significantly, it seems that some states are regressing in terms of provision of voting rights to young people. The Iranian Parliament passed a bill in 2007 increasing the voting age in national elections from 15 to 18.[84] There are claims that this was due to government concerns that reformist opposition parties received a high level of youth votes in the December 2006 elections.[85] However in 2007 a Swiss canton reduced the voting age from 18 to 16 for local elections.[86] There also exist examples of resistance to attempts to decrease voting ages. In New Zealand a Green Party candidate sought to introduce a Civics Education and Voting Age Bill in 2007 but this was abandoned, apparently due to public resistance.[87] In Australia, a report advocating consideration of reducing the voting age to 16 was tabled in the territorial legislature in Canberra in 2007, but was defeated.[88]

Interestingly a legal challenge to the exclusion of under-18s from voting was taken in Canada, albeit unsuccessfully. In *Fitzgerald (Next Friend of) v. Alberta* [2004][89] the Canadian courts were called upon to consider a case taken by a 15 and 16 year old challenging the Election Act 2000

---

82 National Youth Federation, *National Youth Poll* (National Youth Federation, 2004). See www.youth.ie.

83 There is cause for optimism in the fact that in 2009, Mogens Jensen (Danish Member of Parliament) presented a proposed initiative to the Parliamentary Assembly of the Council of Europe to lower the voting age in Europe to 16. It will be followed with interest. See 'Expansion of democracy by lowering the voting age to 16: Motion for a resolution presented by Mr Jensen and others', 4 May 2009. Available online at: http://assembly.coe.int/Documents/WorkingDocs/Doc09/EDOC11895.pdf·

84 'Iran parliament raises voting age to 18', *Iran Focus*, 2 January 2007, available online at: http://www.iranfocus.com/en/index.php?option=com_content&view=article&id=9698:iran-parliament-raises-voting-age-to-18&catid=4:iran-general&Itemid=26.

85 *Ibid.*

86 See Parliamentary Assembly Political Affairs Committee, *Report: Expansion of Democracy by Lowering the Voting Age to 16*, 22 March 2011, available online at: http://assembly.coe.int/Documents/WorkingDocs/Doc11/EDOC12546.pdf.

87 Green Party Press Release, 'Bradford launches Bill to Lower Voting Age to 16', 21 June 2007, available online at: http://www.greens.org.nz/press-releases/bradford-launches-bill-lower-voting-age-16.

88 'ACT to consider lowering voting age', *ABC News*, 26 September 2007, available online at: http://www.abc.net.au/news/stories/2007/09/26/2043628.htm.

89 *Fitzgerald (Next Friend of) v. Alberta* [2004] AJ No 570, 2004 ABCA 184.

of Alberta which prevented them from voting in elections. The applicants claimed that the Act violated the Canadian Charter of Rights and Freedoms which 'guarantees the rights and freedoms set out in it subject only to such reasonable limits prescribed by law as can be demonstrably justified in a free and democratic society.'[90] The Alberta Court of Appeal held that, whilst the age restriction in the Act constituted discrimination, this discrimination was justified as it reflected the 'experiential situation of all citizens when they are young'[91] and because children mature as they age. However, the applicants in this case were two young people who were deeply involved in community and political affairs. This illustrates two points argued throughout this chapter – it is unhelpful and discriminatory to consider all young people as incapable, and children potentially have much to contribute to community and political affairs. Yet perhaps the upholding of age discrimination in the area of voting in *Fitzgerald* was inevitable considering the blanket assumptions at societal level as regards children's capacities.

The examples outlined above highlight that there are isolated efforts at domestic level to challenge existing voting laws around minimum ages. They are notable because they are exceptional, however, and few have been successful. In some cases, there have been steps backwards, and in others, attempts have been met with resistance. It seems unlikely that there will be progress in this area of human rights until change occurs in two respects. Thinking about children's abilities will have to be guided by evidence instead of assumptions and guidance must come from the level of international human rights law.

6. CONCLUSION

It seems clear that the potential for according voting rights to under-18s is a neglected issue in international law as well as at domestic level. Only a small number of states have taken modest steps by lowering the voting age to 16 and there has been a distinct lack of movement at international level. The lack of emphasis on voting rights for under-18s is surprising considering the fact that children have significant decision-making capacities, particularly from the age of 11/12 years. It seems particularly surprising in the context of the EU, considering low voter turnout and the positive

---

90 Section 1.

91 The Court made reference here to *Sauve v. Canada (Chief Election Officer)* [2002] 3 SCR 519, 2002 SCC 68.

effects that earlier education and participation could have. Moreover, most young people wish to be included, and it may well be harmful to deny them that right. Winck refers to the inherent motivation within individuals to be self-determining and holds that '[p]eople who have been labelled incompetent are deprived of their ability to satisfy the basic human need to be self-determining and self-actualizing'.[92] Children are an excluded group whose agency and experiences have been undervalued by the dominant group – adults. Such exclusion can breed resentment and further the apathy that contributes to low voter turnout.

While recognizing that the right to vote alone will not automatically resolve children's rights issues, it will surely go a significant distance towards bringing about greater focus on those issues. Children want to be heard, and they want to feel part of broader society. They are well aware that they are frequently underestimated, excluded and ignored. This view is encapsulated by the observation of one young person who contributed to a consultation with young people on discrimination against them; '[t]here are a lot of people out there who want to have a say but either they don't know enough about how to go about it or they do have a say but are ignored so they won't speak out again'.[93] Perhaps by ignoring children in the area of the right to vote we are discouraging them from 'speaking out' again. In this way, we fail to permit children the right to political influence, and we fail ourselves by imposing a lack of diversity on the civil processes in which we engage.

92 Winck (n28) 22.
93 Lansdown (n20) 5.

15. Cultural rights: A new era

Majella Ní Chríocháin

Cultural rights have long been the most neglected of human rights, in terms of their theoretical treatment and their implementation. While they are invariably included in the triad 'Economic, Social and Cultural Rights', they somehow disappear in the discourse. Even in the scant literature on Economic, Social and Cultural Rights, cultural rights feature little, if at all. In her exhaustive review of human rights institutions and committees, Stamatopoulou found that in most instances they had paid insufficient attention to cultural rights.[1] Her review of the reports of the Commission on Human Rights (now Human Rights Council) since 1990 revealed a lack of understanding and little interest in cultural rights, with very few exceptions.[2] This is despite the fact that cultural rights, particularly the cultural rights of individuals, have been universally recognized in international law as fundamental human rights and are provided for in a host of international and regional instruments.[3] The Vienna Declaration also affirms that all human rights are 'universal, indivisible and interdependent and interrelated' and that they must be treated globally 'in a fair and equal manner, on the same footing, and with the same emphasis.'[4] In this paper, I will first set out the content of cultural rights, before examining why it is that cultural rights have been so long neglected.

Five human rights are generally understood as cultural rights:

---

1 Stamatopoulou's comprehensive review of the right to take part in cultural life is a vital contribution to the scant literature on cultural rights: Elsa Stamatopoulou, *Cultural Rights in International Law – Article 27 of the Universal Declaration of Human Rights and Beyond* (Leiden: Nijhoff, 2007) 512.

2 *Ibid.*, 61.

3 The Observatory of Diversity and Cultural Rights in Fribourg University has published online a useful list of cultural rights, along with references to articles in international instruments pertaining to particular cultural rights, available online at: http://www.unifr.ch/iiedh/assets/files/Publications/ds3cr.pdf.

4 Vienna Declaration and Programme of Action (Part 1, para 5) adopted by the World Conference on Human Rights, Vienna, UN Doc A/CONF. 157/24 (Part 1) chap. III, 25 June 1993.

1. the right to education;
2. the right to participate in cultural life;
3. the right to enjoy the benefits of scientific progress and its applications;
4. the right to benefit from the protection of the moral and material interests resulting from any scientific, literary or artistic production of which the person is the author; and
5. the freedom for scientific research and creative activity.[5]

Other human rights are linked to the right to culture, such as freedom of information and expression, freedom of religion, freedom of assembly and of association, as provided for in the International Covenant on Economic, Social and Cultural Rights (ICESCR) and the International Covenant on Civil and Political Rights (ICCPR), since free participation in cultural life and the practice of one's culture requires that these freedoms are also provided for. It has been argued that the list of cultural rights in the International Bill of Rights should in fact be enlarged to include the right to information and to freedom of opinion and expression.[6] The Fribourg Declaration on Cultural Rights, following that argument, includes rights to communication and information.[7]

1. CULTURAL RIGHTS AS NEGLECTED RIGHTS

Many reasons have been given for the neglect of cultural rights:

1.1 Cultural Rights – A Luxury?

Cultural rights have been viewed as a 'luxury', to be considered only after issues like poverty, hunger and homelessness have been tackled. This view may be informed by a narrow understanding of what cultural rights are –

---

[5] Elissavet Stamatopoulou, 'The Right to Take Part in Cultural Life' (Background Paper submitted to the Committee on Economic, Social and Cultural Rights on its Day of General Discussion on the Right to Take Part in Cultural Life) UN Doc E/C.12/40/9, 9 May 2008, 3.

[6] Janusz Symonides, 'Cultural Rights: A Neglected Category of Human Rights' (1998) 50 (158) *International Social Science Journal* 559, 561–2.

[7] Arts 6 and 7, Fribourg Declaration on Cultural Rights, adopted 7 May 2007, available online at: http://www.unifr.ch/iiedh/assets/files/fr-declaration10.pdf. The Declaration was the fruit of 20 years of work on cultural rights by a group of international experts known as the 'Fribourg Group'. A list of current members of the Group as well as those supporting the Declaration can be accessed online at: http://www.unifr.ch/iiedh/fr.

that they pertain to elite arts or to frivolous pastimes. Cultural rights are however indispensable to human dignity – all communities build cultures through which they express their humanity and their understanding of the world.

It is perhaps not surprising that some of the strongest arguments made in the literature and amongst human rights advocates for implementing cultural rights fully have been from those involved in promoting the rights of minorities and of indigenous peoples. It could be said that minority rights and the rights of indigenous peoples are primarily *cultural* rights, in that they pertain to the protection of the language, traditions, religion and ways of life of groups and of communities. The right to participate in cultural life (Article 15(1), ICESCR) in particular is fundamental to the survival of minority groups and indigenous peoples.

For indigenous peoples, culture is holistic and encompasses all aspects of life[8] – culture is at the heart of their economy, their work, their relationship with the natural and spiritual world, their arts and customary law. Culture is not a luxury – it is fundamental and issues of poverty and exclusion are for many indigenous peoples bound up with the denial of their right to practice their culture, the theft or destruction of their lands and resources and the destruction of their communal structures and relationships.

1.2 Collective Cultural Rights and a Fear of State Fragmentation

States have long feared that granting cultural rights to groups and recognizing their cultural identity will encourage separatism and undermine the unity of the state. Similar arguments have been made regarding the right to self-determination and indeed the cultural rights of groups and collective rights are closely linked to self-determination. The fear of fragmentation, or 'Balkanization' in its contemporary guise, has existed since the drafting of the Universal Declaration of Human Rights (UDHR) and accounts for the omission of the right to self-determination and the reluctance to include group rights in the UDHR.[9] While

---

[8] Kenneth M. Deer, Indigenous World Association, *The Complexities in Practical Terms: Cultural Practices Contrary to Human Rights, Possible Limitations to Cultural Rights, and Tensions Around who Defines Culture and Rights* (Contribution to a seminar organized by the Officer of the High Commissioner for Human Rights on Implementing Cultural Rights: Nature, Issues at Stake and Challenges 2008) 2.

[9] Bruce Robbins and Elsa Stamatopoulou, 'Reflections on Culture and Cultural Rights' (2004) 103 *The South Atlantic Quarterly* 423.

this omission was rectified in the ICCPR and the ICESCR in 1966, former colonies, many of which have within their borders indigenous peoples, have proven just as anxious to preserve their territorial boundaries as older states. The impasse which for many years surrounded the adoption of the UN Declaration on the Rights of Indigenous Peoples has been ascribed to states' reluctance to grant the right to self-determination to indigenous peoples.[10] The Special Rapporteur on the Rights of Indigenous Peoples, James Anaya, has reported that in the course of his work he has heard 'repeated misperceptions . . . that the advancing of indigenous rights will threaten State sovereignty or create so-called "states within a state."'[11]

It has been argued conversely that recognizing group identities and granting cultural rights to minorities and indigenous peoples may *avert* conflict and calls for independence or territorial separation. By granting cultural rights, much of what is sought for by peoples in self-determination will have been achieved within the boundaries of the state.[12] Respecting and implementing fully the cultural rights of minorities and of indigenous peoples could provide stability for the state, acting, as Barth suggests, 'more as a shield than a sword.'[13]

1.3 The Problem of Definition

It has been argued that cultural rights are difficult to define and their content difficult to clarify, as culture is dynamic and ever-changing.[14] There are however difficulties in defining other terms used widely in human rights instruments, like 'indigenous peoples' and yet a reading of human rights instruments and an examination of the jurisprudence associated with indigenous peoples give a good understanding of what

---

[10] *Ibid.* 425. The authors state that the resistance to the Draft Declaration was 'uncannily reminiscent of the original skepticism with regard to group rights by a much smaller number of states in 1948.'

[11] Statement by Professor James Anaya, Special Rapporteur on the Rights of Indigenous Peoples to the Tenth Session of the UN Permanent Forum on Indigenous Issues, 19 May 2011, available online at: http://www.ohchr.org/EN/NewsEvents/Pages/DisplayNews.aspx?NewsID=11037&LangID=E.

[12] Elsa Stamatopoulou, 'Why Cultural Rights Now?', Talk given at Carnegie Council for Ethics in International Affairs, 24 September 2004, available online at: http://www.carnegiecouncil.org/resources/transcripts/5006.html.

[13] William K. Barth, 'Cultural Rights: A Necessary Corrective to the Nation State', in Francesco Francioni and Martin Scheinin, (eds) *Cultural Human Rights* (Leiden: Nijhoff, 2008) 90.

[14] Stamatopoulou, (n1) 4.

type of group is in question, even without their being defined.[15] Not all terms have to be defined in order to have meaning. Human rights language may not be precise, yet this has not prevented judicial organs from deciding human rights cases.[16] Human rights instruments are rightly viewed as 'living instruments', open and responsive to change either in the contemporary understanding of human rights or in the context of new challenges.

The International Commission of Jurists, referring to the alleged lack of clarity of the right to participate in cultural life, has pointed out that the formulation of the right is very similar to that of the right to participate in public affairs in the ICCPR and that no issue of lack of clarity had been raised in regard to that particular right.[17] The Commission also asserts that the right is 'perfectly fit for adjudication' [18] and indeed the many cases decided in national, regional and international courts are testimony to that fact.[19]

1.4 The Spectre of Cultural Relativism

Stamatopoulou found that amongst human rights experts there was a fear that discussion of cultural rights could lead to arguments around cultural relativism and could challenge the 'universality' of human rights[20]

---

15 Patrick Thornberry, 'Cultural Rights and Universality of Human Rights' (Background Paper submitted to the Committee on Economic, Social and Cultural Rights on its Day of General Discussion on the Right to Take Part in Cultural Life) UN Doc E/C.12/40/15, 9 May 2008, 5 ('It would be difficult to read through the whole of the UN Declaration on the Rights of Indigenous Peoples without having, by the end of such a reading, a tolerably clear idea of which groups are comprehended by its terms – even in the absence of "definition". Further, the definition approach may not sit well with the notion of cultural development, hybridization, creolization, interpenetration, etc., in that it might tend to suggest limits on cultural development within the parameters of the right.').

16 *Ibid.*, 6.

17 International Commission of Jurists, 'Submission to the Day of Discussion on the Right to Take Part in Cultural Life', UN Doc E/C.12/$0/7, 8 May 2008, para 5.

18 *Ibid.*, para 23.

19 *Ibid.*, paras 19–22.

20 Stamatopoulou (n5) 7. Stamatopoulou also found that the question of cultural relativism and the potential clash between cultural practices and international human rights has been answered clearly, by international law and by the practice of intergovernmental bodies, in favour of internationally proclaimed human rights (*Ibid.*, 18).

– a concern that promoting the cultural rights of groups would lead to 'cultural wrongs', where cultural practices violate human rights. The Vienna Declaration is unequivocal on this question:

> While the significance of national and regional particularities and various historical, cultural and religious backgrounds must be borne in mind, it is the duty of States, regardless of their political, economic and cultural systems, to promote and protect all human rights and fundamental freedoms.[21]

Numerous international and regional instruments place limitations on the right to engage in cultural practices which violate the human rights of others, be they the rights of women, the child or of minorities or other groups.[22] The non-discrimination element included in many instruments, including under Article 4 of the ICESCR, limits cultural expressions which might infringe the rights of others.[23]

Provisions of non-discrimination in human rights instruments notwithstanding, the tension around cultural rights and relativism is a real one. Human rights are not served by a reluctance to tackle head-on tensions between what may be perceived as Western imposed norms or values and local practices. Both academics and activists in the field have however warned of the dangers of conflating cultures with some of their cultural practices, or of damning particular groups because of a particular practice.[24] There are few cultures which have not included practices which violate human rights, and communities are far more likely to engage in debate and to be open to change if they do not feel externally threatened.[25]

---

[21] Vienna Declaration and Programme of Action, UN Doc A/CONF.157/23, 12 July 1993 (Part I, para 5).

[22] Art. 5(a), Convention on the Elimination of Discrimination Against Women, adopted and opened for signature, ratification and accession by UN GA Res 34/180 of 18 December 1979, entered into force 3 September 1981; Art. 4, UN Declaration on the Rights of Persons belonging to Minorities, UNGA Res 47/135, 18 December 1992; Art. 4, UNESCO Universal Declaration on Cultural Diversity, adopted by the 31st session of the General Conference, 2 November 2001; Art. 2, UNESCO Convention on the Protection and Promotion of the Diversity of Cultural Expressions, adopted by the 33rd session of the General Conference, 20 October 2005; Art. 24.2, Convention on the Rights of the Child, 1577 UNTS 3, 20 November 1989, entered into force 2 September 1990.

[23] Thornberry (n15) 14.

[24] *Ibid.*, 20.

[25] Ephraim Nimni, 'Collective Dimensions of the Right to take Part in Cultural Life' (Background Paper submitted to the Committee on Economic, Social and Cultural Rights on its Day of General Discussion on the Right to Take Part in Cultural Life) UN Doc E/C.12/40/17, 9 May 2008, 8–10.

Recourse to law alone simply may not be effective. There is a need for 'cultural negotiation' around disputed practices, involving families and community leaders.[26] Important aspects of particular practices, such as rites of passage for young people, where traditions and knowledge are passed on, can be maintained, while harmful practices, such as genital mutilation, can be removed and replaced with other ceremonies.[27] This is not to claim that this is an easy process, but that human rights are better served where there is dialogue on controversial or difficult issues, as happened during the development of the UN Declaration on the Rights of Indigenous Peoples,[28] where, for the first time, the subjects of the human rights instrument were involved in its drafting.[29]

In summary, then, cultural rights are not a luxury; they are indispensable to human dignity. Recognizing cultural rights, far from leading to state fragmentation, may in fact provide greater stability for the state. Difficulties in definition need not be a barrier to their implementation. Tensions between cultural practices and individual human rights can be and are being negotiated. It seems that the international community and human rights bodies have become alert to these arguments in recent years, as evidenced by three major developments in the field which, I believe, herald a new era for cultural rights.[30]

---

[26] Human Rights Council, 'Report of the Independent Expert in the Field of Cultural Rights, Ms. Farida Shaheed', UN Doc A/HRC/14/36, 22 March 2010, para 36.

[27] For an interesting insight into approaches to eradicating FGM in Sierra Leone, see Chi Mgbako *et al.*, 'Penetrating the Silence in Sierra Leone: A Blueprint for the Eradication of Female Genital Mutilation' (2010) 23 *Harvard Hum. Rts J.* 111.

[28] UN Declaration on the Rights of Indigenous Peoples, UN Doc A/RES/61/295, 2 October 2007.

[29] Kenneth M. Deer, 'The Complexities in Practical Terms: Cultural Practices Contrary to Human Rights, Possible Limitations to Cultural Rights, and Tensions Around who Defines Culture and Rights', Working Doc 2, Seminar organized by the Office of the High Commissioner for Human Rights, in partnership with the International Organization of La Francophonie and UNESCO, in collaboration with the Observatory of diversity and cultural rights, 1–2 February 2010, 9.

[30] There have been other important developments in the last decade, including the adoption by UNESCO of the Declaration on Cultural Diversity (n22), the UNESCO Convention for the Safeguarding of the Intangible Cultural Heritage adopted by the 32nd session of the General Conference, 17 October 2003, and the Convention on the Protection and Promotion of the Diversity of Cultural Expressions (n22).

2. THE DECLARATION ON THE RIGHTS OF INDIGENOUS PEOPLES

The adoption by the UN of the Declaration on the Rights of Indigenous Peoples in 2007 (UNDRIP) marked a significant move in international law and in the views of states, in that it asserts the right of indigenous peoples to self-determination[31] and affirms that peoples are holders of cultural rights.[32] Its adoption by an overwhelming majority of states signified an acceptance that respecting individual human rights is not enough to protect peoples' cultures, as it also requires a recognition that 'indigenous peoples possess collective rights which are indispensable for their existence, well-being and integral development as peoples . . .'[33]

The rights to self-determination and to autonomy,[34] along with rights to own their lands and to have redress for lands which have been 'confiscated, taken, occupied, used or damaged without their free, prior and informed consent'[35] are potentially transformative. Yet the Declaration provides safety for states in Article 46 (1), which states that nothing in the Declaration

> may be interpreted as implying for any State, people, group or person any right to engage in any activity or to perform any act contrary to the Charter of the United Nations or construed as authorizing or encouraging any action which would dismember or impair, totally or in part, the territorial integrity or political unity of sovereign and independent States.[36]

The Declaration manages to deal deftly with states' fears that granting collective rights and self-determination to sub-state groups would lead to the breaking up of states, by addressing the rights of indigenous peoples within the context and within the boundaries of existing states. This limitation on the right to self-determination imposed by the Declaration has led one commentator to argue that it represents 'the continued power and persistence of an international human rights paradigm that eschews strong forms of indigenous self-determination and privileges individual civil and

---

31 Art. 3, UNDRIP (n28).

32 Matthias Ahren, 'Protecting Peoples' Cultural Rights: A Question of Properly Understanding the Notion of States and Nations?', in Francesco Francioni and Martin Sheinin (eds) *Cultural Human Rights* (Leiden: Nijhoff, 2008) 115.

33 Preamble, UNDRIP (n28).

34 Art. 4, *ibid.*

35 Art. 26, *ibid.*

36 Art. 46, *ibid.*

political rights.'[37] While many indigenous peoples seek to exercise their right to self-determination through autonomy and self-government, there are those for whom any measure short of full political and territorial independence is unacceptable.[38] The Declaration does not however differ from other international legal instruments in that the right to self-determination is limited to remedies short of secession. It does differ in that it is the first time that sub-national groups have been accorded the unqualified right to self-determination.[39] That the Declaration requires states to obtain the free, prior and informed consent of indigenous peoples for any developments on their lands or territories and for any legislative or administrative measures which might affect them is also a powerful indicator that the *collective* rights of indigenous peoples are at the heart of the Declaration.[40]

The Declaration is, however, non-binding. The choice of a soft law instrument for indigenous peoples' rights is one of many examples where advocates of human rights and states negotiate the risks of non-ratification of hard law instruments with non-compliance with soft law. The fact that ILO Convention No 169 on Indigenous and Tribal Peoples (1989) had only been ratified by 18 states by the time the UNDRIP was adopted suggests that a hard law instrument, if agreed, might not yet have sufficient ratifications to enter into force, a situation which would suggest that indigenous peoples' rights were not universally recognized. The choice of a soft law instrument, containing strong obligations and clearly defined rights and which has attracted virtual universal international support may achieve more for indigenous peoples than a binding instrument with few ratifications or weak obligations. Soft law also offers greater opportunity for the participation of non-state actors[41] and in the case of the UNDRIP its content was fundamentally influenced by the part played by representatives of indigenous peoples in its drafting.

The International Law Association asserts that the adoption of the UNDRIP confirms that the international community has come to a consensus that indigenous peoples are a concern of customary international

---

[37] Karen Engle, 'On Fragile Architecture: The UN Declaration on the Rights of Indigenous Peoples in the Context of Human Rights' (2011) 22(1) *EJIL* 142.

[38] John B. Henriksen, 'Implementation of the Right of Self-Determination of Indigenous Peoples' (2001) 3/01 *Indigenous Affairs* 16.

[39] Alexandra Xanthaki, 'Indigenous Rights in International Law over the Last Ten Years and Future Developments' (2009) 10(1) *Melb. JIL* 27.

[40] Arts 10, 11, 19, 28, 29 and 32, UNDRIP (n28).

[41] Mauro Barelli, 'The Role of Soft Law in the International Legal System: The Case of the United Nations Declaration on the Rights of Indigenous Peoples' (2009) 58(4) *ICLQ* 965.

law and that it is therefore, 'indisputable that "customary norms concerning indigenous peoples and their pull toward compliance" are actually a reality in the context of the contemporary international legal order.' [42] According to the Association, under the rules of customary law, indigenous peoples have the right:

- to self-determination
- to autonomy or self-government
- to recognition and preservation of their cultural identity
- to their traditional lands and natural resources
- to reparation and redress for the wrongs suffered
- to expect that all treaties, and other agreements to which they are a direct party with a state, that were fairly negotiated, shall be honoured and fully implemented in a manner respecting the spirit and intent of the understanding of the indigenous negotiators as well as the living nature of the solemn undertakings made by all parties.[43]

The fact that the Declaration was the result of 22 years of negotiation and discussion, that it received the support of large majorities at the Human Rights Council and the General Assembly and that its contents reflect existing international law standards and practice[44] suggests that there is a great degree of international consensus on its contents. It stands as a strong statement of universal recognition of the rights of indigenous peoples. A supportive statement from an indigenous representative notes: 'The Declaration is the most comprehensive international instrument addressing the rights of Indigenous peoples . . . As distinct peoples, we now have a principled international legal framework that affirms our human rights.'[45]

The four states that initially opposed the declaration, New Zealand, Australia,[46] US and Canada have since announced their

---

[42] International Law Association, 'The Hague Conference (2010) Rights of Indigenous Peoples – Interim Report', available online at: http://www.ila-hq.org/en/committees/index.cfm/cid/1024, 51.

[43] *Ibid.*, 51–2.

[44] Barelli (n41) 971–4.

[45] Grand Chief Matthew Mukash, Grand Council of the Crees, 'Supportive Statement on the UN Declaration of the Rights of Indigenous Peoples', 26 September 2007, available online at: http://issuu.com/karinzylsaw/docs/un_declaration_rights_indigenous_peoples/20?mode=a_p.

[46] Amnesty International, 'Australia to support UN Declaration on the Rights of Indigenous Peoples', 27 March 2009, available online at: http://www.amnesty.org.au/news/comments/20640/.

support.[47] Despite caveats entered by Canada and New Zealand, that four of the major states who were built on the colonization of indigenous peoples and the dispossession of their lands and territories should finally join the other 143 states supporting the Declaration indicates broad recognition of the rights of indigenous peoples.

There are signs that human rights institutions are already directing states to endorse the Declaration. It has been interpreted by the Committee on the Elimination of Racial Discrimination (CERD) as being a guide to interpreting State Parties' obligations under the Convention with regard to indigenous peoples.[48] The Committee on Economic, Social and Cultural Rights, in its concluding observations on Nicaragua's country report in 2008, encouraged Nicaragua to apply the principles of the UNDRIP.[49] The Human Rights Council, in its recent Universal Periodic Reviews (UPRs) of states, including Kenya,[50] Panama[51] and Australia[52] recommended the Declaration be fully implemented and in 2010 it recommended that the US ratify the Declaration.[53]

More important perhaps is the impact the Declaration has domestically, as it is in the realm of the domestic state that questions of indigenous peoples' rights are primarily fought. Bolivia has adopted a law giving full legal effect to the provisions of the Declaration in its domestic law. It has also been referenced in constitutional reform measures in Bolivia, Ecuador and Nepal.[54] Both upper and lower houses of the Japanese Diet voted unanimously in 2008 to recognize the Ainu as an indigenous people

---

47 Anaya (n11).

48 Bartolomé Clavero, 'The UN Declaration on the Rights of Indigenous Peoples: Its First Year', in Kathrin Wessendorf (ed.) *IWGIA – The Indigenous World 2009* (Copenhagen: IWGIA, 2009) 584.

49 *Ibid.*, 585

50 Human Rights Council, 'Report of the Working Group on the Universal Periodic Review: Kenya' UN Doc A/HRC/15/8, 17 June 2010.

51 Human Rights Council, 'Report of the Working Group on the Universal Periodic Review: Panama' UN Doc A/HRC/16/6, 4 January 2011, 16.

52 Human Rights Council, 'Report of the Working Group on the Universal Periodic Review: Australia' UN Doc A/HRC/17/10, 24 March 2011, 20.

53 Human Rights Council, 'Report of the Working Group on the Universal Periodic Review: United States of America' UN Doc A/HRC/16/11, 11 January 2011, 13.

54 James Anaya, *The Human Rights of Indigenous Peoples, in the Light of the New Declaration, and the Challenge of Making Them Operative*, Report of the Special Rapporteur on the Situation of Human Rights and Fundamental Freedoms of Indigenous Peoples, UN Doc A/HRC/9/9, 5 August 2008, paras 52–53.

in light of the adoption of the Declaration.[55] There are some signs that domestic courts are also referring to the Declaration in their judgments. In September 2007 the Chief Justice of the Supreme Court of Belize cited Article 26 of the Declaration and the fact that Belize had voted for the Declaration when finding that traditional lands should be returned by the government to the Maya people.[56]

To what extent the Declaration is implemented will depend as much on the actions of non-state actors, like transnational corporations, as it will on the response of states.[57] The UN Permanent Forum on Indigenous Issues has highlighted serious gaps in the implementation of the Declaration, stating that violence and brutality, continuing assimilation policies, dispossession of land, forced removal, the denial of land rights and the impacts of large scale development are still a reality for indigenous peoples throughout the world.[58]

Whether the Declaration is viewed as 'an interpretative mechanism through which to view and apply fundamental human rights'[59] in the

---

[55] Asia Pacific Human Rights Information Center, 'Upper and Lower Houses of the Diet of Japan recognize the Ainu as an indigenous people', 7 June 2008, available online at: http://www.hurights.or.jp/archives/newsinbrief-en/section2/2008/06/upper-and-lower-houses-of-the-diet-of-japan-recognize-the-ainu-as-indigenous-people.html.

[56] United Nations Permanent Forum on Indigenous Issues, 'Advances in the Recognition of Indigenous Rights since the Adoption of the UN Declaration', available online at: http://www.un.org/en/events/indigenousday/pdf/Indigenous_Advances_Eng.pdf.

[57] The Special Rapporteur on Indigenous Peoples, James Anaya, in his third annual report analysed the impact of corporate activities and in particular those of transnational corporations on the rights of indigenous peoples. Asserting that the absence of clarity regarding corporate responsibility has led to numerous abuses of indigenous peoples' rights worldwide, he clearly sets out the nature of these responsibilities. This is another important step towards protecting indigenous peoples' cultures. Other important themes he will explore are legal pluralism and indigenous customary law, the situation of voluntarily isolated indigenous peoples, and the situation of indigenous communities and individuals living in urban areas. See Report of the Special Rapporteur on the situation of human rights and fundamental freedoms of indigenous people, James Anaya, UN Doc A/HRC/15/37, 19 July 2010.

[58] Permanent Forum on Indigenous Issues, Report on Tenth Session 16–27 May 2011, UN Docs E/2011/43 – E/C. 19/2011/14, available online at: http://www.un.org/esa/socdev/unpfii/documents/session_10_report_EN.pdf.

[59] Stephen Allen, 'The UN Declaration on the Rights of Indigenous Peoples and the Limits of the International Legal Project in the Indigenous Context', in Stephen Allen and Alexandra Xanthaki (eds) *Reflections on the United Nations Declaration on the Rights of Indigenous Peoples and International Law* (Oxford: Hart Publishing, 2011) 231.

context of indigenous peoples, or primarily as a political tool with which to seek consensus at a domestic level on the rights of indigenous peoples, as proposed by Allen,[60] indigenous peoples and human rights experts alike agree that the Declaration is the most important development internationally in terms of the rights of indigenous peoples.[61] For all its limitations and the challenges to its full implementation, it is a potentially powerful tool in the growing armoury that advocates of indigenous peoples' rights have at their disposal to defend and promote the rights of indigenous peoples.

3. GENERAL COMMENT 21 OF THE COMMITTEE ON ECONOMIC, SOCIAL AND CULTURAL RIGHTS

One of the obstacles to promoting cultural rights has been the relative neglect of the right by the Committee on Economic, Social and Cultural Rights (CESCR), the human rights body charged with overseeing the implementation of the ICESCR. This has however recently been rectified and the Committee, in consideration of a draft General Comment on the right of everyone to take part in cultural life (CESCR Art. 15(1) (a))[62] called a Day of General Discussion in May 2008, aimed at:

- exploring the definition of cultural life in the context of human rights
- analysing the right to have access to cultural life and to participate in cultural life
- identifying the interlinkages between cultural rights and the universality of human rights
- assessing the individual and collective dimensions of the right to take part in cultural life.[63]

The discussion examined many of the issues identified as contributing to the neglect of cultural rights and was intended to inform the content

---

60 *Ibid.*, 225.

61 For an excellent collection of essays providing a comprehensive review of the Declaration, see Allen and Xanthaki (eds) (n59).

62 Committee on Economic, Social and Cultural Rights, 'Day of General Discussion on "The right to take part in cultural life"', 9 May 2008, available online at: http://www2.ohchr.org/english/bodies/cescr/discussion090508.htm.

63 *Ibid.*

of General Comment 21, later adopted by the Committee in November 2009.

It could be said that General Comment 21 represents a summation of interpretations of the right to date and a fusion of the most persuasive and influential theoretical discussions in the field. Space does not allow for a comprehensive analysis of the Comment and I will limit discussion to how it addresses questions of definition, of cultural relativism and of collective rights.

3.1 Definition of Culture and of Cultural Life

The Committee does not shy away from the difficulty of defining what is meant by culture or by cultural life, nor is it fazed by the fact that many definitions of culture have been given in the past and others may arise in the future.[64] It presents culture as a spectrum covering all aspects of human life and cultural life as a dynamic process stretching back to the past and on into the future.[65] It gives a very broad definition for culture, covering virtually every aspect of human existence:

> The Committee considers that culture, for the purpose of implementing article 15(1)(a), encompasses, inter alia, ways of life, language, oral and written literature, music and song, non-verbal communication, religion or belief systems, rites and ceremonies, sport and games, methods of production or technology, natural and man-made environments, food, clothing and shelter and the arts, customs and traditions through which individuals, groups of individuals and communities express their humanity and the meaning they give to their existence, and build their world view representing their encounter with the external forces affecting their lives. Culture shapes and mirrors the values of well-being and the economic, social and political life of individuals, groups of individuals and communities.[66]

---

[64] General Comment 21, 'The Right of Everyone to take part in Cultural Life', CESCR 43rd Session, 21 December 2009, para 10. The Committee references definitions given in UNESCO's Universal Declaration on Cultural Diversity, in UNESCO's recommendation on participation by the people at large in cultural life and their contribution to it, the Nairobi recommendation, the Fribourg Declaration on Cultural Rights and Rodolfo Stavenhagen's definition in 'Cultural Rights: A Social Science Perspective', in Halina Niec (ed.) *Cultural Rights and Wrongs: A Collection of Essays in Commemoration of the 50th Anniversary of the Universal Declaration of Human Rights* (Paris and Leicester: UNESCO Publishing and Institute of Art and Law 1998).

[65] *Ibid.* para 11.

[66] *Ibid.*

Such a broad definition is consistent with jurisprudence in domestic, regional and international courts.[67] Stamatopoulou, in her submission to the General Day of Discussion, spoke of the UN human rights system 'striving to realize a double aspiration of combining rootedness with freedom' in its attention to cultural rights.[68] The General Comment manages to encompass both – providing a very broad definition of culture which, of its nature, is ever-changing, while bedding the right down by clearly specifying the normative content of the right and States Parties' obligations.

3.2 The Normative Content of the Right

3.2.1 Choice

The decision whether or not to exercise the right to take part in cultural life individually, or in association with others, is a cultural choice to be recognized, respected and protected on the basis of equality.[69] The Committee thus recognizes the potential for conflict between individuals and communities and asserts the right of the individual to abstain from participation.[70]

3.2.2 The meaning of 'participation'

Participation has three main components – participation in, access to and contribution to cultural life. *Participation* covers the right to choose one's own identity, to identify or not with one or several communities and to change that choice.[71] This is particularly important in that the Committee hereby recognizes that one's identity is defined by oneself, not imposed from without, that identities can change and that the nature of multicultural societies is such that one may have a number of identities.

Access includes the right to know and understand one's own culture and that of others, to learn about forms of expression and dissemination through any technical medium of information or communication, to receive quality education and training with due regard for cultural identity and to follow a way of life associated with the use of cultural goods such as land, water, biodiversity, language or specific institutions.[72] *Contribution* includes the right to take part in creating cultural expressions and in the

---

67 International Commission of Jurists (n17) para 7.
68 Stamatopoulou (n5) 11.
69 General Comment 21 (n64) para 7.
70 International Commission of Jurists (n17) para 13.
71 General Comment 21 (n64) para 15(a).
72 *Ibid.* para 15(b).

'definition, elaboration and implementation of policies and decisions that have an impact on the exercise of a person's cultural rights.'[73] This, taken with the condition of *acceptability* ensures that individuals and communities have an input into policies and programmes directed at protecting cultural diversity.[74]

3.3 Core Obligations

The core obligations outlined in the Comment include those of non-discrimination and gender equality in the enjoyment of the right, of respect of the right to identify or not identify with one or more communities and to change that choice, of respect of the right to engage in one's own cultural practices, to eliminate barriers to accessing one's own or other cultures and to allow persons belonging to minorities, indigenous peoples and other communities to participate in the design and implementation of laws and policies which affect them.[75]

A member of the CESCR, Virginia Bonoan Dandan, in a presentation in 2007, spoke of the 'delicate and extremely contentious path' which the Committee would have to negotiate in its interpretation of the normative content of the right to take part in cultural life.[76] While the Committee may have approached the task with trepidation, they have boldly outlined what the legal obligations of States Parties are and what constitutes violations of the right. They also dealt unequivocally with the question of cultural relativism.

3.4 Cultural Relativism and Limitations to the Right

The Committee essentially restates the Vienna Declaration regarding the duty of States to promote and protect all human rights regardless of local particularities and also states that cultural diversity may not be invoked to infringe upon human rights guaranteed by international law.[77]

Limitations to the right may be necessary in certain circumstances, 'in

---

[73] *Ibid.* para 15(c).

[74] *Ibid.* para 16(c).

[75] *Ibid.* para 55.

[76] Virginia Bonoan Dandan, *Finding Meaning in Cultural Life* (Speech by Virginia Bonoan Dandan (Philippines) member of the Committee on Economic, Social and Cultural Rights (CESCR) on the Occasion of Human Rights Day, UNESCO Headquarters, Paris, 2007) UN Doc SHS/RSP/HRS-GED/2007/PI/H/2, 5.

[77] General Comment 21 (n64) para 18.

particular in the case of negative practices, including those attributed to customs and traditions that infringe upon other human rights.'[78] Such limitations must however pursue a legitimate aim, be compatible with the nature of the right and be strictly necessary for the promotion of general welfare in a democratic society. They must also be proportionate. The Committee also essentially reiterates Article 5(1) of the Covenant that the right may not be interpreted as implying for any state, group or person any right to engage in any activity or perform any act aimed at the destruction of any of the rights and freedoms recognized in the Covenant or at their limitation to a greater extent than is provided for therein.[79]

In perhaps the most important interpretation relating to cultural relativism, the Committee states that a violation of the right also occurs when a State Party fails to take steps to combat practices harmful to the well-being of a person or group of persons. 'These harmful practices, including those attributed to customs and traditions, such as female genital mutilation and allegations of the practice of witchcraft, are barriers to the full exercise by the affected persons of the right enshrined in article 15, paragraph 1(a)'.[80]

In his contribution to the General Day of Discussion, Thornberry referred to the Committee on the Elimination of Racial Discrimination (CERD)'s approach to violations of human rights arising out of cultural practices and to difficulties in deciding what recommendations to make following a determination 'that practice X violates human rights norm Y'. CERD generally opts for 'non-coercive, educative strategies', preferring to work through states rather than directly criticizing cultural groups.[81]

It remains to be seen whether or not cultural practices which infringe on human rights are tackled in the reporting process of the Committee and if so, how the Committee deals with the issue.[82] The fact that General Comment 21 is unequivocal in its assertion that culture cannot be used as a cover for legitimizing practices which infringe on human rights must however assuage those concerned that the spectre of cultural relativism would overshadow the universality of human rights.

---

78 *Ibid.* para 19.

79 *Ibid.* para 20.

80 *Ibid.* para 64.

81 Thornberry (n15) 19.

82 At the time of writing the Committee, since its adoption of General Comment 21, had issued Concluding Observations on country reports from Germany, the Republic of Moldova, the Russian Federation and Yemen and there was no reference made to harmful practices. It is however as yet too soon to discern any particular approach.

3.5 The Individual and Collective Nature of the Right

The Committee recognizes the individual and collective components of the right, stating that it may be exercised 'by a person (a) as an individual, (b) in association with others, or (c) within a community or group, as such.'[83] The use of the phrase 'alone, or in association with others or as a community' elsewhere in the General Comment reaffirms both aspects of the right.[84]

The collective rights of indigenous peoples are also recognized – ' [they] have the right to the full enjoyment, as a collective or as individuals, of all human rights and fundamental freedoms . . .'[85] The communal aspect of the right for indigenous peoples is also recognized as being 'indispensable to their existence, well being and development . . .'[86] The Committee recognizes the central importance of indigenous peoples' relationship with their ancestral lands and states that this must be protected 'in order to prevent the degradation of their particular way of life, including their means of subsistence, the loss of their natural resources and, ultimately, their cultural identity.'[87] This interpretation draws heavily on the UNDRIP's provisions on land rights and collective rights.

3.6 Cultural Rights of Minorities and Migrants

The Committee calls on states, as a first step towards the elimination of discrimination, to recognize the existence of diverse cultural identities of individuals and communities in their territories.[88] Minorities have the right to conserve, promote and develop their own culture and there is an obligation on states to recognize, respect and protect minority cultures 'as an essential component of the identity of the States themselves.'[89] Furthermore, programmes directed at integrating minorities into society should be based on inclusion, non-discrimination and participation, with a view to preserving minority cultures.[90] States should also pay particular attention to the protection of the cultural identity of migrants, their

83 General Comment 21 (n64) para 9.
84 *Ibid.* para 15(a) and (b).
85 *Ibid.* para 7.
86 *Ibid.* para 36.
87 *Ibid.* para 36.
88 *Ibid.* para 23.
89 *Ibid.* para 32.
90 *Ibid.* para 33.

language, religion and folklore and should not prevent migrants from maintaining their cultural links with their countries of origin.[91]

The Committee thus strongly asserts the individual and collective aspects of the right to take part in cultural life and affirms the equality between different cultures, challenging the notion that states have a dominant culture into which every individual should be subsumed and presenting as essentially multifaceted the cultural identity of the state.

General Comment 21 addresses authoritatively the three issues of difficulty of definition, cultural relativism and collective rights which have dogged cultural rights for decades. It represents the most authoritative interpretation of the right available to State Parties and acts as guidance to State Parties in fulfilling their reporting requirements under Article 15(1)(a) of the Convention. The adoption of this General Comment is significant and along with the other developments referred to in this chapter goes a considerable way to addressing the historical neglect of cultural rights.

4. INDEPENDENT EXPERT IN THE FIELD OF CULTURAL RIGHTS

The adoption by the Human Rights Council of Resolution 10/23 of 23 March 2009, establishing the mandate of an Independent Expert in the Field of Cultural Rights marked another important step towards fuller implementation of cultural rights.[92] The Independent Expert assumed her functions on 1 November 2009 and her mandate includes identifying best practices in and possible obstacles to the promotion and protection of cultural rights, submitting proposals to the Council on actions in that regard, working with states to foster the adoption of measures to promote and protect cultural rights, studying the relationship between cultural rights and cultural diversity and integrating a gender and disability perspective into her work.[93]

The appointment of the Independent Expert, just as the CESCR adopted its General Comment 21 means that there has recently been an unprecedented focus on the part of UN institutions and international

---

91 *Ibid.* para 34.

92 Human Rights Council Resolution 10/23, 'Independent Expert in the Field of Cultural Rights', 26 March 2009.

93 The Independent Expert, Ms. Farida Shaheed, is a Pakistani sociologist, a recipient of several national and international human rights awards and the Deputy Director of a research project on Women's Empowerment in Muslim Contexts.

legal experts on the right to culture. In her first report to the Human Rights Council, the Independent Expert drew heavily on contributions to the General Day of Discussion which preceded the adoption of General Comment 21 and indeed on the Comment itself in her discussion on the content and scope of cultural rights.[94] The General Comment is of course limited to the right to take part in cultural life and she identified other areas of work in the field of cultural rights which she proposes to explore during the term of her mandate.

She notes that little has been done on the right to enjoy the benefits of scientific progress and its applications and proposes to further explore this right.[95] She also proposes to explore the existence, meaning and scope of a cultural dimension of human rights.[96] Cognizant perhaps of the work of the Special Rapporteur on Indigenous Rights in the area of corporate responsibility, she proposes to follow developments in relation to the roles and responsibilities of corporate actors with regard to human rights, with a specific focus on cultural rights.[97] Other topics she proposes to explore include cultural rights, cultural diversity and globalization; the relationship between individual and collective human rights; cultural rights within the education system; a gendered perspective on cultural rights; the cultural rights of people with disabilities; and the cultural rights of non-nationals, particularly migrant workers and their families.[98] While this is an ambitious plan of work, it is necessary to fill the *lacuna* in which cultural rights have languished for decades.[99]

Effecting change in terms of human rights is as much about political advocacy and discourse as it is about the law, and the new attention to cultural rights which will undoubtedly arise from the work of the

---

94 Report of the independent expert in the field of cultural rights, Ms. Farida Shaheed, submitted pursuant to Resolution 10/23 of the Human Rights Council, UN Doc A/HRC/14/36, 22 March 2010.

95 *Ibid.*, para 13. She describes the Venice Statement on the Right to Enjoy the Benefits of Scientific Progress and its applications as an important first step in elaborating the normative content of the right.

96 *Ibid.*, para 19.

97 *Ibid.*, para 20.

98 *Ibid.*, paras 15–20.

99 The Independent Expert has produced a comprehensive report on the extent to which the right of access to and enjoyment of cultural heritage forms part of international human rights law, which includes a compilation of references in international law, a summary of information received from states on national initiatives and an analysis of the right. See further, Report of the independent expert in the field of cultural rights, Ms. Farida Shaheed, submitted pursuant to Resolution 10/23 of the Human Rights Council, UN Doc A/HRC/17/38, 21 March 2011.

Independent Expert should highlight obstacles to their implementation and encourage states to act on their obligations.

5. CONCLUSION

Cultural rights are fundamental to the survival of minorities and indigenous peoples. For indigenous peoples, their culture, their way of life and their world view define them as distinct peoples. The UN Declaration on the Rights of Indigenous Peoples, providing as it does a legal framework for the recognition of the collective rights of indigenous peoples to self-determination and to ownership of their lands and territories, marked an historic step in redressing centuries of oppression, destruction and abandonment.

The denial of cultural rights to minorities has led to violent conflicts in many parts of the world, from Kashmir to Spain and from Bosnia to China. While states had feared that granting cultural rights to sub-state groups would lead to the eventual break-up of the state, the adoption of the Declaration suggests that they may be persuaded that recognizing cultural and collective rights could in fact secure the future stability of the state.

Difficulties of definition and fears of cultural relativism have dogged cultural rights for decades and have been major factors in their neglect. The adoption of General Comment 21, which defines the normative content of the right to take part in cultural life and deals authoritatively with the question of cultural relativism, has removed these further obstacles to its implementation. The appointment of an Independent Expert will ensure that cultural rights remain on the agenda of the UN Human Rights Council and that as yet unexplored aspects of the rights are given due attention.

These three developments herald a new era for cultural rights. From being virtually ignored in the literature and routinely neglected by human rights institutions, cultural rights have finally come into their own.

16. Intellectual property: A human (not corporate) right

Megan M. Carpenter[*]

There is a discord between intellectual property and human rights, which begins in the human rights instruments themselves. In its General Comment 17, for example, the Committee on Economic, Social, and Cultural Rights distinguishes intellectual property rights from human rights. Human rights, on the one hand, are 'fundamental, inalienable and universal entitlements belonging to individuals and, under certain circumstances, groups of individuals and communities'[1] and are 'timeless expressions of fundamental entitlements of the human person.'[2] Intellectual property rights, on the other hand, are described as 'first and foremost means by which States seek to provide incentives for inventiveness and creativity'[3] and 'primarily protect business and corporate interests and investments.'[4]

The temptation to categorize intellectual property rights as solely a vehicle for protection of corporate interests is great. Pharmaceutical companies participate in a multi-billion dollar industry while indigenous communities with traditional medicines see little benefit. Media companies enjoy increasing market share while independent creators who struggle to find time and energy to work on their art outside of their day jobs are marginal to the operation of intellectual property rules. Sacred religious and

---

* I would like to thank Kathryn Murphy, my (tirelessly hardworking) research assistant.

1 UN Committee On Economic, Social & Cultural Rights, 'General Comment No. 17: The Right of Everyone to Benefit from the Protection of the Moral and Material Interests Resulting from any Scientific, Literary or Artistic Production of Which He or She Is the Author (Art. 15(1)(c) of the Covenant)' 21 November 2005, UN Doc E/C.12/GC/17, available online at: http://portal.unesco.org/culture/en/files/30545/11432142221comment_en.pdf/comment_en.pdf (hereinafter, 'General Comment No. 17') para 1.

2 *Ibid.*, para 2.

3 *Ibid.*

4 *Ibid.*

cultural images are mass-produced on household goods while the communities from which those images are taken are left with neither recourse nor compensation. However, intellectual property rights should not protect primarily corporate interests. Rather, intellectual property law serves as the vehicle for protection of human creativity. And while corporate interests may dominate, as they do in other related areas of human rights such as the food industry or the health industry, it is crucial not to lose sight of the fundamental policies behind intellectual property law, particularly the interests of the humans behind human creativity.

This chapter seeks to distinguish between intellectual property rights – the existing legal mechanisms for intellectual property protection – and the right to intellectual property. The right to intellectual property is a human right. Intellectual property rights, instrumental in nature and codified in legal frameworks around the world, are not. Rather, intellectual property rights as they exist are both over- and under-inclusive in their protection of the right to intellectual property. However, the right to intellectual property exists for everyone, and a human rights perspective on IP should change the framework by which we evaluate and construct the legal system, expose the flaws of a system designed to primarily protect corporate interests, and present possibilities for a more inclusive approach.

The analysis begins in Part 1 with a discussion of the human right to the moral and material interests of creators, as that right has been embodied in an international human rights framework over time.[5] In Part 2, I discuss intellectual property rights – their importance and relevance to the human rights detailed in Article 15(1)(c) of the International Covenant on Economic, Social, and Cultural Rights. Creations of the mind are not only fundamental to personhood and community, but they serve as a primary economic vehicle on the global stage and have the potential to facilitate the ability of creators to access an adequate standard of living in remote areas and disadvantaged communities. In Part 3, I discuss General Comment 17 of the CESCR, which gives guidance and effect to the human rights provisions found in Article 15(1)(c). I conclude that for the rights in Article 15(1)(c) to be realized, they must be perceived as a fundamental aspect of intellectual property law and policy. Protection and respect for the moral and material interests of creators, the right to intellectual property, is a human right; and as such, human rights discourse must inform

[5] Part 1 is excerpted from Megan Carpenter, 'Trademarks and Human Rights: Oil and Water? Or Chocolate and Peanut Butter?' (2009) 99(4) *Trademark Reporter* 892.

intellectual property policy.[6] This conclusion has implications both for the intellectual property law community and the human rights community: to forget that human creators are at the centre of scientific and artistic innovation works to the detriment of effective IP policy; to avoid the legal mechanism by which the rights of creators are protected works to the detriment of human rights.

1. THE RIGHT TO INTELLECTUAL PROPERTY EXISTS WITHIN THE HUMAN RIGHTS FRAMEWORK

1.1 Human Rights Are Fundamental Rights Inherent to All Human Beings

Human rights are thought of, at a fundamental level, as rights inherent to all human beings, whatever the nationality, place of residence, sex, national or ethnic origin, colour, religion, language, or any other status. They are, quite simply, 'timeless expressions of fundamental entitlements of the human person.'[7] As a matter of first steps, when we consider whether or not anything is a human right, a logical place to turn to is the United Nations, which has played a definitional role with regard to the promotion of international human rights since the mid-twentieth century. The United Nations has created a global framework for protecting fundamental human rights, including multiple declarations and multilateral treaties on human rights. These instruments, both declarations and treaties, contain provisions commonly cited when asserting that intellectual property is a human right.[8]

---

[6] See, for example, Laurence R. Helfer, 'Human Rights and Intellectual Property: Conflict or Coexistence?' (2003) 5 *Minnesota Intellectual Property Rev.* 47; Laurence R. Helfer, 'Toward a Human Rights Framework for Intellectual Property' (2007)16 *U.C. Davis L. Rev.* 971; Peter K. Yu, 'Reconceptualizing Intellectual Property Interests in a Human Rights Framework' (2007) 40 *U.C. Davis L. Rev.* 1039; Mary W.S. Wong, 'Toward an Alternative Normative Framework for Copyright: From Private Property to Human Rights' (2009) 26 *Cardozo Arts & Ent. L.J.* 775.

[7] General Comment No. 17 (n1). For an interpretation, see Helfer 'Toward a Human Rights Framework for Intellectual Property' (n6) 997–1000.

[8] See, for example, Universal Declaration of Human Rights, UNGA Res 217 A(III) UN Doc A/810 91, UN General Assembly, 10 December 1948 (UDHR), Art. 27 ('(1) Everyone has the right freely to participate in the cultural life of the community, to enjoy the arts and to share in scientific advancement and its

1.1.1 Universal Declaration on Human Rights

The Universal Declaration on Human Rights, and the entire United Nations international human rights regime, were born from the wreckage of a post-World War II environment and culture and very much reflected the political climate of the time.[9] The Allied nations were determined to establish a peace-keeping structure for international cooperation that would prevent widespread trauma and violence from occurring in the future.[10] After US President Franklin Delano Roosevelt, British Prime Minister Winston Churchill, and Russian Premier Joseph Stalin met at Yalta and agreed to form 'a general international organization to maintain peace and security,' the United Nations was established; the UN Charter was drafted and signed in 1945.[11]

Following the establishment of the United Nations, the Universal Declaration on Human Rights became one of the first international documents based on the tenet that human beings have inherent and fundamental rights.[12] While the UDHR is not legally binding, it is the

---

benefits. (2) Everyone has the right to the protection of the moral and material interests resulting from any scientific, literary or artistic production of which he is the author'); International Covenant on Economic, Social and Cultural Rights (adopted 16 December 1966, entered into force 3 January 1976) 993 UNTS 3 (ICESCR), Arts 15(1)(b) and (c) (recognizing the right 'to enjoy the benefits of scientific progress and its applications' and 'to benefit from the protection of the moral and material interests resulting from any scientific, literary or artistic production of which he is the author').

[9] Paul Gordon Lauren, *The Evolution of International Human Rights* (Philadelphia: University of Pennsylvania Press, 1998) 181 notes that those who endured the traumas of the Depression, Hitler's Third Reich, and World War II sought to learn from the perceived mistakes of the past to create a lasting peace with rights. See also Yu (n6) 1050 (citing Matthew C.R. Craven, *The International Covenant on Economic, Social, and Cultural Rights: A Perspective on Its Development* (Oxford: Clarendon Press, 1995) 6 ('As a reaction to events prior to and during the Second World War, the allies, and later the international community as a whole, came to the belief that the establishment of the new world order should be based upon a commitment to the protection of human rights and fundamental freedoms'); Johannes Morsink, *The Universal Declaration of Human Rights: Origins, Drafting, and Intent* (Philadelphia: University of Pennsylvania Press, 1999) xiv ('[W]ithout the delegates' shared moral revulsion against [the Holocaust] the Declaration would never have been written')).

[10] Lauren (n9) 181.

[11] Department of Public Information, Milestones in United Nations History: Yalta Conference (1997) available online at: http://www.un.org/Overview/milesto4.htm.

[12] Previous international agreements were generally based in positivism, the idea that international rights and obligations only exist after those rights are rec-

cornerstone, if not the foundation, of our contemporary human rights regime, setting standards that are codified in multiple international treaties. It contains 30 articles specifying particular individual rights; the first two articles set a foundation of equality and basic dignity for all people, and the remaining rights encompass both civil and political rights and economic, social, and cultural rights.

The United Nations was itself an unprecedented effort at international cooperation, and the drafting of the main human rights instruments at the heart of this effort was an amalgamation of cooperation and conflicting ideologies. The first draft of provisions for the UDHR, which were compiled by John Humphrey, the director of the Division on Human Rights at the United Nations, did not include protection for the moral and/or material interests of creators, but did include 'the right to participate in the cultural life of the community, to enjoy the arts and to share in the benefits of science,'[13] a version of which eventually became Article 27(1). There was little controversy over Article 27(1). There was some discussion as to whether to stipulate that 'the development of science must serve the interests of progress and democracy and the cause of international peace and cooperation,' which grew out of concern by the Soviet Union regarding the United States' sharing secrets about the atomic bomb.[14] The additional phrase was rejected in the final version of the document, in part because of (unsurprising) widespread difficulties defining precisely the word 'democracy'.[15] Some delegates were further passionate about the inclusion of the word 'freely'; they believed that it was inadequate to state that everyone has the right to cultural participation without further emphasizing complete freedom 'to protect . . . from harmful pressures which were only too frequent in recent history.'[16] The final provision, a product of cooperation and compromise, reads 'everyone has the right freely to participate

ognized in national legislation. See Yu (n6) 1045–6 (citing Richard Falk, 'Cultural Foundations for the International Protection of Human Rights', in Abdullahi Ahmed An-Naim (ed.) *Human Rights in Cross-Cultural Perspectives: A Quest for Consensus* (Philadelphia: University of Pennsylvania Press, 1992) 44).

13 Mary Ann Glendon, *A World Made New: Eleanor Roosevelt and the Universal Declaration of Human Rights* (New York: Random House, 2002) 274 (quoting Art. 44 of the Humphrey Draft).

14 Yu (n6) 1053 (citing Morsink (n9) 61–2. For a detailed history of the drafting process of the UDHR, see Yu (n6) 1047–75.

15 Yu (n6) 1053 (citing Morsink (n9) 61–2).

16 Yu (n6) 1053 (citing Morsink (n9) 218 (quoting Peruvian delegate José Encinas)).

in the cultural life of the community, to enjoy the arts and to share in scientific advancement and its benefits.'[17]

Professor Peter Yu notes that, in contrast to the relatively smooth adoption of 27(1), the process for inclusion of 27(2) was fraught with controversy.[18] The protection of creators' moral interests did not arise in the first draft, but was added in a later draft compiled by Rene Cassin after further discussions of the Drafting Committee.[19] The Cassin draft provided initially that 'authors of all artistic, literary, scientific works and inventors shall retain, in addition to just remuneration for their labour, a moral right on their work and/or discovery which shall not disappear, even after such a work or discovery shall have become the common property of mankind.'[20] The draft article seems to implicate material interests in addition to moral ones, through the use of the phrase 'just and favourable remuneration,' as well as the seeming negative implication that creators will, at least for a time, have exclusive property rights in their creations.[21] (Some scholars have suggested that the Humphrey draft assumed material interests in intellectual property as well, by virtue of other property rights provisions.[22]) The draft Article 27(2) was the subject of much debate, and was objected to by various states on multiple grounds, including particularly the moral rights provisions.[23] Delegates split over growing Cold War ideologies. In the end, the product of compromise afforded individuals 'the right to the protection of the moral and material interests resulting from any scientific, literary or artistic production of which he is the author.'[24] This provision has served as the model language for both international and regional human rights instruments for the last half-century.

It is no surprise to discover that enforcement mechanisms for international human rights are categorically inadequate. Setting aspirational standards for human rights in the interest of international cooperation and the well-being of citizens around the world is achievable but creating legally cognizable individual rights *vis-à-vis* domestic sovereign entities is

---

17 Art. 27(1) UDHR (n8).
18 Yu (n6) 1054.
19 *Ibid.*
20 Glendon (n13) 275–80 (quoting Art. 43 of the Cassin Draft).
21 Art. 23(3) UDHR (n8).
22 Yu (n6) 1052.
23 *Ibid.*, 1054 ('While the additional element of moral rights provided the provision's *raison d'être*, it raised considerable concern for the United Kingdom and United States').
24 Art. 27(2) UDHR (n8).

more complex. The Universal Declaration, as such, does not and is not intended to create specific, legal, binding rights and duties between individuals and the states.[25] Rather, as a Declaration, it is intended to establish what Eleanor Roosevelt called a common standard of rights 'for all peoples and all nations.'[26] In contrast to a legally enforceable instrument, the UDHR was designed to proclaim a united vision of human rights for the world, a world which, looking forward, would believe in the 'inherent dignity' of the individual and the 'inalienable rights of all members of the human family.'[27] The Declaration has served this function well, and has become a means of guiding states, both collectively and individually, in the direction of fundamental human rights.

1.1.2 International Covenant on Economic, Social and Cultural Rights

The International Covenant on Economic, Social, and Cultural Rights was adopted by the United Nations in 1966, although it did not enter into force for another decade, a delay due in large part to the escalating Cold War and ideological conflicts between Western capitalist democracies and Communist regimes.[28] The ICESCR is a legal instrument binding upon its more than 150 States Parties.[29] There has been some debate as to why (and how) intellectual property protection ended up in the final version of the ICESCR. The ideological conflicts of the Cold War had only intensified in the time since the passage of the UDHR and the future of intellectual property in a human rights framework was uncertain. In Article 15, however, the final version of the ICESCR sets out binding protection

---

[25] See Audrey R. Chapman, 'A Human Rights Perspective on Intellectual Property, Scientific Progress, and Access to the Benefits of Science' (2002) 5 *Journal of International Economic Law* 861–82, noting that although 'the UDHR is aspirational or advisory in nature' and 'does not legally bind member states of the U.N. to implement it,' over time, it 'has gradually assumed the status of customary international law'); Paul Torremans, 'Is Copyright a Human Right?' (2007) *Michigan State L. Rev.* 271, 277.

[26] Lauren (n9) 234 (citing 'Searching Study of Human Rights Declaration' (1948) 5 *United Nations Weekly Bulletin* No. 858, 1 November 1948).

[27] Preamble, UDHR (n8).

[28] Yu (n6) 1069 (quoting Maria Green, Int'l Anti-Poverty Law Centre, *Drafting History of Article 15(1)(c) of the International Covenant*, 6, UN Doc E/C.12/2000/15 (9 October 2000) available online at: http://www.unhchr.ch/tbs/doc.nsf/(Symbol)/E.C.12.2000.15.En?Opendocument ('The final vote was straight down Cold War fault lines, with the opposed roster holding Romania, Ukrainian Soviet Socialist Republic, USSR, Albania, Bulgaria, Byelorussian Soviet Socialist Republic, Czechoslovakia, Hungary, and Iraq')).

[29] Helfer 'Toward a Human Rights Framework for Intellectual Property' (n6) 988.

for the intellectual property rights detailed in the UDHR.[30] The Covenant provides:

> 1. The States Parties to the present covenant recognize the right of everyone:
>   a. To take part in cultural life;
>   b. To enjoy the benefits of scientific progress and its applications;
>   c. To benefit from the protection of the moral and material interests resulting from any scientific, literary or artistic production of which he is the author.
> 2. The steps to be taken by the States Parties to the present Covenant to achieve the full realization of this right shall include those necessary for the conservation, the development and the diffusion of science and culture.
> 3. The States Parties to the present Covenant undertake to respect the freedom indispensable for scientific research and creative activity.[31]

The Committee on Economic, Social, and Cultural Rights is the body charged with monitoring the implementation of the Covenant.[32] The Committee is composed of 18 independent experts, and while it does not have a mechanism to adjudicate individual complaints, it is responsible for receiving and reviewing individual reports by States Parties, which detail the actions a state has taken to implement the provisions of the Covenant on a domestic level.[33] Thus, the CESCR is charged with both interpreting the provisions of the Covenant and monitoring its implementation by more than 150 States Parties. As part of its interpretative duties, the CESCR publishes 'General Comments' interpreting specific treaty articles or specific human rights issues.[34] While the General Comments do not create legally binding obligations on the part of States Parties, they do serve a standard-setting function for the CESCR in reviewing compliance with the treaty.[35]

1.1.3 Regional human rights treaties

Regional human rights treaties buttress the IP provisions found in the UN instruments, and often contain language modeled after the UDHR and the ICESCR. The American Declaration on the Rights and Duties of Man, for example, parallels the ICESCR and provides that 'every

---

30 The language in Art. 15 of the ICESCR (n8) closely tracks that of Art. 27 of the UDHR (n8).

31 Art. 15, ICESCR (n8).

32 Helfer, 'Toward a Human Rights Framework for Intellectual Property' (n6) 988.

33 *Ibid.*

34 *Ibid.*

35 *Ibid.*

person . . . has the right to the protection of his moral and material interests as regards his inventions or any literary, scientific or artistic works of which he is the author.'[36] The American Declaration was innovative in providing protection for the moral and material interests of creators of intellectual property. The Additional Protocol to the American Convention on Human Rights in the Area of Economic, Social and Cultural Rights of 1988 provides protection for the interests of creators, as well.[37]

The European Convention for the Protection of Human Rights and Fundamental Freedoms of 1952 ('ECHR') is perhaps the most influential regional human rights instrument. The ECHR creates legal obligations within the Council of Europe, and has judicial oversight by the European Court of Human Rights. Like the American Declaration, the ECHR protects intellectual property rights, albeit through a different approach – the right to property.[38] The European Court of Human Rights has held that intellectual property is protected by Article 1 of Protocol 1 to the ECHR, which provides that '[e]very natural or legal person is entitled to the peaceful enjoyment of his possessions.'[39] The ECHR is a powerful regional mechanism for the enforcement of human rights, including 'tens of thousands of complaints each year, and its jurisdiction extends the length and breadth of the continent, encompassing 800 million people in forty-seven nations from Azerbaijan to Iceland and from Portugal to Russia.'[40]

---

36 American Declaration of the Rights and Duties of Man, OAS Res. XXX, adopted by Ninth International Conference of American States, 2 May 1948, available online at: http://www.unhcr.org/refworld/type,RESOLUTION,OAS,,3ae6b3710,0.html, Art. 13(2).

37 Additional Protocol to the American Convention on Human Rights in the area of Economic, Social and Cultural Rights, 'Protocol of San Salvador', OASTS No. 69, 17 November 1988, available online at: http://www.oas.org/juridico/English/treaties/a-52.html, Art. 14(1)(c).

38 Laurence R. Helfer, 'The New Innovation Frontier? Intellectual Property and the European Court of Human Rights' (2008) 49 *Harv. Int'l L.J.* 1, 2 (citing Protocol 1 to the European Convention for the Protection of Human Rights and Fundamental Freedoms (4 November 1950, entered into force 3 September 1953) 213 UNTS 222, Art. 1 ('Every natural or legal person is entitled to the peaceful enjoyment of his possessions. No one shall be deprived of his possessions except in the public interest and subject to the conditions provided for by law and by the general principles of international law').

39 Helfer (n38) 2.

40 *Ibid.*, 1.

2. INTELLECTUAL PROPERTY IS HUMAN CREATIVITY

The subjects of intellectual property are creations of the mind.[41] At a basic level, intellectual property rights share many characteristics of other property rights – including that they are often misconstrued as a form of dominion but are in fact representative of a structured relationship between people *vis-à-vis* a given asset. Intellectual property is generally considered to be an asset, and as such can, to the extent of the rights, often be bought, sold, licensed, exchanged, or given away, and the intellectual property rights-holder has a limited right to exclude, including in some cases the ability to prevent unauthorized use or sale.[42] While intellectual property rights are similar to other forms of property rights in operation and structure, the objects of intellectual property are unique, in that they are intangible in nature and cannot generally be identified by their own physicality.[43]

The World Intellectual Property Organization divides intellectual property into two categories: industrial property, which includes inventions (patents), trademarks, industrial designs, and geographic indications of source; and copyright, which includes literary and artistic works such as novels, poems, plays, films, musical works, software, drawings, paintings, photographs, sculptures, and architectural designs.[44] Copyrights have many layers that can coexist in separate parties even within the context of a singular work: rights of a performing artist, for example, can coexist with rights in the underlying composition, rights in the sound recording, and rights of radio broadcasters.[45] Intellectual property may include medicines, genetic resources, sacred religious and cultural knowledge, plants, costumes, chain letters and secret diaries. Intellectual property flies airplanes and fills libraries; it vaccinates children and facilitates viral internet videos. Simply put, intellectual property is the fruit of human creativity and invention.[46]

---

41 General Comment 17 (n1) para 4; WIPO, 'What Is IP?', available online at: http://www.wipo.int/about-ip/en/.

42 Carpenter (n5) 57.

43 *Ibid.*

44 *Ibid.* (citing WIPO (n41)).

45 Carpenter (n5) 57 (citing WIPO (n41)).

46 Carpenter (n5) 57 (citing WIPO, 'At Home with Invention', available online at: http://www.wipo.int/about-ip/en/athome.htm).

2.1 Trademarks are not the Subject of Human Rights *Per Se*

In the last decade, there has been increasing discussion about the relationship (or lack thereof) between intellectual property and human rights.[47] There is one category of intellectual property rights that is clearly not supported by the fundamental purposes of Article 15 – namely, trademarks and associated rights.[48] Trademarks are symbols and signs that serve a consumer protection function by enabling entities to identify and distinguish their goods and services from those of others. Trademarks are distinct from patents and copyrights, and unique as a form of intellectual property, because the policy underlying trademarks is not one of personhood or incentive, but rather commercial dealing and unfair competition. '[A] creator's personal interests on the one hand and the protection of a trademark on the other hand have completely different foundations,'[49] and IP law does not seek to incentivize the creation of trademarks, nor does it endow the creator of a trademark with a moral connection to that mark in the marketplace. Thus, as subjects of intellectual property that are neither literary nor scientific works, trademarks simply do not fall within the purview of Article 15.

The connection between trademarks and human rights has been explored in case law, to the extent that it exists, through the right to property. In recent years, for example, the European Court of Human Rights (ECtHR) extended the protection of fundamental property rights under Article 1, Protocol 1 of the European Convention on Human Rights (the 'Convention') to trademark applications and registrations.[50] In *Anheuser-Busch v. Portugal*, the ECtHR held that a trademark application constituted a 'legitimate expectation' of a 'possession' under the Convention, because of the bundle of financial interests and rights that arise upon its filing, including transactions with substantial financial value.[51] And while trademarks certainly represent a form of limited property interest, the only relationship trademarks have to human rights is by virtue of that property interest, not by their nature *per se*. The right to peaceful enjoyment of

---

47 See above (n6) and accompanying text.

48 For a more complete discussion on this point, see Carpenter (n5).

49 Burkhart Goebel, 'Trademarks and Fundamental Rights – Europe' (2009) 99(4) *Trademark Reporter* 931 (noting a decision of the German Constitutional Court in 1979, which recognized the human rights protection of artists' personal achievements as distinct from the industrial effort and function of trademarks).

50 *Anheuser-Busch v. Portugal*, App. No. 73049/01, 44 EHRR 42, 855–56 (Grand Chamber, 11 January 2007) reviewing in part Chamber Judgment of 11 October 2005.

51 *Ibid.*, 849.

one's possessions may be a human right; the right to have that possession in the first place, however, is not.

Article 15 has particular relevance defensively in the trademark context. Indigenous cultural heritage sometimes finds itself in conflict with trademark rights, exemplifying the importance of Article 15 considerations. Indigenous cultural heritage is often the subject of intellectual property, including artistic works, cultural practices, designs, songs, stories, and dances. Indigenous signs and symbols are increasingly used as trademarks in a commercial market for a wide variety of goods and services.[52] The moral and material interests of indigenous creators should be protected by intellectual property rights, but without trademark laws that safeguard indigenous culture, there will be little restriction on the appropriation of indigenous creations for commercial use. Two particular safeguards have emerged in various intellectual property schemes to protect indigenous peoples in this context (albeit to a limited extent): (1) restrictions on trademark registration for significant indigenous symbols; and (2) the implementation of authenticity provisions.[53]

In countries such as New Zealand and Canada, trademark law prevents registration of certain marks that are significant to indigenous peoples. Trademarks that contain an emblem or mark of a 'public authority' in Canada cannot be registered, for example, and 'public authority' in that context includes indigenous groups.[54] The Lanham Act in the United States, on the other hand, does not have a specific provision addressing the rights of indigenous peoples, although it does prevent registration of marks that create a false association with a particular group or are disparaging.[55] Indigenous groups have had a difficult time in the United States using these provisions to prevent registration of particular marks, however, including the renowned case of the Washington Redskins, which upheld the trademark interest of the football franchise in the mark over the complaints of a group of Native Americans.[56] Another mechanism

---

[52] Peter J. Chalk and Alexander Dunlop, 'Indigenous Trade Marks and Human Rights: An Australian and New Zealand Perspective' (2009) 99(4) *Trademark Reporter* 956 (citing M. Solomon, 'Indigenous People's Rights Versus Intellectual Property Rights', in Nin Thomas (ed.) *Collective Human Rights of Pacific Peoples* (International Research Unit for Maori and Indigenous Education, Conference Proceedings for Conference on Collective Human Rights of Pacific Peoples, December 1998, University of Auckland, 2000) 46, 51).

[53] See generally, Chalk and Dunlop (n52).

[54] *Ibid.*, at 961.

[55] 15 U.S.C. § 1052(a).

[56] *Pro Football v. Harjo*, Civ. Action No. 99-1395 (D.D.C. June 25, 2008) affirmed, 565 F.3d 880 (D.C. Cir. 2009).

that has been employed in trademark law to protect the moral and material interests of indigenous creators is a system of labels of authenticity. Australia and New Zealand, for example, both allow for the creation and enforcement of a label of authenticity for works of indigenous origin. The United States also has a similar law; the Indian Arts and Crafts Act is designed to prevent the sale of goods misidentified as being 'Indian made'.[57] Due to the limited scope and application of the law, however, many appropriations of indigenous cultural heritage fall outside the parameters of the Act. Recently, for example, Texas has seen the production of what the distiller calls the world's first Hopi blue corn whiskey, called Baby Blue.[58] Blue corn is the most sacred of substances to the Hopi people, and the symbolism of blue corn is central to the Hopi religion.[59] Despite a strong moral interest in protecting their cultural heritage and its association with the Hopi people, neither trademark law nor the Indian Arts and Crafts Act offers any protection.

2.2 The Subjects of Copyright and Patent Law Overlap with Article 15(1)(c)

In contrast to trademark law, whose function is based in commercial dealing and unfair competition, copyrights and patent rights are the means by which the Article 15 creators' rights are made manifest. The 'right of everyone to benefit from the protection of the moral and material interests resulting from any scientific, literary or artistic production of which he or she is the author' is a human right, and the means by which that right is legislated and implemented (to varying degrees of effectiveness or ineffectiveness) for the most is through copyright and patent protection.

The policies behind copyrights and patent rights are two-fold, related both to an incentive theory of intellectual property and a personality

---

57 Indian Arts and Crafts Act of 1990 (P.L. 101-644).

58 See William M. Dowd, 'Texas distiller has 1st blue corn whiskey,' *The Examiner*, available online at: http://www.examiner.com/drinks-in-national/texas-distiller-has-1st-blue-corn-whiskey (21 September 2009); see also Addie Broyles, 'Texas' (sic) First Whiskey Hits the Shelves,' *Austin 360*, available online at: http://www.austin360.com/blogs/content/shared-gen/blogs/austin/food2/entries/2009/09/16/texas_first_whiskey_hits_the_s.html (16 September 2009); see also Jennifer McInnis, 'Texas' (sic) first whiskey, Baby Blue, wins double gold in San Francisco,' *My SA Taste*, available online at: http://www.mysanantonio.com/life/food/Texas_first_whisky_Baby_Blue_wins_double_gold_in_San_Francisco.html (7 April 2010).

59 John D. Loftin, *Religion and Hopi Life* (2nd edn, Bloomington, IN: Indiana University Press, 2003) 5.

theory. The incentive theory seeks to advance innovation and creativity of humankind. If creators are afforded exclusive rights for limited times, they will be incentivized to create (and have the material capability to do so). The incentive theory supports all forms of creativity, whether a song or a pharmaceutical drug. Article 7 of the Agreement on Trade-Related Aspects of Intellectual Property Rights (TRIPS Agreement), which establishes minimum standards for intellectual property protection and enforcement for members of the World Trade Organization, includes reference to the incentive theory: 'The protection and enforcement of intellectual property rights should contribute to the promotion of technological innovation and to the transfer and dissemination of technology.'[60] Estimating the effect of intellectual property protection on the quantity or quality of works created is a difficult proposition, but, as an example, in the United States, a recent study 'found that 60% of the pharmaceutical inventions made between 1981 and 1983 would not have been developed at all and 65% of those inventions would not have been introduced into commerce if patent protection had been unavailable.'[61] Indeed, regarding patent rights, '[a]ll of the empirical and historical studies of the drug business conclude that [they] have been crucial in fostering high rates of innovation and progress.'[62]

In addition to the utilitarian theory of intellectual property law is personality theory, which gained wide popularity in the realm of tangible property after Professor Margaret Jane Radin published her 1982 essay entitled *Property and Personhood.*[63] Radin drew philosophical inspiration from Hegel and his view that a person has no concrete existence until that person exercises his will on the outside world.[64] Professor Radin revisits the writings of Hegel and expands them to the intellectual property context: '[T]he personality theory has an intuitive appeal when applied to intellectual property: an idea belongs to its creator because the idea is a manifestation of the creator's personality or self.'[65] In order to actualize one's personality, thus, '[a] person must translate his freedom onto an

---

60 Art. 7, TRIPS: Agreement on Trade-Related Aspects of Intellectual Property Rights, 15 April 1994.

61 William Fisher, 'Intellectual Property and Innovation: Theoretical, Empirical, and Historical Perspectives', paper prepared for the Programme Seminar on *Intellectual Property and Innovation in the Knowledge-based Economy*, The Hague, 2 May 2001.

62 *Ibid.*

63 Margaret Radin, 'Property and Personhood' (1982) 34 *Stan. L. Rev.* 957.

64 *Ibid.*, 972 (citing Georg Hegel, *Philosophy of Right* (T. Knox tr, Oxford: Clarendon Press, 1952)).

65 *Ibid.*

external sphere in order to exist as an Idea.'[66] In Professor Radin's interpretation, creation of and control over one's intellectual property is what makes us human: '[B]ecause the person . . . is merely an abstract unit of free will or autonomy, it has no concrete existence until that will acts on the external world. . . The person becomes a real self only by engaging in a property relationship with something external.'[67] Freedom is increasingly realized by the individual through her expression; the more expressive one can be through property, the more free and *real* a person becomes. It is personality theory that comes most into play in concepts of moral rights in artistic works, which protect rights of attribution and integrity (and sometimes more). It is also personality theory that focuses on the connection between the creator and the work, which is the focus also of Article 15(1)(c). Personality theory can be seen in international treaties like the Berne Convention,[68] and the US Copyright Act,[69] which extend copyright protection even to works that remain private without formalities or publication requirements.

2.3 Intellectual Property is the Currency of the New Economy

Intellectual property and the laws surrounding its development, protection, and enforcement have an unparalleled effect on individuals and communities in contemporary society. A global economy based in information and content is, simply, an economy built on intellectual property.[70] And as the way that we define rights over ideas and their control and use, intellectual property rights are of key importance. Intellectual property is unique as a driver of economic development, in part because it is not as geographically limiting as traditional economic resources are and can be as available to people in isolated or developing communities as to those in urban or more developed areas. The new economy presents opportunities that were heretofore impossible; areas isolated by geography, by their rural character, or by other socio-economic demographics

---

66 *Ibid.*, 331 (citing Hegel (n64) 41).

67 M. Scott Boone, 'Virtual Property and Personhood' (2008) 24 *Santa Clara Computer & High Tech. L.J.* 715, 726–7 (citing Radin (n63) 972–3).

68 Berne Convention for the Protection of Literary and Artistic Works, 1 B.D.I.E.L. 715.

69 17 U.S.C. § 101 *et seq.*

70 Alan Greenspan, 'Intellectual Property Rights', Stanford Institute for Economic Policy Research Economic Summit (27 February 2004) (positing that '[i]deas are at the center of productivity growth,' and stating that, '[i]n essence, the growth of productivity . . . is largely a measure of the contribution of ideas to economic growth and to our standards of living.'

are no longer economically isolated. Accordingly, the Director General of the World Intellectual Property Organization (WIPO) has emphasized 'the importance of developing the infrastructure of the international intellectual property system as a means of increasing participation in the knowledge economy and reducing the knowledge gap.'[71] The new economy, based on information and content, is potentially open and accessible to all. In light of this new accessibility and rapid change, the moral and material interests of creators are of utmost importance from both an offensive and a defensive perspective. Because 'the intellectual property system offers an essential framework for defining the rights and obligations of multiple participants in collective knowledge-generation and knowledge-sharing projects,'[72] it is imperative that it be structured with conscious regard for the moral and material interests of the holders of that knowledge.

One example of what the WIPO Director-General has heralded as a 'dramatic shift in models of innovation, and specifically, the arrival of open and networked innovation . . . [that] . . . offers great opportunities for developing countries to share in innovation' can be seen in Thailand.[73] The Fiscal Policy Research Institute of Thailand just released a study 'conclud[ing] that 10% of Thailand's economy is reliant on intellectual property rights, and, with an improved IP climate, this number could grow substantially.'[74] The study 'found that IP is not only a driving economic force in the nation, but it is also a contributor to job growth in other non-IP sectors as well.'[75] The study included nine intellectual property industries, including printing and publishing, information technology, wooden furniture, medicines, jewellery, research, movie production, movie theatres, and radio and television.[76] The study concluded that these industries directly contributed about 1 trillion baht ($30 billion) to the economy, amounting to nearly 10 per cent of Thailand's gross domestic

---

[71] See Francis Gurry, *WIPO Director-General Highlights Importance of Intellectual Property for Innovation and Technology Transfer* 10 May 2010, Press Release PR/2010/640, available online at: http://www.wipo.int/pressroom/en/articles/2010/article _0013.html.

[72] *Ibid.*

[73] *Ibid.*

[74] US Chamber of Commerce & Global Intellectual Property Center, *New Study Demonstrates Importance of Intellectual Property Rights to Emerging Economy*, 28 January 2010, available online at: http://www.theglobalipcenter.com/pressreleases/new-study-demonstrates-importance-intellectual-property-rights-emerging-economy.

[75] *Ibid.*

[76] *Ibid.*

product.[77] The study notes that '[p]romoting creative industries is a key element in the needed transition to a more advanced economy that can provide higher per capita income and greater quality of life for the Thai people.'[78] The study also concluded that increased IP enforcement would further promote IP and incentivize an already growing field.[79] Intellectual property is no longer an area that can be marginalized and if Article 15(1)(c) is to have any meaning, it is of vital importance that intellectual property law and policy be drafted with regard to its policies.

3. GENERAL COMMENT 17

General Comment No. 17 notes that States Parties have the obligation to respect, protect, and fulfil the obligations contained in Article 15(c) of the ICESCR:

> The obligation to *respect* requires States parties to refrain from interfering directly or indirectly with the enjoyment of the right to benefit from the protection of the moral and material interests of the author. The obligation to *protect* requires States parties to take measures that prevent third parties from interfering with the moral and material interests of authors. Finally, the obligation to *fulfil* requires States parties to adopt appropriate legislative, administrative, budgetary, judicial, promotional and other measures towards the full realization of article 15, paragraph 1 (c).[80]

Just as other human rights are mutually reinforcing and reciprocally limitative, such as the right to health, the right to food, and the right to education, Article 15 rights are similarly reinforcing and limitative, including the right to take part in cultural life, the right to enjoy the benefits of scientific progress and its applications and the freedom for scientific research and creative activity. Finding a balance between and among human rights as they are implemented into law is a natural part of

---

77 *Ibid.*

78 *Ibid.*

79 *Ibid.*

80 General Comment No. 17 (n1) para 28 (citing General Comment No. 13 (1999) at paras 46 and 47, and General Comment No. 14 (2000) para 33. See also, Maastricht Guidelines on Violations of Economic, Social and Cultural Rights, unanimously adopted by a group of more than 30 experts in Maastricht at the invitation of the International Commission of Jurists (Geneva, Switzerland), the Urban Morgan Institute on Human Rights (Cincinnati, Ohio, USA) and the Centre for Human Rights of the Faculty of Law of Maastricht University, Maastricht, The Netherlands, 22–26 January 1997 (hereinafter, 'Maastricht Guidelines') para 6.

implementing domestic legislation, and often mirrored by similar balances in domestic legislative documents, such as the constitution. The Brazilian Constitution, for example, includes scientific, artistic, and technological creations as part of the nation's cultural heritage, and also declares the right of citizens to the enjoyment of an ecologically well-balanced environment.[81] Thus, the development and protection of both natural (environmental) and technological (intellectual property) resources must be encouraged, two goals that are reciprocally limitative.[82]

In General Comment 17, the CESCR astutely notes, as we have discussed, that the scope of protection of the moral and material interests of authors provided for in Article 15 'does not necessarily coincide with what is referred to as intellectual property rights under national legislation or international agreements.'[83] Thus, the CESCR says that it is 'therefore important not to equate intellectual property rights with the human right recognized in article 15, paragraph 1(c).'[84] And indeed while the two should not be equated *per se*, they are inextricably related insofar as the moral and material interests of creators are a policy basis for intellectual property rights. IP rights give legal effect to the language in 15(1)(c), and conversely 15(1)(c) provides a policy justification for IP rights.

It is dangerous and detrimental to think of these two concepts as being wholly distinct. Human rights are aspirational rights, and there are a variety of legal mechanisms by which those rights are realized. Human rights are mutually reinforcing and reciprocally limitative, and so are the legal mechanisms that seek to make these rights manifest in positive law. Intellectual property rights frameworks are the primary mechanisms by which states deal with creative works and scientific innovations, including the interests of their authors or inventors. And thus, rather than viewing the moral and material interests of creators as separate from intellectual property rights, it is important that they be part of the analysis in creating and implementing IP law generally.

General Comment 17 defines the individual who receives protection under this Article as a 'creator, whether man or woman, individual or

---

81 See *State Report of Brazil to CESCR*, 5 August 2001, UN Doc. E/1990/5/Add.53.

82 *Ibid.* As manifested, government sectors thus have the duty to preserve both assets, including (1) protecting the environment and combating pollution in any form whatsoever; (2) preserving forests, plant life and wildlife; and (3) recording, monitoring and overseeing the granting of prospecting and exploration rights for water and mineral resources within their territories.

83 General Comment 17 (n1) para 2.

84 *Ibid.* para 3.

group of individuals, of scientific, literary or artistic productions, such as, *inter alia*, writers and artists.'[85] The CESCR further interprets 'any scientific, literary or artistic production' to include 'creations of the human mind, that is to "scientific productions," such as scientific publications and innovations, including knowledge, innovations and practices of indigenous and local communities, and "literary and artistic productions," such as, *inter alia*, poems, novels, paintings, sculptures, musical compositions, theatrical and cinematographic works, performances and oral traditions.'[86] The creator of Article 15 is the author or the inventor of intellectual property law; and, the scientific, literary, or artistic productions which are the objects of creativity in Article 15 are the objects of intellectual property law. It is imperative that we recognize that the right to intellectual property is not a corporate right; rather, IP rights are legal instruments that have at their base the right of individuals to the moral and material interests of their creations, which is, quite simply, the right to intellectual property – a human right, borne of human creativity, connected with the human being, and contributing to a larger global community.

---

85 General Comment 17 (n1) para 7: 'This follows from the words "everyone", "he" and "author", which indicate that the drafters of that article seemed to have believed authors of scientific, literary or artistic productions to be natural persons, without at that time realizing that they could also be groups of individuals. Under the existing international treaty protection regimes, legal entities are included among the holders of intellectual property rights. However, as noted above, their entitlements, because of their different nature, are not protected at the level of human rights.'

86 *Ibid.*, para 9.

Index